D1130379

THE WASHINGTON PAPERS

THE WASHINGTON PAPERS

Basic Selections from the Public and Private Writings of George Washington

EDITED AND ARRANGED, WITH AN INTRODUCTION, BY

SAUL K. PADOVER

DEAN, SCHOOL OF POLITICS,

NEW SCHOOL FOR SOCIAL RESEARCH

HARPER & BROTHERS PUBLISHERS NEW YORK

THE WASHINGTON PAPERS

Printed in the United States of America

FIRST EDITION

A-E

Library of Congress catalog card number: 54-12149

Contents

THE WASHINGTON PAPERS

Introduction

GEORGE WASHINGTON: A Political Portrait and a Re-Appraisal

I

For more than a century and a half the granite reputation of George Washington has withstood the attentions of his idolizers. Few other national heroes have ever been greater targets of assiduous idolatry, hagiography, iconolatry, myth-making, and breathless patriotic oratory. Washington was made into a graven image for the nation to worship.

This sanctification has done a grave injustice to a good and great man. It has stripped him of the common humanity with which he was so abundantly endowed. A passionate, sensitive, earthy, deeply feeling human being was transformed into an idol that, presumably, had never experienced anything but the loftiest patriotic emotions.

The person and character of Washington did, of course, easily lend themselves to national deification. He was of the stuff of heroes. He even looked the way a hero should look—tall and handsome, powerfully built and graceful. Jefferson said of him: "His person . . . was fine, his stature exactly what one would wish, his deportment easy, erect and noble; the best horseman of his age, and the most graceful figure that could be seen on horseback."

His sheer presence impressed everybody. Abigail Adams thought he had more grace and dignity than King George III. John Page, a Governor of Virginia, considered him greater than Cicero. Benjamin Franklin, bequeathing to him his gold-headed crabtree walking stick, said: "If it were a sceptre, he has merited it and would become it." And his Negro servant, recalling the twenty-seven-year-old Washington's marriage to Martha Custis, exclaimed that there was nobody, in that glittering wedding assemblage, like the young Colonel: "So tall, so straight! and . . . with such an air! Ah, sir; he was like no one else! Many of the grandest gentlemen in their gold lace were at the wedding, but none looked like the man himself."

His dignity and self-esteem were such that to a superficial observer he appeared to be cold. Actually he was emotional, tender, and capable of outbursts of violence. An iron discipline, which he imposed upon himself all his life, kept a leash on his passions. "All the muscles of his face," Captain George Mercer, a fellow-soldier, wrote of him "[are] under perfect control, though flexible and expressive of deep feeling when moved by emotion." His infrequent outbursts of anger were legendary. On the occasions when his rigid self-control broke under stress, he was, according to a contemporary, "most tremendous in his wrath."

One such occasion is recorded in Jefferson's diary. At an important Cabinet meeting in August, 1793, Secretary of War Knox referred to some particularly nasty abuse of the President that had just been printed in Freneau's *National Gazette* and Bache's *General Advertiser*. The mention of these hostile newspapers so inflamed Washington's "irritable and high toned" temper that it finally broke up the session. Jefferson relates:

> The Presdt . . . got into one of those passions when he cannot command himself, ran on much on the personal abuse which had been bestowed on him, defied any man on earth to produce one single act of his since he had been in the govmt which was not done on the purest motives, that he had never repented but once the having slipped the moment of resigning his office, & that was every moment since, that *by god* he had rather be on his farm than be made *emperor of the world,* and yet they were charging him with wanting to be a king [*Anas,* August 2].

Washington had the aloofness of the very shy. He was a poor public speaker, slow in expression, and unequipped with quips or glibness. Strangers were likely to embarrass him and to reduce him to a slightly awkward silence. Only among friends would he warm up and show the gentle, and sometimes whimsical, side of his nature. At best, however, he was a mediocre conversationalist, possessing, in the words of a contemporary, "neither copiousness of ideas nor fluency of words."

In person-to-person contact he was a gentleman of considerable charm, invariably courteous and attentive. His voice was pleasant and well modulated. In conversation he would look you full in the face, weigh your words carefully, and show you an engaging deference. Ladies found him charming and he, in turn, could not easily resist them. His letters to women show him to be something of a romantic where they were concerned, curiously coy and surprisingly sentimental. A strong, masculine man, he liked women unabashedly. "When once the woman has tempted us," he wrote to a lady at the age of fifty-one, "and we have tasted the forbidden fruit, there is no such thing as checking our appetites, whatever the consequences may be."

An emotional man at bottom, Washington, the seemingly frosty hero, was capable of the grand, dramatic gesture. His farewell to his officers, on December 4, 1783, at Fraunces' Tavern in New York, was a scene out of a classic play. Standing before the men he had commanded for eight perilous and finally triumphant years, his customary self-control deserted him. Tears filled his eyes as he stood up, filled a glass with a shaking hand, and said in a trembling voice: "I cannot come to each of you to take my leave, but shall be obliged if you will each come and shake me by the hand." Silently they lined up and shook his hand. Then he returned home to Mount Vernon, journeying through communities that moved him deeply with their outpourings of homage, determined to retire from public life. He had started his military career more than thirty years back, and now that he had won independence for his country the American Cincinnatus, as the newspapers and the orators called him, felt that he merited retirement to the plow. He was only fifty-one and, as he wrote to his friend Lafayette, his sole desire was to be a private citizen, sitting under his "own vine and fig-tree" and "move gently down the stream of life until I sleep with my fathers."

Retirement, however, was a luxury that destiny did not permit him to enjoy.

II

What was there in George Washington that attracted so many diverse men and that made his countrymen turn to him, almost as if by instinct, in any crisis? He was not a particularly great general; some of the most important battles of the Revolution were won by others. He was not, like Alexander Hamilton, a brilliant man; his mind, on the contrary, was slow in operation. Nor was he an educated man; in literary culture and knowledge he could in no way be compared to such colleagues and contemporaries as Adams, Jefferson, and Madison.

Indeed, he had little formal education. A non-wealthy orphan, he had left school at the age of about fifteen, having acquired merely the rudiments of arithmetic, the art of reading and a rather limited skill in writing. It was only after he grew older, and by dint of hard application, that he learned to write without doing too much violence to spelling and structure. When he was a lad his literary compositions left much to be desired, as is shown especially in his early diaries. An interesting example is taken from his diary of March 15, 1748, covering his first surveying trip at the age of sixteen:

> We got our suppers & was Lighted into a Room & I not being so good a woodsman as ye rest of my company, striped myself very orderly and went into ye Bed, as they calld it, when to my surprize, I found it to be nothing but a little straw matted together without sheets or anything else, but only one thread bear blanket with double its weight of vermin, such as Lice, Fleas, &. I was glad to get up. . . . I put on my cloths & lay as my companions.

What gives Washington his special distinction, what, in fact, accounts for his peculiar greatness and appeal, is not book learning but character. In the course of a busy and active life he found little time and had small inclination to read; what reading he did was confined mainly to books of history and agricultural proceedings. But his character and personality were molded by a different kind of education—the living world around him. Washington carefully observed the best examples of proper behavior and deliberately modelled himself after the well-bred, class-conscious, and almost feudally elegant Virginia gentry, particularly the aristocratic Fairfax family. In the virtually self-contained plantation world of eighteenth-century Virginia a man was in a position to learn values that form the basic ingredients of leadership. There was hardly a better school anywhere in which to acquire the habits of sane command, the importance of good manners and dignified behavior, and, above all, that special noblesse oblige which fortifies the sense of leadership, no matter how self-sacrificing, and of responsibility, no matter how onerous. Among members of his family and neighbors young Washington chose models of manliness, ambition, self-respect, and practicality.

He set himself gentlemanly standards of behavior early in life. At the age of thirteen he elaborately copied a set of 110 "Rules of Civility and Decent Behaviour in Company and Conversation." The Rules are an amalgam of Calvinistic morals, Franklinian maxims, Chesterfieldian manners. The significant thing about this handbook of behavior is not that Washington copied it as a schoolboy but that he seriously strove to live up to its rules as a man. A few examples will convey the flavor of the maxims:

Every Action done in Company, ought to be with some Sign of Respect, to those that are Present.

Sleep not when others Speak, Sit not when others stand, Speak not when you should hold your Peace.

At Play and at Fire its Good manners to Give Place to the last Commer.

Come not near the Books or Writings of Another so as to read them unless desired or give your opinion of them unask'd.

Let your countenance be pleasant but in serious matters somewhat grave.

Reproach none for the Infirmaties of Nature.

Shew not yourself glad at the Misfortune of another though he were your enemy.

When you meet with one of Greater Quality than yourself, Stop, and . . . give way for him to Pass.

Let your Discourse with Men of Business be Short and Comprehensive.

In writing or Speaking, give to every Person his due Title according to his Degree & the Custom of the Place.

Strive not with your superiors in argument, but always submit your Judgment to others with Modesty.

Undertake not to teach your Equal in the Art himself professes; it savors Arrogancy.

In your Apparel be Modest and endeavour to accomodate Nature, rather than to procure Admiration.

Associate yourself with Men of good Quality if you Esteem your own Reputation; for 'tis better to be alone than in bad Company.

Let your Conversation be without Malice or Envy. . . . And in all Causes of Passion admit Reason to Govern.

Be not apt to relate News if you know not the truth thereof.

Undertake not what you cannot Perform but be Careful to keep your Promise.

Speak not Evil of the Absent for it is unjust.

Be not tedious in Discourse.

When you Speak of God or his Attributes, let it be Seriously & with Reverence.

Let your Recreations be Manfull not Sinfull.

Labour to keep alive in your Breast that Little Spark of Celestial fire Called Conscience.

The virtues Washington adopted and developed were an integral part of his massive character. His qualities were not those of a wild-eyed dreamer or frenetic patriot. They were, rather, those of a tough-minded man of the world, ambitious to acquire wealth and honor, practical and conservative in all his dealings, always accepting the world exactly as it was, and generally untroubled by illusions of human nobility. "We may," he would tell his impatient friends, "lament that things are not consonant with our wishes, but cannot change the nature of man." In all his dealings with people he acted on the assumption that follies and foibles were inherent in mankind. "We must," he said repeatedly, "take the passions of men as nature has given them."

It was imperative for a gentleman to recognize the limitations of human nature and to act so as not to be entrapped by the weakness or greed of others. The weak and the unfortunate called for assistance, but not for personal involvement in their ill luck. Washington practiced charity, but lost no emotions over its recipients. It was out of his sharply developed sense of duty that he often helped the needy even when he could hardly afford it. In his relations with individuals he carefully calculated their characters and gave them the exact respect they deserved.

Typical of his practical attitude is the letter he wrote to his twenty-one-years old nephew, Bushrod Washington, who went to

Philadelphia to study law. Washington gave the future Justice of the Supreme Court advice worthy of Polonius.

> Let the object, which carried you to Philadelphia [the General wrote] be always before your Eyes. Remember, that it is not the mere study of the Law, but to become eminent in the profession of it, which is to yield honor and profit. The first was your choice; let the second be your ambition. . . . Dissipation is incompatible with both; . . . the Company, in which you will improve most, will be least expensive to you; and yet I am not such a Stoic as to suppose that you will, or to think it right that you should, always be in Company with senators and philosophers; but of the young and juvenile kind let me advise you to be choice. It is easy to make acquaintances, but very difficult to shake them off, however irksome and unprofitable they are found. . . . The indiscretions and scrapes, which very often they involuntarily lead one into, prove equally distressing and disgraceful.
>
> Be courteous to all, but intimate with few; and let those few be well tried before you give them your confidence. True friendship is a plant of slow growth, and must undergo and withstand the shocks of adversity before it is entitled to the appellation. . . .
>
> Do not conceive that fine clothes make fine men any more than fine feathers make fine Birds. A plain genteel dress is more admired, and obtains more credit than lace and embroidery. . . .
>
> The last thing, which I shall mention, is first in importance; and that is, to avoid Gaming. This is a vice which is productive of every possible evil; equally injurious to the morals and health of its votaries. It is the child of avarice, the brother of iniquity, and father of mischief. It has been the ruin of many worthy families, the loss of many a man's honor, and the cause of Suicide. . . . In a word, few gain by this abominable practice . . . while thousands are injured.

If this sounds like mere moralizing, it should be kept in mind that Washington himself practiced his preachings. From early youth he imposed upon himself a severe code of conduct which formed a kind of frame into which he fitted himself. Instead of repressing his character, the strong discipline and conscious purpose of his life elevated it. Of him it could be said that he learned to command himself so that he could command others.

The towering character of the man—that compound of Calvinistic morality and aristocratic obligation—enabled him to play the commanding role that he did in the early years of the United States. It is perhaps hazardous to speak of individual indispensability in history, but if there ever was an indispensable leader at a critical moment in history, it was George Washington. In the formative years of the American republic, roughly between 1776 and 1796, the man, the moment, and the crisis coincided.

It was the sheer personality of Washington that was the decisive element in the three crucial events of early America—the Revolutionary War, the Constitutional Convention, and the first national administration. Hardly anything more than his will power held together the ragged Revolutionary army in times of darkest despair; a weaker man would have given way to hopelessness as the troops deserted, provisions gave out and funds dwindled to near-nothingness. The Commander-in-Chief complained with furious bitterness, but stuck to his guns. Similarly, it was his presence that helped to weld the Constitutional Convention in 1787. Chairman of the Convention, he was a silent member, but the fact that he was there was a guarantee of the importance of the meeting and cemented the disparate viewpoints. Washington's immense prestige was a major factor in the adoption of the bitterly assailed Constitution, especially in the Virginia legislature, where the instrument, eloquently battered by the formidable Patrick Henry, was adopted by a mere majority of 5 out of a total of 168 votes. Rejection of the Constitution by Virginia, Washington knew, would have been a fatal blow to national union. Thus in June, 1788, he helped to save the union just before it began its operations. Finally, it was Washington's personality—recognized far and wide for his integrity and impartiality—that launched the Republic under the Constitution. His exquisite sense of balance and steadying wisdom reconciled clashing interests and opposing sections and gave the new nation the fundamental shape that it has retained to this day.

III

Small wonder that so many of his countrymen began to deify him. The process of canonization started soon after his death. In 1800, a few months after he was buried in the family vault at Mount Vernon, there appeared the first eulogistic biography that was to set a pattern. The title is descriptive of the book—*A History of the Life and Death, Virtues and Exploits of General George Washington, with Curious Anecdotes Equally Honourable to Himself and Exemplary to his Young Countrymen.* The author, Mason

Locke Weems, described himself on the title page as "Formerly Rector of Mount Vernon Parish," an identification with Washington's own church that undoubtedly had much to do with the book's fabulous success. Young America, in the second decade of its nationhood, was hungry for a hero, especially one as ready-made as George Washington, and devoured Weems' rhapsodic production. As edition succeeded edition—there were about seventy of them altogether—the good parson kept on inventing more "curious anecdotes" until the figure of Washington was smothered in a morass of sentimental and moralistic extravaganza. Weems even appealed to future generations to genuflect before the sacred idol he helped to create. On the title page he urged: "Lisp! lisp his name, ye children yet unborn!"

Probably the most famous Weemsey (if the reader will excuse the expression) was the cherry tree story. It is a gem of Americana that is worth recalling:

> The following anecdote . . . is too valuable to be lost, and too true to be doubted; for it was communicated to me by the same excellent lady to whom I am indebted for the last.
>
> "When George," says she, "was about six years old, he was made the wealthy master of a hatchet! of which, like most little boys, he was immoderately fond, and was constantly going about chopping everything that came in his way. One day, in the garden, where he often amused himself hacking his mother's pea-sticks, he unluckily tried the edge of his hatchet on the body of a beautiful young English cherry-tree, which he barked so terribly, that I don't believe the tree ever got the better of it. The next morning the old gentleman, finding out what had befallen his tree, which, by the way, was a great favourite, came into the house; and with much warmth asked for the mischievous author, declaring at the same time, that he would not have taken five guineas for his tree. Nobody could tell him anything about it. Presently George and his hatchet made their appearance. "George," said his father, "do you know who killed that beautiful little cherry tree yonder in the garden?" This was a tough question; and George staggered under it for a moment; but quickly recovered himself: and looking at his father, with the sweet face of youth brightened with the inexpressible charm of all-conquering truth, he bravely cried out, "I can't tell a lie, Pa; you know I can't tell a lie. I did cut it with my hatchet."—"Run to my arms, you dearest boy," cried his father in transports, "run to my arms; glad am I, George, that you killed my tree; for you have paid me for it a thousand fold. Such an act of heroism in my son is more worth than a thousand trees, though blossomed with silver, and their fruits of purest gold."

It is not easy to survive this kind of prose, and George Washington—as a human being—was immolated by it. If there is such a thing as a crime of herocide, Washington was its victim. To his countrymen he became an embalmed image, a figure of wood, a mindless icon. When, in recent years, I told friends and students that I was preparing a book on George Washington's political and social ideas, I was invariably asked the surprised and sceptical question: "Why, did Washington have any ideas?"

IV

He had definite ideas, especially about the kind of world he wished to see established in America. He was not a systematic thinker; nor did he take the trouble to formulate his ideas. But scattered through his utterances, addresses, and letters there are strains of thought that show considerable consistency.

At bottom, George Washington was an eighteenth-century rationalist, a firm believer in the rule of reason and of justice, and a champion of republicanism. Despite his aristocratic habits and predilections, he detested the very idea of monarchical or autocratic government; the suggestion that he should become a king outraged him deeply. Unlike some of his distinguished contemporaries, Washington was a genuine republican. Talk about a possible American monarchy made him angry and ashamed.

> I am told [he wrote to John Jay a year before the Constitutional Convention] that even respectable characters speak of a monarchical form of government without horror. From thinking proceeds speaking; thence to acting is often but a single step. What a triumph for our enemies to verify their predictions! What a triumph for the advocates of despotism to find that we are incapable of governing ourselves.

He was resolved that, in so far as he could have anything to do about it, America would not become an autocracy. He knew that there was no such thing as an ideal government, but he was convinced that a constitutional republic, run by responsible and honest men, was, as he told James Madison, "as near to perfection as any human institution ever approximated." Hence the American Republic, which he did so much to create, must succeed at all costs.

General Washington . . . [Jefferson said of him] sincerely wished the people to have as much self government as they were competent to exercise themselves. The only point on which he and I ever differed in opinion, was, that I had more confidence then he had in the natural integrity and discretion of the people, and in the safety and extent to which they might trust themselves with a control over their government. He has asseverated to me a thousand times his determination that the existing government should have a fair trial, and that in support of it he would spend the last drop of his blood.

To Washington, the experiment in self-government was more than a purely American affair. It was, he felt, of importance to mankind, because if it succeeded here it would serve as an example to others. For, in common with other eighteenth-century minds, he took a world view. He was, indeed, a Mason at a time when Masonry was reputed to be actively revolutionist, that is, opposed to the established autocracies and tyrannies. As a Mason, he had, he said, "true Brothers in all parts of the world."

An admirer of Thomas Paine's writings, he wrote him, in 1792:

No one can feel a greater interest in the happiness of mankind than I do. . . . It is the first wish of my heart, that the enlightened policy of the present age may diffuse to all men those blessings, to which they are entitled, and lay the foundation of happiness for future generations.

He had a definite philosophy of republican self-government. Republicanism, to him, meant a way of life that guaranteed personal freedom, the enjoyment of private property, and equal justice for all individuals. Although himself a Southerner and a planter, Washington, unlike most of his neighbors, was no agrarian. He took a national view of the republic, realizing that there were other interests and other honorable ways of making a living than agriculture. He was pleased to observe the initial growth of industry in Pennsylvania and New England; it meant a strengthening of the Republic.

Paradoxical as it may sound, the owner of several hundred slaves was also opposed to the institution of slavery. Washington found slavery abhorrent, but, as a Southern landowner, he was trapped in its tragedy. "There is not a man living," he wrote to Robert Morris in 1786, "who wishes more sincerely than I do to see a plan adopted for the abolition of it." He played with a number of plans for emancipation; for economic and political reasons nothing came of them. But in his will he provided for the manumission of his own slaves.

In matters of religion, too, Washington was a child of the eighteenth-century Enlightenment. With Jefferson, Madison, and the other liberals of his day, he shared the idea of complete religious toleration. He was totally free of the vulgarity of religious or racial bias. Once in trying to get some servants, he said that he did not care where they came from or what Deity they worshipped or did not worship. "If they are good workmen," he wrote, "they may be from Asia, Africa, or Europe; they may be Mahometans, Jews, or Christians of any sect, or they may be Atheists."

He knew that in the past religious persecutions had caused great misery. "Of all the animosities which have existed among mankind," he wrote, "those which are caused by difference of sentiments in religion appear to be the most inveterate and distressing, and ought most to be deprecated." For himself, he did not particularly care which, if any, path a man took to get to heaven. Referring to the conflicting sects of Christendom, he told Lafayette: "Being no bigot myself, I am disposed to indulge the professors of Christianity . . . with that road to heaven, which to them shall seem the most direct, plainest, easiest."

It was a matter of special pride to Washington that the American Republic guaranteed full religious liberty to all, particularly such persecuted groups as the Quakers and the Jews. To the Philadelphia Quakers he wrote a characteristic letter:

> The liberty enjoyed by the People of these States, of worshipping Almighty God agreeable to their consciences is not only among the choicest of their *blessings* but also of their *rights*. While men perform their social duties faithfully, they do all that Society or the State can with propriety demand or expect; and remain responsible only to their Maker for the religion or modes of faith which they may prefer to profess. . . . I assure you very explicitly that in my opinion the conscientious scruples of all men should be treated with delicacy and tenderness.

In a similar vein he wrote to the Hebrew Congregation at Newport, Rhode Island. In that famous letter he rejected the idea of mere toleration, stressing that freedom of religious worship was one of the "inherent natural rights." America, he said, required only good civic behavior, and not spiritual conformity. "For happily the Government of the United States . . . gives to bigotry no sanction, to persecution no assistance."

He was touchingly proud of America, proud that it was his country that had been given the historic chance of serving as a model of republican freedom, which was the only way of attaining happiness. As he wrote to a French friend during the third year of his Presidency: "The United States are making great progress towards national happiness; and, if it is not attained here in as high a degree as human nature will admit . . . , I think we may conclude, that political happiness is unattainable."

In retrospect, we can say that it is now clear that the victorious American Revolution inspired not only the French Revolution of 1789 but also republican movements in many parts of the world, and most particularly throughout Latin America. It started a world-wide chain reaction the end of which has not yet been reached. We also know that the American Republic, which Washington did so much to create, showed itself to be so enduring and successful that it became an example to many other nations. Hence we may conclude that George Washington, the eighteenth-century Virginia planter, is more than a national American figure. He may be truly regarded as a giant in the history of human freedom.

A methodical and scrupulously careful man, Washington wrote voluminously and kept a full record of his transactions. This collection is based on his writings that have been published over the years in many and scattered volumes. Here are Washington's speeches and addresses, his essential diaries, many of his more important letters and comments. The editor has tried to eliminate the irrelevant but to omit nothing that is of importance for an understanding of the essential Washington. Here we see him in his capacity as surveyor and planter, as general and patriot, as President and statesman, as family man and friend. The editor's aim has been to produce a one-volume treasury of Washington, to show him in his fullness and many-sidedness.

Chronology

GEORGE WASHINGTON (1732-1799)

1732	February 22 (February 11, Old Style)	Born, Bridges Creek, Westmoreland County, Virginia
1747		Left school
1749	July 20	Official surveyor, Culpeper County, Virginia
1752	November 6	Appointed major in Virginia Militia
1753	October 31	Sent by Governor Robert Dinwiddie as agent to warn French against Ohio Valley encroachments
1754	March 15	Lieutenant-Colonel of Virginia Regiment in the Ohio campaign
1755	May 10	General Edward Braddock's Aide-de-Camp
	August 14	Colonel of Virginia Regiment and Commander in Chief of Virginia Forces
1756	February-March	Trip to Boston to see Governor William Shirley
1758		Participated in John Forbes expedition to Fort Duquesne
	July 24	Elected Burgess for Frederick County
	December	Resigned commission as Colonel of Virginia Regiment
1759	January 6	Married Mrs. Martha Dandridge Custis
1761	May 18	Re-elected Burgess for Frederick County
1762	October 25	Vestryman, Truro Parish, Fairfax County
1763	October 3	Warden, Pohick Church, Truro Parish
1765	July 16	Elected Burgess for Fairfax County
1768	December 1	Re-elected Burgess for Fairfax County
1769	September 14	Re-elected Burgess
1770	October	Justice of the Peace for Fairfax County

1770	October 5 December 1	Trip to the Ohio and the Great Kanawha
1771	December 4	Re-elected Burgess for Fairfax County
1773	May 10 June 8	Trip to New York City
1774	July 14	Re-elected Burgess for Fairfax County
1774	July 18	Chairman, Fairfax County mass meeting that adopted Fairfax County Resolves
1774	August 1	Attended first Virginia Provincial Convention at Williamsburg
1774	August 5	Elected Delegate to First Continental Congress
1774	September 5 October 26	Attended Congress at Philadelphia
1775	March 25	Elected Delegate to Second Continental Congress
1775	May 10 June 22	Attended Congress at Philadelphia
1775	June 15	Elected by Congress General and Commander-in-Chief of Army of the United Colonies (accepted June 16; commissioned June 19)
1775	July 3	Took command at Cambridge, Mass.
1783	June 19	Elected President-General of Society of the Cincinnati
1783	December 23	Surrendered commission to Congress at Annapolis
1783	December 24	Arrived at Mount Vernon to resume private life
1787	March 28	Elected Virginia Delegate to Federal Convention
1787	May 25	Unanimously elected President of Convention
1788	January 18	Elected Chancellor of William and Mary College
1788	December 20	Elected Master of the Freemasons Lodge in Alexandria
1789	February 4	Unanimously elected President of the United States
1789	April 30	Inaugurated President in New York

1792	December 5	Unanimously re-elected President
1793	March 4	Inaugurated President in Philadelphia
1793	September 18	Laid cornerstone of Federal Capitol in Washington
1796	September 17	Issued Farewell Address
1797	March 9-15	Returned home to Mount Vernon
1798	July 4	Appointed Lieutenant General and Commander-in-Chief of the armies by President Adams
1799	December 14	Died at Mount Vernon
1799	December 18	Buried in family vault

Part I

PERSONAL

Chapter I

FAMILY ORIGINS

To Sir Isaac Heard, Philadelphia, May 2, 1792

I have often heard others of the family, older than myself, say that our ancestor who first settled in this country came from some one of the northern counties of England, but whether from Lancashire, Yorkshire, or one still more northerly I do not precisely remember.

The Arms enclosed in your letter are the same that are held by the family here—though I have also seen, and have used as you may perceive by the seal to this packet, a flying griffen for the Crest.

If you can derive any information from the enclosed lineage which will enable you to complete your Table, I shall be well pleased in having been the means to assist you in those researches which you have had the politeness to undertake.

Lawrence Washington, from whose will you enclosed an abstract, was my grandfather.

In the year 1657, or thereabouts, and during the usurpation of Oliver Cromwell, John and Lawrence Washington, brothers, emigrated from the north of England, and settled at Bridges Creek, on Potomac River, in the county of Westmoreland. But from whom they descended, the subscribed is possessed of no document to ascertain.

John Washington [George Washington's great-grandfather] was employed as General agent to the Indians in Maryland, and as a reward for his services was made a Colonel; and the parish wherein he lived was called after him.

He married Ann Pope, and left issue, two sons, Lawrence and

John, and one daughter, Ann, who married Major Francis Wright. . . .

Lawrence Washington [George Washington's grandfather], his eldest son, married Mildred Warner, daughter of Col. Augustine Warner of Gloucester County, by whom he had two sons, John and Augustine, and one daughter named Mildred. He died in 1697 and was interred in the family vault at Bridges Creek. . . . Augustine [George Washington's father], son of Lawrence and Mildred Washington, married Jane Butler, the daughter of Caleb Butler, of Westmoreland, April 20, 1715, by whom he had three sons: Butler (who died young), Lawrence, and Augustine, and one daughter, Jane, who died when a child. Jane, wife of Augustine, died Nov. 24, 1728, and was buried in the family vault at Bridges Creek.

Augustine then married (Mary) Ball [George Washington's mother], March 6, 1730, by whom he had issue George, born February 11 (old style), 1732; Betty, born June 20, 1733; Samuel, born Nov. 16, 1734; John Augustine, born Jan. 13, 1736; Charles, May 1, 1738; and Mildred, June 21, 1739, who died Oct. 28, 1740. Augustine departed this life April 12, 1743, aged 49 years, and was interred at Bridges Creek in the vault of his ancestors.

Lawrence [George Washington's half-brother, who left him Mount Vernon], son of Augustine and Jane Washington, married July 19, 1743, Ann, eldest daughter of the Hon. William Fairfax of Fairfax County, by whom he had issue Jane, born Sept. 27, 1744, who died Jan. 7, 1745; Fairfax, born August 22, 1747, who died in Oct., 1747; Mildred, born Sept. 28, 1748, who died in 1749; Sarah, born Nov. 7, 1750, who died in 175–. In 1752 Lawrence himself died, aged about 34, and was interred in a vault which he had caused to be erected at Mount Vernon in Fairfax County, where he settled after he returned from the Cartagena Expedition and died. . . .

George, eldest son of Augustine Washington by the second marriage [to Mary Ball], was born in Westmoreland County, and married Jan. 6, 1759, Martha Custis, widow of Danl. Parke Custis, and daughter of John Dandridge, both of New Kent County. Has no issue. . . .

The above is the best account the subscriber [George Washington] is able to give at present, absent as he is, and at so great a distance from Virginia, and under circumstance too which allows no time for enquiry, of the family of Washington from which he is lineally descended.

The descendants of the first named Lawrence, and the second John, are also numerous; but for the reasons before mentioned and from not having the same knowledge of them, and being moreover more remote from their place of residence, and in truth not having enquired much into the names or connection of the lateral branches of the family, I am unable to give a satisfactory account of them. But if it be in any degree necessary, or satisfactory to Sir Isaac Heard, Garter Principal King of Arms, I will upon intimation thereof, set on foot an enquiry, and will at the same time endeavor to be more particular with respect to the births, names, ages and burials of those of the branch to which the subscriber belongs.

To William Augustine Washington, February 27, 1798

Did you ever receive a letter from me transmitting the request of Sir Isaac Heard of the Heraldry Office in England respecting Genealogy of our family? and my own desire to be furnished with the Inscriptions on the Tombs of our Ancestors at—Bridge Creek? Among your father's papers, I thought it likely, you might obtain some information on this head. From the coming over of John and Lawrence Washington in the year 1657—I have [been] able to trace the descendants of the former, being the one from whom our family came, those of Lawrence from whom the Chotankers proceeded I have not been able to give any correct account: and that is the branch to which Sir Isaac Heard's enquiry's particularly point. . . . The enquiry is in my opinion of very little moment, but as Sir Isaac has interested himself in the matter and seems desirous of tracing the family from whom we are descended—back—I wish to give him as correct information of it—as I am able to procure.

To William Augustine Washington, October 3, 1798

I thank you for the old documents you sent me respecting the family of our ancestors, but I am possessed of papers which prove beyond a doubt, that of the two brothers who emigrated to this country in the year 1657, during the troubles of that day, that John Washington from whom we are descended was the eldest. The pedigree from him I have, and I believe very correct: but the descendants of Lawrence in a regular course, I have not been able to trace. All those of our name in and about Chotank are from the latter. John was the grandfather of my father, and uncle and great grandfather to Warren [Warner] and me. He left two sons, Lawrence and John, the former who was the eldest, was the father of my father.

Chapter 2

EXTRACTS FROM DIARIES

Diary, Surveying Trip to Blue Ridge Mountains, Which Started Out on March 11, 1748

Began my Journey in Company with George Fairfax, Esqr., we travell'd this day 40 Miles to Mr. George Neavels in Prince William County . . . This Morning Mr. James Genn ye. surveyor came to us we travell'd over ye. Blue Ridge to Capt. Ashbys on Shannondoah River, Nothing remarkable happen'd . . . Rode to his Lordships Quarter about 4 Miles higher up y. River we went through most beautiful Groves of Sugar Trees and spent ye. best part of y. Day in admiring ye. Trees and richness of ye land . . . We . . . went ourselves down ye River about 16 miles to Capt. Isaac Penningtons (the Land exceeding Rich and Fertile all ye. way produces abundance of Grain Hemp Tobacco &ca.) in order to lay of some Lands on Cates Marsh and Long Marsh . . .

We set out early with Intent to Run round ye sd. Land but being taken in a Rain and it Increasing very fast obliged us to return it clearing about one oClock and our time being too Precious to Loose we a second time ventur'd out and Worked hard till Night and then return'd to Penningtons we got our Supper and was lighted into a Room and I not being so good a Woodsman as ye rest of my Company striped myself very orderly and went in to ye Bed as they called it when to my Surprise I found it to be nothing but a Little Straw-Matted together without Sheets or any thing else but only one thread Bear blanket with double its Weight of Vermin such as Lice Fleas &c I was glad to get up (as soon as y. Light was carried from us) I put on my Cloths and Lay as my Companions. Had we not been very tired I am sure we should not have slep'd much that night I made a Promise not to

Sleep so from that time forward chusing rather to sleep in y. open Air before a fire as will appear hereafter. . . .

Survey'd for George Fairfax Esqr. a Tract of Land lying on Cates Marsh and Long Marsh. . . . We set out early and finish'd about one oClock and then Travell'd up to Frederick Town [Winchester] where our Baggage came to us we cleaned ourselves (to get Rid of y. Game we had catched y. Night before) and took a Review of y. Town and thence return'd to our Lodgings where we had a good Dinner prepar'd for us Wine and Rum Punch in Plenty and a good Feather Bed with clean Sheets which was a very agreeable regale . . .

We Travell'd up about 35 Miles to Thomas Barwicks on Potomack where we found y. River so excessively high by Reason of y. Great Rains that had fallen up about y. Alleghany Mountains as they told us which was then bringing down y. melted Snow and that it would not be fordable for severall Days it was then above Six foot Higher than usual and was rising we agreed to stay till Monday we this day call'd to see y. Fam'd Warm Springs we camped out in y. field . . .

finding y. River not much abated we in y. Evening Swam our horses over and carried them to Charles Polks in Maryland for Pasturage till y. next Morning . . . We went over in a Canoe and travell'd up Maryland side all y. Day in a Continued Rain to Collo Cresaps right against y. Mouth of y. South Branch about 40 Miles from Polks I believe y. worst Road that ever was trod by Man or Beast . . .

Rain'd till about two oClock and Clear'd when we were agreeably surpris'd at y. sight of thirty odd Indians coming from War with only one Scalp We had some Liquor with us of which we gave them Part it elevating their Spirits put them in y. Humour of Dauncing of whom we had a War Daunce there manner of Dauncing is as follows Viz They clear a Large Circle and make a Great Fire in y. middle then seats themselves around it y. Speaker makes a grand speech telling them in what Manner they are to Daunce after he has finished y. best Dauncer jumps up as one awaked out of a Sleep and runs and Jumps about y. Ring in a most comical Manner he is followed by y. Rest then begins there Musicians to Play ye. Musick is a Pot half [full] of Water with a Deerskin

Streched over it as tight as it can and a goard with some Shott in it to Rattle and a Piece of an horses Tail tied to it to make it look fine y. one keeps Rattling and y. other Drumming all y. while y. others is Dauncing . . .

This Morning went out and Survey'd five Hundred Acres of Land and went down to one Michael Stumps on ye. So Fork of ye. Branch on our way Shot two Wild Turkies. . . . Survey'd for Mr. James Rutlidge ye following a piece of Land . . .

Last Night was a blowing and Rainy night Our Straw catch'd a Fire yt. we were laying upon and was luckily Preserv'd by one of our Mens awaking when it was in a [blaze] . . .

Last Night was a much more blostering night then ye. former we had our Tent Carried Quite of with ye. Wind and was obliged to Lie ye. Latter part of ye. night without covering . . .

Last Night was so Intolerable smoky that we were obliged all hands to leave ye Tent to ye. Mercy of ye Wind and Fire this day was attended by our afored Company untill about 12 oClock when we finish'd we travell'd down ye Branch to Henry Vanmetris's on our Journey was catched in a very heavy Rain we got under a Straw House untill ye Worst of it was over and then continued our Journey . . .

Rain'd Successively all Last night this Morning one of our men Killed a Wild Turkie that weight 20 Pounds we went and Survey'd 15 Hundred Acres of Land and Return'd to Vanmetris's about 1 oClock about two I heard that Mr. Fairfax was come up and at 1 Peter Casseys about 2 Miles of in ye. same Old Field I then took my Horse and went up to see him . . .

we breakfasted at Casseys and Rode down to Vanmetris's to get all our Company together which when we had accomplished we Rode down below ye. Trough in order to Lay of Lots there we laid of one this day The Trough is [a] couple of Ledges of Mountain Impassable running side and side together for above 7 or 8 Miles and ye River down between them you must Ride Round ye back of ye. Mountain for to get below them we Camped this Night in ye Woods near a Wild Meadow where was a Large Stack of Hay after we had Pitched our Tent and made a very Large Fire we pull'd out our Knapsack in order to Recruit ourselves every [one] was his own Cook our Spits was Forked Sticks our Plates was a Large Chip as for Dishes we had none

Barbados Diary, 1751

[October] 7th . . . Saw many fish swimming abt. us of which a Dolphin we catchd at Noon but cou'd not intice with a baited hook two Baricootas which played under our Stern for some Hours; the Dolphin being small we had it dressed for Supper . . .

20th. A Constant succession of hard Winds, Squals of Rain, and Calms was the remarkable attendants of this day which was so sudden and flighty we durst not go under any but reef'd Sails and those that we cou'd D R [double reef]. At 6 A M put abt. to the Eastward A sloop that for the two preceding Days was [in] sight of us hung out a Signal but wheth[er] distress or not we are uncertain; if it had [been we] were incapable of reliving them by ye contrs. of [the wind?] . . .

[30th] This Morning arose with agreeable assurances of a certain and steady trade Wind which after near five Weeks of buffiting and being toss'd by a fickle and Merciless ocean was glad-ening knews: the preceeding night we separated from sloop abe mentioned . . .

[Nov. 2d] We were grea . . . larm'd with the cry of Land at 4 A: M: we quitted ourbeds with surprise and found ye land plainly appearing at [a]bout 3 leauges distance . . .

[4th. Early this morning came Dr. Hilary, an eminent physician recommended by Major Clarke, to pass his opinion on my brother's disorder, which he did in a favorable light, giving great assurance, that it was not so fixed but that a cure might be effectually made. In the cool of the evening we rode out accompanied by Mr. Carter to seek lodgings in the country, as the Doctor advised,] and was perfectly rav . . . the beautiful prospects which on every side presented to our view The fields of Cain, Corn, Fruit Trees &c in a delightful Green. We return'd without accomplishing our intentions. . . .

6th. . . . Receiv'd a Card from Majr. Clarke wherein our companys were desir'd to Dinner to morrow and myself an invitation from Mrs. Clarke and Miss Robts. to come and see the seprts fir'd being gunpd. . . .

9th. We receiv'd a card from Majr. Clarke inviting us to dine with him at Judge Maynards on the Morrow he had a right to ask being a Member of the Club call'd the Beefstake and tripe instituted by himself. . . .

[10th] . . . After Dinner was the greatest Collection of Fruits I have yet seen on the Table there was Granadella the Sappadilla Pomgranate Sweet Orange Water Lemmon forbidden Fruit apples Guavas &ca. &ca. &ca. . . .

15*th.* Was treated with a play ticket by Mr. Carter to see the Tragedy of George Barnwell acted: the character of Barnwell and several others was said to be well perform'd there was Musick a Dapted and regularly conducted by Mr. . . .

17*th.* Was strongly attacked with the small Pox: sent for Dr. Lanahan whose attendance was very constant till my recovery, and going out which was not 'till thursday the 12th of December. . . .

[Dec.] 22*d.* Took my leave of . . . Majr. Clarke &ca. and Imbar[ked] in the Industry Captn. John Saund[ers] for Virginia wai'd anchor and got out of Carlile Bay abt. 12. . . . How wonderful that such people shou'd be in debt! and not be able to indulge themselves in all the Luxurys as well as necessarys of Life Yet so it happens Estates are often alienated for the debts . . . Hospitality and a Genteel behav[ior] is shewn to every gentlemen stranger by the Gentlemen Inhab[itants. . . .] Taverns they have none but in their Towns so that Travellers is oblig'd to go to private houses however the Island being but abt. 22 Miles in length and 14 in width preven[ts] their being much infested with ym. . . . There are few who may be calld midling people they are either very rich or very poor for by a Law of the Island Every Gentn. is oblig'd to keep a white person for ten Acres capable of acting in the Militia and consequently those persons so kept cant but [be] very poor. . . .

[Jan. 29?, 1752] Early this Morning . . . Wind sprang up at Sp. Et. made Sail under easy Gales past the Cape abt. Sun's Rising and got to the Mouth of York River abt. 11 P. M. and was met by a pilot boat.

JOURNAL TO THE OHIO, 1753

ADVERTISEMENT

As it was thought adviseable by his Honour the Governor to have the following Account of my Proceedings to and from the FRENCH *on* OHIO, *committed to Print; I think I can do no less than apologize, in some Measure, for the numberless Imperfections of it.*

There intervened but one Day between my Arrival in WILLIAMSBURG, *and the Time for the Council's Meeting, for me to prepare and transcribe, from the rough Minutes I had taken in my Travels, this Journal; the writing of which only was sufficient to employ me closely the whole Time, consequently admitted of no Leisure to consult of a new and proper Form to offer it in, or to correct or amend the Diction of the old: Neither was I apprised, nor did in the least conceive, when I wrote this for his Honour's Perusal, that it ever would be published, or even have more than a cursory Reading; till I was informed, at the Meeting of the present General Assembly, that it was already in the Press.*

There is nothing can recommend it to the Public, but this. Those Things which came under the Notice of my own Observation, I have been explicit and just in a Recital of:—Those which I have gathered from Report, I have been particularly cautious not to augment, but collected the Opinions of the several Intelligencers, and selected from the whole, the most probable and consistent Account.

G. WASHINGTON.

Wednesday, October 31, 1753.

I was commissioned and appointed by the Honourable *Robert Dinwiddie,* Esq; Governor, &c., of *Virginia,* to visit and deliver a letter to the Commandant of the *French* forces on the *Ohio,* and set out on the intended Journey the same day: The next, I arrived at *Fredericksburg,* and engaged Mr. *Jacob Vanbraam,*[1] to

[1] Van Braam was a Hollander, and had served under Lawrence Washington in the Cartagena expedition.

be my *French* interpreter; and proceeded with him to *Alexandria,* where we provided Necessaries. From thence we went to *Winchester,* and got Baggage, Horses, &c; and from thence we pursued the new Road to *Wills-Creek,*[2] where we arrived the 14th of *November.*

Here I engaged Mr. *Gist*[3] to pilot us out, and also hired four others as Servitors, *Barnaby Currin* and *John Mac-Quire,* Indian Traders, *Henry Steward,* and *William Jenkins;* and in company with those persons, left the Inhabitants the Day following.

The excessive Rains and vast Quantity of Snow which had fallen, prevented our reaching Mr. *Frazier's,* an Indian Trader, at the Mouth of *Turtle Creek,* on *Monongahela* [River], till *Thursday,* the 22d. We were informed here, that Expresses had been sent a few Days before to the Traders down the River, to acquaint them with the *French* General's death, and the Return of the major Part of the *French* Army into Winter Quarters.

The Waters were quite impassable, without swimming our Horses; which obliged us to get the Loan of a Canoe from *Frazier,* and to send *Barnaby Currin* and *Henry Steward* down the *Monongahela,* with our Baggage, to meet us at the Forks of *Ohio,* about 10 miles, there to cross the *Aligany.*

As I got down before the Canoe, I spent some time in viewing the Rivers, and the Land in the Fork; which I think extremely well situated for a Fort, as it has the absolute Command of both Rivers. The Land at the Point is 20 or 25 Feet above the common Surface of the Water; and a considerable Bottom of flat, well-timbered land all around it, very convenient for Building: The Rivers are each a Quarter of a Mile, or more, across, and run here very near at right Angles: *Aligany* bearing N. E. and *Monongahela* S. E. The former of these two is a very rapid and swift running Water; the other deep and still, without any perceptible Fall.

About two Miles from this, on the South East Side of the river, at the Place where the *Ohio* Company intended to erect a Fort, lives *Shingiss,* king of the *Delawares:* We called upon him, to invite him to Council at the *Loggs*-Town.

As I had taken a good deal of Notice Yesterday of the Situation

[2] Now Cumberland, Md.
[3] Christopher Gist.

at the *Forks,* my Curiosity led me to examine this more particularly, and I think it greatly inferior, either for Defence or Advantages; especially the latter: For a Fort at the *Forks* would be equally well situated on the *Ohio,* and have the entire Command of the *Monongahela;* which runs up to our Settlements and is extremely well designed for Water Carriage, as it is of a deep still Nature. Besides a fort at the *Fork* might be built at a much less Expence, than at the other Place.

Nature has well contrived this lower Place, for Water Defence; but the Hill whereon it must stand being about a Quarter of a Mile in Length, and then descending gradually on the Land Side, will render it difficult and very expensive, to make a sufficient Fortification there.—The whole Flat upon the Hill must be taken-in, the Side next the Descent made extremely high, or else the Hill itself cut away: Otherwise, the Enemy may raise Batteries within that Distance without being exposed to a single Shot from the Fort.

Shingiss attended us to the *Loggs*-Town, where we arrived between Sun-setting and Dark, the 25th Day after I left *Williamsburg.* We travelled over some extreme good and bad Land, to get to this Place.—

As soon as I came into Town, I went to *Monakatoocha* (as the Half-King was out at his hunting-Cabbin on little *Beaver*-Creek, about 15 Miles off) and informed him by *John Davison,* my *Indian* Interpreter, that I was sent a Messenger to the *French* General; and was ordered to call upon the Sachems of the *Six Nations,* to acquaint them with it.—I gave him a String of Wampum, and a Twist of Tobacco, and desired him to send for the Half-King; which he promised to do by a Runner in the Morning, and for other Sachems.—I invited him and the other great Men present to my Tent, where they stay'd about an Hour and return'd.

According to the best Observations I could make, Mr. *Gist's* new Settlement (which we pass'd by) bears about W. N. W. 70 Miles from *Wills*-Creek; *Shanapins,* or the Forks N. by W. or N. N. W. about 50 Miles from that; and from thence to the *Loggs*-Town, the course is nearly West about 18 or 20 Miles: so that the whole Distance, as we went and computed it, is at least 135 or 140 Miles from our back Inhabitants.

25th. Came to Town four or ten *Frenchmen* who had deserted from a Company at the *Kuskuskas,* which lies at the Mouth of this River. I got the following Account from them. They were sent from *New-Orleans* with 100 men, and 8 Canoe-Loads of Provisions to this Place; where they expected to have met the same Number of Men, from the Forts on this Side Lake *Erie,* to convey them and the Stores up, who were not arrived when they ran-off.

I enquired into the Situation of the *French,* on the *Mississippi,* their Number, and what Forts they had built. They inform'd me, That there were four small Forts between *New Orleans* and the *Black-Islands,* garrison'd with about 30 or 40 Men, and a few small Pieces in each. That at *New Orleans,* which is near the Mouth of the *Mississippi,* there are 35 Companies, of 40 Men each, with a pretty strong Fort mounting 8 Carriage Guns; and at the *Black-Islands* there are several Companies, and a Fort with 6 Guns. The *Black-Islands* are about 130 Leagues above the Mouth of the *Ohio,* which is about 350 above *New-Orleans.* They also acquainted me that there was a small pallisado'd Fort on the *Ohio,* at the Mouth of the *Obaish* about 60 Leagues from the *Mississippi.* The *Obaish* heads near the West End of Lake *Erie,* and affords the Communication between the *French* on *Mississippi* and those on the Lakes. These Deserters came up from the lower *Shanoah* Town with one *Brown,* an *Indian* Trader, and were going to *Philadelphia.*

About 3 o'Clock this Evening the Half-King came to Town. I went up and invited him with *Davison,* privately, to my Tent; and desir'd him to relate some of the Particulars of his Journey to the *French* Commandant, and Reception there: Also to give me an account of the Ways and Distance. He told me that the nearest and levellest Way was now impassable, by Reason of many large mirey Savannas; that we must be obliged to go by *Venango,*[4] and should not get to the near Fort under 5 or 6 Nights Sleep, good Travelling. When he went to the Fort, he said he was received in a very stern Manner by the late Commander; who ask'd him very abruptly, what he had come about, and to declare his Business: Which he said he did in the following Speech:—

[4] Venango was at the meeting of French Creek and the Allegheny River.

Fathers, I am come to tell you your own Speeches; what your own Mouths have declared. Fathers, You in former Days, set a silver Bason before us, wherein there was the Leg of a Beaver, and desir'd all the Nations to come and eat of it; to eat in Peace and plenty, and not to be churlish to one another: and that if any such Person should be found to be a Disturber, I here lay down by the Edge of the Dish a Rod, which you must scourge them with; and if I your Father, should get foolish, in my old Days, I desire you may use it upon me as well as others.

Now Fathers, it is you who are the Disturbers in this Land, by coming and building your Towns; and taking it away unknown to us, and by Force.

Fathers, We kindled a fire a long Time ago, at a Place called *Montreal,* where we desired you to stay, and not to come and intrude upon our Land. I now desire you may dispatch to that Place; for be it known to you, Fathers, that this is our Land, and not yours.

Fathers, I desire you may hear me in Civilness; if not, we must handle that Rod which was laid down for the Use of the abstreperous. If you had come in a peaceable Manner, like our Brothers the *English,* we should not have been against your trading with us, as they do; BUT TO COME, FATHERS, AND BUILD HOUSES UPON OUR LAND, AND TO TAKE IT BY FORCE, IS WHAT WE CANNOT SUBMIT TO.

Fathers, Both you and the *English* are white, we live in a Country between; therefore the Land belongs to neither one nor t'other: But the Great Being above allow'd it to be a place of Residence for us; so Fathers, I desire you to withdraw, as I have done our Brothers the *English*: For I will keep you at Arm's length. I lay this down as a Trial for both, to see which will have the greatest Regard to it, and that Side we will stand by and make equal shares with us. Our Brothers, the *English,* have heard this, and I come now to tell it to you; for I am not afraid to discharge you off this Land.

This he said was the substance of what he spoke to the General, who made this Reply.

Now my child, I have heard your Speech: you spoke first, but it is my Time to speak now. Where is my Wampum that you took away, with the Marks of towns in it? This wampum I do not know, which you have discharged me off the Land with; but you need not put yourself to the Trouble of speaking, for I will not hear you. I am not afraid of Flies, or Musquitos, for *Indians* are such as those. I tell you, down that River I will go, and will build upon it, according to my command. If the River was block'd up, I have Forces sufficient to burst it open and tread under my Feet all that Stand in Opposition, together with their Alliances; for my Force is as the Sand upon the Sea Shore: therefore, here is your Wampum, I fling it at you. Child, you talk foolish; you say this Land belongs to you, but there is not the Black of my Nail yours. I saw that Land sooner than you did, before the Shannoahs and you were at War: *Lead* was the Man who went down and took Possession of that River: It is my Land, and I will have it, let who will stand-up for, or say-against it. I'll buy and sell with the *English* (*mockingly*). If People will be rul'd by me, they may expect kindness, but not else.

The Half-King told me he enquired of the General after two *Englishmen* who were made Prisoners, and received this Answer.

Child, you think it is a very great Hardship that I made Prisoners of those two People at *Venango*. Don't you concern yourself with it: We took and carried them to *Canada*, to get Intelligence of what the *English* were doing in *Virginia*.

He informed me that they had built two Forts, one on Lake *Erie*,[5] and another on *French*-Creek[6] near a small Lake about 15 Miles asunder, and a large Waggon Road between: They are both built after the same Model, but different in the Size; that on the Lake the largest. He gave me a Plan of them, of his own drawing.

The *Indians* enquired very particularly after their Brothers in *Carolina* Goal.

They also asked what sort of Boy it was who was taken from the *South*-Branch; for they were told by some *Indians*, that a Party of *French Indians* had carried a white Boy by the Kuskuska Town, towards the Lakes.

26th. We met in Council at the *Long-House*, about 9 o'clock, where I spoke to them as follows:

Brothers, I have called you together in Council by order of your Brother, the Governor of *Virginia*, to acquaint you, that I am sent, with all possible Dispatch, to visit, and deliver a Letter to the *French* Commandant, of very great Importance to your Brothers, the *English;* and I dare say, to you their Friends and allies.

I was desired, Brothers, by your Brother the Governor, to call upon you, the Sachems of the Nations, to inform you of it, and to ask your Advice and Assistance to proceed the nearest and best Road to the *French*. You see, Brothers, I have gotten thus far on my Journey.

His Honour likewise desired me to apply to you for some of your young Men, to conduct and provide Provisions for us on our Way; and be a safeguard against those *French Indians* who have taken up the hatchet against us. I have spoke this particularly to you Brothers, because his Honour our

[5] Fort Presque Isle.

[6] Fort le Boêuf.

Governor treats you as good Friends and Allies; and holds you in great Esteem. To confirm what I have said, I give you this String of Wampum.

After they had considered for some Time on the above Discourse, the Half-King got up and spoke:—

Now, my Brothers, in regard to what my Brother the Governor has desired me, I return you this answer.

I rely upon you as a Brother ought to do, as you say we are Brothers and one People: We shall put Heart in Hand and speak to our Fathers the *French* concerning the Speech they made to me; and you may depend that we will endeavour to be your Guard.

Brother, as you have asked my Advice, I hope you will be ruled by it and stay till I can provide a Company to go with you. The *French* Speech-Belt is not here, I have it to go for to my hunting Cabbin: Likewise the People whom I have ordered in, are not yet come, nor cannot till the third Night from this: till which Time, brother, I must beg you to stay.

I intend to send a Guard of *Mingo's Shannoah's* and *Delawares,* that our Brothers may see the Love and Loyalty we bear them.

As I had Orders to make all possible Dispatch, and waiting here was very contrary to my Inclinations, I thanked him in the most suitable Manner I could; and told him, that my Business required the greatest Expedition, and would not admit of that Delay. He was not well pleased that I should offer to go before the Time he had appointed, and told me, that he could not consent to our going without a Guard, for Fear some Accident should befal us and draw a Reflection upon him. Besides, says he, this is a Matter of no small Moment, and must not be entered into without due Consideration: For now I intend to deliver up the *French*-Speech-Belt, and make the *Shanoahs* and *Delawares* do the same. And accordingly he gave orders to King *Shingiss,* who was present, to attend on *Wednesday* Night with the Wampum; and two Men of their Nation to be in Readiness to set-out with us next Morning. As I found it was impossible to get-off without affronting them in the most egregious Manner, I consented to stay.

I gave them back a String of Wampum which I met with at Mr. *Frazier's,* and which they had sent with a Speech to his Honour the Governor, to inform him, that three Nations of *French Indians,* viz: *Chippoways, Ottoways,* and *Orundaks* had taken-up the Hatchet against the *English;* and desired them to repeat it over again: But this they postponed doing till they met in full Council with the *Shannoahs* and *Delaware* Chiefs.

27*th*. Runners were now dispatched very early for the *Shannoah* Chiefs. The Half-King set out himself to fetch the *French*-Speech-Belt from his hunting Cabbin.

28*th*. He returned this Evening, and came with *Monokatoocha*, and two other Sachems to my Tent, and begged (as they had complied with his Honour the Governor's Request, in providing Men, &c.) to know on what Business we were going to the *French?* this was a Question I all along expected, and had provided as satisfactory Answers to, as I could; which allayed their Curiosity a little.

Monokatoocha informed me, that an *Indian* from *Venango* brought News, a few Days ago, that the *French* had called all the *Mingo's, Delawares,* &c., together at that Place; and told them, that they intended to have been down the River this Fall, but the Waters were growing cold, and the Winter advancing, which obliged them to go into Quarters: But that they might assuredly expect them in the Spring with a far greater Number; and desired that they might be quite passive, and not to intermeddle, unless they had a Mind to draw all their Force upon them: For that they expected to fight the *English* three Years (as they supposed there would be some Attempts made to stop them), in which Time they should conquer: But that if they should prove equally Strong, they and the *English* would join to cut them all off, and divide the Land between them: That though they had lost their General, and some few of their Soldiers, yet there were Men enough to reinforce them, and make them masters of the *Ohio*.

This Speech, he said, was delivered to them by one Captain *Joncaire,* their Interpreter in Chief, living at *Venango,* and a Man of Note in the Army.

29th. The Half-King and Monokatoocha came very early, and begged me to stay one Day more: For notwithstanding they had used all the Diligence in their Power, the *Shanoah* Chiefs had not brought the Wampum they ordered, but would certainly be in To-night; if not, they would delay me no longer, but would send it after us as soon as they arrived.—When I found them so pressing in their Request, and knew that returning of Wampum was the abolishing of Agreements; and giving this up, was shaking-off all Dependance upon the *French,* I consented to stay, as I believed an Offence offered at this Crisis, might be attended with greater ill Consequence, than another Day's Delay. They also informed me, that *Shingiss* could not get-in his Men; and was prevented from coming himself by his Wife's Sickness (I believe, by Fear of the *French*); but that the Wampum of that Nation was lodged with *Kustaloga* one of their Chiefs at *Venango.*

In the Evening late they came again and acquainted me that the *Shannoahs* were not yet arrived, but that it should not retard the Prosecution of our Journey. He delivered in my Hearing, the Speeches that were to be made to the *French* by *Jeskakake,* one of their old Chiefs, which was giving-up the Belt the late Commandant had asked for, and repeating near the same Speech he himself had done before.

He also delivered a String of Wampum to this Chief, which was sent by King *Shingiss,* to be given to *Kustaloga,* with orders to repair to the *French,* and deliver up the Wampum.

He likewise gave a very large String of black and white Wampum, which was to be sent up immediately to the Six Nations, if the *French* refused to quit the Land at this Warning; which was the third and last Time, and was the Right of this *Jeskakake* to deliver.

30th. Last Night the great Men assembled to their Council-House, to consult further about this Journey, and who were to go: The Result of which was, that only three of their Chiefs, with one of their best Hunters, should be our Convoy. The Reason they gave for not sending more, after what had been proposed at Council the 26th, was, that a greater Number might give the *French* Suspicions of some bad Design, and cause them to be treated rudely: But I rather think they could not get their Hunters in.

We set out about 9 o'Clock with the Half-King *Jeskakake, White Thunder,* and the Hunter; and travelled on the Road to *Venango,* where we arrived the 4th of *December,* without any Thing remarkable happening but a continued Series of bad Weather.

This is an old *Indian* Town, situated at the Mouth of *French* Creek on *Ohio;* and lies near N. about 60 Miles from the *Loggs*-Town, but more than 70 the Way we were obliged to go.

We found the *French* Colours hoisted at a House from which they had driven Mr. *John Frazier,* an *English* Subject. I immediately repaired to it, to know where the Commander resided. There were three Officers, one of whom, Capt. *Joncaire,* informed me, that he had the Command of the *Ohio:* But that there was a General Officer at the near Fort, where he advised me to apply for an Answer. He invited us to sup with them; and treated us with the greatest Complaisance.

The Wine, as they dosed themselves pretty plentifully with it, soon banished the Restraint which at first appeared in their Conversation; and gave a Licence to their Tongues to reveal their Sentiments more freely.

They told me, That it was their absolute Design to take Possession of the *Ohio,* and by G—— they would do it: For that altho' they were sensible the *English* could raise two Men for their one; yet they knew their Motions were too slow and dilatory to prevent any Undertaking of theirs. They pretend to have an undoubted Right to the River, from a Discovery made by one *La Salle* 60 Years ago; and the Rise of this Expedition is, to prevent our settling on the River or Waters of it, as they had heard of some Families moving-out in Order thereto. From the best Intelligence I could get, there have been 1500 Men on their Side *Ontario* Lake: But upon the Death of the General all were recalled to about 6 or 700, who were left to garrison four Forts, 150 or there abouts in each. The first of them is on *French*-Creek near a small Lake, about 60 Miles from *Venango,* near N.N.W. the next lies on Lake *Erie,* where the greater Part of their Stores are kept, about 15 Miles from the other. From this it is 120 Miles to the carrying Place at the Falls of Lake *Erie* where there is a small Fort;[7] which they lodge their Goods at, in bringing them from *Montreal,* the Place whence all their Stores come from. The next Fort lies about 20 Miles from this, on *Ontario*-Lake.[8] Between this Fort and *Montreal* there are three others, the first[9] of which is near opposite to the *English* Fort *Oswego.* From the Fort on Lake *Erie* to *Montreal* is about 600 Miles, which they say requires no more, if good Weather,

[7] Fort Niagara.
[8] Fort Toronto.
[9] Fort Frontenac.

than four Weeks Voyage, if they go in Barks or large Vessels, so that they may cross the Lake: But if they come in Canoes it will require 5 or 6 Weeks, for they are obliged to keep under the Shore.

5th. Rain'd excessively all Day, which prevented our Travelling. Capt. *Joncaire* sent for the Half-King, as he had but just heard that he came with me: He affected to be much concerned that I did not make free to bring them in before. I excused it in the best Manner I was capable, and told him, I did not think their company agreeable, as I had heard him say a good deal in Dispraise of *Indians* in general. But another Motive prevented me from bringing them into his Company: I knew he was Interpreter, and a Person of very great Influence among the *Indians,* and had lately used all possible Means to draw them over to their Interest; therefore I was desirous of giving no Opportunity that could be avoided.

When they came in, there was great Pleasure expressed at seeing them. He wondered how they could be so near without coming to visit him; made several trifling Presents; and applied Liquor so fast, that they were soon rendered incapable of the Business they came about, notwithstanding the Caution which was given.

6th. The Half-King came to my Tent, quite sober, and insisted very much that I should stay and hear what he had to say to the *French.* I fain would have prevented his speaking any Thing till he came to the Commandant, but could not prevail. He told me that at this Place a Council Fire was kindled, where all their Business with these People was to be transacted; and that the Management of the *Indian* affairs was left solely to Monsieur *Joncaire.* As I was desirous of knowing the Issue of this, I agreed to stay: But sent our Horses a little way up *French* Creek to raft over and encamp; which I knew would make it near Night.

About 10 o'Clock they met in Council. The King spoke much the same as he had before done to the General; and offered the *French* Speech-Belt which had before been demanded, with the Marks of four Towns on it, which Monsieur *Joncaire* refused to receive; but desired him to carry it to the Fort to the Commander.

7th. Monsieur *La Force,* Commissary of the *French* Stores, and three other Soldiers came over to accompany us up. We found it extremely difficult to get the *Indians* off To-day, as every Stratagem had been used to prevent their going-up with me. I had last Night, left *John Davison* (the *Indian* Interpreter whom I brought with me from Town), and strictly charged him not to be out of their Company, as I could not get them over to my Tent; for they had some Business with *Kustaloga,* and chiefly to know the Reason why he did not deliver up the *French* Belt which he had in Keeping: But I was obliged to send Mr. *Gist* over To-day to fetch them; which he did with great Persuasion.

At 11 o'Clock we set out for the Fort, and were prevented from arriving there till the 11th by excessive Rains, Snows, and bad Travelling, through many Mires and Swamps. These we were obliged to pass, to avoid crossing the Creek, which was impossible, either by fording or rafting, the Water was so high and rapid.

We passed over much good Land since we left *Venango,* and through several extensive and very rich Meadows; one of which I believe was near four Miles in Length, and considerably wide in some Places.

12th. I prepared early to wait upon the Commander, and was received and conducted to him by the second Officer in Command. I acquainted him with my Business, and offered my Commission and Letter: Both of which he desired me to keep till the Arrival of Monsieur *Riparti* Captain, at the next Fort, who was sent for and expected every Hour.

This Commander is a Knight of the military Order of St. *Lewis,* and named *Legardeur de St. Pierre.* He is an elderly Gentleman, and has much the Air of a Soldier. He was sent over to take the Command immediately upon the Death of the late General, and arrived here about seven Days before me.

At 2 o'Clock the Gentleman who was sent for arrived, when I offered the Letter, &c., again; which they received, and adjourned into a private Apartment for the Captain to translate, who understood a little *English.* After he had done it, the Commander desired I would walk-in, and bring my Interpreter to peruse and correct it; which I did.

13th. The chief Officers retired, to hold a Council of War; which gave me an Opportunity of taking the Dimensions of the Fort, and making what Observations I could.

It is situated on the South or West Fork of *French* Creek, near the Water; and is almost surrounded by the Creek, and a small

Branch of it which forms a Kind of Island. Four Houses compose the Sides. The Bastions are made of Piles driven into the Ground, standing more than 12 Feet above it, and sharp at Top: with Port-Holes cut for Cannon, and Loop-Holes for the small Arms to fire through. There are eight 6 *lb.* Pieces mounted, in each Bastion; and one Piece of four Pound before the Gate. In the Bastions are a Guard-House, Chapel, Doctor's Lodging, and the Commander's private Store: Round which are laid Plat-Forms for the Cannon and Men to stand on. There are several Barracks without the Fort, for the Soldiers Dwelling; covered, some with Bark and some with Boards, made chiefly of Loggs. There are also several other Houses, such as Stables, Smiths Shop, &c.

I could get no certain Account of the Number of Men here: But according to the best Judgment I could form, there are an Hundred exclusive of Officers, of which there are many. I also gave Orders to the People who were with me, to take an exact Account of the Canoes which were hauled-up to convey their Forces down in the Spring. This they did, and told 50 of Birch Bark, and 170 of Pine; besides many others which were blocked-out, in Readiness to make.

14th. As the Snow encreased very fast, and our Horses daily became weaker, I sent them off unloaded; under the Care of *Barnaby Currin,* and two others, to make all convenient Dispatch to *Venango,* and there wait our Arrival, if there was a Prospect of the Rivers freezing: If not, then to continue down to Shanapin's Town, at the Forks of *Ohio,* and there to wait till we came to cross *Aliganey;* intending myself to go down by Water, as I had the Offer of a Canoe or two.

As I found many Plots concerted to retard the *Indians* Business, and prevent their returning with me; I endeavor'd all that lay in my Power to frustrate their Schemes, and hurry them on to execute their intended Design. They accordingly pressed for Admittance this Evening, which at Length was granted them, privately, with the Commander and one or two other officers. The Half-King told me, that he offer'd the Wampum to the Commander, who evaded taking it, and made many fair Promises of Love and Friendship; said he wanted to live in Peace, and trade amicably with them, as a Proof of which he would send some Goods immediately down to the *Logg's*-Town for them. But I rather think the Design of that is, to bring away all our straggling Traders they meet with, as I privately understood they intended to carry an Officer, &c, with them. And what rather confirms this Opinion, I was enquiring of the Commander, by what Authority he had made Prisoners of several of our *English* Subjects. He told me that the Country belong'd to them; that no *Englishman* had a Right to trade upon those Waters; and that he had Orders to make every Person Prisoner who attempted it on the *Ohio,* or the Waters of it.

I enquir'd of Capt. *Riparti* about the Boy who was carried by this Place, as it was done while the Command devolved on him, between the Death of the late General, and the Arrival of the present. He acknowledged, that a Boy had been carried past; and that the *Indians* had two or three white Men's Scalps (I was told by some of the *Indians* at *Venango* Eight) but pretended to have forgotten the Name of the Place which the Boy came from, and all the Particular Facts, though he had question'd him for some Hours, as they were carrying him past. I likewise enquired what they had done with *John Trotter* and *James MacClocklan,* two *Pensylvania* Traders, whom they had taken, with all their Goods. They told me, that they had been sent to *Canada,* but were now returned Home.

This Evening I received an Answer to his Honour the Governor's Letter from the Commandant.

15th. The Commandant ordered a plentiful Store of Liquor, Provision, &c., to be put on Board our Canoe; and appeared to be extremely complaisant, though he was exerting every Artifice which he could invent to set our own *Indians* at Variance with us, to prevent their going 'till after our Departure. Presents, Rewards, and every Thing which could be suggested by him or his Officers—I can't say that ever in my Life I suffered so much Anxiety as I did in this Affair: I saw that every Stratagem which the most fruitful Brain could invent, was practised, to win the Half-King to their Interest; and that leaving him here was giving them the Opportunity they aimed at.—I went to the Half-King and press'd him in the strongest Terms to go: He told me the Commandant would not discharge him 'till the Morning. I then went to the Commandant, and desired him to do their Business; and complain'd of ill Treatment: For keeping them, as they were Part of my Company, was detaining me. This he promised not to do, but to forward my Journey as much as he could. He protested he did not keep them, but was ignorant of the Cause of their Stay; though I soon found it out:—He had promised them a present of Guns, &c, if they would wait 'till the morning.

As I was very much press'd, by the *Indians,* to wait this Day for them, I consented, on a Promise, That nothing should hinder them in the Morning.

16th. The *French* were not slack in their Inventions to keep the *Indians* this Day also: But as they were obligated, according to Promise, to give the Present, they then endeavoured to try the Power of Liquor; which I doubt not would have prevailed at any other Time than this; But I urged and insisted with the King so closely upon his Word, that he refrained, and set off with us as he had engaged.

We had a tedious and very fatiguing Passage down the Creek. Several Times we had like to have been staved against Rocks; and many Times were obliged all Hands to get out and remain in the Water Half an Hour or more, getting over the Shoals. At one Place the Ice had lodged and made it impassable by Water; therefore we were obliged to carry our Canoe across a Neck of Land, a quarter of a Mile over. We did not reach *Venango,* till the 22d, where we met with our Horses.

This Creek is extremely crooked, I dare say the Distance between the Fort and *Venango* can't be less than 130 Miles, to follow the Meanders.

23d. When I got Things ready to set-off, I sent for the Half King, to know whether he intended to go with us, or by Water. He told me that *White-Thunder* had hurt himself much, and was sick and unable to walk; therefore he was obliged to carry him down in a Canoe. As I found he intended to stay here a Day or two, and knew that Monsieur *Joncaire* would employ every Scheme to set him against the *English* as he had before done; I told him I hoped he would guard against his Flattery, and let no fine Speeches influence him in their Favour. He desired I might not be concerned, for he knew the *French* too well, for any Thing to engage him in their Behalf; and that though he could not go down with us, he yet would endeavour to meet at the Forks with *Joseph Campbell,* to deliver a Speech for me to carry to his Honour the Governor. He told me he would order the young Hunter to attend us, and get Provisions, &c. if wanted.

Our Horses were now so weak and feeble, and the Baggage so heavy (as we were obliged to provide all the Necessaries which the Journey would require) that we doubted much their performing it; therefore myself and others (except the Drivers, who were obliged to ride) gave up our Horses for Packs, to assist along with the Baggage. I put myself in an *Indian* walking Dress, and continued with them three Days, till I found there was no Probability of their getting home in any reasonable Time. The Horses grew less able to travel every Day; the Cold increased very fast; and the Roads were becoming much worse by a deep Snow, continually freezing: Therefore as I was uneasy to get back, to make Report of my Proceedings to his Honour, the Governor, I determined to prosecute my Journey the nearest Way through the Woods, on Foot.

Accordingly I left Mr. Vanbraam in Charge of our Baggage: with Money and Directions to Provide Necessaries from Place to Place for themselves and Horses, and to make the most convenient Dispatch in Travelling.

I took my necessary Papers; pulled off my Cloaths; and tied myself up in a Match Coat. Then with Gun in Hand and Pack at my Back, in which were my Papers and Provisions, I set-out with Mr. *Gist,* fitted in the same Manner, on *Wednesday* the 26th.

The Day following, just after we had passed a Place called the *Murdering*-Town (where we intended to quit the Path, and steer across the Country for *Shannapins* Town) we fell in with a Party of *French* Indians, who had lain in Wait for us. One of them fired at Mr. *Gist* or me, not 15 steps off, but fortunately missed. We took this Fellow into Custody, and kept him till about 9 o'clock at Night; Then let him go, and walked all the remaining Part of the Night without making any Stop; that we might get the Start, so far, as to be out of the Reach of their Pursuit the next Day, since we were well assured they would follow our Tract as soon as it was light. The next Day we continued travelling till quite dark, and got to the River about two Miles above *Shannapins.*

We expected to have found the River frozen, but it was not, only about 50 Yards from each Shore; The Ice I suppose had broken up above, for it was driving in vast Quantities.

There was no Way for getting over but on a Raft; Which we set about with but one poor Hatchet, and finished just after Sun-setting. This was a whole Day's Work. Then set off; But before we were Half Way over, we were jammed in the Ice, in such a Manner that we expected every Moment our Raft to sink, and ourselves to perish. I put-out my setting Pole to try to stop the Raft, that the Ice might pass by; when the Rapidity of the Stream threw it with so much Violence against the Pole, that it jerked me out into ten Feet Water: but I fortunately saved myself by catching hold of one of the Raft Logs. Notwithstanding all our Efforts we could not get the Raft to either Shore; but were obliged, as we were near an Island, to quit our Raft and make to it.

The Cold was so extremely severe, that Mr. *Gist* had all his Fingers, and some of his Toes frozen; but the water was shut up so hard, that we found no Difficulty in getting-off the Island, on the Ice, in the Morning, and went to Mr. *Frazier's*. We met here with 20 Warriors who were going to the *Southward* to War, but coming to a Place upon the Head of the great *Kunnaway,* where they found seven People killed and scalped (all but one Woman with very light Hair) they turned about and ran back for fear the Inhabitants should rise and take them as the Authors of the Murder. They report that the Bodies were lying about the House, and some of them much torn and eaten by Hogs. By the Marks which were left, they say they were *French* Indians of the *Ottaway* Nation, &c., who did it.

As we intended to take Horses here, and it required some Time to find them, I went-up about three Miles to the Mouth of *Yaughyaughane* to visit Queen *Aliquippa,* who had expressed great Concern that we passed her in going to the Fort. I made her a Present of a Matchcoat and a Bottle of Rum; which latter was thought much the best Present of the Two.

Tuesday the 1st Day of January, we left Mr. *Frazier's* House, and arrived at Mr. *Gist's* at *Monongahela* the 2d, where I bought a Horse, Saddle, etc: the 6th we met 17 Horses loaded with Materials and Stores, for a Fort at the Forks of *Ohio,* and the Day after some Families going out to settle: This Day we arrived at

Wills Creek, after as fatiguing a Journey as it is possible to conceive, rendered so by excessive bad Weather. From the first Day of December to the 15th, there was but one Day on which it did not rain or snow incessantly: and throughout the whole Journey we met with nothing but one continued Series of cold wet Weather, which occasioned very uncomfortable Lodgings: especially after we had quitted our Tent, which was some Screen from the Inclemency of it.

On the 11th I got to Belvoir: where I stopped one Day to take necessary Rest; and then set out and arrived in Williamsburgh the 16th; when I waited upon his Honour the Governor with the Letter I had brought from the French Commandant; and to give an Account of the Success of my Proceedings. This I beg leave to do by offering the foregoing Narrative as it contains the most remarkable Occurrences which happened in my Journey.

I hope what has been said will be sufficient to make your Honour satisfied with my Conduct; for that was my Aim in undertaking the Journey, and chief Study throughout the Prosecution of it.

Journal, 1754

June the 1st [1754]. Arrived here an *Indian* Trader with the *Half-King:* They said that when Mr. *de Jumonville* was sent here, another Party had been detached towards the lower Part of the River, in order to take and kill all the *English* they should meet.

We are finishing our Fort.

Towards Night arrived Ensign *Towers,* with the *Half-King,* Queen *Aliquippa,* and about twenty-five or Thirty Families, making in all about Eighty or One Hundred Persons, including Women and Children. The old King, being invited to come in to our Tents, told me that he had sent *Monacatoocha* to *Log's-Town,* with Wampum, and four French scalps, which were to be sent to the *Six Nations,* to the *Wyandotts,* & to inform them that they had attacked the French, and to demand their Assistance to maintain the first advantage.

He also told me he had something to say at the Council but

would stay till the Arrival of the Shawanese whom we expected next Morning.

The 2d. Arrived two or three Families of the *Shawanese* and *Loups:* We had Prayers in the Fort.

The 3d. The *Half-King* assembled the Council, and informed me that he had received a Speech from the Big Kettle (*Grand-Chaudiere*) in Answer to the one he had sent him.

Diary, 1771. Annapolis Races

Sept. 21. Set out with Mr. Wonneley for the Annapolis races. Dined at Mr. William Digges, and lodged at Mr. Ignatius Digges.

22. Dined at Mr. Sam Galloway's, and lodged with Mr. Boucher in Annapolis.

23. Dined with Mr. Loyd Dulany, and spent the evening at the Coffee House.

24. Dined with the Govr., and went to the play and ball afterwards.

25. Dined at Doctor Stewards, and went to the play and ball afterwards.

26. Dined with Mr. Ridouts, and went to the play after it.

27. Dined at Mr. Carroll's, and went to the ball.

28. Dined at Mr Boucher's, and went from thence to the play, and afterwards to the Coffee House.

29. Dined with Major Jenifer, and supped at Dan'l Dulany, Esqs.

30. Left Annapolis, and dined and supped with Mr. Sam'l Galloway.

October 1. Dined at Upper Marlborough, and reached home in the afternoon.

Journey in the Central Colonies, 1773

[May] 9. At home all day, Messrs. Ramsay, Rumney, and Herbert dind here; the last of whom went away, the others stayd all Night.

10. Those two Gentlemen stayd to Dinner; after which I set out on my journey for New York. Lodgd at Mr. Calvert's.

11. Breakfasted at Mr. Igns. Digge's. Dind at the Coffee Ho. in Annapolis and lodgd at the Govr's.

12. Dined, Supped and lodgd at the Governor's.

13. After Breakfast and abt. 8 Oclock, set out for Rockhall where we arrived in two hours and 25 Minutes. Dind on Board the Annapolis at Chester Town, and Supped and lodged at Ringold's.

14. Stopd at George Town on Sassafras, and dind and lodgd at Mr. Dl. Heath's.

15. Dined at Newcastle and lodged at Wilmington.

16. Breakfasted at Chester and Dined at Govr. Penn's in Philadelphia.

17. Dined again at Govr. Penn's and spent the Evening at the Jocky Club.

18. Dined with sevl. Gentlemen at our own lodgings and went to the Assembly in the Evening.

19. Dined at the Govr's. and spent the Evening at Allan's.

20. Dined with Mr. Cadwalader and went to the Ball.

21. Dined with Mr. Merideth and Spent the Evening at Mr. Mease's.

22. Dined at Mr. Morris's and Spent the Evening at the Club.

23. Set out for New York with Lord Sterling, Majr. Bayard and Mr. Custis, after Breakfasting with Govr. Penn. Dind with Govr. Franklin at Burlington and lodgd at Trenton.

24. Breakfasted at Princeton. Dined at Bound Brooke, and Reachd Lord Sterling's at Basking Bridge in the Afternoon.

25. Din'd and Lodg'd at Lord Sterling's. Drank Tea at Mr. Kimble's.

26. Din'd at Elizabeth Town, and reach'd New York in the Evening wch. I spent at Hull's Tavern. Lodgd at a Mr. Farmer's.

27. Din'd at the Entertainment given by the Citizens of New York to Genl' Gage.

28. Dined with Mr. James Dillancey and went to the Play and Hull's Tavern in the Evening.

29. Dined with Majr. Bayard and Spent the Evening with the Old Club at Hull's.

30. Dined with Genl. Gage and Spent the Evening in my own Room writing.

31. Set out on my return home.

Diary, 1774

1774. Aug. 1. Went from Colo. Bassett's to Williamsburg to the meeting of the Convention. Dined at Mrs. Campbell's, spent ye evening in my lodgings.

2. At the convention; dined at the Treasurer's. At my lodgings in the evening.

3. Dined at the Speaker's, and spent the evening at my own lodgings.

4. Dined at the Attorney's, and spent the evening at my own lodgings.

5. Dined at Mrs. Dawson's, and spent the evening at my own lodgings.

6. Dined at Mrs. Campbell's, and spent the evening at my own lodgings.

7. Left Williamsburg about 9 o'clock.

The Frontier, 1783

October 12. I have lately made a tour through the Lakes George and Champlain, as far as Crown Point. Then returning to Schenectady, I proceeded up the Mohawk River to Fort Schuyler (formerly Fort Stanwix), and crossed over to the Wood Creek, which empties into the Oneida Lake, and affords the water communication with Ontario. I then traversed the country to the head of the eastern branch of the Susquehanna, and viewed the Lake Otsego, and the portage between that Lake and the Mohawk River at Canajoharie. Prompted by these actual observations, I could not help taking a more contemplative and extensive view of the vast inland navigation of these United States, from maps and the information of others; and could not help but be struck with the immense diffusion and importance of it, and with the goodness of that Providence, which has dealt her favors to us with so profuse a hand. Would to God we may have wisdom enough to improve them. I shall not rest contented, till I have explored the western country, and traversed those lines, or great part of them, which have given bounds to a new empire.

I have it in contemplation to make a tour thro' all the Eastern States, thence into Canada, thence up the St. Laurence and thro' the lakes to Detroit, thence to Lake Michigan by land or water, thence through the Western Country, by the river Illinois to the river Mississippi, and down the same to New Orleans, thence into Georgia by the way of Pensacola, and then thro' the two Carolinas home. A great tour this, you will say. Probably it may take place nowhere but in imagination, tho' it is my *wish* to begin it in the latter end of April of next year.

Advice on the Tours, 1789

October 5, 1789. Had conversation with Colo. Hamilton on the propriety of making a tour through the Eastern States during the recess of Congress, to acquire knowledge of the face of the Country, the growth and agriculture thereof—and the temper and disposition of the inhabitants towards the new government, who thought it a very desirable plan, and advised it accordingly.

October 6. Conversed with Gen. Knox, Secretary at War, on the above tour, who also recommended it accordingly.

October 7. Upon consulting Mr. Jay on the propriety of my intended tour into the Eastern States, he highly approved of it, but observed, a similar visit w'd be expected by those of the Southern.

October 8. Mr. Madison took his leave today. He saw no impropriety in my trip to the eastward . . .

Diary, 1789. New England Trip

Tuesday [October] 20th [1789]. After breakfast, accompanied by Colo. Wadsworth, Mr. Ellsworth and Colo. Jesse Root, I viewed the Wollen Manufactory at this place, which seems to be going on with spirit. Their Broad-cloths are not of the first quality, as yet, but they are good; as are their Coatings, Cassimeres, Serges and Everlastings; of the first, that is, broad-cloth, I ordered a suit to be sent to me at New York—and of the latter a whole piece, to make breeches for my servants. All the parts of this business are performed at the Manufactory except the spinning—this is done by the Country people, who are paid by the cut.

Hartford is more compactly built than Middletown, and contains more souls; the computed number of which amount to about dble. The number of Houses in Middletown are said to be 250 or 60—these reckoning eight persons to a house, would make two thousand at least. The depth of water which Vessels can bring to the last place, is about ten feet; and is as much as there is over Saybrook bar. From Middletown to Hartford there is not more than 6 feet water.

Wednesday, 28th. Went after breakfast, to visit the duck manufacture [at Boston], which appeared to be carrying on with spirit, and is in a prosperous way. They have manufactured 32 pieces of Duck 30 or 40 yds. each in a week; and expect in a short time to increase it to [ ]. They have 28 looms at work, and 14 Girls spinning with Both hands, (the flax being fastened to their waste.) Children (girls) turn the wheels for them, and with this assistance each spinner can turn out 14 lbs. of Thread pr. day when they stick to it, but as they are pd. by the piece, or work they do, there is no other restraint upon them but to come at 8 o'clock in the morning, and return at 6 in the evening. They are the daughters of decayed families, and are girls of Character—none others are admitted.

Diary of Trip to D.C., March, 1791

March 28, 1791. Left Bladensburgh at half after six, and breakfasted at George Town about 8; where, having appointed the Commissioners under the Residence Law to meet me, I found Mr. Johnson one of them (and who is Chief Justice of the State) in waiting—and soon after came in David Stuart, and Dan'l Carroll, Esqrs. the other two. A few miles out of Town I was met by the principal Citizens of the place and escorted in by them; and dined at Suter's tavern (where I also lodged) at a public dinner given by the Mayor and Corporation—previous to which I examined the Surveys of Mr. Ellicott who had been sent on to lay out the district of ten miles square for the federal seat; and also the works of Majr. L'Enfant who had been engaged to examine and make a draught of the grds. in the vicinity of George Town and Carrollsburg on the Eastern branch making arrangements for examining the ground myself to morrow with the Commissioners.

Tuesday, 29th. . . . Finding the interests of the Landholders about George Town and those about Carrollsburg much at variance and that their fears and jealousies of each were counteracting the public purposes and might prove injurious to its best interests, whilst if properly managed they might be made to subserve it, I requested them to meet me at six o'clock this afternoon at my lodgings, which they accordingly did.

To this meeting I represented that the contention in which they seemed engaged, did not in my opinion comport either with the public interest or that of their own; that while each party was aiming to obtain the public buildings, they might by placing the matter on a contracted scale, defeat the measure altogether; not only by procrastination but for want of the means necessary to effect the work; That neither the offer from George-town or Carrollsburgh, separately, was adequate to the end of insuring the object. That both together did not comprehend more ground nor would afford greater means than was required for the federal City; and that, instead of contending which of the two should have it they had better, by combining more offers make a common cause of it, and thereby secure it to the district; other arguments were used to show the danger which might result from delay and the good effects that might proceed from a Union.

An Accident on the Road, 1791

Thursday, [April] 7th. . . . In attempting to cross the ferry at Colchester with the four horses hitched to the Chariot by the neglect of the person who stood before them, one of the leaders got overboard when the boat was in swimming water and 50 yards from the shore—with much difficulty he escaped drowning before he could be disengaged. His struggling frightened the others in such a manner that one after another and in quick succession they all got overboard harnessed and fastened as they were and with the utmost difficult they were saved and the Carriage escaped being dragged after them, as the whole of it happened in swimming water and at a distance from the shore. Providentially—indeed miraculously—by the exertions of people who went off in Boats and jumped into the River as soon as the Batteau was forced into wading water—no damage was sustained by the horses, Carriage or harness.

Public Opinion in the South, 1791

Richmond, April 12. In the course of my enquiries, chiefly from Colo. Carrington, I cannot discover that any discontents prevail among the people at large, at the proceedings of Congress. The conduct of the Assembly respecting the assumption he thinks is condemned by them as intemperate and unwise; and he seems to have no doubt but that the Excise law, as it is called, may be executed without difficulty—nay more, that it will become popular in a little time. His duty as Marshall having carried him through all parts of the State lately, and of course given him the best means of ascertaining the temper and disposition of its Inhabitants, he thinks them favorable towards the General Government, and that they only require to have matters explained to them in order to obtain their full assent to the measures adopted by it.

Wednesday, 13th. Fixed with Colo. Carrington (the supervisor of the district) the surveys of Inspection for the District of this State and named the characters for them, an acct. of which was transmitted to the Secretary of the Treasury.

Escape from an Escort, 1791

Friday, [April] 15th. Having suffered very much by the dust yesterday, and finding that parties of Horse, and a number of other Gentlemen were intending to attend me part of the way to day, I caused their enquiries respecting the time of my setting out, to be answered that, I should endeavor to do it before eight o'clock; but I did it a little after five, by which means I avoided the inconveniences above mentioned.

Southern Commerce, 1791

Sunday, [April] 24th. . . . Wilmington is situated on the Cape Fear River, about 30 miles *by water* from its mouth, but much less by land. It has some good houses pretty compactly built. The whole under a hill; which is formed entirely of sand. The number of Souls in it amount by the enumeration to about 1000, but it is agreed on all hands that the Census in this State has been very inaccurately and Shamefully taken by the Marshall's deputies . . . Wilmington, unfortunately for it, has a Mud bank—miles below, over which not more than 10 feet of water can be brought at common tides, yet it is said vessels of 250 Tons have come up. The qu'ty. of Shipping, which load here annually, amounts to about 1200 Tonns. The exports consist chiefly of Naval Stores and lumber. Some Tobacco, Corn, Rice, and flax seed with Porke. It is at the head of the tide navigation, but inland navigation may be extended 115 miles farther to and above Fayettesville which is from Wilmington 90 miles by land, and 115 by Water as above. Fayettesville is a thriving place containing near [ ] Souls. 6000 Hhds. of Tobacco and 3000 Hhds. of Flax Seed have been recd. at it in the course of the year.

Diary, D.C. Trip, June, 1791

Monday [June] 27th. Left Mount Vernon for Georgetown before Six oclock;—and according to appointment met the Commissioners at that place by 9—then calling together the Proprietors of those Lands on which the federal City was proposed to be built who had agreed to cede them on certain conditions at the last meeting I had with them at this place but from some misconception with respect to the extension of their grants had refused to make conveyances and recapitulating the principles upon which my comns. to them at the former meeting were made and giving some explanation of the present State of matters and the consequences of delay in this business they readily waved their objections and agd. to convey to the utmost extent of what was required.

Tuesday, 28th. Whilst the Commissioners were engaged in preparing the Deeds to be signed by the Subscribers this afternoon, I went out with Majr. L'Enfant and Mr. Ellicot to take a more perfect view of the ground, in order to decide finally on the spots on which to place the public buildings and to direct how a line which was to leave out a Spring (commonly known by the name of the Cool Spring) belonging to Majr. Stoddart should be run.

Wednesday, 29th. The Deeds which remained unexecuted yesterday were signed to day and the Dowers of their respective wives acknowledged according to Law.

This being accomplished, I called the several subscribers together and made known to them the spots on which I meant to place the buildings for the P: and Executive departments of the Government—and for the Legislature of Do.—A Plat was also laid before them of the City in order to convey to them general ideas of the City but they were told that some deviation from it would take place—particularly in the diagonal streets or avenues, which would not be so numerous; and in the removal of the Presidents house more westerly for the advantage of higher ground—they were also told that a Town house, or exchange wd be placed on some convenient ground between the spots designated for the public buildings, before mentioned.—and it was with much pleasure that a general approbation of the measure seemed to pervade the whole.

Diary, Last Days, December, 1799

7th. Rainy morning, with the wind at north; mercury at 37. Afternoon, clear and pleasant; wind westerly. Mercury 41 at night. Dined at Lord Fairfax's.

8th. Morning perfectly clear, calm, and pleasant; but about nine o'clock the wind came from the northwest and blew frost. Mercury 38 in the morning, and 40 at night.

9th. Morning clear and pleasant, with a light wind from northwest. Mercury at 33. Pleasant all day; afternoon calm. Mercury 39 at night . . .

10th. Morning clear and calm; mercury at 31. Afternoon lowering; mercury at 42, and wind brisk from the southward. A very large hoar-frost this morning.

11th. But little wind, and raining. Mercury 44 in the morning and 38 at night. About nine o'clock the wind shifted to the northwest, and it ceased raining, but continued cloudy. Lord Fairfax, his son Thomas, and daughters, Mrs. Warner Washington and son Whiting, and Mr. John Herbert, dined here and returned after dinner.

12th. Morning cloudy; wind at northeast; mercury 33. A large circle round the moon last night. About one o'clock it began to snow; soon after, to hail, and then turned to a settled cold rain. Mercury 28 at night.

13th. Morning snowing, and about three inches deep. Wind at northwest, and mercury at 30. Continued snowing till one o'clock, and about four it became perfectly clear. Wind the same place, but not hard. Mercury 28 at night.

[That previous evening Washington caught the sore throat (then known as Quincy) from which he died at 11 P.M., December 14.]

Chapter 3

SELF-PORTRAIT: AUTOBIOGRAPHIC GLIMPSES

Arranged Chronologically

To "Dear Friend Robin," 1748[1]

My place of Residence is at present at His Lordship's [Fairfax] where I might, was my heart disengag'd, pass my time very pleasantly as there's a very agreeable Young Lady Lives in the same house [Mary Cary]. But as that's only adding Fuel to fire, it makes me the more uneasy, for by often, and unavoidably, being in Company with her revives my former Passion for your Low Land Beauty; whereas, was I to live more retired from young Women, I might in some measure eliviate my sorrows, by burying that chast and troublesome Passion in the grave of oblivion or etarnall forgetfulness, for as I am very well assured, that's the only antidote or remedy that I shall be releivd by or only recess that can administer any cure or help to me, as I am well convinced, was I ever to attempt anything, I should only get a denial which would be only adding grief to uneasiness.

Was my affections disengaged I might perhaps form some pleasure in the conversation of an agreeable Young Lady, as there's one now Lives in the same house with me; but as that is only nourishment to my former affecn, for by often seeing her brings the other into my remembrance. Whereas perhaps, was she not often & (unavoidably) presenting herself to my view, I might in some measure aliviate my sorrows by burying the other in the grave of Oblivion. I am well convinced my heart stands in defiance

[1] The punctuation is slightly edited here.

of all others, but only she thats given it cause enough to dread a second assault and from a different Quarter; tho I well know let it have as many attacks as it will from others, they cant be more fierce than it has been.

Acrostic [in honor of Frances Alexander], 1748

From your bright sparkling Eyes, I was undone;
Rays, you have more transparent than the sun,
Amidst its glory in the rising Day,
None can you equal in your bright array;
Constant in your calm and unspotted Mind;
Equal to all, but will to none Prove kind,
So Knowing, seldom one so Young, you'l Find
Ah! woe's me, that I should love and conceal,
Long have I wish'd, but never dare reveal,
Even though severely Loves Pains I feel;
Xerxes that great, was't free from Cupid's Dart,
And all the greatest Heroes, felt the smart.

Sonnet [to Frances Alexander], 1748

Oh Ye Gods why should my Poor Resistless Heart
Stand to oppose thy might and Power
At Last surrender to cupid's feather'd Dart
And now lays Bleeding every Hour
For her that's Pityless of my grief and Woes
And will not one me Pity take
Ile sleep amongst my most Inveterate Foes
And with gladness never with [*sic*] to Wake
In deluding sleepings let my Eyelids close
That in an enraptured Dream I may
In a soft lulling sleep and gentle repose
Possess those joys denied by Day.

Refuses Commission

To Colonel William Fitzhugh, November 15, 1754

You make mention in your letter of my continuing in the service, and retaining my colonel's commission. This idea has filled me with surprise; for, if you think me capable of holding a commission, that has neither rank or emolument annexed to it, you must entertain a very contemptible opinion of my weakness, and believe me to be more empty than the commission itself.

Besides, Sir, if I had time, I could enumerate many good reasons, that forbid all thoughts of my returning; and which to you, or any other, would, upon the strictest scrutiny, appear to be well founded. I must be reduced to a very low command, and subjected to that of many, who have acted as my inferior officers. In short, every captain, bearing the King's commission, every half-pay officer, or others appearing with such commission, would rank before me. . . .

I herewith enclose Governour [of Maryland] Sharpe's [commander in chief of all British forces engaged against the French] letter, which I beg you will return to him, with my acknowledgments for the favour he intended me. Assure him, Sir . . . of my reluctance to quit the service . . . Also inform him, that it was to obey the call of honour, and the advice of my friends, I declined it, and not to gratify any desire I had to leave the military line. My inclinations are strongly bent to arms.

With Braddock

To William Byrd, Mount Vernon, May 25, 1755

I am now preparing for, and shall in a few days set off, to serve in the ensuing campaign, with different views, however, from those I had before. For here, if I gain any credit, or if I am entitled to the least countenance or esteem, it must be from serving my country without fee or reward; for I can truly say, I have no expectation of either. To merit its esteem, and the good will of my friends, is the sum of my ambition, having no prospect of attaining a commission . . .

Yet to have a family just settling [referring to his younger brother, John Augustine], and in the confusion and disorder mine is at present, is not a pleasing thing and may be hurtful. Be this as it may, it shall be no hindrance to my making *this* campaign.

To John Augustine Washington, Fort Cumberland, July 18, 1755

Dear Brother, As I have heard, since my arrival at this place, a circumstantial account of my death and dying speech, I take this early opportunity of contradicting the first, and of assuring you, that I have not as yet composed the latter. But, by the all-powerful dispensations of Providence, I have been protected beyond all human probability and expectation; for I had four bullets through my coat, and two horses shot under me, yet escaped unhurt, altho' death was levelling my companions on every side of me!

We have been most scandalously beaten by a trifling body of men, but fatigue and want of time will prevent me from giving you any of the details, until I have the happiness of seeing you at Mount Vernon, which I now most ardently wish for, since we are drove in thus far. A weak and feeble state of health obliges me to halt here for two or three days, to recover a little strength, that I may thereby be enabled to proceed homewards with more ease.

Continued Illness

To Colonel Stanwix, Mount Vernon, March 4, 1758

I have never been able to return to my command since I wrote to you last, my disorder at times returning obstinately upon me, in spite of the efforts of all the sons of Aesculapius, whom I have hitherto consulted. At certain periods I have been reduced to great extremity, and have now too much reason to apprehend an approaching decay, being visited with several symptoms of such a disease.

I am now under a strict regimen, and shall set out tomorrow for Williamsburg to receive the advice of the best physicians there. My constitution is certainly greatly impaired, and as nothing can retrieve it, but the greatest care and the most circumspect conduct, as I now have no prospect left of preferement in the military way, and as I despair of rendering that immediate service, which my country may require . . . I have some thoughts of quitting my command, and retiring from all public business.

Wants Distinction

To Brigadier General Stanwix, Fort Loudoun, April 10, 1758

I must . . . beg that you will add one more kindness to the many I have experienced, and that is, to mention me in favorable terms to General [John] Forbes . . . not as a person, who would depend upon him for . . . military preferment . . . but as a person, who would gladly be distinguished in some measure from the ***common run*** of provincial officers.

Election to Office—Duty

To Colonel James Wood, July, 1758

If thanks flowing from a heart replete with joy and Gratitude can in any Measure compensate for the fatigue, anxiety and Pain you had at my Election, be assured you have them . . .

How I shall thank Mrs. Wood for her favorable Wishes, and how acknowledge my sense of obligation to the People in general for their choice of me, I am at a loss to resolve on. But why? Can I do it more effectually than by making their Interest (as it really is) my own, and doing everything that lyes in my little Power for the Honor and welfare of the Country? I think not; and my best endeavors they may always command . . .

I am extremely thankful to you and my other friends for entertaining the Freeholders in my name. I hope no Exception was taken to any that voted against me, but that all were alike treated, and all had enough. It is what I much desired.

Love Letter

To Mrs. Martha Custis, July 20, 1758

We have begun our march for the Ohio. A courier is starting for Williamsburg, and I embrace the opportunity to send a few words to one whose life is now inseparable from mine. Since that happy hour when we made our pledges to each other, my thoughts have been continually going to you as another Self. That an all-powerful Providence may keep us both in safety is the prayer of your ever faithful and affectionate friend.

On Love—and Wife

To Mrs. George William Fairfax, September 12, 1758

'Tis true, I profess myself a votary of love. I acknowledge that a lady is in the case, and further I confess that this lady is known to you . . . I feel the force of her amiable beauties in the recollection of a thousand tender passages that I could wish to obliterate, till I am bid to revive them. But experience, alas! sadly reminds me how impossible this is, and evinces an opinion which I have long entertained, that there is a Destiny which has the control of our actions, not to be resisted by the strongest efforts of Human Nature.

You have drawn me, dear Madame, or rather I have drawn myself, into an honest confession of a simple Fact. Misconstrue not my meaning; doubt it not, nor expose it. The world has no business to know the object of my love, declared in this manner to you, when I want to conceal it . . . Adieu to this till happier times, if I ever shall see them. The hours at present are melancholy dull . . . I dare believe you are as happy as you say. I wish I was happy also.

Personal Orders from London

To Robert Cary & Company, London, Williamsburg, May 1, 1759

Gentln., The inclosed is the minister's certificate of my marriage with Mrs. Martha Custis, properly . . . authenticated. You will, therefore for the future please to address all your letters, which relate to the affairs of the late Daniel Parke Custis, Esqr., to me, as by marriage I am entitled to a third part of that estate, and invested likewise with the care of the other two thirds by a decree of our General Court, which I obtained in order to strengthen the power I before had in consequence of my wife's administration. . . .

On the other side is an invoice of some goods which I beg of you to send me by the first ship, bound either to Potomack or Rappahanock, as I am in immediate want of them. Let them be insured, and, in case of accident, re-shipped without delay. Direct for me at Mount Vernon, Potomack River, Virginia; the former is the name of my seat, the other of the river on which t'is situated.

Invoice of Sundry Goods to be Ship'd by Robt. Cary, Esq., and Company for the use of George Washington—viz:

1 Tester Bedstead 7½ feet pitch with fashionable bleu or blue and white curtains . . .

Window curtains of the same for two windows . . .

1 fine Bed Coverlid to match the Curtains. 4 Chair bottoms of the same . . .

1 Fashionable Sett of Desert Glasses and Stands for Sweet meats Jellys & . . .

2 Setts of Chamber, or Bed Carpets—Wilton.

4 Fashionable China Branches & Stands for Candles.

2 Neat fire Screens—

50 lbs Spirma Citi Candles—

6 Carving Knives and Forks—handles of Stained Ivory and bound with Silver.

A pretty large Assortment of Grass Seeds . . .

1 Large neat and Easy Couch for a Passage.

50 yards of best Floor Matting.

2 pair of fashionable mixd. or Marble Cold Silk Hose.

6 pair of finest cotton Ditto.

6 pair of finest threat Ditto.

6 pair of midling Do. to cost abt 5/

6 pair of worsted Do . . .

N.B. All the above Stockings to be long, and tolerably large.

1 piece of finest and most fashionable Stock Tape.

1 suit of Cloaths of the finest Cloth & fashionable colour made by the Inclos'd measure.

The newest and most approvd Treatise of Agriculture—besides this, send me a Small piece in Octavo—called a New System of Agriculture, or a Speedy Way to grow Rich.

Langley's Book of Gardening.

Gibson, upon Horses, the latest Edition in Quarto—

Half a dozen pair of Men's neatest shoes, and Pumps, to be made by one Didsbury, on Colo. Baylor's Last—but a little larger than his—and to have high heels.—

6 pr Mens riding Gloves—rather large than the Middle size.

One neat Pocket Book, capable of receiving Memorandoms & Small Cash accts. to be made of Ivory, or any thing else that will admit of cleaning.

Fine Soft Calf Skin for a pair of Boots—

Ben leathr. for Soles.

Six Bottles of Greenhows Tincture.

Order from the best House in Madeira a Pipe of the best old Wine, and let it be securd from Pilferers.

Happily Married

To Richard Washington, September 20, 1759

I am now I believe fixd at this seat [Mount Vernon] with an agreeable Consort for Life. And hope to find more happiness in retirement than I ever experienced amidst a wide and bustling World.

Orders Shoes

To Didsbury, November 30, 1759

The first Shoes which I desird might be made by you for me on Colo. Baylors Last are come in, and fit me tolerably well except that some of them are rather too Short—as I imagine you will now be able to suit my foot exactly—I beg you will for the future observe the following Directions in Making the Shoes.

Let the hind Quarters always be high and very Short so that they may Buckle high up on the Instep—the Heels midling high also.

Never more make any of Dog leather except one pair of Pumps in a Cargoe unless you send better Leather than they were made of before—for the two pairs of Shoes scarcely lasted me twice as many days & had very fair wearing. If I should find occasion to alter at any time these directions you shall be timely advisd of it at present please to send me,

2 pair Strong Shoes. 1 pr. dble Channel Pumps.
2 pr. neat & fine Do. 1 pr very neat turnd Ditto.

Visit to Warm Springs

To Reverend Charles Green,[2] Warm Springs, August 26, 1761

We arrived here yesterday, and our journey as you may imagine was not of the most agreeable sort, through such weather and such roads as we had to encounter; these last for 20 or 25 miles from hence are almost impassible for carriages, not so much from the mountainous country (but this in fact is very rugged), as from trees that have fallen across the road and rendered the way intolerable.

We found of both sexes about 200 people at this place, full of all manner of diseases and complaints; some of which are much benefited, while others find no relief from the waters.—Two or three doctors are here, but whether attending as physicians or to drink of the waters I know not.

It is thought the Springs will soon begin to lose their vitues, and the weather get too cold for people not well provided to remain here. They are situated very badly on the East side of a steep Mountain, and inclosed by hills on all sides, so that the afternoon's Sun is hid by 4 o'clock and the fogs hang over us till 9 or 10 which occasion great damps, and the mornings and evenings to be cool.

The place . . . is supplyed with provisions of all kinds; good beef and venison, fine veal, lambs, fowls, &, may be bought at almost any time, but lodgings can be had on no terms but building for them; and I am of opinion that numbers get more hurt by their manner of lying, than the waters can do them good. Had we not succeeded in getting a tent and marquee from Winchester we should have been in a most miserable situation here.

In regard to myself I must beg leave to say, that I was much overcome with the fatigue of the ride and weather together. However I think my fevers a good deal abated, although my pains grow rather worse, and my sleep equally disturbed. What effect the waters may have upon me I can't say at present, but I expect nothing from the air—this certainly must be unwholesome. I purpose to stay here a fortnight and longer if benefitted.

[2] Minister of old Pohick Church from 1738 to 1765.

Orders Clothes

To Richard Washington, Mount Vernon, October 20, 1761

On the other side [of this letter] is an invoice of clothes, which I beg the favor of you to purchase for me, and to send them by the first ship bound to this river. As they are designed for wearing-apparel for myself, I have committed the choice of them to your fancy, having the best opinion of your taste. I want neither lace nor embroidery. Plain clothes, with a gold or silver button (if worn in genteel dress), are all I desire. I have hitherto had my clothes made by one Charles Lawrence, in Old Fish Street. But whether it be the fault of the tailor, or the measure sent, I cant say, but, certain it is, my clothes have never fitted me well. I therefore leave the choice of the workman to your care likewise. I enclose a measure, and, for a further insight, I dont think it amiss to add, that my stature is six feet; otherwise rather slender than corpulent.

Orders a Suit

To Charles Lawrence, tailor in London, April 26, 1763

Be pleased to send me a genteel suit of cloaths made of superfine broad cloth, handsomely chosen. I should have inclosed you my measure, but in a general way they are so badly taken here, that I am convinced it would be of very little service. I would have you, therefore, take measure of a gentleman who wares well-made cloaths of the following size: to wit, 6 *feet* high, and proportionably made;—if any thing rather slender than thick, for a person of that highth, with pretty long arms and thighs. You will take care to make the breeches longer than those you sent me last, and I would have you keep the measure of the cloaths you now make, by you, and if any alteration is required, in my next it shall be pointed out.

Economic Difficulties

To Robert Stewart, April 27, 1763

I wish, my dear Stewart, that the circumstances of my affairs would have permitted me to have given you an order . . . for £400 . . . or even twice that sum . . . But, alas! to show my inability in this respect, I enclose you a copy of Mr. Cary's last account current against me, which upon my honor and the faith of a Christian, is a true one . . .

This, upon my soul, is a genuine account of my affairs in England. Here they are a little better, because I am not much in debt. I doubt not but you will be surprized at the badness of their condition unless you will consider under what terrible management and disadvantages I found my estate when I retired from the publick service of this Colony; and that besides some purchases of Lands and Negroes I was necessitated to make adjoining me (in order to support the expences of a large family), I had Provisions of all kinds to buy for the first two or three years; and my Plantation to stock in short with every thing;—buildings to make and other matters which swallod up before I well knew where I was, all the money I got by marriage, nay more, brought me in debt.

Selling a Negro

To Captain John Thompson, Mount Vernon, July 2, 1766

With this letter comes a negro (Tom), which I beg the favor of you to sell in any of the Islands you may go to, for whatever he will fetch, and bring me in return from him

One hhd[3] of best molasses
One ditto of best rum
One barrel of lymes, if good and cheap

[3] Hogshead: a cask containing from 63 to 140 gallons.

One pot of tamarinds, containing about 10 lbs.

Two small ditto of mixed sweetmeats, about 5 lbs each.

And the residue, much or little, in good old spirits. That this fellow is both a rogue and a runaway (tho' he was by no means remarkable for the former, and never practised the latter till of late) I shall not pretend to deny. But that he is exceeding healthy, strong, and good at the hoe, the whole neiborhood can testify, and particularly Mr. Johnson and his son, who have both had him under them as foreman of the gang; which gives me reason to hope he may with your good management sell well, if kept clean and trim'd up a little when offered for sale.

I shall very chearfully allow you the customary commissions on this affair, and must beg the favor of you (lest he should attempt his escape) to keep him handcuffed till you get to sea, or in the bay, after which I doubt not but you make him very useful to you.

Orders a Chariot

To Robert Cary & Company, June 6, 1768

Gentn: My old Chariot havg. run its race, and gone through as many stages as I could conveniently make it travel, is now renderd incapable of any further Service; The intent of this Letter therefore is to desire you will bespeak me a New one, time enough to come out with the Goods (I shall hereafter write for) by Captn. Johnstown, or some other Ship.

As these are kind of Articles, that last with care agst. number of years, I woud willingly have the Chariot you may now send me made in the newest taste, handsome, genteel and light; yet not slight and consequently unserviceable. To be made of the best Seasond Wood, and by a celebrated Workman. The last Importation which I have seen, besides the customary steel springs have others that play in a Brass barrel, and contribute at one and the same time to the ease and Ornament of the Carriage; One of this kind therefore woud be my choice; and Green being a colour little apt, as I apprehend to fade, and grateful to the Eye, I woud give it the preference, unless any other colour more in vogue and equally lasting is entitled to precedency, in that case I woud be governd by fashion. A light gilding on the mouldings (that is, round the Pannels) and any other Ornaments that may not have a heavy and tawdry look (together with my Arms agreeable to the Impression here sent) might be added, by way of decoration. A lining of a handsome, lively cold. leather of good quality, I sh'd also prefer; such as green, blew, or &ca., as may best suit the col'r of the outside, Let the box that slips under Seat, be as large as it conveniently can be made (for the benefit of Storage upon a journey), and to have a Pole (not shafts) for the Wheel Horses to draw by; together with a handsome sett of Harness for four middle sized Horses orderd in such a manner as to suit either two Postilions (without a box) or a box and one Postilion. The box being made to fix on, and take off occasionally, with a hammel Cloth &ca., suitable to the lining. On the Harness let my Crest be engravd.

If such a Chariot as I have here describd cd. be got at 2d. hand little or nothg. the worse of wear, but at the same time a good deal under the first cost of a new one[4] (and sometimes tho perhaps rarely it happens so), it wd. be very desirable; but if I am obligd to go near to the origl. cost I wd. even have one made; and have been thus particular, in hopes of gettg. a handsome Chart. through your direction, good taste, and managt.; not of Copper however, for these do not stand the powerful heat of our sun.

Hunting

Diary, January and February, 1769

Jan. 4, Fox hunting; 10, Fox hunting; 11, Fox hunting; 12, Fox hunting; 16, Went a ducking; 17, Fox hunting; 18, Fox hunting; 19, Fox hunting; 20, Fox hunting; 21, Fox hunting;

[4] The new chariot was shipped to Washington in September, 1768, and cost altogether £133.

25, Hunting below Accotinck; 28, Fox hunting; Feb. 3, Went a Gunning up the Creek; 9, Went a Ducking; 10, Went a shooting again; 11, Ducking till Dinner; 14, Fox hunting; 17, Rid out with my hounds; 18, Went a hunting with Doctr. Rumney [.] Started a fox or rather 2 or 3 & catched none—Dogs mostly got after deer & never joind; 27, Fox hunting.

Sits for Portrait

To Dr. Boucher, May 21, 1772

Inclination having yielded to Importunity, I am now contrary to all expectation under the hands of Mr. [Charles Willson] Peale; but in so grave—so sullen a mood—and now and then under the influence of Morpheus, when some critical strokes are making, that I fancy the skill of this Gentleman's Pencil, will be put to it, in describing to the World what manner of man I am.[5]

Overwhelmed with Personal Affairs

To John West, Mount Vernon, January 13, 1775

I can solemnly declare to you, that, for a year or two past, there has been scarce a moment, that I could properly call my own. What with my own business, my present ward's, my mother's, which is wholly in my hands, Colonel Colvill's, Mrs. Savage's, Colonel Fairfax's, Colonel Mercer's, and the little assistance I have undertaken to give in the management of my brother Augustine's concerns (for I have absolutely refused to qualify as an executor), together with the share I take in public affairs, I have been kept constantly engaged in writing letters, settling accounts, and nego-

[5] Peale painted Washington in the uniform of a colonel of the Virginia Militia —wearing a blue coat faced with red, a dark red waistcoat, and breeches. On May 30 he paid Peale £18 4*s*. for the picture.

tiating one piece of business or another; by which means I have really been deprived of every kind of enjoyment, and had almost fully resolved to engage in no fresh matter, till I had entirely wound up the old.

Accepts Appointment as Commander in Chief[6]

Speech to Congress, June 16, 1775

Mr. President,

Though I am truly sensible of the high honor done me in this appointment, yet I feel great distress from a consciousness that my abilities and military experience may not be equal to the extensive and important trust. However, as the Congress desire it, I will enter upon the momentous duty and exert every power I possess in the service and for support of the glorious cause. I beg they will accept my most cordial thanks for this distinguished testimony of their approbation. But lest some unlucky event should happen unfavourable to my reputation, I beg it may be remembered by every gentleman in the room, that I this day declare with the utmost sincerity I do not think myself equal to the command I am honored with.

As to pay, Sir, I beg leave to assure the Congress, that as no pecuniary consideration could have tempted me to accept this arduous employment at the expense of my domestic ease and happiness, I do not wish to make any profit from it. I will keep an exact account of my expenses. Those I doubt not they will discharge, and that is all I desire.

[6] On June 15, 1775, Congress unanimously elected Washington general and commander of "all the continental forces raised or to be raised for the defence of American liberty." Washington was informed of it on the following day and, standing in his place at the Congress, made the above reply.

Farewell to Home—Goes to Army

To John Augustine Washington, Philadelphia, June 20, 1775

I am now to bid adieu to you, and to every kind of domestic ease, for a while. I am embarked on a wide ocean, boundless in its prospect, and in which, perhaps, no safe harbor is to be found. I have been called upon by the unanimous voice of the Colonies to take the command of the Continental army; an honor I have neither sought after, nor desired, as I am thoroughly convinced, that it requires greater abilities and much more experience, than I am master of, to conduct a business so extensive in its nature, and arduous in its execution. But the partiality of the Congress, joined to a political motive, really left me without a choice; and I am now commissioned a General and Commander-in-chief of all the forces now raised, or to be raised, for the defense of the United Colonies. That I may discharge the trust to the satisfaction of my employers, is my first wish; that I shall aim to do it, there remains as little doubt of. How far I shall succeed, is another point; but this I am sure of, that, in the worst event, I shall have the consolation of knowing, if I act to the best of my judgment, that the blame ought to lodge upon the appointers, not the appointed, as it was by no means a thing of my seeking, or proceeding from any hint of my friends . . . I shall hope that my friends will visit and endeavor to keep up the spirits of my wife, as much as they can, as my departure will, I know, be a cutting stroke upon her;[7] and on this account alone I have many disagreeable sensations. I hope you and my sister (although the distance is great) will find as much leisure this summer as to spend a little time at Mount Vernon.

[7] Washington did not return to Mount Vernon until six years later.

WIFE

To Martha Washington, Philadelphia, June 23, 1775

My Dearest: As I am within a few minutes of leaving this city, I would not think of departing from it with out dropping you a line, especially as I do not know whether it may be in my power to write again till I get to the camp at Boston. I go fully trusting in that providence, which has been more bountiful to me than I deserve and in full confidence of a happy meeting with you some time in the fall. I have no time to add more as I am surrounded with company to take leave of me. I return an unalterable affection for you which neither time or distance can change my best love to Jack and Nelly and regard for the rest of the family; conclude me with the utmost truth and Sincerity,

Yr. entire,

G. WASHINGTON.

DINING IN WARTIME

To Dr. John Cochran, Surgeon General, West Point, August 16, 1779

I have asked Mrs. Cochran & Mrs. Livingston to dine with me tomorrow; but am I not in honor bound to apprize them of their fare? As I hate deception, even where the imagination only is concerned; I will. It is needless to premise, that my table is large enough to hold the ladies. Of this they had ocular proof yesterday. To say how it is usually covered, is rather more essential; and this shall be the purport of my Letter.

Since our arrival at this happy spot, we have had a ham, (sometimes a shoulder) of Bacon, to grace the head of the Table; a piece of roast Beef adorns the foot; and a dish of beans, or greens, (almost imperceptible) decorates the center. When the cook has a mind to cut a figure, (which I presume will be the case tomorrow), we have two Beef-steak pyes, or dishes of crabs, in addition, one on each side the center dish, dividing the space & reducing the distance between dish & dish to about 6 feet, which without them would be near 12 feet apart. Of late he has had the surprising sagacity to discover, that apples will make pyes; and its a question, if, in the violence of his efforts, we do not get one of apples, instead of having both of Beef-steaks. If the ladies can put up with such entertainment, and will submit to partake of it on plates, once Tin but now Iron—(not become so by the labor of scouring), I shall be happy to see them; and am, dear Doctor, yours, &.

Warm Friendship for Lafayette

To Lafayette, West Point, September 30, 1779

Your forward zeal in the cause of liberty; Your singular attachment to this infant world; your ardent and persevering efforts, not only in America, but since your return to France, to serve the United States; your polite attention to Americans, and your strict and uniform friendship for *me,* has ripened the first impressions of esteem and attachment, which I imbibed for you, into such perfect love and gratitude, that neither time nor absence can impair. Which will warrant my assuring you, that, whether in the character of an officer at the head of a corps of gallant French (if circumstances should require this), whether as a major-genl. commanding a division of the American army, or whether, after our Swords and spears have given place to the ploughshare and pruning-Hook, I see you as a private gentleman, a friend and companion, I shall welcome you in all the warmth of friendship to Columbia's shores; and, in the latter case, to my rural cottage, where homely fare and a cordial reception shall be substituted for delicacies of costly living. This, from past experience, I know *you* can submit to; and if the lovely partner of your happiness will consent to participate with *us* in such rural entertainment and amusemem'ts, I can undertake, in behalf of Mrs. Washington, that she will do every thing in her power to make Virginia agreeable to the Marchioness. . . . I assure you, that I love every body that is dear to you . . .

You are pleased, my dear Marquis, to express an earnest desire of seeing me in France (after the establishment of our independency) . . . Let me entreat you to be persuaded, that to meet you any where . . . would contribute to my happiness; and that to visit a country, to whose generous aid we stand so much indebted, would be an additional pleasure; but remember, my good friend, that I am unacquainted with your language, that I am too far advanced in years to acquire a knowledge of it, and that, to converse through the medium of an interpreter upon common occasions, especially with the Ladies, must appear so extremely awkward, insipid, and uncouth, that I can scarce bear it in idea. I will, therefore, hold myself disengaged for the present; but when I see you in Virginia, we will talk of this matter and fix our plans.

His Mother

To Benjamin Harrison, New Windsor, March 21, 1781

I do not delay a moment to thank you for [your letter] . . . and to express surprize at that part which respects a pension for my mother.

True it is, I am but little acquainted with her *present* situation or distresses, if she is under any. As true it is, a year or two before I left Virginia (to make her latter days comfortable and free from care) I did, at her request, but at my own expence, purchase a commodious house, garden and Lotts (of her own choosing) in Fredericksburg, that she might be near my sister Lewis, her only daughter—and did moreover agree to take her land and negroes at a certain yearly rent, to be fixed by Colo. Lewis and others (of her own nomination) which has been an annual expence to me ever since, as the estate never raised one half the rest I was to pay. Before I left Virginia I answered all her calls for money; and since that period have directed my steward to do the same.

Whence her distresses can arise, therefore, I know not, never having received any complaint of his inattention or neglect on that head; tho' his inability to pay my own taxes, is such I know, as to oblige me to sell negroes for this purpose—the taxes being the most unequal (I am told) in the world—some persons paying for things of equal value, four times, nay ten times, the rate that others do. But putting these things aside, which I could not avoid mentioning in exculpation of a presumptive want of duty on my part; confident I am that she has not a child that would not divide the last sixpence to relieve her from *real* distress. This she has been repeatedly assured of by me; and all of us I am certain, would feel much hurt, at having our mother a pensioner, while we had the means of supporting her; but in fact she has an ample income of her own.

I lament accordingly that your letter, which conveyed the first hint of this matter, did not come to my hands sooner; but I request, in pointed terms, if the matter is now in agitation in your Assembly, that all proceedings on it may be stopped, or in case of a decision in her favor, that it may be done away and repealed at my request.

Hopes to Retire

To Archibald Cary, H. Q., Newburgh, June 15, 1782

I pant for retirement, and am persuaded that an end of our warfare is not to be obtained but by vigorous exertions . . . I can truly say, that the first wish of my Soul is to return speedily into the bosom of that country, which gave me birth, and, in the sweet enjoyment of domestic happiness and the company of a few friends, to end my days in quiet, when I shall be called from this stage.

His Brother, Mother

To John Augustine Washington, Newburgh, January 16, 1783

Since the letter which Bushrod delivered to me in Philadelphia, I have received your favors of the 24th of July from Westmoreland, and 12th of Novr. from Berkley.

The latter gave me extreme pain. In God's name, how did my brother Samuel contrive to get himself so enormously in debt? Was it by making purchases? By misfortunes? or sheer indolence and inattention to business? From whatever cause it proceeded, the matter is now the same, and curiosity only prompts me to the enquiry, as it does to know what will be saved, and how it is disposed of. In the list of his debts, did it appear that I had a claim upon him for the purchase money of the land I sold to Pendleton on Bullskin? I have never received a farthing for it yet, and think I have been informed by him, that he was to pay it.

I have heard a favorable account of Bushrod, and doubt not but his prudence will direct him to a proper line of conduct; I have given him my sentiments on this head, and persuade myself that with the advice of Mr. Wilson, to whose friendship, as well as instruction in his profession, I recommended him; and the admonition of others: he will stand as good a chance as most youth of his age, to avoid the vices of large cities, which have their advantages and disadvantages in fitting a man for the great theater of public life.

I have lately received a letter from my mother, in which she complains much of the knavery of the overseer at the Little Falls quarter. She says she can get nothing from him. It is pretty evident, I believe, that I get nothing from thence, while I have the annual rent of between eighty and an hundred pounds to pay. The whole profit of the plantation, according to her account, is applied to his own use; which is hard upon me, as I had no earthly inducement to meddle with it, but to comply with her wish and to free her from care. This, like very other matter of private concern to me, has been totally neglected; but it is too much, while I am suffering in every other way (and hardly able to keep my own estate from sale) to be saddled with all the expence of hers, and not be able to derive the smallest return from it. She has requested that I should get somebody to attend to it: I must therefore ask the favor of you, to take it under your care. I know of none in whose hands it can be better placed; none to whom it will be less inconvenient; and who is more interested in the good management of the land . . .

While I am talking of my mother and her concerns, I am impelled to mention some things which have given, and still continue to give me pain. About two years ago, a gentleman of my acquaintance [Benjamin Harrison; see Washington's letter to him: March 21, 1781] informed me, that it was in contemplation, to move for a pension for her in the Virginia Assembly; that he did not suppose I knew of the measure proposed; and that he did not believe it would be very agreeable to me to have it done; but wished, however, to know my sentiments thereon. I instantly wrote him, that it was new and astonishing to me, and begged that he would prevent the motion if possible; or oppose it, if made; for I was sure she had not a child that would not be hurt at the idea of her becoming a pensioner—or in other words, receiving *charity* from the public. Since then I have heard nothing of *that* matter; but learn from very good authority, that she is, upon all occasions and in all companies, complaining of the hardness of the times, of her wants and difficulties; and if not in direct terms, at least by strong innuendoes, endeavors to excite a belief that times are much altered, &c., &c, which not only makes *her* appear in an unfaborable point of view, but *those also* who are connected with her. That she can have no *real* wants, that may not easily be supplied, I am sure of. *Imaginary* wants are indefinite; and oftentimes insatiable; because they sometimes are boundless, and always changing. The reason of my mentioning these matters, is that you may enquire into her real wants, and see what is necessary to make her comfortable. If the rent is insufficient to do this, while I have anything, I will part with it to make her so; and wish you to take measures in my behalf accordingly. At the same time, I wish you to represent to her in delicate terms, the impropriety of her complaints, and *acceptance* of favors, even where they are voluntarily offered, from any but relations. It will not do to touch upon this subject in a letter to her, and therefore I have avoided it.

Insists upon Accounts of Management of His Estate

To Lund Washington, Newburgh, February 12, 1783

You do not seem to have considered the force and tendency of the words of yr. letter when you talk of the probability *only* of sending me 'the long promised account.' . . .

Delicacy hitherto, and a hope that you long ago would have seen into the propriety of the measure without a hint of it from me, has restrained me from telling you, that annual accounts of my Crops, together with the receipts and expenditure of my Money, State of my stocks, &, ought to have been sent to me as regularly as the year came about. It is not to be supposed, that all the avocations of my public duties, great and laborious as they have been, could render me totally insensible to the *only means* by which myself and family, and the character I am to maintain in life hereafter, is to be supported; or that a precise account of these matters would not have been exceedingly satisfactory to me. Instead of this, except the accounts rendered at Valley Forge in the year 1778, I have received none since I left home . . .

I have often told you, and I repeat it with much truth, that the entire confidence which I placed in your integrity made me easy, and I was always happy at thinking that my affairs were in your hands—which I could not have been if they had been under the care of a common manager. But this did not exempt me from the desires which all men have, of knowing the exact state of them. I have now to beg that you will not only send me the account of your receipts and expenditures of specie, but of every other kind of money subsequent to the account exhibited at Valley Forge . . . I want to know before I come home (as I shall come home with empty pockets, whenever Peace shall take place) how affairs stand with me, and what my dependence is.

Wishes to Retire

To Robert Stewart, New York, August 10, 1783

I only wait (and with anxious impatience) the arrival of the definitive treaty, that I may take leave of my Military Employments and by bidding adieu to Public life, forever enjoy in the shades of retirement that ease and tranquillity to which, for more than eight years, I have been an entire stranger, and for which, a mind which has been constantly on the stretch during that period, and perplexed with a thousand embarrassing circumstances, often times without a ray of light to guide it, stands much in need.

Poetry, Lady, Badinage

To Mrs. Richard Stockton,[8] Rocky Hill, September 2, 1783

You apply to me, my dear Madam, for absolution as tho' I was your father Confessor; and as tho' you had committed a crime, great in itself, yet of the venial class. You have reason good—for I find myself strangly disposed to be a very indulgent ghostly adviser on this occasion; and, notwithstanding 'you are the most offending Soul alive' (that is, if it is a crime to write elegant Poetry), yet if you will come and dine with me on Thursday, and go thro' the proper course of penitence which shall be prescribed, I will strive hard to assist you in expiating these poetical trespasses on this side of purgatory. Nay more, if it rests with me to direct your future lucubrations, I shall certainly urge you to a repetition of the same conduct, on purpose to shew what an admirable knack you have at confession and reformation; and so without more hesitation, I shall venture to command the muse, not to be restrained by ill-grounded timidity, but to go on and prosper.—You see, Madam, when once the woman has tempted us, and we

[8] Annis Stockton, sister of Elias Boudinot, was a New Jersey lady who wrote verse.

have tasted the forbidden fruit, there is no such thing as checking our appetites, whatever the consequences may be. . . .

Before I come to the more serious conclusion of my Letter—I must beg leave to say a word about these fine things you have been telling [i.e., in a poem praising George Washington] in such harmonious and beautiful numbers. Fiction is to be sure the very life and Soul of Poetry—all Poets and Poetesses have been indulged in the free and indisputable uses of it, time out of mind. And to oblige you to make such an excellent Poem on such a subject, without any materials but those of simple reality, would be as cruel as the Edict of Pharaoh which compelled the children of Israel to manufacture Bricks without the necessary Ingredients.

Thus are you sheltered under the authority of prescription, and I will not dare to charge you with an intentional breach of the Rules of the decalogue in giving so bright a coloring to the services I have been enabled to render my Country.

At Length, a Private Citizen

To Lafayette, February 1, 1784

At length, my dear marquis, I am become a private citizen on the banks of the Potomac, and under the shadow of my own vine and my own fig-tree, free from the bustle of a camp and the busy scenes of public life, I am solacing myself with those tranquil enjoyments of which the soldier who is ever in pursuit of fame, the statesman whose watchful days and sleepless nights are spent in devising schemes to promote the welfare of his own, perhaps the ruin of other countries, as if the globe was insufficient for us all . . . can have very little conception. I have not only retired from all public employments, but I am retiring within myself, and shall be able to view the solitary walk of private life with heartfelt satisfaction. Envious of none, I am determined to be pleased with all; and this, my dear friend, being the order of my march, I will move gently down the stream of life until I sleep with my fathers.

Has No Money

To Fielding Lewis, Mount Vernon, February 27, 1784

You very much mistake my circumstances when you suppose me in a condition to advance money. I made no money from my Estate during the nine years I was absent from it, and brought none home with me. Those who owed me, for the most part, took advantage of the depreciation, and paid me off with six pence in the pound. Those to whom I was indebted, I have yet to pay, without other means, if they will not wait, than selling part of my Estate; or distressing those who were too honest to take advantage of the tender Laws to quit scores with me.

His Simple Way of Living

To Marquise de Lafayette, Mount Vernon, April 4, 1784

From the clangor of arms and the bustle of a camp, freed from the cares of public employment and the responsibility of office, I am now enjoying domestic ease under the shadow of my own vine and my own fig tree; and in a small villa, with the implements of husbandry and lambkins around me, I expect to glide gently down the stream of life, till I am entombed in the dreary mansion of my fathers.

Mrs. Washington is highly honored by your participations, and feels very sensibly the force of your polite invitation to Paris; but she is too far advanced in life, and is too much immersed in the care of her little progeny, to cross the Atlantic. This, my dear Marchioness . . . is not the case with you. You have youth . . . and must have a curiosity to see the country, young, rude, and uncultivated as it is, for the liberties of which your husband has fought, bled, and acquired much glory, where every body admires, every body loves him. Come, then, let me entreat it, and call my cottage your home; for your own doors do not open to you with more readiness than mine would. You will see the plain manner in which we live, and meet the rustic civility; and you shall taste the simplicity of rural life. It will diversify the scene, and may give you a higher relish for the gayeties of the court, when you return to Versailles.

Affection for Lafayette

To Lafayette, November, 1784

In the moment of our separation,[9] upon the road as I travelled, and every hour since, I have felt all that love, respect and attachment for you, with which length of years, close connection, and your merits have inspired me. I often asked myself, as our carriages separated, whether that was the last sight I ever should have of you? And though I wished to answer No, my fears answered Yes. I called to mind the days of my youth, and found they had long since fled to return no more! that I was now descending the hill I had been fifty two years in climbing, and that, though I was blessed with a good constitution, I was of a short lived family, and might soon expect to be entombed in the mansion of my fathers. These thoughts darkened the shades, and gave a gloom to the picture, and consequently, to my prospect of ever seeing you again.

Sits for His Portrait

To Francis Hopkinson, Mount Vernon, May 16, 1785

In for a penny, in for a pound, is an old adage. I am so hackneyed to the touches of the painter's pencil, that I am *now* altogether at their beck; and sit, 'like Patience on a monument,' whilst

[9] On his return to America in 1784, Lafayette made two visits to Mount Vernon, one in August and one in November, when he spent one week there

they are delineating the lines of my face. It is a proof, among many others, of what habit and custom can accomplish. At first I was as impatient at the request, and as restive under the operation, as a colt is of the saddle. The next time I submitted very reluctantly, but with less flouncing. Now, no dray-horse moves more readily to his thill than I to the painter's chair.

No Compensation for Himself

To Patrick Henry, Mount Vernon, October 29, 1785

When I was first called to the station, with which I was honored during the late conflict for our liberties . . . I thought it my duty to . . . shut my hand against every pecuniary recompense. To this resolution I have invariably adhered, and from it, if I had the inclination, I do not feel at liberty now to depart.

Costume for His Monument

To Thomas Jefferson, Mount Vernon, August 1, 1786

In answer to your obliging inquiries respecting the dress, attitude, &, which I would wish to have given to the statue in question, I have only to observe, that, not having sufficient knowledge in the art of sculpture to oppose my judgment to the taste of connoisseurs, I do not desire to dictate in the matter. On the contrary, I shall be perfectly satisfied with whatever may be judged decent and proper. I should even scarcely have ventured to suggest, that perhaps a servile adherence to the garb of antiquity might not be altogether so expedient, as some little deviation in favor of the modern costume, if I had not learnt from Colonel Humphreys, that this was a circumstance hinted in conversation by Mr. West to Mr. Houdon. This taste, which has been introduced in painting by West, I understand is received with applause, and prevails extensively.

His Money Difficulties

To Mrs. Mary Washington, Mount Vernon, February 15, 1787

I take the (first safe) conveyance . . . to send you 15 guineas, which believe me is all I have, and which indeed ought to have been paid many days ago to another . . . I have now demands upon for more than 500 £, three hundred and forty odd of which is due for the tax of 1786; and I know not where or when, I shall receive one shilling with which to pay it. In the last two years I made no crops. In the first I was obliged to buy corn and this year have none to sell, and my wheat is so bad, I cannot neither eat it myself nor sell it to others, and Tobacco I make none. Those who owe me money cannot or will not pay it without suits, and to sue is to do nothing; whilst my expences, not from any extravagance, or an inclination on my part to live splendidly, but for the absolute support of my family and the visitors who are constantly here, are exceedingly high; higher indeed than I can support without selling part of my estate, which I am disposed to do, rather than run in debt, or continue to be so; but this I cannot do, without taking much less than the lands I have offered for sale are worth. This is really and truely my situation.

On Marriage

To Marquis de Chastellux, April 25, 1788

In reading your very friendly and acceptable letter . . . which came to hand by the last mail, I was, as you may well suppose, not less delighted than surprised to meet the plain American words, 'my wife.' A wife! Well, my dear Marquis, I can hardly refrain from smiling to find you are caught at last. I saw, by the eulogium you often made on the happiness of domestic life in America, that you had swallowed the bait, and that you would as surely be taken, one day or another, as that you were a philosopher and a soldier. So your day has at length come. I am glad of it, with all my heart and soul. It is quite good enough for you. Now you are well served for coming to fight in favor of the American rebels, all the way across the Atlantic Ocean, by catching that terrible contagion—domestic felicity—which time, like the small pox or the plague, a man can have only once in his life: because it commonly lasts him (at least with us in America—I dont know how you manage these matters in France) for his whole life time. And yet after all the maledictions you so richly merit on the subject, the worst wish which I can find in my heart to make against Madame de Chastellux and yourself is, that you may neither of you ever get the better of this same—domestic felicity during the entire course of your mortal existence.

Desire to Retire from Presidency

To James Madison, Mount Vernon, May 20, 1792

I have not been unmindful of the sentiments expressed by you in conversation. . . . I have again, and again revolved them with thoughtful anxiety; but without being able to dispose my mind to a longer continuation in the office I now have the honor to hold. I therefore still look forward to the fulfilment of my fondest and most ardent wishes to spend the remainder of my days (which I cannot expect will be many) in ease and tranquillity.

Nothing short of conviction that my dereliction of the Chair of Government . . . would involve the Country in serious disputes respecting the chief Magestrate . . . could, in any wise, induce me to relinquish the determination I have formed . . .

Under these impressions then, permit me to reiterate the request I made to you at our last meeting—namely, to think of the proper time, and the best mode of announcing the intention; and that you would prepare the latter. In revolving this subject myself, my judgment has always been embarrassed.—On the one hand, a previous declaration to retire, not only carries with it the appearance of vanity and self-importance, but it may be construed into a manoeuvre to be invited to remain.—And on the other hand, to say nothing, implys consent; or, at any rate, would leave the matter in doubt; and to decline afterwards might be deemed as bad, and uncandid.

Has No Money

To Charles Carter, Philadelphia, March 10, 1795

My friends entertain a very erroneous idea of my pecuniary resources, when they set me down for a money lender, or one who (now) has a command of it. You may believe me when I assert that the bonds which were due to me before the Revolution, were discharged during the progress of it—with a few exceptions in depreciated paper (in some instances as low as a shilling in the pound). That such has been the management of my Estate, for many years past, especially since my absence from home, now six years, as scarcely to support itself. That my public allowance (whatever the world may think of it) is inadequate to the expence of living in this City; to such an extravagant height has the necessaries as well as the conveniences of life arisen. And, moreover that to keep myself out of debt; I have found it expedient now and then to sell lands, or something else to effect this purpose.

These are facts I have no inclination to publish to the world, nor should I have disclosed them on this occasion, had it not been due to friendship, to give you some explanation of my inability to comply with your request. If, however by joining with nine others, the sum required can be obtained—notwithstanding my being under these circumstances—and notwithstanding the money will have to be withdrawn from another purpose—I will contribute one hundred pounds towards the accommodation of your son's wants, without any view to the receipt of interest therefrom.

Impervious to Personal Attack

To David Humphreys, June 12, 1796

I am attacked for a steady opposition to every measure which has a tendency to disturb the peace and tranquillity of [the country]. But these attacks, unjust and unpleasant as they are, will occasion no change in my conduct; nor will they work any other effect in my mind, than to increase the anxious desire which has long possessed my breast to enjoy in the shades of retirement the consolation of having rendered my country every service my abilities were competent to, uninfluenced by pecuniary or ambitious considerations. . . . Malignity therefore may dart her shafts; but no earthly power can deprive me of the consolation of knowing that I have not in the course of my administration been guilty of a wilful error, however numerous they may have been from other causes.

Bitterness at Personal Attack

To Thomas Jefferson, Mount Vernon, July 6, 1796

Until within the last year or two, I had no conception that [political] parties would or even could go the length I have been witness to; nor did I believe until lately, that . . . while I was using my utmost exertions to establish a national character of our own, independent . . . of every nation of the earth, and wished, by steering a steady course, to preserve this country from the horrors of a desolating war, I should be accused of being the enemy of one nation [France], and subject to the influence of another [England]; and . . . that every act of my administration would be tortured, and the grossest and most insidious misrepresentations of them be made, by giving one side *only* of a subject, and that too in such exaggerated and indecent terms as could scarcely be applied to a

Nero, a notorious defaulter, or even to a common pickpocket. But enough of this, I have already gone farther in the expression of my feelings than I intended.

Anticipates Pleasure of Retirement

To Henry Knox, Philadelphia, March 2, 1797

To the wearied traveller, who sees a resting-place, and is bending his body to lean thereon, I now compare myself . . . To misrepresent my motives, to reprobate my politics, and to weaken the confidence which has been reposed in my administration, are objects, which cannot be relinquished by those who will be satisfied with nothing short of a change in our political system. The consolation, however, which results from conscious rectitude, and the approving voice of my country . . . deprives their sting of its poison . . .

Although the prospect of retirement is most grateful to my soul, and I have not a wish to mix again in the great world, or to partake in its politics, yet I am not without my regrets at parting with (perhaps never more to meet) the few intimates, whom I love, and among these, be assured, you are one.

. . . The remainder of my life (which in the course of nature cannot be long) will be occupied in rural amusement; and, though I shall seclude myself as much as possible from the noisy and bustling crowd, none more than myself would be regaled by the company of those I esteem, at Mount Vernon; more than twenty miles from which, after I arrive there, it is not likely I ever shall be.

Returns Home from Presidency

To James McHenry, April 3, 1797

We got home without accident, and found the Roads drier, and better than I ever travelled them at that season of the year. The attentions we met with on our journey were very flattering, and to some, whose minds are differently formed from mine would have been highly relished; but I avoided in every instance, where I had any previous knowledge of the intention, and could by earnest entreaties prevail, all parade or escorts. Mrs. Washington took a violent cold in Philadelphia, which hangs upon her still; but it is not as bad as it has been.

I find myself in the situation nearly of a young beginner; for, although I have not houses to build (except one, which I must erect for the accommodation and security of my Military, Civil, and private Papers, which are voluminous and may be interesting), yet I have not one, or scarcely anything else about me that does not require considerable repairs. In a word, I am already surrounded by Joiners, Masons, Painters, &, &; and such is my anxiety to get out of their hands, that I have scarcely a room to put a friend into, or to sit in myself, without the music of hammers, or the odoriferous smell of paint.

Retirement

To Oliver Wolcott, Mount Vernon, May 15, 1797

For myself, having turned aside from the broad walks of political, into the narrow paths of private life, I shall leave it with those, whose duty it is to consider subject of this sort [public affairs], and (as every good citizen ought to do) conform to whatsoever the ruling powers shall decide. To make and sell a little flour annually, to repair houses (going fast to ruin), to build one for the security of my papers of a public nature, and to amuse myself in agricultural and rural pursuits, will constitute employment for the few years I have to remain on this terrestrial globe. If, to these, I could now and then meet the friends I esteem, it would fill the measure and add zest to my enjoyments; but, if ever this happens, it must be under my own vine and fig-tree. . .

Last Years

To James McHenry, May 29, 1797

I am indebted to you for several unacknowledged letters; but never mind that; go on as if you had them. You are at the source of information, and can find many things to relate; while I have nothing to say, that could either inform or amuse a Secretary of War in Philadelphia.

I might tell him, that I begin my diurnal course with the sun; that, if my hirelings are not in their places at that time I send them messages expressive of my sorrow for their indisposition; that, having put these wheels in motion, I examine the state of things further; and the more they are probed, the deeper I find the wounds are which my buildings have sustained by an absence and neglect of eight years; by the time I have accomplished these matters, breakfast (a little after seven o'clock, about the time I presume you are taking leave of Mrs. McHenry), is ready; that, this being over, I mount my horse and ride round my farms, which employs me until it is time to dress for dinner, at which I rarely miss seeing strange faces, come as they say out of respect for me. Pray, would not the word curiosity answer as well? And how different this from having a few social friends at a cheerful board! The usual time of sitting at table, a walk, and tea, brings me within the dawn of candlelight; previous to which, if not prevented by company, I resolve, that, as soon as the glimmering taper supplies the place of the great luminary, I will retire to my writing-table and acknowledge the letters I have received; but when the lights are brought, I feel tired and disinclined to engage in this work, conceiving that the next night will do as well. The next comes, and with it the same causes for postponement, and effect, and so on.

This will account for your letter remaining so long unacknowledged; and, having given you the history of a day, it will serve for a year, and I am persuaded you will not require a second edition of it. But it may strike you, that in this detail no mention is made of any portion of time allotted for reading. The remark would be just, for I have not looked into a book since I came home; nor shall I be able to do it until I have discharged my workmen, probably not before the nights grow longer, when possibly I may be looking in Doomsday-Book . . . I am always and affectionately yours.

Lending Money

To Samuel Washington, Mount Vernon, July 12, 1797

I perceive by your letter of the 7th Instant that you are under the same mistake that many others are—in supposing that I have money always at command.

The case is so much the reverse of it, that I found it expedient, before I retired from public life, to sell all my Lands (near 5000 acres) in Pennsylvania . . . and my lands in the Great Dismal Swamp in Virginia, in order to enable me to defray the expenses of my station, and to raise money for other purposes. . .

A third [of the lands] having within these few days paid me an installment of three thousand Dollars, I will, rather than you should be compelled to sell your land, lend you a third of them, altho' it will be inconvenient for me to do so . . .

It is because you have assured me that misfortunes have brought on your present difficulties (tho' by the by let me observe if you had inspected as you ought, the staking of your wheat more closely, the spoiling thereof might have been avoided) and because I have heard that you are industrious and sober that I put myself to the inconvenience of parting with the above sum; for I would not lend it for the purpose to enable you to indulge in any thing that is not strictly oeconomical and proper; and I shall add further, that it will be my expectation that the money be immediately applied to the uses for which you have required it—for you may be assured that there is no practice more dangerous than that of borrowing money . . . For when money can be had in this way, repayment is seldom thought of in time;—the Interest becomes a moth;—exertions to raise it by dint of Industry ceases—it comes easy and is spent freely; and many things indulged in that would never be thought of, if to be purchased by the sweat of the brow.— In the mean time the debt is accumulating like a snow ball in rolling.

I mention these things to you, because your inexperience may not have presented them to your mind—but you may rely on it that they are indubitable facts, and have proved the ruin of thousands before suspected. Great speculations and sometimes trade may be benefitted of obtaining money on Interest, but no landed Estate will bear it. . . .

All that I shall require is, that you will return the nett sum when in your power, without interest.

Engaging a Housekeeper

To Bushrod Washington, Mount Vernon, November 3, 1797

Your aunt's distresses for want of a good housekeeper are such as to render the wages demanded by Mrs. Forbes (though unusually high) of no consideration . . .

If you are in habits of free communication with Mr. Brooke or with others who had opportunities of judging completely of the qualifications and conduct of Mrs. Forbes as a housekeeper, I would thank you for ascertaining and giving it to me in as precise a manner as you can obtain it. Among other things it would be satisfactory to know—

What countrywoman she is?
Whether Widow or Wife? if the latter
Where her husband is?
What family she has?
What her age is?
Of what temper?
Whether active and spirited in the execution of her business?
Whether sober and honest?
Whether much knowledge in Cookery, and understands ordering and setting out a table?
What her appearance is?

With other matters which may occur to you to ask—and necessary for me to know.

Mrs. Forbes will have a warm, decent and comfortable room to herself, to lodge in, and will eat of the victuals of our Table, but not set at it, at any time *with us,* be her appearance what it may; for if this was *once admitted,* no line satisfactory to either party, perhaps, could be drawn thereafter. . . .

Is it practicable do you think to get a good and well-disposed negro cook on hire, or purchase?

[*To George Lewis, November 13, 1797:* The running off of my cook has been a most inconvenient thing to this family, and what rendered it more disagreeable, is that I had resolved never to become the Master of another slave by purchase, but this resolution I fear I must break. I have endeavored to hire, black or white, but am not yet supplied.]

Relations with Estate Manager

To James Anderson, Federal City, May 22, 1798

I had no intention . . . to part with you as a manager; but . . . I have no wish to retain any person in my service who is discontented with my conduct . . . Strange and singular indeed would it be, if the proprietor of an estate . . . should have nothing to say in, or control over, his own expenditures; should not be at liberty to square his oeconomy thereto; nor should, without hurting the feelings of a manager, point to such alterations . . . as he might incline to adopt . . . I have no hesitation in declaring that I shall never relinquish the right of judging in my own concerns . . . to any man living, while I have health and strength to look into my own business . . .

Where have I been deficient? or in what have you just cause to complain? If I cannot remark upon my own business passing every day under my own eyes, without hurting your feelings, I must discontinue my rides, or become a cypher on my own estate . . . If your feelings have been hurt by my remarks on the bad clover seed that was purchased, I cannot help that; my views and plans have been much more hurt by it . . . It is not my wish to hurt the feelings of anyone, where it can be avoided.

Commander in Chief's Uniform

To James McHenry, Mount Vernon, January 27, 1799

On reconsidering the uniform for the Commander-in-Chief, it has become a matter of doubt with me (although, as it respects myself *personally,* I was against *all* embroidery), whether embroidery on the Cape, Cuffs, and Pockets of the Coat, and none on the buff waistcoat, would not have a disjointed and awkward appearance. It is neither required nor forbidden . . . To *you* I submit the matter, as I also do whether the coat shall have slash Cuffs (with blue flaps passing through them), and slash pockets, or both shall be in the usual manner.

These apparently are trifling matters to trouble you with; but, as it is the commencement of a new scene, it is desirable that the thing should take a right direction. I have therefore . . . determined to direct Mr. McAlpin [Philadelphia tailor] to apply to and follow your directions in making the uniform. I should not prefer a heavy embroidery, or one containing much work. A light and neat one would in my opinion be more elegant and more desirable, as well for the Coat as the Waistcoat . . .

The eagle, too, having become part of the American cockade; have any of them been brought into use yet? My idea of the size is, that it ought not to be larger than would cover a quarter of a dollar at most, and should be represented (for the officers) as clothed with feathers. This any ingenious silversmith can execute; and, if four were sent to me, I would thank you, and would remit the cost as soon as known to me.

I must further beg, that proper stars for the epaulets . . . may be sent to me with the other articles, that I may be equipped in dress *at least;* and if there are any handsome cockades (but not whimsically foolish) in wear, or any one who can make them,

I should be glad if they were sent with the eagles fixed thereon, ready to be placed in the hats. Does the Presid[en]t and yourself wear them?

Expects Death

To Burges Ball, Mount Vernon, September 22, 1799

Your letter of the 16th inst. has been received, informing me of the death of my brother [Charles Washington].

The death of near relations always produces awful and affecting emotions, under whatsoever circumstances it may happen. That of my brother has been so long expected, and his latter days so uncomfortable to himself [that they] must have prepared all around him for the stroke though painful in the effect.

I was the first, and am, now, the last of my father's children by the second marriage who remain.

When I shall be *called upon to follow them,* is known only to the Giver of Life. When the summons comes I shall endeavor to obey it with good grace.[10]

[10] Washington died eleven weeks after he wrote these lines.

Chapter 4

BRIEF COMMENTS ON HIMSELF

Arranged Chronologically

Humor

To John Augustine Washington, July 18, 1755

As I have heard . . . a circumstantial account of my death and dying speech, I take this early opportunity of contradicting the first, and of assuring you, that I have not as yet composed the latter.

His Character

To Earl of Loudoun, March, 1757

Do not think, my Lord, that I am going to flatter; notwithstanding I have exalted sentiments of your Lordship's character and respect your rank, it is not my intention to adulate. My nature is open and honest and free from guile.

Reproof

To Governor Dinwiddie, August 27, 1757

It is with pleasure I receive reproof, when reproof is due, because no person can be readier to accuse me, than I am to acknowledge an error, when I am guilty of one; nor more desirous for atoning for a crime, when I am sensible of having committed it. But, on the other hand, it is with concern I remark, that my best endeavors lose their reward, and that my conduct, although I have uniformly studied to make it unexceptionable as I could, does not appear to you in a favorable point of light.

His Conduct

To Major Francis Halket, August 2, 1758

I am uninfluenced by prejudice, having no hopes or fears but for the general good.

To John Armstrong, May 18, 1779

To please everybody is impossible; were I to undertake it, I should probably please nobody. If I know myself I have no partialities. I have from the beginning, and I hope I shall to the end, pursued to the utmost of my judgment and abilities, one steady line of conduct for the good of the great whole.

To President of Congress, December 20, 1776

I have no lust for power.

Public Service

Speech to Army officers, March, 1783

I have grown gray in your service, and now find myself growing blind.

No Vanity

To Dr. James Craik, March 25, 1784

I will frankly declare to you, my dear Doctor, that any memoirs of my life, distinct and unconnected with the general history of the [Revolutionary] war, would rather hurt my feelings than tickle my pride whilst I lived. I had rather glide gently down the stream of life, leaving it to posterity to think and say what they please of me, than by any act of mine to have vanity or ostentation imputed to me . . . I do not think vanity is a trait of my character.

Not Educated

To David Humphreys, July 25, 1785

If I had the *talents* for it, I have not *leisure* to turn my thoughts to Commentaries [on the American Revolution]. A consciousness of a defective education, and a certainty of the want of time, unfit me for such an undertaking.

World Citizen

To Lafayette, August 15, 1786

[I am] a philanthropist by character, and . . . a citizen of the great republic of humanity at large.

Takes Abuse

To Henry Lee, July 21, 1793

The result [of public abuse], as it respects myself, I care not; for I have a consolation within, that no earthly efforts can deprive me of, and that is, that neither ambitious nor interested motives have influenced my conduct. The arrows of malevolence, therefore, however barbed and well pointed, never can reach the most vulnerable part of me; though, whilst I am *up* as a *mark,* they will be continually aimed.

Duty and Conscience

To Selectmen of Boston, July 28, 1795

While I feel the most lively gratitude for the many instances of the approbation from my country, I can not otherwise deserve it, than by obeying the dictates of my conscience.

Seeks Truth

To Edmund Randolph, July 31, 1795

I am [not] disposed to quit the ground I have taken, unless circumstances more imperious than have yet come to my knowledge should compel it; for there is but one straight course, and that is to seek truth and pursue it steadily.

Not Infallible

To Henry Knox, September 20, 1795

If any power on earth could . . . erect the standard of infallibility in political opinions, there is no being . . . that would resort to it with more eagerness than myself, so long as I remain a servant of the public. But as I have found no better guide hitherto, than upright intentions and close investigation, I shall adhere to those maxims, while I keep the watch; leaving it to those who will come after me, to explore new ways, if they like or think them better.

Manners

To Ferdinand Ferot, April 15, 1798

Not being conscious of having merited the reprehension you have judged it expedient to inflict on me, I shall not give you the trouble of reading an answer in detail. I cannot forbear observing however that . . . it is not usual with me, to treat any gentleman with incivility or even with indifference (especially under my own roof).

Prepare for the Worst

To James Anderson, July 25, 1798

I, believing that man was not designed by the all-wise Creator to live for himself alone, prepare for the worst that can happen.

His Politics

To Lafayette, December 25, 1798

I wish well to all nations and to all men. My politics are plain and simple. I think every nation has a right to establish that form of government under which it conceives it shall live most happy; provided it infracts no right, or is not dangerous to others; and that no governments ought to interfere with the internal concerns of another, except for the security of what is due to themselves.

General Welfare

To James McHenry, April 23, 1799

I have no object separated from the general welfare to promote. I have no predilections, no prejudices to gratify, no friends, whose interests or views I wish to advance at the expence of propriety.

Chapter 5

LAST WILL AND TESTAMENT, JULY 9, 1799

IN THE NAME OF GOD, AMEN!

I GEORGE WASHINGTON of Mount Vernon, a citizen of the United States and lately President of the same do make ordain and declare this Instrument, which is written with my own hand and every page thereof subscribed with my name to be my last Will & Testament, revoking all others.[1]

—Imprimus—All my debts, of which there are but few, and none of magnitude, are to be punctually and speedily paid, and the legacies hereinafter bequeathed are to be discharged as soon as circumstances will permit, and in the manner directed.

ITEM. To my dearly beloved wife, Martha Washington I give and bequeath the use profit and benefit of my whole Estate, real and personal, for the term of her natural life, except such parts thereof as are specially disposed of hereafter,—My improved lot in the Town of Alexandria, situated on Pitt and Cameron Streets, I give to her & her heirs forever, as I also do my [2][2] household and kitchen furniture of every sort and kind with the liquors and groceries which may be on hand at the time of my decease, to be used and disposed of as she may think proper.

ITEM—Upon the decease of wife it is my will and desire, that all the slaves which I hold in *my own right* shall receive their freedom—To emancipate them during her life, would tho earnestly wished by me, be attended with such insuperable difficulties, on account of their intermixture by marriages with the Dower negroes

[1] At the bottom of every page—with one exception—he signed his name. On the one page, the last word was Washington, which probably led him to assume he had signed.

[2] These figures in brackets mark the beginning of each page of the MS. will.

as to excite the most painful sensations—if not disagreeable consequences from the latter while both descriptions are in the occupancy of the same proprietor, it not being in my power under the tenure by which the dower Negroes are held to manumit them—And whereas among those who will receive freedom according to this devise there may be some who from old age, or bodily infirmities & others who on account of their infancy, that will be unable to support themselves, it is my will and desire that all who come under the first and second description shall be comfortably clothed and fed by my heirs while they live and [3] that such of the latter description as have no parents living, or if living are unable, or unwilling to provide for them, shall be bound by the Court until they shall arrive at the age of twenty five years, and in cases where no record can be produced whereby their ages can be ascertained, the Judgment of the Court upon it's own view of the subject shall be adequate and final.—The negroes thus bound are (by their masters and mistresses) to be taught to read and write and to be brought up to some useful occupation, agreeably to the laws of the commonwealth of Virginia, providing for the support of orphans and other poor children—and I do hereby expressly forbid the sale or transportation out of the said Commonwealth of any Slave I may die possessed of, under any pretence, whatsoever—and I do moreover most positively, and most solemnly enjoin it upon my Executors hereafter named, or the survivors of them to see that this clause respecting slaves and every part thereof be religiously fulfilled at the Epoch at which it is directed to take place without evasion neglect or delay after the crops which may then be on the ground are harvested, particularly as it respects [4] the aged and infirm, seeing that a regular and permanent fund be established for their support so long as there are subjects requiring it, not trusting to the uncertain provisions to be made by individuals.—And to my mulatto man, William (calling himself William Lee) I give immediate freedom or if he should prefer it (on account of the accidents which have befallen him and which have rendered him incapable of walking or of any active employment) to remain in the situation he now is, it shall be optional in him to do so—In either case however I allow him an annuity of thirty dollars during his natural life which shall be independent of the victuals and *cloaths* he has been accustomed to receive; if he *chuses* the last alternative, but in full with his freedom, if he prefers the first, and this I give him as a testimony of my sense of his attachment to me and for his faithful services during the Revolutionary War.

ITEM—To the Trustees, (Governors or by whatsoever other name they may be designated) of the academy in the Town of Alexandria, I give and bequeath, in Trust, Four thousand dollars, or in other words twenty of the shares which I [5] hold in the Bank of Alexandria towards the support of a Free School, established at, and annexed to the said academy for the purpose of educating such orphan children, or the children of such other poor and indigent persons as are unable to accomplish it with their own means, and who in the judgment of the trustees of the said Seminary, are best entitled to the benefits of this donation—The aforesaid twenty shares I give and bequeath in perpetuity—the dividends only of which are to be drawn for and applied by the said Trustees for the time being, for the uses above mentioned, the stock to remain entire and untouched unless indications of a failure of the said Bank should be so apparent or discontinuance thereof should render a removal of this fund necessary, in either of these cases the amount of the stock here devised is to be vested in some other bank or public institution whereby the interest may with regularity and certainty be drawn and applied as above.—And to prevent misconception, my meaning is, and is hereby declared to be that, these twenty shares are in lieu of and not in addition to the Thousand pounds given by a missive letter some years ago in consequence whereof an an[6]nuity of fifty pounds has since been paid towards the support of this institution.

ITEM—Whereas by a law of the Commonwealth of Virginia, enacted in the year 1785, the Legislature thereof was pleased (as an evidence of it's approbation of the services I had rendered the public, during the Revolution—and partly, I believe in consideration of my having suggested the vast advantages which the community would derive from the extension of its Inland navigation, under legislative patronage) to present me with one hundred shares, of one hundred dollars each, in the incorporated company established for the purpose of extending the navigation of James

River from tide water to the mountains; and also with fifty shares of one hundred pounds sterling each in the corporation of another company likewise established for the similar purpose of opening the navigation of the River Potomac from tide water to Fort Cumberland; the acceptance of which, although the offer was highly honorable and grateful to my feelings, was refused, as inconsistent with a principle which I had adop[7]ted, and had never departed from, namely not to receive pecuniary compensation for any services I could render my country in it's arduous struggle with Great Britain for it's Rights; and because I had evaded similar propositions from other States in the Union—adding to this refusal however an intimation, that, if it should be the pleasure of the Legislature to permit me to appropriate the said shares to *public uses,* I would receive them on those terms with due sensibility—and this it having consented to in flattering terms, as will appear by a subsequent law and sundry resolutions, in the most ample and honorable manner, I proceed after this recital for the more correct understanding of the case to declare—

That as it has always been a source of serious regret with me to see the youth of these United States sent to foreign countries for the purpose of education, often before their minds were formed or they had imbibed any adequate ideas of the happiness of their own, contracting too frequently not only habits of dissipation and *extravagance,* but principles unfriendly to Republican Governm't and to the true and genuine liberties [8] of mankind, which thereafter are rarely overcome.—For these reasons it has been my ardent wish to see a plan devised on a liberal scale which would have a tendency to spread systematic ideas through all parts of this rising Empire, thereby to do away local attachments and state prejudices as far as the nature of things would, or indeed ought to admit, from our national councils—Looking anxiously forward to the accomplishment of so desirable an object as this is, (in my estimation) my mind has not been able to contemplate any plan more likely to effect the measure than the establishment of a University in a central part of the United States to which the youth of fortune and talents from all parts thereof might be sent for the completion of their education in all the branches of polite literature in arts and sciences—in acquiring knowledge in the principles of Politics and good Government and (as a matter of infinite importance in my judgment) by associating with each other and forming friendships in Juvenile years, be enabled to free themselves in a proper degree from those local prejudices and habit[9]ual jealousies which have just been mentioned and which when carried to excess are never failing sources of disquietude to the Public mind and pregnant of mischievous consequences to this country:—under these impressions so fully dilated,—

Item—I give and bequeath in perpetuity the fifty shares which I hold in the Potomac Company (under the aforesaid Acts of the Legislature of Virginia) towards the endowment of a University to be established within the limits of the District of Columbia, under the auspices of the General Government, if that Government should incline to extend a fostering hand towards it,—and until such seminary is established, and the funds arising on these shares shall be required for its support, my further will and desire is that the profit accruing therefrom shall whenever the dividends are made be laid out in purchasing stock in the Bank of Columbia or some other Bank at the discretion of my Executors, or by the Treasurer of the United States for the time being under the direction of Congress, provided that Honorable body should [10] *patronize* the measure. And the dividends proceeding from the purchase of such Stock is to be vested in more Stock and so on until a sum adequate to the accomplishment of the object is obtained, of which I have not the smallest doubt before many years pass away, even if no aid or *encouraged* is given by Legislative authority or from any other source.[3]

Item—The hundred shares which I held in the James River Company I have given and now confirm in perpetuity to and for the use and benefit of Liberty Hall Academy in the County of Rockbridge, in the Commonwealth of *Virga.*

Item—I release exonerate and discharge the estate of my deceased brother, Samuel Washington, from the payment of the money which is due to me for the land I sold to Philip Pendleton (lying in the County of Berkley) who assigned the same to him the said Samuel, who by agreement was to pay me therefor.—And whereas by some contract (the purport of which was never com-

[3] This provision of the will was never carried out.

municated to me) between the said Samuel and his son Thornton Washington, the latter became possessed of the aforesaid land without [11] any conveyance having passed from me either to the said Pendleton the said Samuel or the said Thornton and without any consideration having been made, by which neglect neither the legal or equitable title has been alienated;—it rests therefore with me to declare my intentions concerning the premises—And these are to give and bequeath the said land to whomsoever the said Thornton Washington (who is also dead) devised the same or to his heirs forever, if he died intestate.—Exonerating the estate of the said Thornton, equally with that of the said Samuel from payment of the purchase-money, which with Interest agreeably to the original contract with the said Pendleton would amount to more than a thousand pounds—and whereas two other sons of my said deceased brother Samuel,—namely, George Steptoe Washington and Lawrence Augustine Washington were by the decease of those to whose care they were committed, brought under my protection, and in consequence have occasioned advances on my part for their education at college and other schools for their board *cloathing* and other incidental expenses to the amount of near [12] five thousand dollars over and above the sums furnished by their estate, *wch* sum may be inconvenient for them or their father's Estate to refund—I do for these reasons acquit them and the said Estate from the payment thereof.—My intention being that all accounts between them and me and their father's Estate and me shall stand balanced.

Item—The balance due to me from the Estate of Bartholomew Dandridge deceased, (my wife's brother) and which amounted on the first day of October, 1795, to Four hundred and twenty-five pounds (as will appear by an account rendered by his deceased son, John Dandridge, who was the Executor of his father's will) I release and acquit from the payment thereof.—And the *negros* (then thirty three in number) formerly belonging to the said Estate who were taken in Execution,—sold—and purchased in, on my account in the year [1795?] and ever since have remained in the possession and to the use of Mary, widow of the said Bartholomew Dandridge with their increase, it is my will and desire shall continue and be in her possession, without paying hire or making [13] compensation for the same for the time past or to come during her natural life, at the expiration of which, I direct that all of them who are forty years old and upwards shall receive their freedom, all under that age and above sixteen shall serve seven years and no longer, and all under sixteen years shall serve until they are twenty-five years of age and then be free.—And to avoid disputes respecting the ages of any of these *negros* they are to be taken to the Court of the County in which they reside and the judgment thereof in this relation shall be final and a record thereof made, which may be adduced as evidence at any time thereafter if disputes should arise concerning the same.—And I further direct that the heirs of the said Bartholomew Dandridge shall equally share the benefits arising from the services of the said *negros* according to the tenor of this devise upon the decease of their mother.

ITEM—If Charles Carter who intermarried with my niece, Betty Lewis, is not sufficiently secured in the title to the lots he had of me in the town of Fredericksburg, it is my will and desire that my Executors shall make such conveyances [14] of them as the law requires to render it perfect.

ITEM—To my nephew, Wm. Augustine Washington and his heirs (if he should conceive them to be objects worth prosecuting) *and to his heirs* a lot in the town of Manchester (opposite to Richmond) No. 265—drawn on my sole account and also the tenth of one or two hundred acre lots and two or three half-acre lots in the City and *vicinity* of Richmond, drawn in partnership with nine others, all in the lottery of the deceased William Byrd are given—as is also a lot which I purchased of John Hood conveyed by William Willie and Samuel Gordon, Trustees of the said John Hood, numbered 139 in the town of Edenburgh in the county of Prince George, State of Virginia.

ITEM—To my nephew, Bushrod Washington I give and bequeath all the papers in my possession which relate to my civil and military administration of the affairs of this Country:—I leave to him also such of my private papers as are worth preserving;—and at the decease [of] my wife and before, if she is not inclined to retain them, I give and bequeath my library of Books and pamphlets of every kind.

[15] ITEM—Having sold lands which I possessed in the State of Pennsylvania and part of a tract held in equal right, with George

Clinton, late Governor of New York, in the State of New York;—my share of land and interest in the great Dismal Swamp and a tract of land which I owned in the County of Gloucester;—withholding the legal titles thereto until the consideration money should be paid—and having moreover leased and conditionally sold, (as will appear by the tenor of the said leases) all my lands upon the Great *Kanawha* and the tract upon Difficult Run in the County of Loudon, it is my will and direction that whensoever the contracts are fully and respectively complied with according to the spirit, true intent, and meaning thereof on the part of the purchaser, their heirs, or assigns, that then and in that case conveyances are to be made agreeably to the terms of the said contracts and the money arising therefrom when paid to be vested in Bank stock, the dividends whereof, as of that also which is already vested therein, is to inure to my said wife during her life but the stock it'self is to remain & [16] be subject to the general distribution hereafter directed.

ITEM—To the Earl of Buchan I recommit, "The Box made of the Oak that sheltered the Great Sir William Wallace after the battle of Falkirk"—presented to me by his Lordship in terms too flattering for me to repeat,—with a request "To pass it, on the event of my decease to the man in my Country who should appear to merit it best, upon the same conditions that have induced him to send it to me"—Whether easy or not to select *the man* who might comport with his Lordship's opinion in this respect, is not for me to say, but conceiving that no disposition of this valuable curiosity, can be more eligible than the recommitment of it to his own cabinet agreeably to the original design of the Goldsmith's Company of Edinburgh, who presented it to him, and at his request, consented that it should be transferred to me; I do give and bequeath the same to his Lordship, and in case of his decease, to his heir with my grateful thanks for the distinguished honor of presenting it to me, and more especially for the favorable sentiments [17] with which he accompanied it—

ITEM—To my brother Charles Washington I give and bequeath the Gold-headed cane left me by Doct'r Franklin in his will— I add nothing to it because of the ample provision I have made for his issue.—To the acquaintances and friends of my juvenile years,

Lawrence Washington and Robert Washington of *Chotanck,* I give my other two gold-headed canes, having my arms engraved on them, and to each (as they will be useful where they live), I leave one of the spy glasses which constituted part of my Equipage during the late war—To my compatriot in arms and old and intimate friend Doct'r Craik, I give my Bureau (or as the Cabinet makers called it Tambour Secretary) and the circular chair, an appendage of my study—To Doct'r David Stuart I give my large shaving and dressing Table, and my Telescope—To the Reverend, now Bryan Lord Fairfax I give a Bible in three large folio volumes with notes, presented to me by the Right Reverend Thomas Wilson, Bishop of Sodor & Man—To General de la Fayette I give a pair of finely wrought steel pistols taken from the enemy in the Revolutionary war—To my sisters in law [18] Hannah Washington, and Mildred Washington;—To my friends Eleanor Stuart; Hannah Washington of Fairfield and Elizabeth Washington of Hayfield, I give each a mourning Ring of the value of one hundred dollars—These bequests are not made for the intrinsic value of them, but as *mementos* of my esteem and regard—To Tobias Lear I give the use of the farm which he now holds in virtue of a lease from me to him and his deceased wife (for and during their natural lives) free from Rent during his life, at the expiration of which it is to be disposed as is hereafter directed—To Sally B. Haynie (a distant relation of mine) I give and bequeath three hundred dollars—To Sarah Green daughter of the deceased Thomas Bishop and to Ann Walker, daughter of John Alton, also deceased I give each one hundred dollars in consideration of the attachment of their father[s] to me, each of whom having lived nearly forty years in my family.—To each of my nephews William Augustine Washington, George Lewis, George Steptoe Washington, Bushrod Washington, and Samuel Washington, I give one of the swords or *cutteaux* of which I may die pos[19]sessed, and they are to *chuse* in the order they are named.—These swords are accompanied with an injunction not to unsheath them for the purpose of shedding blood except it be for self-defence, or in defence of their Country and it's rights, and in the latter case to keep them unsheathed, and prefer falling with them in their hands to the relinquishment thereof.

AND NOW,

Having gone through these specific devises, with explanations for the more correct understanding of the meaning and design of them, I proceed to the distribution of the more important parts of my Estate, in manner following

First—To my nephew Bushrod Washington and his heirs (partly in consideration of an intimation to his deceased father, while we were bachelors and he had kindly undertaken to superintend my estate, during my military services in the former war between Great Britain and France, that if I should fall therein, Mt. Vernon (then less extensive in dominion than at present, should become his property) I give and bequeath all that part thereof which is comprehen[20]ded within the following limits—viz:—Beginning at the ford of Dogue Run near my mill and extending along the road and bounded thereby as it now goes, and ever has gone since my recollection of it, to the ford of little hunting Creek, at the gum spring until it comes to a knowl opposite to an old road which formerly passed through the lower field of Muddy-Hole Farm; at which, on the north side of the said road are three red or Spanish oaks marked as a corner, and a stone placed—thence by a line of trees to be marked rectangular to the black line, or outer boundary of the tract between Thomson Mason and myself,—thence with that line easterly (*now double* ditching with a post and rail fence thereon) to the run of little hunting Creek, thence with that run, which is the boundary of the lands of the late Humphrey Peake and *me,* to the tide water of the said Creek thence by that water to Potomac River, thence with the River to the mouth of Dogue Creek, and thence with the said Dogue Creek to the place of beginning, at the aforesaid ford, containing upwards of Four thousand acres, be the same more or less together with the Mansion House, [21] and all other buildings and *improvemts.* thereon.—

Secondly—In consideration of the consanguinity between them and my wife, being as nearly related to her as to myself, as on account of the affection I had for, and the obligation I was under to their father when living, who from his youth had attached himself to my person and followed my fortunes through the vicissitudes of the late Revolution, afterwards devoting his time to the superintendence of my private concerns for many years whilst my public employments rendered it impracticable for me to do it myself, thereby affording me essential services, and always performing them in a manner the most filial and respectful; for these reasons I say, I give and bequeath to George Fayette Washington and Lawrence Augustine Washington & their heirs my Estate East of little hunting creek lying on the River Potomac, including the farm of 360 acres, leased to Tobias Lear as noticed before and containing in the whole, by deeds, Two thousand & twenty seven acres be it more or less which said Estate, it is my will and desire should be equitably and advantageously divided between them, according to quantity, quality & other circumstances when [22] the youngest shall have arrived at the age of twenty one years, by three judicious and disinterested men, one to be chosen by each of the brothers and the third by these two.—In the mean time if the termination of my wife's interest therein should have ceased the profits, arising therefrom are to be applied for their joint uses and benefit.

Third—And whereas it has always been my intention, since my expectation of having issue has ceased, to consider the grand children of my wife in the same light as I do my own relations and to act a friendly part by them, more especially by the two whom we have reared from their earliest infancy, namely, Eleanor Parke Custis and George Washington Parke Custis; and whereas the former of these hath lately intermarried with Lawrence Lewis, a son of my deceased sister Betty Lewis, by which union the inducement to provide for them both has been increased.—Wherefore I give and bequeath to the said Lawrence Lewis and Eleanor Parke Lewis, his wife, and their heirs, the residue of my Mount Vernon Estate, not already devised to my nephew Bushrod Washington comprehended within the fol[23]lowing description.—viz—all the land north of the Road leading from the ford of Dogue Run to the Gum Spring as described in the devise of the other part of the tract to Bushrod Washington until it comes to the stone and three red or Spanish oaks on the knowl,—thence with the rectangular line to the back line (between Mr. Mason and *me*)—thence with that line westerly, along the new double ditch to Dogue Run, by the tumbling dam of my mill,—thence with the said Run to the ford afore mentioned;—to which I add all the land I possess west of the said Dogue Run & Dogue Crk bonded, Easterly & Southerly thereby—

together with the mill, Distillery and all other houses and improvements on the premises making together about two thousand acres be it more or less.

Fourth—Actuated by the principle already mentioned, I give and bequeath to George Washington Parke Custis the Grand son of my wife and my ward and to his heirs, the tract I hold on four mile Run in the *vicinity* of Alexandria containing one thousd two hundred acres more or less;—and my entire square, numbering twenty one, in the city of Washington.

[24] *Fifth*—All the rest and residue of my Estate, real and personal, not disposed of in manner aforesaid—In whatsoever consisting—wheresoever lying, and wheresoever found—a Schedule of which as far as is recollected, with a reasonable estimate of its value is hereunto annexed—I desire may be sold by my Executors at such times—in such manner, and in such credits (if an equal valid and satisfactory distribution of the specific property cannot be made without) as, in their judgment shall be most conducive to the interests of the parties concerned, and the monies arising therefrom to be divided into twenty three equal parts and applied as follows—viz:—

To William Augustine Washington, Elizabeth Spotswood, Jane Thornton, and the heirs of Ann Ashton; son and daughters of my deceased brother Augustine Washington, I give and bequeath four parts—that is—one part to each of them.

To Fielding Lewis, George Lewis, Robert Lewis, Howell Lewis, & Betty Carter, sons and daughter of my deceased sister Betty Lewis I give & bequeath five other parts—one to each of them.

To George Steptoe Washington, Lawrence Augustine Washington, Harriot [25] Parks, and the heirs of Thornton Washington, sons and daughter of my deceased brother Samuel Washington, I give and bequeath other four parts, one part to each of them.—

To Corbin Washington, and the heirs of Jane Washington, I give and bequeath two parts;—one part to each of them;—

To Samuel Washington, Frances Ball, & Mildred Hammond, son and daughters of my brother Charles Washington I give and bequeath three parts—one part to each of them.—And to George Fayette Washington, Charles Augustine Washington and Maria Washington, sons and daughter of my deceased nephew, Geo: Augustine Washington, I give one other part—that is—to each a third of that part.

To Elizabeth Parke Law, Martha Parke Peter, and Eleanor Parke Lewis, I give and bequeath three other parts—that is, a part to each of them.

And to my nephew Bushrod Washington & Lawrence Lewis,—and to my ward, the grandson of my wife,[4] I give and bequeath one other part;—that is a third part to each of them—And if it should so happen, that any of the persons whose names are here enumerated (unknown to me) should now [26] be deceased, or should die before me, that in either of these cases, the heirs of such deceased persons shall, notwithstanding derive all the benefit of the bequest, in the same manner as if he, or she was actually living at the time.

And by way of advice, I recommended it to my Executors not to be precipitate in disposing of the landed property (herein directed to be sold) if from temporary causes the sale thereof should be dull, experience having fully evinced, that the price of land (especially above the Falls of the Rivers & on the Western Waters) have been progressively rising, and cannot be long checked in its increasing value.—and I particularly recommend it to such of the Legatees (under this clause of my will) as can make it convenient, to take each a share of my stock in the Potomac Company in preference to the amount of what it might sell for; being thoroughly convinced myself, that no uses to which the money can be applied will be so productive as the Tolls arising from this navigation when in full operation (and this from the nature of things it must be 'ere long) and more especially if that of the Shenandoah is added thereto.

[27] The family Vault at Mount Vernon requiring repairs, and being improperly situated besides, I desire that a new one of Brick, and upon a larger scale, may be built at the foot of what is commonly called the Vineyard Inclosure,—on the ground which is marked out.—In which my remains, with those of my deceased relatives (now in the Old Vault) and such others of my family as may *chuse* to be entombed there, may be deposited.—And it is my

[4] George Washington Parke Custis.

express desire that my corpse may be interred in a private manner, without parade or funeral oration.

Lastly—I constitute and appoint my dearly beloved wife Martha Washington, my nephews William Augustine Washington, Bushrod Washington, George Steptoe Washington, Samuel Washington & Lawrence Lewis, & my ward, George Washington Parke Custis, (when he shall have arrived at the age of twenty years) Executrix and Executors of this Will & Testament,—In the construction of which it will readily be perceived that no professional character has been consulted or has had any agency in the draught—and that, although it has occupied [28] many of my leisure hours to digest & to *through* it into its present form, it may notwithstanding, appear crude and incorrect—But having endeavored to be plain and explicit in all the Devises—even at the expense of prolixity, perhaps of tautology, I hope, and trust, that no disputes will arise concerning them; but if contrary to expectation the case should be otherwise from the want of legal expression, or the usual technical terms, or because too much or too little, has been said on any of the devises to be consonant with law, my will and direction expressly is, that all disputes (if unhappily any should arise) shall be decided by three impartial and intelligent men, known for their probity and good understanding; two to be chosen by the disputants, each having the choice of one, and the third by those two.—which three men thus chosen, shall unfettered by Law, or legal constructions declare their sense of the Testator's intention; and such decision is, to all intents and purposes to be as binding on the Parties as if it had been given in the Supreme Court of the United States.

[29] In witness of all and of each of the things herein contained I have set my hand and seal this ninth day of July, in the year one thousand seven hundred and ninety [nine[5]] and of the Independence of the United States, the Twenty fourth.

GO. WASHINGTON.

[5] A word omitted by Washington.

Part II

POLITICAL

Chapter 6

THE AMERICAN REVOLUTION

Stamp Act

To Francis Dandridge, September 20, 1765

The Stamp Act, imposed on the colonies by the Parliament of Great Britain, engrosses the conversations of the speculative part of the colonists, who look upon this unconstitutional method of taxation, as a direful attack upon their liberties and loudly exclaim against the violation. What may be the result of this, and of some other (I think I may add) ill-judged measures, I will not undertake to determine; but this I may venture to affirm, that the advantage accruing to the mother country will fall greatly short of the expectations of the ministry; for certain it is, that our whole substance does already in a manner flow to Great Britain, and that whatsoever contributes to lessen our importations must be hurtful to their manufacturers. And the eyes of our people, already beginning to open, will perceive, that many luxuries, which we lavish our substance in Great Britain for, can well be dispensed with, whilst the necessaries of life are (mostly) to be had within ourselves. This, consequently, will introduce frugality, and be a necessary stimulation to industry. If Great Britain, therefore, loads her manufactories with heavy taxes, will it not facilitate these measures? They will not compel us, I think, to give our money for their exports, whether we will or not; and certain, I am, none of their traders will part from them without a valuable consideration. Where, then, is the utility of these restrictions? As to the Stamp Act, taken in a single view, one and the first bad consequence attending it, I take to be this, our courts of judicature must inevitably be shut up; for it is impossible (or next of kin to it), under our present circumstances, that the act of Parliament can be complied with, were we ever so willing to enforce the execution; for, not to say, which alone would be sufficient, that we have not money to pay the stamps, there are many cogent reasons to prevent it; and if a stop be put to our judicial proceedings, I fancy the merchants of Great Britain, trading to the colonies, will not be among the last to wish for a repeal of it.

Refuses to Buy British-Taxed Articles

To Robert Cary & Company, 1769

If there are any articles contained in either of the respective invoices (paper only excepted) which are taxed by act of Parliament for the purpose of raising revenue in America, it is my express desire and request, that they may not be sent, as I have very heartily entered into an association (copies of which I make no doubt you have seen, otherwise I should have enclosed one) not to import any article which now is, or hereafter shall be taxed for this purpose until the said act or acts are repealed. I am therefore particular in mentioning this matter as I am fully determined to adhere religiously to it, and may perhaps have wrote for some things unwittingly which may be under these circumstances.

Nonimportation

To George Mason, April 5, 1769

At a time, when our lordly masters in Great Britain will be satisfied with nothing less than the deprivation of American freedom, it seems highly necessary that something should be done to avert the stroke, and maintain the liberty, which we have derived from our ancestors. But the manner of doing it, to answer the purpose effectually, is the point in question. That no man should scruple, or hesitate a moment, to use arms in defence of so valuable a blessing, on which all the good and evil of life depends, is clearly my opinion. Yet arms, I would beg leave to add, should be the last resource, the dernier resort. Addresses to the throne, and remonstrances to Parliament, we have already, it is said, proved the inefficacy of. How far, then, their attention to our rights and privileges is to be awakened or alarmed, by starving their trade and manufactures, remains to be tried. . . .

The more I consider a scheme of this sort, the more ardently I wish success to it, because I think there are private as well as public advantages to result from it,—the former certain, however precarious the other may prove. For in respect to the latter, I have always thought, that by virtue of the same power, (for here alone the authority derives) which assumes the right of taxation, they may attempt at least to restrain our manufactories, especially those of a public nature, the same equity and justice prevailing in the one case as the other, it being no greater hardship to forbid my manufacturing, than it is to order me to buy goods of them loaded with duties, for the express purpose of raising a revenue. But as a measure of this sort would be an exertion of arbitrary power, we cannot be worsted, I think, but by putting it to the test.

Boston Port Bill

To Bryan Fairfax, July 4, 1774

As to your political sentiments, I would heartily join you in them, so far as relates to a humble and dutiful petition to the throne, provided there was the most distant hope of success. But have we not tried this already? Have we not addressed the Lords, and remonstrated to the Commons? And to what end? Did they deign to look at our petitions? Does it not appear, as clear as the sun in its meridian brightness, that there is a regular, systematic plan formed to fix the right and practice of taxation upon us? Does not the uniform conduct of Parliament for some years past confirm this? Do not all the debates, especially those just brought to us, in the House of Commons on the side of government, expressly declare that America must be taxed in aid of the British funds, and that she has no longer resources within herself? Is there any thing to be expected from petitioning after this? Is not the attack upon the liberty and property of the people of Boston, before restitution of the loss to the India Company was demanded, a plain and self-evident proof of what they are aiming at? Do not the subsequent bills (now I dare say acts), for depriving the Massachusetts Bay of its charter, and transporting offenders into other colonies or to Great Britain for trial, where it is impossible from the nature of the thing that justice can be obtained, convince us that the administration is determined to stick at nothing to carry its point? Ought we not, then, to put our virtue and fortitude to the severest test?

COMMISSION AS COMMANDER IN CHIEF

In Congress.

The *delegates of the United Colonies of New-Hampshire, Massachusetts bay, Rhode Island, Connecticut, New-York, New Jersey, Pennsylvania, New Castle, Kent & Sussex on Delaware, Maryland, Virginia, North Carolina and South Carolina*

To **George Washington** *Esquire*

We *reposing especial trust and confidence in your patriotism, conduct and fidelity* Do *by these presents constitute and appoint you to be* **General and Commander in Chief** *of the Army of the United Colonies and of all the forces raised or to be raised by them and of all others who shall voluntary offer their service and join the said army for the defence of American Liberty and for repelling every hostile invasion thereof.* AND *you are hereby vested with full power and authority to act as you shall think for the good and welfare of the service.*

And *we do hereby strictly charge and require all officers and soldiers under your command to be obedient to your orders & diligent in the exercise of their several duties.*

And *we do also enjoin and require you to be careful in executing* *the great trust reposed in you, by causing strict discipline and order to be observed in the army and that the soldiers are duly exercised and provided with all convenient necessaries.*

And *you are to regulate your conduct in every respect by the rules and discipline of war (as herewith given you) and punctually to observe and follow such orders and directions from time to time as you shall receive from this or a future Congress of the said United Colonies or a committee of Congress for that purpose appointed.*

THIS COMMISSION *to continue in force until revoked by this or a future Congress.*

By order of the Congress
JOHN HANCOCK *President*

Dated, Philadelphia June 19th 1775.
Attest CHAS. THOMSON *Secr.*

INSTRUCTIONS TO COLONEL BENEDICT ARNOLD

Cambridge, September 14, 1775

1. You are immediately on their march from Cambridge to take the command of the detachment from the Continental army against Quebec, and use all possible expedition, as the winter season is now advancing, and the success of this enterprise, under God, depends wholly upon the spirit with which it is pushed, and the favorable dispositions of the Canadians and Indians.

2. When you come to Newburyport you are to make all possible inquiry, what men-of-war or cruisers there may be on the coast . . . and, if you should find that there is danger of your being intercepted, you are not to proceed by water, but by land . . .

3. You are, by every means in your power, to endeavor to discover the real sentiments of the Canadians towards our cause . . . bearing in mind, that if they are averse to it and will not cooperate, or at least willingly acquiesce, it must fail of success. In this case you are by no means to prosecute the attempt . . .

4. In order to cherish those favorable sentiments to the American

cause, that they have manifested, you are, as soon as you arrive in their country, to disperse a number of the addresses you will have with you, particularly in those parts, where your route shall lie; and observe the strictest discipline and good order, by no means suffering any inhabitant to be abused, or in any manner injured, either in his person or property, punishing with exemplary severity every person, who shall transgress, and making ample compensation to the party injured.

5. You are to endeavor, on the other hand, to conciliate the affections of those people, and such Indians as you may meet with, by every means in your power; convincing them that we come . . . not as robbers or to make war upon them, but as the friends and supporters of their liberties as well as ours. . . .

6. Check every idea and crush in its earliest stage every attempt to plunder even those, who are known to be enemies to our cause. It will create dreadful apprehensions in our friends, and, when it is once begun, no one can tell where it will stop. . . .

7. Any King's stores, which you shall be so fortunate as to possess yourself of, are to be secured for the Continental use, agreeably to the rules and regulations of war published by the honorable Congress . . .

8. Spare neither pains nor expense to gain all possible intelligence on your march, to prevent surprises and accidents of every kind, and endeavor if possible to correspond with General Schuyler, so that you may act in concert with him . . .

9. In case of a union with General Schuyler, or if he should be in Canada upon your arrival there, you are by no means to consider yourself as upon a separate and independent command, but are to put yourself under him and follow his directions. Upon this occasion, and all others, I recommend most earnestly to avoid all contention about rank. In such a cause every post is honorable, in which a man can serve his country.

10. If Lord Chatham's son should be in Canada, and in any way should fall into your power, you are enjoined to treat him with all possible deference and respect . . . Any other prisoners . . . you will treat with as much humanity and kindness, as may be consistent with your own safety and the public interest. Be very particular in restraining, not only your own troops, but the Indians,

from all acts of cruelty and insult, which will disgrace the American arms . . .

11. You will be particularly careful to pay the full value for all provisions, or other accommodations, which the Canadians may provide for you on your march. By no means press them or any of their cattle into your service, but amply compensate those who voluntarily assist you . . .

12. You are by every opportunity to inform me of your progress, your prospects, and intelligence, and upon any important occurrence to send an express.

13. As the season is now far advanced, you are to make all possible dispatch; but if unforeseen difficulties should arise, or if the weather should become so severe, as to render it hazardous to proceed . . .—you are to return, giving me as early notice as possible . . .

14. As the contempt of the religion of a country by ridiculing any of its ceremonies, or affronting its ministers or votaries, has ever been deeply resented, you are to be particularly careful to restrain every officer and soldier from such imprudence and folly, and to punish every instance of it. On the other hand, as far as lies in your power, you are to protect and support the free exercise of the religion of the country, and the undisturbed enjoyment of the rights of conscience in religious matters, with your utmost influence and authority.

A Naked Army

To the President of Congress, September 21, 1775

It gives me great pain to be obliged to solicit the attention of the honorable Congress to the state of this army, in terms which imply the slightest apprehension of being neglected. But my situation is inexpressibly distressing, to see the winter fast approaching upon a naked army, the time of their service within a few weeks of expiring, and no provision yet made for such important events. Added to these, the military chest is totally exhausted; the paymaster has not a single dollar in hand; the commissary-general assures me he has strained his credit, for the subsistence of the army, to the utmost. The quartermaster-general is precisely in the same situation; and the greater part of the troops are in a state not far from mutiny, upon the deduction from their stated allowance. I know not to whom I am to impute this failure; but I am of opinion, if the evil is not immediately remedied, and more punctually observed in future, the army must absolutely break up. I hoped I had expressed myself so fully on this subject, both by letter, and to those members of the Congress, who honored the camp with a visit, that no disappointment could possibly happen. I therefore hourly expected advice from the paymaster, that he had received a fresh supply, in addition to the hundred and seventy-two thousand dollars delivered him in August; and thought myself warranted to assure the public creditors, that in a few days they should be satisfied. But the delay has brought matters to such a crisis, as admits of no farther uncertain expectations. I have therefore sent off this express with orders to make all possible despatch. It is my most earnest request, that he may be returned with all possible expedition, unless the honorable Congress have already forwarded what is so indispensably necessary. I have the honor to be, &c.

To Joseph Reed, November 28, 1775

What an astonishing thing it is, that those who are employed to sign the Continental bills should not be able, or inclined, to do it as fast as they are wanted. They will prove the destruction of the army, if they are not more attentive and diligent. Such a dearth of public spirit, and want of virtue, such stock-jobbing, and fertility in all the low arts to obtain advantages of one kind or another, in this great change of military arrangement, I never saw before, and pray God I may never be witness to again. What will be the ultimate end of these manoeuvres is beyond my scan. I tremble at the prospect. We have been till this time enlisting about three thousand five hundred men. To engage these I have been obliged to allow furloughs as far as fifty men a regiment, and the officers I am persuaded indulge as many more. The Connecticut troops will not be prevailed upon to stay longer than their term (saving those who have enlisted for the next campaign, and mostly on furlough), and such a dirty, mercenary spirit pervades the whole, that I should not be at all surprised at any disaster that may happen. In short, after the last of this month our lines will be so weakened, that the minute-men and militia must be called in for their defence; these, being under no kind of government themselves, will destroy the little subordination I have been laboring to establish, and run me into one evil whilst I am endeavoring to avoid another; but the lesser must be chosen. Could I have foreseen what I have, and am likely to experience, no consideration upon earth should have induced me to accept this command. . . .

To Joseph Reed, January 14, 1776

These are evils, but small in comparison of those, which disturb my present repose. Our enlistments are at a stand; the fears I ever entertained are realized; that is, the discontented officers (for I do not know how else to account for it) have thrown such difficulties or stumbling-blocks in the way of recruiting, that I no longer entertain a hope of completing the army by voluntary enlistments, and I see no move or likelihood of one, to do it by other means. In the last two weeks we have enlisted but about a thousand men; whereas I was confidently bid to believe, by all the officers I conversed with, that we should by this time have had the regiments nearly completed. Our total number upon paper amounts to about ten thousand five hundred; but as a large portion of these are returned not joined, I never expect to receive them, as an ineffectual order has once issued to call them in. Another is now gone forth, peremptorily requiring all officers under pain of being cashiered, and recruits as being treated as deserters, to join their respective regiments by the 1st day of next month, that I may know my real strength; but if my fears are not imaginary, I shall have a dreadful account of the advanced month's pay. In consequence of the assurances given, and my expectation of having at least men enough enlisted to defend our lines, to which may be added my unwillingness of burthening the cause with unnecessary expense, no relief of militia has been ordered in, to supply the places of those, who are released from their engagements to-morrow, and on whom, though many have promised to continue out the month, there is no security for their stay.

Thus am I situated with respect to men. With regard to arms I am yet worse off. Before the dissolution of the old army, I issued an order directing three judicious men of each brigade to attend, review, and appraise the good arms of every regiment; and finding a very great unwillingness in the men to part with their arms, at the same time not having it in my power to pay them for the months of November and December, I threatened severely, that every soldier, who carried away his firelock without leave, should never receive pay for those months; yet so many have been carried off, partly by stealth, but chiefly as condemned, that we have not at this time one hundred guns in the stores, of all that have been taken in the prize-ship and from the soldiery, notwithstanding our regiments are not half complete. At the same time I am told, and believe it, that to restrain the enlistment to men with arms, you will get but few of the former, and still fewer of the latter, which would be good for any thing.

How to get furnished I know not. I have applied to this and the neighboring colonies, but with what success time only can tell. The reflection on my situation, and that of this army, produces many an uneasy hour when all around me are wrapped in sleep. Few people know the predicament we are in, on a thousand accounts; fewer still will believe, if any disaster happens to these lines, from what causes it flows. I have often thought how much happier I should have been, if, instead of accepting of a command under such circumstances, I had taken my musket on my shoulder and entered the ranks, or, if I could have justified the measure to posterity and my own conscience, had retired to the back country, and lived in a wigwam. If I shall be able to rise superior to these and many other difficulties, which might be enumerated, I shall most religiously believe, that the finger of Providence is in it, to blind the eyes of our enemies; for surely if we get well through this month, it must be for want of their knowing the disadvantages we labor under.

Could I have foreseen the difficulties, which have come upon us;

could I have known, that such a backwardness would have been discovered in the old soldiers to the service, all the generals upon earth should not have convinced me of the propriety of delaying an attack upon Boston till this time. When it can now be attempted, I will not undertake to say; but thus much I will answer for, that no opportunity can present itself earlier than my wishes. But as this letter discloses some interesting truths, I shall be somewhat uneasy until I hear it gets to your hands, although the conveyance is thought safe. . . .

To Joseph Reed, Cambridge, February 10, 1776

Your obliging favors of the 28th ult. and 1st inst. are now before me, and claim my particular thanks for the polite attention you pay to my wishes in an early and regular communication of what is passing in your quarter.

If you conceive, that I took any thing wrong, or amiss, that was conveyed in any of your former letters, you are really mistaken. I only meant to convince you, that nothing would give more real satisfaction, than to know the sentiments, which are entertained of me by the public, whether they be favorable or otherwise; and I urged as a reason, that the man, who wished to steer clear of shelves and rocks, must know where they lay. I know—but to declare it, unless to a friend, may be an argument of vanity—the integrity of my own heart. I know the unhappy predicament I stand in; I know that much is expected of me; I know, that without men, without arms, without ammunition, without any thing fit for the accommodation of a soldier, little is to be done; and, which is mortifying, I know, that I cannot stand justified to the world without exposing my own weakness, and injuring the cause, by declaring my wants, which I am determined not to do, further than unavoidable necessity brings every man acquainted with them.

If, under these disadvantages, I am able to keep above water, (as it were) in the esteem of mankind, I shall feel myself happy; but if, from the unknown peculiarity of my circumstances, I suffer in the opinion of the world, I shall not think you take the freedom of a friend, if you conceal the reflections that may be cast upon my conduct. My own situation feels so irksome to me at times, that, if I did not consult the public good, more than my own tranquillity, I should long ere this have put every thing to the cast of a Dye. So far from my having an army of twenty thousand men well armed, I have been here with less than half of it, including sick, furloughed, and on command, and those neither armed nor clothed, as they should be. In short, my situation has been such, that I have been obliged to use art to conceal it from my own officers. The Congress, as you observe, expect, I believe, that I should do more than others,—for whilst they compel me to inlist men without a bounty, they give 40 to others, which will, I expect, put a stand to our Inlistments; for notwithstanding all the publick virtue which is ascrib'd to these people, there is no nation under the sun, (that I ever came across) pay greater adoration to money than they do—I am pleas'd to find that your Battalions are cloathed and look well, and that they are filing off for Canada. I wish I could say that the troops here had altered much in Dress or appearance. Our regiments are little more than half compleat, and recruiting nearly at a stand—In all my letters I fail not to mention of Tents, and now perceive that notice is taken of yr. application. I have been convinced, by General Howe's conduct, that he has either been very ignorant of our situation (which I do not believe) or that he has received positive orders (which, I think, is natural to conclude) not to put anything to the hazard till his reinforcements arrive; otherwise there has [not] been a time since the first of December, that we must have fought like men to have maintained these Lines, so great in their extent.

The party to Bunker's Hill had some good and some bad men engaged in it. One or two courts have been held on the conduct of part of it. To be plain, these people—among friends—are not to be depended upon if exposed; and any man will fight well if he thinks himself in no danger. I do not apply this only to these people. I suppose it to be the case with all raw and undisciplined troops. You may rely upon it, that transports left Boston six weeks ago with troops; where they are gone, unless driven to the West Indies, I know not. You may also rely upon General Clinton's sailing from Boston about three weeks ago, with about four or five hundred men; his destination I am also a stranger to. I am sorry to hear of the failures you speak of from France. But why will not Congress forward part of the powder made in your province? They seem to look upon this as the season for action, but will not furnish the means. I will not blame them. I dare say the demands upon them are greater than they can supply. The cause must be starved till our resources are greater, or more certain within ourselves.

With respect to myself, I have never entertained an idea of an accommodation, since I heard of the measures, which were adopted in consequence of the Bunker's Hill fight. The King's speech has confirmed the sentiments I entertained upon the news of that affair; and, if every man was of my mind, the ministers of Great Britain should know, in a few words, upon what issue the cause should be put. I would not be deceived by artful declarations, nor specious pretences; nor would I be amused by unmeaning propositions; but in open, undisguised, and manly terms proclaim our wrongs, and our resolution to be redressed. I would tell them, that we had borne much, that we had long and ardently sought for reconciliation upon honorable terms, that it had been denied us, that all our attempts after peace had proved abortive, and had been grossly misrepresented, that we had done everything which could be expected from the best of subjects, that the spirit of freedom beat too high in us to submit to slavery, and that, if nothing else could satisfy a tyrant and his diabolical ministry, we are determined to shake off all connexions with a state so unjust and unnatural. This I would tell them, not under covert, but in words as clear as the sun in its meridian brightness. . . .

To John Augustine Washington, Cambridge, March 31, 1776

. . . The want of arms and powder is not peculiar to Virginia. This country of which doubtless you have heard large and flattering accounts, is more deficient in both than you can conceive. I have been here months together, with (what will scarcely be believed) not thirty rounds of musket cartridges to a man; and have been obliged to submit to all the insults of the enemy's cannon for want of powder, keeping what little we had for pistol distance. Another thing has been done, which, added to the above, will put in it the power of this army to say, what perhaps no other with justice ever could say. We have maintained our ground against the enemy, under this want of powder, and we have disbanded one army, and recruited another, within musket-shot of two and twenty regiments, the flower of the British army, whilst our force has been but little if any superior to theirs; and, at last, have beaten them into a shameful and precipitate retreat out of a place the strongest by nature on this continent, and strengthened and fortified at an enormous expense.

As some account of the late manoeuvres of both armies may not be unacceptable, I shall, hurried as I always am, devote a little time to it. Having received a small supply of powder, very inadequate to our wants, I resolved to take possession of Dorchester Point, lying east of Boston, looking directly into it, and commanding the enemy's lines on Boston Neck. To do this, which I knew would force the enemy to an engagement, or subject them to be enfiladed by our cannon, it was necessary, in the first instance, to possess two heights (those mentioned in General Burgoyne's letter to Lord Stanley, in his account of the battle of Bunker's Hill), which had the entire command of the point. The ground at this point being frozen upwards of two feet deep, and as impenetrable as a rock, nothing could be attempted with earth. We were obliged, therefore, to provide an amazing quantity of chandeliers and fascines for the work; and, on the night of the 4th, after a previous severe cannonade and bombardment for three nights together, to divert the enemy's attention from our real design, we removed every material to the spot, under cover of darkness, and took full possession of those heights, without the loss of a single man.

Upon their discovery of the works next morning, great preparations were made for attacking them; but not being ready before the afternoon, and the weather getting very tempestuous, much blood was saved, and a very important blow, to one side or the other, was prevented. That this most remarkable interposition of Providence is for some wise purpose, I have not a doubt. But, as the principal design of the manoeuvre was to draw the enemy to an engagement under disadvantages to them, as a premeditated plan was laid for this purpose, and seemed to be succeeding to my utmost wish, and as no men seem better disposed to make the appeal than ours did upon that occasion, I can scarcely forbear lamenting the disappointment, unless the dispute is drawing to an accommodation, and the sword going to be sheathed. But, to return, the enemy thinking, as we have since learnt, that we had got too securely posted, before the second morning, to be much hurt by them, and apprehending great annoyance from our new works, resolved upon a retreat, and accordingly on the 17th embarked in as much hurry, precipitation, and confusion, as ever troops did, not taking time to fit their transports, but leaving the King's property in Boston, to the amount, as is supposed, of thirty or forty thousand pounds in provisions and stores. Many pieces of cannon, some mortars, and a number of shot and shells are also left; and baggage-wagons and artillery-carts, which they have been eighteen months preparing to take the field with, were found destroyed, thrown into the docks, and drifted upon every shore. In short, Dunbar's destruction of stores after General Braddock's defeat, which made so much noise, affords but a faint idea of what was to be met with here.

The enemy lay from the 17th to the 27th in Nantasket and King's Roads, about nine miles from Boston, to take in water from the islands thereabouts, and to prepare themselves for sea. Whither they are now bound, and where their tents will be next pitched, I know not; but, as New York and Hudson's River are the most important objects they can have in view, as the latter secures the communication with Canada, at the same time that it separates the northern and southern colonies, and the former is thought to abound in disaffected persons, who only wait a favorable opportunity and support to declare themselves openly, it becomes equally important for us to prevent their gaining possession of these advantages; and, therefore, as soon as they embarked, I detached a brigade of six regiments to that government, and, when they sailed, another brigade composed of the same number; and to-morrow another brigade of five regiments will march. In a day or two more, I shall follow myself, and be in New York ready to receive all but the first.

The enemy left all their works standing in Boston and on Bunker's Hill; and formidable they are. The town has shared a much better fate than was expected, the damage done to the houses being nothing equal to report. But the inhabitants have suffered a good deal, in being plundered by the soldiery at their departure. All those who took upon themselves the style and title of government-men in Boston, in short, all those who have acted an unfriendly part in the great contest, have shipped themselves off in the same hurry, but under still greater disadvantages than the King's troops, being obliged to man their own vessels, as seamen enough could not be had for the King's transports, and submit to every hardship that can be conceived. One or two have done, what a great number ought to have done long ago, committed suicide. By all accounts, there never existed a more miserable set of beings, than these wretched creatures now are. Taught to believe, that the power of Great Britain was superior to all opposition, and, if not, that foreign aid was at hand, they were even higher and more insulting in their opposition than the regulars. When the order issued, therefore, for embarking the troops in Boston, no electric shock, no sudden explosion of thunder, in a word, not the last trump could have struck them with greater consternation. They were at their wits' end, and, conscious of their black ingratitude, they chose to commit themselves, in the manner I have above described, to the mercy of the waves at a tempestuous season, rather than meet their offended countrymen.

I believe I may with great truth affirm, that no man perhaps since the first institution of armies ever commanded one under more difficult circumstances, than I have done. To enumerate the particulars would fill a volume. Many of my difficulties and distresses were of so peculiar a cast, that, in order to conceal them from the enemy, I was obliged to conceal them from my friends, and indeed from my own army, thereby subjecting my conduct to interpretations unfavorable to my character, especially by those at a distance, who could not in the smallest degree be acquainted with the springs that governed it. I am happy, however, to find, and to hear from different quarters, that my reputation stands fair, that my conduct hitherto has given universal satisfaction. The addresses, which I have received, and which I suppose will be published, from the General Court of this colony, and from the selectmen of Boston upon the evacuation of the town, and my approaching departure from the colony, exhibit a pleasing testimony of their approbation of my conduct, and of their personal regard, which I have found in various other instances, and which, in retirement, will afford many comfortable reflections.

The share you have taken in the public disputes is commendable and praiseworthy. It is a duty we owe our country; a claim which posterity has upon us. It is not sufficient for a man to be a passive friend and well-wisher to the cause. This, and every other cause of such a nature, must inevitably perish under such an opposition. Every person should be active in some department or other, without paying too much attention to private interest. It is a great stake we are playing for, and sure we are of winning, if the cards are well managed. Inactivity in some, disaffection in others, and timidity in many, may hurt the cause. Nothing else can; for unanimity will carry us through triumphantly, in spite of every exertion of Great Britain, if we are linked together in one indissoluble bond. This the leaders know, and they are practising every stratagem to divide us, and unite their own people. Upon this principle it is, that the restraining bill is passed, and commissioners are coming over. The device, to be sure, is shallow, the covering thin, but they will hold out to their own people, that the acts complained of are repealed, and commissioners sent to each colony to treat with us, and that we will attend to neither of them. This, upon weak minds among us, will have its effect. They wish for reconciliation; or, in other words, they wish for peace without attending to the conditions.

General [Charles] Lee, I suppose, is with you before this. He is the first officer, in military knowledge and experience, we have in the whole army. He is zealously attached to the cause, honest and well-meaning, but rather fickle and violent, I fear, in his temper. However, as he possesses an uncommon share of good sense and spirit, I congratulate my countrymen upon his appointment to that department. As I am now nearly at the end of my eighth page, I think it time to conclude; especially, as I set out with prefacing the little time I had for friendly correspondences. I shall only add, therefore, my affectionate regards to my sister and the children, and compliments to friends; and that I am, with every sentiment of true affection, your loving brother and faithful friend.

Military Morale and Payments

To the President of Congress, New York, April 23, 1776

I take the liberty, unsolicited by, and unknown to my aids-de-camp, to inform your honorable body, that their pay is not by any means equal to their trouble and confinement.

No person wishes more to save money to the public, than I do; and no person has aimed more at it. But there are some cases in which parsimony may be ill-placed; and this I take to be one. Aids-de-camp are persons in whom entire confidence must be placed; it requires men of abilities to execute the duties with propriety and despatch . . . Persuaded I am, that nothing but the zeal of those gentlemen, who live with me and act in this capacity, for the great American cause, and personal attachment to me, have induced them to undergo the trouble and confinement they have experienced, since they have become members of my family.

I give in to no kind of amusements myself; and consequently those about me can have none, but are confined from morning till eve, hearing and answering the applications and letters of one and another. . . . If these gentlemen had the same relaxation from duty as other officers have in their common routine, there would not be so much in it. But, to have the mind always upon the stretch, scarce ever unbent, and no hours for recreation, makes a material odds. Knowing this, and at the same time how inadequate the pay is, I can scarce find inclination to impose the necessary duties of their office upon them . . . The duty is hard and the pay small.

Military Behavior

To Colonel Fisher Gay, New York, September 4, 1776

Sir, Whether you do not get the General Orders with that regularity which is to be wished, or whether (which is hard to suppose) you do not attend to them, I will not undertake to determine; but it is a melancholy truth that returns essentially necessary for the commanding officers to govern himself by, and which might be made in an hour after they are called for . . . are obtained with so much difficulty. Nor can I help regretting, that not only regular returns, but that orders, in instances equally important, should be so little attended to. I therefore address myself to you in this manner, requesting in express and peremptory terms, that you do without delay make out and return to the Adjutant General's office immediately an exact state of the regiment or corps under your command, and that the like return be given in every Saturday, at orderly time, without fail.

I also desire, in terms equally express, that you do not suffer the men of your corps to straggle from their quarters, or be absent from camp without leave, and even then but a few at a time. Your own reputation, the safety of the army, and the good of the cause, depend, under God, upon our vigilance and readiness to oppose a crafty and enterprising enemy, who are always upon the watch to take advantages. To prevent straggling, let your rolls be called over three times a day, and the delinquents punished. I have one thing more to urge, and that is, that every attempt of the men to plunder houses, orchards, gardens, etc., be discouraged, not only for the preservation of property and sake of good order, but for the prevention of those fatal consequences which usually follow such diabolical practices. In short, Sir, at a time when every thing is at stake, it behoves every man to exert himself. It will not do for a commanding officer of a regiment to content himself with barely giving orders; he should see (at least know) they are executed. He should call his men out frequently, and endeavor to impress them with a just sense of their duty, and how much depends upon subordination and discipline.

Let me, therefore, not only command, but exhort you and your officers, as you regard your reputation, your country, and the sacred cause of freedom in which you are engaged, to manly and vigorous exertions at this time, each striving to excel the other in the respective duties of his department. I trust it is unnecessary for me to add further, and that these and all other articles of your duty you will execute with a spirit and punctuality becoming your station. I am, etc.

Military Discipline

To the President of Congress, Camp near Kingsbridge, September 22, 1776

I had flattered myself that the Congress would before this Time have forwarded the Amended Articles for the Government of the Army. But as they have not I think it my indispensable Duty to lay before them the Necessity, the absolute Necessity of forming an Article against plundering, marauding and burning of Houses. Such a Spirit has gone forth in our Army that neither publick or private Property is secure. Every Hour brings the most distressing complaints of the Ravages of our own Troops who are becoming infinitely more formidable to the poor Farmers and Inhabitants than the common Enemy. Horses are taken out off the Continental Teams; the Baggage of Officers and the Hospital Stores, even the Quarters of General Officers are not exempt from Rapine.

Some severe and exemplary Punishment to be inflicted in a summary way must be immediately administered, or the Army will be totally ruined.

Morale and Militia

To the President of Congress, Colo. Morris's, on the Heights of Haerlem, September 24, 1776

From the hours allotted to sleep, I will borrow a few moments to convey my thoughts on sundry important matters to Congress. I shall offer them with the sincerity, which ought to characterize a man of candor, and with the freedom, which may be used in giving useful information without incurring the imputation of presumption.

We are now, as it were, upon the eve of another dissolution of our army. The remembrance of the difficulties, which happened upon that occasion last year, and the consequences, which might have followed the change if proper advantages had been taken by the enemy, added to a knowledge of the present temper and situation of the troops, reflect but a very gloomy prospect in the appearances of things now, and satisfy me beyond the possibility of doubt, that, unless some speedy and effectual measures are adopted by Congress, our cause will be lost. It is in vain to expect, that any more than a trifling part of this army will again engage in the service on the encouragement offered by Congress. When men find that their townsmen and companions are receiving twenty, thirty, and more dollars for a few months' service, which is truly the case, it cannot be expected, without using compulsion; and to force them into the service would answer no valuable purpose. When men are irritated, and their passions inflamed, they fly hastily and cheerfully to arms; but, after the first emotions are over, to expect among such people as compose the bulk of an army, that they are influenced by any other principles than those of interest, is to look for what never did, and I fear never will happen; the Congress will deceive themselves, therefore, if they expect it. A soldier, reasoned with upon the goodness of the cause he is engaged in, and the inestimable rights he is contending for, hears you with patience, and acknowledges the truth of your observations, but adds that it is of no more importance to him than to others. The officer makes you the same reply, with this further remark, that his pay will not support him, and he cannot ruin himself and family to serve his country, when every member of the community is equally interested, and benefited by his labors. The few, therefore, who act upon principles of disinterestedness, comparatively speaking, are no more than a drop in the ocean.

It becomes evident to me then, that, as this contest is not likely to be the work of a day, as the war must be carried on systematically, and to do it you must have good officers, there are in my judgment no other possible means to obtain them but by establishing your army upon a permanent footing, and giving your officers good pay. This will induce gentlemen and men of character to engage; and, till the bulk of your officers is composed of such persons as are actuated by principles of honor and a spirit of enterprise, you have little to expect from them. They ought to have such allowances, as will enable them to live like and support the character of gentlemen, and not be driven by a scanty pittance to the low and dirty arts, which many of them practise, to filch from the public more than the difference of pay would amount to, upon an ample allowance. Besides, something is due to the man, who puts his life in your hands, hazards his health, and forsakes the sweets of domestic enjoyment. Why a captain in the Continental service should receive no more than five shillings currency per day for performing the same duties, that an officer of the same rank in the British service receives ten shillings for, I never could conceive; especially when the latter is provided with every necessary he requires upon the best terms, and the former can scarce procure them at any rate. There is nothing that gives a man consequence and renders him fit for command, like a support that renders him independent of every body but the state he serves.

With respect to the men, nothing but a good bounty can obtain them upon a permanent establishment; and for no shorter time, than the continuance of the war, ought they to be engaged; as facts incontestably prove, that the difficulty and cost of enlistments increase with time. When the army was first raised at Cambridge, I am persuaded the men might have been got, without a bounty, for the war. After this, they began to see that the contest was not likely to end so speedily as was imagined, and to feel their consequence by remarking, that, to get in their militia in the course of the last year, many towns were induced to give them a bounty. Foreseeing the evils resulting from this, and the destructive consequences, which unavoidably would follow short enlistments, I took the liberty in a long letter written by myself (date not now recollected as my Letter Book is not here) to recommend the enlistments for and during the war, assigning such reasons for it as experience has since convinced me were well founded. At that time, twenty dollars would, I am persuaded, have engaged the men for this term. But it will not do to look back; and, if the present opportunity is slipped, I am persuaded that twelve months more will increase our difficulties fourfold. I shall therefore take the freedom of giving it as my opinion, that a good bounty should be immediately offered, aided by the proffer of at least a hundred or a hundred and fifty acres of land, and a suit of clothes and blanket to each non-commissioned officer and soldier; as I have good authority for saying, that, however high the men's pay may appear, it is barely sufficient, in the present scarcity and dearness of all kinds of goods, to keep them in clothes, much less afford support to their families.

If this encouragement then is given to the men, and such pay allowed the officers as will induce gentlemen of character and liberal sentiments to engage, and proper care and precaution are used in the nomination, (having more regard to the characters of persons, than to the number of men they can enlist,) we should in a little time have an army able to cope with any that can be opposed to it, as there are excellent materials to form one out of. But while the only merit an officer possesses is his ability to raise men, while those men consider and treat him as an equal, and, in the character of an officer, regard him no more than a broomstick, being mixed together as one common herd, no order nor discipline can prevail; nor will the officer ever meet with that respect, which is essentially necessary to due subordination.

To place any dependence upon militia is assuredly resting upon a broken staff. Men just dragged from the tender scenes of domestic life, unaccustomed to the din of arms, totally unacquainted with every kind of military skill, (which being followed by want of confidence in themselves, when opposed to troops regularly trained, disciplined, and appointed, superior in knowledge and superior in arms,) makes them timid and ready to fly from their own shadows. Besides the sudden change in their manner of living, (particularly in the lodging,) brings on sickness in many, impatience in all, and such an unconquerable desire of returning to their respective homes, that it not only produces shameful and scandalous desertions among themselves, but infuses the like spirit in others. Again, men accustomed to unbounded freedom and no control cannot brooke the restraint, which is indispensably necessary to the good order and government of an army; without which, licentiousness and every kind of disorder triumphantly reign. To bring men to a proper degree of subordination is not the work of a day, a month, or even a year, and, unhappily for us and the cause we are engaged in, the little discipline I have been laboring to establish in the army under my immediate command is in a manner done away, by having such a mixture of troops, as have been called together within these few months.

Relaxed and as unfit as our rules and regulations of war are for the government of an army, the militia (those properly so called, for of these we have two sorts, the six-months' men, and those sent in as a temporary aid) do not think themselves subject to them, and therefore take liberties, which the soldier is punished for. This creates jealousy; jealousy begets dissatisfaction; and these by degrees ripen into mutiny, keeping the whole army in a confused and disordered state, rendering the time of those, who wish to see regularity and good order prevail, more unhappy than words can describe. Besides this, such repeated changes take place, that all arrangement is set at nought, and the constant fluctuation of things deranges every plan as fast as adopted.

These, Sir, Congress may be assured, are but a small part of the inconveniences, which might be enumerated, and attributed to militia; but there is one, that merits particular attention, and that is the expense. Certain I am, that it would be cheaper to keep fifty or a hundred thousand in constant pay, than to depend upon half the number and supply the other half occasionally by militia. The time the latter are in pay before and after they are in camp, assembling and marching, the waste of ammunition, the consumption of stores, which, in spite of every resolution or requisition of Congress, they must be furnished with, or sent home, added to other incidental expenses consequent upon their coming and conduct in camp, surpasses all idea, and destroys every kind of regularity and economy, which you could establish among fixed and settled troops, and will, in my opinion, prove, if the scheme is adhered to, the ruin of our cause.

The jealousy of a standing army, and the evils to be apprehended from one, are remote, and, in my judgment, situated and circumstanced as we are, not at all to be dreaded; but the consequence of wanting one, according to my ideas formed from the present view of things, is certain and inevitable ruin. For, if I was called upon to declare upon oath, whether the militia have been most serviceable or hurtful upon the whole, I should subscribe to the latter. I do not mean by this, however, to arraign the conduct of Congress; in so doing I should equally condemn my own measures, if I did not my judgment; but experience, which is the best criterion to work by, so fully, clearly, and decisively reprobates the practice of trusting to militia, that no man, who regards order, regularity, and economy, or who has any regard for his own honor, character, or peace of mind, will risk them upon this issue.

No less attention should be paid to the choice of surgeons, than of other officers of the army. They should undergo a regular examination, and, if not appointed by the director-general and surgeons of the hospital, they ought to be subordinate to and governed by his directions. The regimental surgeons I am speaking of, many of whom are very great rascals, countenancing the men in sham complaints to exempt them from duty, and often receiving bribes to certify indispositions, with a view to procure discharges or furloughs; but, independent of these practices, while they are considered as unconnected with the general hospital, there will be nothing but continual complaints of each other; the director of the hospital charging them with enormity in their drafts for the sick, and they him with the same for denying such things as are necessary. In short, there is a constant bickering among them, which tends greatly to the injury of the sick, and will always subsist till the regimental surgeons are made to look up to the director-general of the hospital as a superior. Whether this is the case in regular armies or not, I cannot undertake to say; but certain I am, there is a necessity for it in this, or the sick will suffer. The regimental surgeons are aiming, I am persuaded, to break up the general hospital, and have, in numberless instances, drawn for medicines and stores in the most profuse and extravagant manner for private purposes.

Another matter highly worthy of attention is, that other rules and regulations may be adopted for the government of the army, than those now in existence; otherwise the army, but for the name, might as well be disbanded. For the most atrocious offences, one or two instances only excepted, a man receives no more than thirty-nine lashes; and these, perhaps, through the collusion of the officer, who is to see it inflicted, are given in such a manner as to become rather a matter of sport than punishment; but, when inflicted as they ought, many hardened fellows, who have been the subjects, have declared that, for a bottle of rum, they would undergo a second operation. It is evident, therefore, that this punishment is inadequate to many crimes it is assigned to. As a proof of it, thirty or forty soldiers will desert at a time, and of late a practice prevails (as you will see by my letter of the 22d) of the most alarming nature and which will, if it cannot be checked, prove fatal both to the country and army; I mean the infamous practice of plundering. For, under the idea of Tory property, or property that may fall into the hands of the enemy, no man is secure in his effects, and scarcely in his person. In order to get at them, we have several instances of people being frightened out of their houses, under pretence of those houses being ordered to be burnt, and this is done with a view of seizing the goods; nay, in order that the villainy may be more effectually concealed, some houses have actually been burnt, to cover the theft. I have, with some others, used my utmost endeavors to stop this horrid practice; but under the present lust after plunder, and want of laws to punish offenders, I might almost as well attempt to remove Mount Atlas. I have ordered instant corporal punishment upon every man, who passes our lines, or is seen with plunder, that the offenders might be punished for disobedience of orders; and enclose to you the proceedings of a court-martial held upon an officer [Ensign Matthew McCumber] who, with a party of men, had robbed a house a little beyond our lines of a number of valuable goods, among which (to show that nothing escapes) were four large pier looking-glasses, women's clothes, and other articles, which, one would think, could be of no earthly use to him. He was met by a major of brigade, [Box] who ordered him to return the goods, as taken contrary to general orders, which he not only peremptorily refused to do, but drew up his party, and swore he would defend them at the hazard of his life; on which I ordered him to be arrested and tried for plundering, disobedience of orders, and mutiny. For the result, I refer to the proceedings of the court, whose judgment appeared so exceedingly extraordinary, that I ordered a reconsideration of the matter, upon which, and with the assistance of a fresh evidence, they made a shift to cashier him. I adduce this instance, to give some idea to Congress of the current sentiments and general run of the officers, which compose the present army; and to show how exceedingly necessary it is to be careful in the choice of the new set, even if it should take double the time to complete the levies.

An army formed of good officers moves like clock-work; but there is no situation upon earth less enviable, nor more distressing, than that person's, who is at the head of troops which are regardless of order and discipline, and who are unprovided with almost every necessary. In a word, the difficulties, which have for ever surrounded me since I have been in the service, and kept my mind constantly upon the stretch, the wounds, which my feelings as an officer have received by a thousand things, which have happened contrary to my expectation and wishes; the effect of my own conduct, and present appearance of things, so little pleasing to myself, as to render it a matter of no surprise to me if I should stand capitally censured by Congress; added to a consciousness of my inability to govern an army composed of such discordant parts, and under such a variety of intricate and perplexing circumstances; —induces not only a belief, but a thorough conviction in my mind, that it will be impossible, unless there is a thorough change in our military system, for me to conduct matters in such a manner as to give satisfaction to the public, which is all the recompense I aim at, or ever wished for. . . .

Army Situation Drives Him to Despair

To Lund Washington, H. Q., Harlem, September 30, 1776

At present our numbers fit for duty (by this day's report) amount to 14,759, besides 3,427 on command, and the enemy within stone's throw of us . . . I discharged a regiment the other day that had in it fourteen rank and file fit for duty only, and several that had less than fifty. In short, such is my situation that if I were to wish the bitterest curse to an enemy on this side of the grave, I should put him in my stead with my feelings; and yet I do not know what plan of conduct to pursue. I see the impossibility of serving with reputation, or doing any essential service to the cause by continuing in command, and yet I am told that if I quit the command inevitable ruin will follow from the distraction that will ensue. In confidence I tell you that I never was in such an unhappy, divided state since I was born . . . I am wearied to death all day with a variety of perplexing circumstances—disturbed at the conduct of the militia, whose behavior and want of discipline has done great injury to the other troops, who never had officers, except in a few instances, worth the bread they eat.

To John Augustine Washington, November 19, 1776

I am wearied almost to death with the retrograde motion of things, and I solemnly protest, that a pecuniary reward of twenty thousand pounds a year would not induce me to undergo what I do; and after all, perhaps, to lose my character, as it is impossible, under such a variety of distressing circumstances, to conduct matters agreeably to public expectation, or even to the expectation of those, who employ me, as they will not make proper allowances for the difficulties their own errors have occasioned. . . .

Censure

To Major General William Heath, Morristown, February 3, 1777

This letter is in addition to my public one of this date. It is to hint to you, and I do it with concern, that your conduct is censured (and by men of sense and judgment, who have been with you on the expedition to Fort Independence), as being fraught with too much caution, by which the army has been disappointed, and in some degree disgraced. Your summons, as you did not attempt to fulfil your threats, was not only idle but farcical, and will not fail of turning the laugh exceedingly upon us. These things I mention to you as a friend, for you will perceive that they have composed no part of my public letter. Why you should be so apprehensive of being surrounded, even if Lord Percy had landed, I cannot conceive.

To Major Appolos Morris, H. Q., Middle Brooke, June 6, 1777

I think it very odd, that . . . you should . . . conclude that matters between this Country and Great Britain might have been adjusted, had any terms short of Independence been insisted upon. I must tell you in plain terms, that at this time a neutral character is looked upon as a suspicious one; and I would therefore advise you to leave a Country with a Majority of whom you cannot agree in Sentiment, and who are determined to assert their liberties by the ways and means which necessity and not the love of War has obliged them to adopt.

The Art of War

To General George Clinton, July 31, 1778

Sir, With the detachment under your command . . . you are to move towards Kings Bridge and the Enemy's lines thereabouts.—

The principal objects in view are, to cover the Engineers and Surveyors, while they reconnoiter and as far as time will permit, survey the ground & roads in your rear, and in front of the Camp—to countenance and encourage that spirit of desertion which seems so prevalent at present—to discover, if possible, those unfriendly, and ill disposed inhabitants who make a practice of apprehending, and conveying within the Enemy's line such deserters from their Army as happen to fall into their hands and with such witnesses as are necessary to elucidate the facts send them to the Head Quarters of this Army—and lastly to try what effect the detachments approach may have upon the Enemy.

I do not mean, or wish, that you should encamp very near the Enemy of nights, but wherever you do encamp, that you do it in proper order of battle, so that your officers and men may rise at once upon the ground they are to defend. Your flanks and front sufficiently advanced upon every possible approach; always remembering how disgraceful a thing it is for an officer to be surprised, and believing, that if the enemy are in force at the Bridge, they will certainly attempt it.

When I speak of your flanks, I have an eye particularly to the North River, as the enemy can, with facility move with both secrecy & dispatch by water . . .

Have your evening's position well reconnoitred before hand, and unless there are good reasons to the contrary, I would advise against kindling fires at night, as the weather is warm, & your position would be discovered, & advantages taken from the knowledge of it.

To Lieutenants William Bird, Richard Dorsey, John Craig, N. Buxton Moore, and George Gray, Camp at Cross Roads, August 15, 1777

Your wishes to resign at such a period as this . . . will be sufficient evidence with me, that it is a disinclination to the Service, and not the mere disappointments of Rank and pay, that causes it; and therefore it may be unnecessary for me to add, that any future application from either of you to get into the Continental Service will be improper, and as far as it is in my power to make it so unavailing.

Tactics

To General George Clinton, August 16, 1777

I should not be very uneasy for the issue if I could once see our northern army recovered from their present dejection, and restored to a tolerable degree of confidence and animation. In addition to the two regiments, which are gone from Peekskill, I am forwarding as fast as possible, to join the northern army, Colonel Morgan's corps of riflemen, amounting to about five hundred. They are well chosen men, selected from the army at large, well acquainted with the use of rifles, and with that mode of fighting, which is necessary to make a good counterpoise to the Indians; and they have distinguished themselves on a variety of occasions, since the formation of the corps, in skirmishes with the enemy. I expect the most eminent services from them; and I shall be mistaken if their presence does not go far towards producing a general desertion among the savages. I should think it would be well, even before their arrival, to begin to circulate these ideas, with proper embellishments, throughout the country and in the army; and to take pains to communicate them to the enemy. It would not be amiss, among other things, to magnify their numbers. . . .

From some expressions in a letter, which I have seen. . . it is in contemplation to unite all the militia and Continental troops in one body, and make an opposition wholly in front. If this be really the intention, I should think it a very ineligible plan. An enemy can always act with more vigor and effect when they have nothing to apprehend for their flanks and rear, than when they have: and it is one of the most approved and most universally practiced manoeuvres of war, to keep their fears continually awake on these accounts, and, when circumstances permit, to be actually in condition to give them serious annoyance in those parts. Independent of the inconveniences, that attend a situation where the rear and flank are constantly exposed to the insults of light parties, which may at every moment be harassing them; the necessity of never losing sight of the means of a secure retreat, which ought to be the object of an officer's care, must be exceedingly embarrassing, where is a force in such a position as to endanger it.

Need for Supplies

To Lieutenant Colonel Alexander Hamilton, camp, September 22, 1777

The distressed situation of the army for want of blankets, and many necessary articles of cloathing, is truly deplorable; and must inevitably be destructive to it, unless a speedy remedy be applied. Without a better supply than they at present have, it will be impossible for the men to support the fatigues of the campaign in the further progress of the approaching inclement season. This you well know to be a melancholy truth. It is equally the dictate of common sense and the opinion of the Physicians of the army, as well as of every officer in it. No supply can be drawn from the public magazines. We have therefore no resource but from the private stock of individuals. I feel, and I lament, the absolute necessity of requiring the inhabitants to contribute to those wants, which we have no other means of satisfying, and which if unremoved would involve the ruin of the army, and perhaps the ruin of America. Painful as it is to me to order and as it will be to you to execute the measure, I am compelled to desire you immediately to proceed to Philadelphia, and there procure from the inhabitants contributions of blankets and cloathing, and materials to answer the purposes of both, in proportion to the ability of each. This you will do with as much delicacy and discretion, as the nature of the business demands; and I trust the necessity will justify the proceeding in the eyes of every person well affected to the American cause, and that all good citizens will chearfully afford their assistance to soldiers, whose sufferings they are bound to commiserate, and who are eminently exposed to danger and distress, in defence of every thing they ought to hold dear.

As there are also a number of horses in Philadelphia both of public and private property, which would be a valuable acquisition to the enemy, should the city by any accident fall into their hands, you are hereby authorized and commanded to remove them thence into the Country to some place of greater security, and more remote from the operations of the enemy. You will stand in need of assistance from others to execute this commission with despatch and propriety, and you are therefore empowered to employ such persons as you shall think proper to aid you therein. I am, Sir, &c.

To John Augustine Washington, Philadelphia County, October 18, 1777

Your kind and affectionate Letters of the 21st of Septr. & 2d Inst. came safe to hand.

When my last to you was dated I know not; for truly I can

say, that my whole time is so much engrossed, that I have scarcely a moment, but sleeping ones, for relaxation, or to indulge myself in writing to a friend. The anxiety you have been under, on acct of this army, I can easily conceive. Would to God there had been less cause for it; or that our situation at present was such as to promise much from it. The Enemy crossed the Schuylkill which, by the by, above the Falls (& the Falls you know is only five miles from the city) is as easily crossed in any place as Potomac Run, Aquia, or any other broad & shallow water, rather by stratagem; tho I do not know, that it was in our power to prevent it, as their manoeuvres made it necessary for us to attend to our Stores, which lay at Reading, towards which they seemed bending their course, and the loss of which must have proved our Ruin. After they had crossed, we took the first favorable opportunity of attacking them.[1]

This was attempted by a night's march of fourteen miles to surprise them, which we effectually did, so far as to reach their guards before they had notice of our coming; and but for a thick Fog, which rendered so infinitely dark at times as not to distinguish friend from Foe at the distance of thirty yards, we should, I believe, have made a decisive and glorious day of it. But Providence or some unaccountable something designed it otherwise; for after we had driven the Enemy a mile or two, after they were in the utmost confusion and flying before us in most places, after we were upon the point, (as it appeared to every body,) of grasping a compleat victory, our own troops took fright and fled with precipitation and disorder. How to acct for this, I know not; unless, as I before observed, the Fog represented their own Friends to them for a Reinforcement of the Enemy, as we attacked in different Quarters at the same time, and were about closing the wings of our army when this happened. One thing, indeed, contributed not a little to our misfortune, and that was want of ammunition on the right wing, which began the Engagement, and in the course of two hours and forty minutes, which time it lasted, had, (many of them,) expended the forty Rounds, that they took into the Field. After the Engagement we removed to a place about twenty miles from the Enemy, to collect our Forces together, to take care of our wounded, get furnished with necessaries again, and be in a

[1] The battle of Germantown.

better posture, either for offensive or defensive operations. We are now advancing towards the Enemy again, being at this time within twelve miles of them.

Our loss in the late action was, in killed, wounded, and missing, about one thousand men, but of the missing, many, I dare say, took advantage of the times, and deserted. Genl. Nash of No. Carolina was wounded, and died two or three days after. Many valuable officers of ours was also wounded, and some killed. The Enemy's loss is variously reported—none make it less than 1500 (killed & wounded) & many estimate it much larger. Genl. Agnew of theirs was certainly killed—many officers wounded among whom some of distinction. This we certainly know, that the Hospital at Philadelphia & several large Meeting Houses, are filled with their wounded besides private Houses with the Horses. In a word, it was a bloody day. Would to Heaven I could add, that it had been a more fortunate one for us.

Our distress on acct. of Cloathing is great, and in a little time must be very sensibly felt, unless some expedient can be hit upon to obtain them. We have since the Battle got in abt. 1200 Militia from Virginia—about the same number have gone off from this State and Jersey but others are promised in lieu of them—with truth however it may be said, that this State acts most infamously, the People of it, I mean, as we derive little or no assistance, from them. In short they are, in a manner, totally, disaffected, or in a kind of Lethargy.

The Enemy are making vigorous efforts to remove the obstructions in the Delaware, and to possess themselves of the Works which have been constructed for the Defence of them.—I am doing all I can in my present situation to save them, God only knows which will succeed.

I very sincerely congratulate you on the change in your Family. Tell the young couple, after wishing them joy of their union, that it is my sincere hope, that it will be as happy and lasting as their present joys are boundless. The Enclosed Letter of thanks to my sister for her elegant present you will please to deliver; and, with sincere affection for you all, I am &c.

Lack of Supplies

To the President of Congress, Valley Forge, December 23, 1777

Since the month of July we have had no assistance from the quartermaster-general, and to want of assistance from this department the commissary-general charges great part of his deficiency. To this I am to add, that, notwithstanding it is a standing order, and often repeated, that the troops shall always have two days' provisions by them, that they might be ready at any sudden call; yet an opportunity has scarcely ever offered, of taking an advantage of the enemy, that has not been either totally obstructed, or greatly impeded, on this account. And this, the great and crying evil, is not all. The soap, vinegar, and other articles allowed by Congress, we see none of, nor have we seen them, I believe, since the battle of Brandywine. The first, indeed, we have now little occasion for; few men having more than one shirt, many only the moiety of one, and some none at all. In addition to which, as a proof of the little benefit received from a clothier-general, and as a further proof of the inability of an army, under the circumstances of this, to perform the common duties of soldiers (besides a number of men confined to hospitals for want of shoes, and others in farmers' houses on the same account,) we have, by a field-return this day made, no less than two thousand eight hundred and ninety-eight men now in camp unfit for duty, because they are barefoot and otherwise naked. By the same return it appears, that our whole strength in Continental troops, including the eastern brigades, which have joined us since the surrender of General Burgoyne, exclusive of the Maryland troops sent to Wilmington, amounts to no more than eight thousand two hundred in camp fit for duty; notwithstanding which, and that since the 4th instant, our numbers fit for duty, from the hardships and exposures they have undergone, particularly on account of blankets (numbers having been obliged, and still are, to sit up all night by fires, instead of taking comfortable rest in a natural and common way), have decreased near two thousand men.

We find gentlemen, without knowing whether the army was

really going into winter-quarters or not (for I am sure no resolution of mine would warrant the Remonstrance), reprobating the measure as much as if they thought the soldiers were made of sticks or stones, and equally insensible of frost and snow; and moreover, as if they conceived it easily practicable for an inferior army, under the disadvantages I have described ours to be, which are by no means exaggerated, to confine a superior one, in all respects well-appointed and provided for a winter's campaign, within the city of Philadelphia, and to cover from depredation and waste the States of Pennsylvania and Jersey. But what makes this matter still more extraordinary in my eye is, that these very gentlemen,—who were well apprized of the nakedness of the troops from ocular demonstration, who thought their own soldiers worse clad than others, and who advised me near a month ago to postpone the execution of a plan I was about to adopt, in consequence of a resolve of Congress for seizing clothes, under strong assurances that an ample supply would be collected in ten days agreeably to a decree of the State (not one article of which, by the by, is yet come to hand),—should think a winter's campaign, and the covering of these States from the invasion of an enemy, so easy and practicable a business. I can assure those gentlemen, that it is a much easier and less distressing thing to draw remonstrances in a comfortable room by a good fireside, than to occupy a cold, bleak hill, and sleep under frost and snow, without clothes or blankets. However, although they seem to have little feeling for the naked and distressed soldiers, I feel superabundantly for them, and, from my soul, I pity those miseries, which it is neither in my power to relieve or prevent.

It is for these reasons, therefore, that I have dwelt upon the subject; and it adds not a little to my other difficulties and distress to find, that much more is expected of me than is possible to be performed, and that upon the ground of safety and policy I am obliged to conceal the true state of the army from public view, and thereby expose myself to detraction and calumny. The honorable committee of Congress went from camp fully possessed of my sentiments respecting the establishment of this army, the necessity of auditors of accounts, the appointment of officers, and new arrangements. I have no need, therefore, to be prolix upon these subjects, but I refer to the committee. I shall add a word or two to show, first, the necessity of some better provision for binding the officers by the tie of interest to the service, as no day nor scarce an hour passes without the offer of a resigned commission; (otherwise I much doubt the practicability of holding the army together much longer, and in this I shall probably be thought the more sincere, when I freely declare, that I do not myself expect to derive the smallest benefit from any establishment that Congress may adopt, otherwise than as a member of the community at large in the good, which I am persuaded will result from the measure, by making better officers and better troops;) and, secondly, to point out the necessity of making the appointments and arrangements without loss of time. We have not more than three months, in which to prepare a great deal of business. If we let these slip or waste, we shall be laboring under the same difficulties all next campaign, as we have been this, to rectify mistakes and bring things to order.

Military arrangement, and movements in consequence, like the mechanism of a clock, will be imperfect and disordered by the want of a part. In a very sensible degree have I experienced this, in the course of the last summer, several brigades having no brigadiers appointed to them till late, and some not at all; by which means it follows, that an additional weight is thrown upon the shoulders of the Commander-in-chief, to withdraw his attention from the great line of his duty. The gentlemen of the committee, when they were at camp, talked of an expedient for adjusting these matters, which I highly approved and wish to see adopted; namely, that two or three members of the Board of War, or a committee of Congress, should repair immediately to camp, where the best aid can be had, and with the commanding officer, or a committee of his appointment, prepare and digest the most perfect plan, that can be devised, for correcting all abuses and making new arrangements; considering what is to be done with the weak and debilitated regiments, if the States to which they belong will not draft men to fill them, for as to enlisting soldiers it seems to me to be totally out of the question; together with many other things, that would occur in the course of such a conference; and, after digesting matters in the best manner they can, to submit the whole to the ultimate determination of Congress.

If this measure is approved, I would earnestly advise the immediate execution of it, and that the commissary-general of purchases, whom I rarely see, may be directed to form magazines without a moment's delay in the neighborhood of this camp, in order to secure provision for us in case of bad weather. The quartermaster-general ought also to be busy in his department. In short, there is as much to be done in preparing for a campaign, as in the active part of it. Everything depends upon the preparation that is made in the several departments, and the success or misfortunes of the next campaign will more than probably originate with our activity or supineness during this winter. I have the honor to be, &c.

British Policy

To Bryan Fairfax, March 1, 1778

Does not every act of Administration, from the Tea Act to the present session of Parliament, declare this in plain and self-evident characters? Had the commissioners any power to treat with America? If they meant peace, would Lord Howe have been detained in England five months after passing the act? Would the powers of these commissioners have been confined to mere acts of grace, upon condition of absolute submission? No! surely, no! They meant to drive us into what they termed rebellion, that they might be furnished with a pretext to disarm, and then strip us of the rights and privileges of Englishmen and citizens.

If they were actuated by the principles of justice, why did they refuse indignantly to accede to the terms, which were humbly supplicated before hostilities commenced, and this country deluged in blood; and now make their principal officers, and even the commissioners themselves, say that these terms are just and reasonable; nay, that more will be granted, than we have yet asked, if we will relinquish our claim to independency? What name does such conduct as this deserve? And what punishment is there in store for the men, who have distressed millions, involved thousands in ruin, and plunged numberless families in inextricable woe? Could that, which is just and reasonable now, have been unjust four years ago? If not, upon what principles, I say, does Administration act? They must either be wantonly wicked and cruel, or (which is only another mode of describing the same thing) under false colors are now endeavoring to deceive the great body of the people, by industriously propagating a belief, that Great Britain is willing to offer any, and that we will accept of no terms; thereby hoping to poison and disaffect the minds of those, who wish for peace, and create feuds and dissensions among ourselves. In a word, having less dependence now in their arms than in their arts, they are practising such low and dirty tricks, that men of sentiment and honor must blush at their villainy. Among other manœuvres in this way, they are counterfeiting letters, and publishing them as intercepted ones of mine, to prove that I am an enemy to the present measures, and have been led into them step by step, still hoping that Congress would recede from their present claims. I am, dear Sir, your most obedient and affectionate, &c.

Prisoners' Exchange—Principles of Probity and Public Opinion

To the President of Congress, Valley Forge, March 7, 1778

But perhaps it may be thought contrary to our interest to go into an exchange [of war prisoners], as the enemy would derive more immediate advantage from it than we should. This I shall not deny; but it appeared to me, that, on principles of genuine, extensive policy, independent of the considerations of compassion and justice, we were under an obligation not to elude it. I have the best evidence, that an event of this kind is the general wish of the country. I know it to be the wish of the army; and no one can doubt, that it is the ardent wish of the unhappy sufferers themselves. We need only consult the tide of humanity, and the sympathies natural to those connected by the cement of blood, interest, and a common dread of evil, to be convinced, that the prevailing current of sentiment demands an exchange. If the country, the army, and even the prisoners themselves, had a precise idea of our circumstances, and could be fully sensible of the disadvantages, that might attend the giving our enemy a considerable reinforcement without having an equivalent, they might perhaps be willing to make a sacrifice of their feelings to the motives of policy. But they have not this knowledge, and cannot be entrusted with it; and their reasonings, of necessity, will be governed by what they feel.

Were an opinion once to be established . . . that we designedly avoided an exchange, it would be a cause of dissatisfaction and disgust to the country and to the army, of resentment and desperation to our captive officers and soldiers. To say nothing of the importance of not hazarding our national character but upon the most solid grounds, especially in our embryo state, from the influence it may have on our affairs abroad, it may not be a little dangerous to beget in the minds of our own countrymen a suspicion, that we do not pay the strictest observance to the maxims of honor and good faith.

It is prudent to use the greatest caution not to shock the notions of general justice and humanity, universal among mankind, as well in a public as in a private view. In a business on the side of which the passions are so much concerned as in the present, men would be readily disposed to believe the worst, and cherish the most unfavorable conclusions. Were the letters, that have passed between General Howe and myself . . . to be published with proper comments, it is much to be feared, that it would be difficult to prevent our being generally accused of a breach of good faith . . . Imputations of this nature would have a tendency to unnerve our operations, by diminishing that respect and confidence, which are essential to be placed in those, who are at the head of affairs either in the civil or military line. This, added to the prospect of hopeless captivity, would be a great discouragement to the service. The ill consequences of both would be immense, by increasing the causes of discontent in the army, which are already too numerous . . .

If we do not seize the present propitious moment, when the necessities of the enemy press them to reasonable terms . . . it is not impossible . . . that a time may come when we should wish we had embraced it . . . True policy, as well as good faith, in my opinion, binds us to improve the occasion . . .

I cannot doubt that Congress, in preservation of the public faith and my personal honor, will remove all impediments . . . and . . . will authorize me . . . to negotiate a more extensive and competent cartel, upon such principles as may appear advantagous and founded in necessity . . .

To Lieutenant General John Burgoyne, H. Q., March 11, 1778

Your indulgent opinion of my character, and the polite terms in which you are pleased to express it, are peculiarly flattering; and I take pleasure in the opportunity you have afforded me, of assuring you, that, far from suffering the views of national opposition to be embittered and debased by personal animosity, I am ever ready to do justice to the merit of the man and soldier, and to esteem where esteem is due, however the idea of a public enemy may interpose. You will not think it the language of unmeaning ceremony, if I add, that sentiments of personal respect, in the present instance, are reciprocal.

Viewing you in the light of an officer, contending against what I conceive to be the rights of my country, the reverses of fortune you experienced in the field cannot be unacceptable to me; but, abstracted from considerations of national advantage, I can sincerely sympathize with your feelings as a soldier, the unavoidable difficulties of whose situation forbid his success; and as a man, whose lot combines the calamity of ill health, the anxieties of captivity, and the painful sensibility for a reputation exposed, where he most values it, to the assaults of malice and detraction.

. . . Wishing you a safe and agreeable passage, with a perfect restoration of your health, I have the honor to be, very respectfully, &.[2]

[2] April 14, Burgoyne to Washington: "I beg you to accept my sincerest acknowledgments for your obliging letter. I find the character, which I before knew to be respectable, is also perfectly amiable; and I should have few greater private gratifications in seeing our melancholy contest at an end, than that of cultivating your friendship."

Opposes Enlistment of Deserters

To James Bowdoin,[3] *Valley Forge, March 17, 1778*

It gives me inexpressible concern to have repeated information from the best authority, that the committees of the different towns and districts of your State hire deserters from General Burgoyne's army, and employ them as substitutes, to excuse the personal service of the inhabitants. I need not enlarge upon the danger of substituting, as soldiers, men, who have given a glaring proof of a treacherous disposition, and who are bound to us by no motives of attachment, to citizens, in whom the ties of country, kindred, and sometimes property are so many securities for their fidelity. The evils with which this measure is pregnant are obvious, and of such a serious nature, as makes it necessary, not only to stop the farther progress of it, but likewise to apply a retrospective remedy, and if possible to annul it, so far as it has been carried into effect. Unless this is done, although you may be amused for the present with the flattering idea of speedily completing your battalions, they will be found, at or before the opening of the campaign, reduced by the defection of every British soldier to their original weak condition; and the accumulated bounties of the continent and of the State will have been fruitlessly sacrificed.

Indeed, Mr. Burgoyne could hardly, if he were consulted, suggest a more effectual plan for plundering us of so much money, reinforcing General Howe with so many men, and preventing us from recruiting a certain number of regiments; to say nothing of the additional losses, which may be dreaded, in desertions among the native soldiers, from the contagion of ill example and the arts of seduction, which it is more than probable will be put in practice. This matter demands your immediate attention.

[3] President of the Council of Massachusetts.

Problems of the Army and Peace

To John Banister, Delegate in Congress, Valley Forge, April 21, 1778

The difference between our service and that of the enemy is very striking. With us, from the peculiar, unhappy situation of things, the officer, a few instances excepted, must break in upon his private fortune for present support, without a prospect of future relief. With them, even companies are esteemed so honorable and so valuable, that they have sold of late from fifteen to twenty-two hundred pounds sterling; and I am credibly informed, that four thousand guineas have been given for a troop of dragoons. You will readily determine how this difference will operate; what effects it must produce. Men may speculate as they will; they may talk of patriotism; they may draw a few examples from ancient story, of great achievements performed by its influence; but whoever builds upon them, as a sufficient basis for conducting a long and bloody war, will find themselves deceived in the end. We must take the passions of men as nature has given them, and those principles as a guide, which are generally the rule of action. I do not mean to exclude altogether the idea of patriotism. I know it exists, and I know it has done much in the present contest. But I will venture to assert, that a great and lasting war can never be supported on this principle alone. It must be aided by a prospect of interest, or some reward. For a time it may, of itself, push men to action, to bear much, to encounter difficulties; but it will not endure unassisted by interest.

The necessity of putting the army upon a respectable footing, both as to numbers and constitution, is now become more essential than ever. The enemy are beginning to play a game more dangerous, than their efforts by arms (though these will not be remitted in the smallest degree), and which threatens a fatal blow to the independence of America, and to her liberties of course. They are endeavoring to ensnare the people by specious allurements of peace. It is not improbable they have had such abundant cause to be tired of the war, that they may be sincere in the terms they offer, which, though far short of our pretensions, will be extremely flattering to minds, that do not penetrate far into political consequences; but, whether they are sincere or not, they may be equally destructive; for, to discerning men nothing can be more evident, than that a peace on the principles of dependence, however limited, after what has happened, would be to the last degree dishonorable and ruinous. It is however much to be apprehended, that the idea of such an event will have a very powerful effect upon the country, and if not combated with the greatest address will serve, at least, to produce supineness and disunion. Men are naturally fond of peace, and there are symptoms which may authorize an opinion, that the people of America are pretty generally weary of the present war. It is doubtful, whether many of our friends might not incline to an accommodation on the grounds held out, or which may be, rather than persevere in a contest for independence. If this is the case, it must surely be the truest policy to strengthen the army, and place it upon a substantial footing. This will conduce to inspire the country with confidence; enable those at the head of affairs to consult the public honor and interest, notwithstanding the defection of some and temporary inconsistency and irresolution of others, who may desire to compromise the dispute; and, if a treaty should be deemed expedient, will put it in their power to insist upon better terms, than they could otherwise expect.

Besides the most vigorous exertions at home to increase and establish our military force upon a good basis, it appears to me advisable, that we should immediately try the full extent of our interest abroad, and bring our European negotiations to an issue. I think France must have ratified our independence, and will declare war immediately, on finding that serious proposals of accommodation are made; but lest, from a mistaken policy or too exalted an opinion of our power from the representations she has had, she should still remain indecisive, it were to be wished, proper persons were instantly despatched, or our envoys already there instructed to insist pointedly on her coming to a final determination. It cannot be fairly supposed, that she will hesitate a moment to declare war, if she is given to understand, in a proper manner, that a reunion of the two countries may be the consequence of procrastination. A European war and a European alliance would effectually answer our purposes. If the step I now mention should be eligible, despatches ought to be sent at once by different conveyances, for fear of accidents. I confess, it appears to me a measure of this kind could not but be productive of the most salutary consequences. If possible, I should also suppose it absolutely necessary to obtain good intelligence from England, pointing out the true springs of this manœuvre of ministry; the preparations of force they are making; the prospects there are of raising it; the amount, and when it may be expected.

It really seems to me, from a comprehensive view of things, that a period is fast approaching, big with events of the most interesting importance; when the counsels we pursue, and the part we act, may lead decisively to liberty or to slavery. Under this idea, I cannot but regret that inactivity, that inattention, that want of something, which unhappily I have but too often experienced in our public affairs. I wish that our representation in Congress was complete and full from every State, and that it was formed of the first abilities among us. Whether we continue to war or proceed to negotiate, the wisdom of America in council cannot be too great. Our situation will be truly delicate. To enter into a negotiation too hastily, or to reject it altogether, may be attended with consequences equally fatal. The wishes of the people, seldom founded in deep disquisitions, or resulting from other reasonings than their present feelings, may not entirely accord with our true policy and interest. If they do not, to observe a proper line of conduct for promoting the one, and avoiding offence to the other, will be a work of great difficulty.

Nothing short of independence, it appears to me, can possibly do. A peace on other terms would, if I may be allowed the expression, be a peace of war. The injuries we have received from the British nation were so unprovoked, and have been so great and so many, that they can never be forgotten. Besides the feuds, the jealousies, the animosities, that would ever attend a union with them; besides the importance, the advantages, we should derive from an unrestricted commerce; our fidelity as a people, our gratitude, our character as men, are opposed to a coalition with them as subjects, but in case of the last extremity. Were we easily to accede to terms of dependence, no nation, upon future occasions, let the oppressions of Britain be never so flagrant and unjust, would interpose for our relief; or, at most, they would do it with a cautious reluctance, and upon conditions most probably that would be hard, if not dishonorable to us. France, by her supplies, has saved us from the yoke thus far; and a wise and virtuous perseverance would, and I trust will, free us entirely.

I have sent Congress Lord North's speech, and the two bills offered by him to Parliament. They are spreading fast through the country, and will soon become a subject of general notoriety. I therefore think they had best be published in our papers, and persons of leisure and ability set to work to counteract the impressions they may make on the minds of the people.

Before I conclude, there are one or two points more, upon which I will add an observation or two. The first is, the indecision of Congress and the delay used in coming to determinations on matters referred to them. This is productive of a variety of inconveniences; and an early decision, in many cases, though it should be against the measure submitted, would be attended with less pernicious effects. Some new plan might then be tried; but, while the matter is held in suspense, nothing can be attempted. The other point is, the *jealousy,* which Congress unhappily entertain of the army, and which, if reports are right, some members labor to establish. You may be assured, there is nothing more injurious, or more unjustly founded. This jealousy stands upon the commonly received opinion, which under proper limitations is certainly true, that standing armies are dangerous to a State, and from forming the same conclusion of the component parts of all, though they are totally dissimilar in their nature. The prejudices in other countries have only gone to them in time of *peace,* and these from their not having in general cases any of the ties, the concerns, or interests of citizens, or any other dependence, than what flowed from their military employ; in short, from their being mercenaries, hirelings. It is our policy to be prejudiced against them in time of *war;* & though they are citizens, having all the ties and interests of citizens, and in most cases property totally unconnected with the military line.

If we would pursue a right system of policy, in my opinion, there should be none of these distinctions. We should all be considered, Congress and army, as one people, embarked in one cause, in one interest; acting on the same principle, and to the same end. The distinction, the jealousies set up, or perhaps only incautiously let out, can answer not a single good purpose. They are impolitic in the extreme. Among individuals the most certain way to make a man your enemy is to tell him you esteem him such. So with public bodies; and the very jealousy, which the narrow politics of some may affect to entertain of the army, in order to a due subordination to the supreme civil authority, is a likely mean to produce a contrary effect; to incline it to the pursuit of those measures, which they may wish it to avoid. It is unjust, because no order of men in the Thirteen States has paid a more sanctimonious regard to their proceedings than the army; and indeed it may be questioned whether there has been that scrupulous adherence had to them by any other, for without arrogance or the smallest deviation from truth it may be said, that no history now extant can furnish an instance of an army's suffering such uncommon hardships as ours has done, and bearing them with the same patience and fortitude. To see men, without clothes to cover their nakedness, without blankets to lie on, without shoes, by which their marches might be traced by the blood from their feet, and almost as often without provisions as with them, marching through the frost and snow, and at Christmas taking up their winter-quarters within a day's march of the enemy, without a house or hut to cover them, till they could be built, and submitting to it without a murmur, is a proof of patience and obedience, which in my opinion can scarce be paralleled.

There may have been some remonstrances or applications to Congress, in the style of complaint, from the army, and slaves indeed should we be, if this privilege were denied, on account of their proceedings in particular instances; but these will not authorize nor even excuse a jealousy, that they are therefore aiming at unreasonable powers, or making strides dangerous or subversive of civil authority. Things should not be viewed in that light, more especially as Congress in some cases have relieved the injuries complained of, & which had flowed from their own acts. I refer you to my letter to yourself and Colo. Lee which accompanies this upon the subject of money for such of the old Virginia troops as have or may reinlist.

In respect to the volunteer plan, I scarce know what opinion to give at this time. The propriety of a requisition on this head will depend altogether on our operations. Such kind of troops should not be called for, but upon the spur of the occasion, and at the moment of executing an enterprise. They will not endure a long service; and, of all men in the military line, they are the most impatient of restraint and necessary government.

As the propositions and the speech of Lord North must be founded in the despair of the nation of succeeding against us; or from a rupture in Europe, that has actually happened, or certainly will happen; or from some deep political manoeuvre; or from what I think still more likely, a composition of the whole, would it not be good policy, in this day of uncertainty and distress to the Tories, to avail ourselves of the occasion, and for the several States to hold out pardon &c. to all delinquents returning by a certain day? They are frightened, and this is the time to operate upon them. Upon a short consideration of the matter, it appears to me, that such a measure would detach the Tories from the enemy, and bring things to a much speedier conclusion, and of course be a mean of saving much public treasure.

I will now be done and I trust that you excuse, not only the length of my letter, but the freedom with which I have delivered my sentiments in the course of it upon several occasions. The subjects struck me as important and interesting, and I have only to wish, that they may appear to you in the same light.

I am, dear Sir, with great regard, &c.

To Henry Laurens, April 30, 1778

It appears to me, that nothing short of independence can possibly do. The injuries we have received from Britain can never be forgotten, and a peace upon other terms would be the source of perpetual feuds and animosity. Besides, should Britain, from her love of tyranny and lawless domination, attempt again to bend our necks to the yoke of slavery, and there is no doubt but she would, for her pride and ambition are unconquerable, no nation would credit our professions, nor grant us aid. At any rate, their favors would be obtained upon the most disadvantageous and dishonorable terms.

French to Have No Hurt Feelings

To Lafayette, White Plains, September 1, 1778

I feel every thing that hurts the sensibility of a gentleman, and consequently upon the present occasion I feel for you and for our good and great allies the French. I feel myself hurt, also, at every illiberal and unthinking reflection, which may have been cast upon the Count d'Estaing, or the conduct of the fleet under his command; and lastly I feel for my country. Let me entreat you, therefore, my dear Marquis, to take no exception at unmeaning expressions, uttered perhaps without consideration, and in the first transport of disappointed hope. Everybody, Sir, who reasons, will acknowledge the advantages which we have derived from the French fleet, and the zeal of the commander of it; but, in a free and republican government, you cannot restrain the voice of the multitude. Every man will speak as he thinks, or, more properly, without attending to the causes. The censures, which have been levelled at the officers of the French fleet, would more than probably have fallen in a much higher degree upon a fleet of our own (if we had one), in the same situation. It is the nature of man to be displeased with every thing, that disappoints a favorite hope or flattering project; and it is the folly of too many of them to condemn without investigating circumstances. Let me beseech you therefore, my good Sir, to afford a healing hand to the wound, that unintentionally has been made. America esteems your virtues and your services, and admires the principles on which you act.

Can We Win?

To Gouverneur Morris, Fishkill, October 4, 1778

My public Letters to the President of Congress will inform you of the wind that wafted me to this place. Nothing more therefore need be said on that head. Your Letter of the 8th ulto, contains three questions and answers, to wit; Can the Enemy prosecute the war? Do they mean to stay on the Continent? And, is it our interest to put impediments in the way of their departure? To the first you answer in the negative. To the second you are decided in opinion, that they do not. And to the third say clearly, No.

Much, my good Sir, may be said in favor of these answers, and *some* things against the two first of them. By way therefore of dissertation on the first, I will also beg leave to put a question, and give it an answer. Can *we* carry on the war much longer? Certainly NO, unless some measures can be devised & speedily executed to restore the credit of our currency, restrain extortion, & punish forestallers. Without these can be effected, what funds can stand the present expenses of the army? And what officer can bear the weight of prices, that every necessary article is now got to? A Rat in the shape of a horse, is not to be bought at this time for less than £200; A Saddle under Thirty or Forty;—Boots twenty,—and shoes and other articles in the like proportion.—How is it possible, therefore, for officers to stand this without an increase of pay? And how is it possible to advance their Pay, when Flour is selling (at different places) from five to fifteen pounds pr cwt.,—Hay from ten to thirty pounds pr Tunn, and Beef & other essentials in this proportion?

The true point of light, then, to place & consider this matter in is, not simply whether Gt. Britain can carry on the war, but whose Finances, (theirs or ours,) is most likely to fail; which leads me to doubt very much the infallibility of the answer given to your second question, respecting the Enemy's leaving the Continent; for I believe they will not do it, while ever *hope* and the chapter of *accidents* can give them a chance of bringing us to terms short of *Independence*.—But this, *you* will perhaps say, they are now bereft of. I shall acknowledge that many things favor the idea; but add, that, upon a comparative view of circumstances, there is abundant matter to puzzle & confound the judgment. To your third answer I subscribe with hand and heart. The opening is now fair, and God grant that they may embrace the opportunity of bidding an eternal adieu to our (once quit of them) happy Land. If the Spaniards would but join their Fleets to those of France, & commence hostilities, my doubts would all subside. Without it, I fear the British Navy has it too much in its power to counteract the Schemes of France.

The high prices of every necessary; The little, indeed no benefit, which officers have derived from the intended bounty of Congress in the article of cloathing; The change in the establishment, by which so many of them are discontinued; The unfortunate delay of this business, which kept them too long in suspense, and set a number of evil spirits to work; The unsettled Rank, and contradictory modes of adjusting it,—with other causes, which might be enumerated have conspired to sour the temper of the army exceedingly; and has, I am told, been productive of a memorial or representation of some kind to Congress; which neither directly nor indirectly did I know or even hear was in agitation, till some days after it was despatched; owing, as I apprehend, to the secrecy with which it was conducted to keep it from my knowledge, as I had in a similar instance last spring discountenanced and stifled a child of the same illegitimacy in its birth. If you have any news worth communicating, do not put it under a bushel, but give it to, dear Sir, yours sincerely, &c.

To Benjamin Harrison, Speaker of the House of Delegates of Virginia, H. Q., Middlebrook, December 18, 1778

. . . I can assign but two causes for the enemy's continuance among us; and these balance so equally in my mind, that I scarcely know which of the two preponderates. The one is, that they are waiting the ultimate determination of Parliament; the other, that of our distresses, by which I know the Commissioners went home not a little buoyed up, and, sorry I am to add, not without cause.

What may be the effect of such large and frequent emissions, of the dissensions,—parties,—extravagance, and a general lax of public virtue, Heaven alone can tell! I am afraid even to think of it. But it appears as clear to me as ever the Sun did in its meridian brightness, that America never stood in more eminent need of the wise, patriotic, and spirited exertions of her Sons than at this period; and if it is not a sufficient cause for genl. lamentation, my misconception of the matter impresses it too strongly upon me, that the States, separately, are too much engaged in their local concerns, and have too many of their ablest men withdrawn from the general council, for the good of the common weal. In a word, I think our political system may be compared to the mechanism of a clock, and that our conduct should derive a lesson from it; for it answers no good purpose to keep the smaller wheels in order, if the greater one, which is the support and prime mover of the whole, is neglected.

How far the latter is the case, it does not become me to pronounce; but, as there can be no harm in a pious wish for the good of one's Country, I shall offer it as mine, that each State wd. not only choose, but absolutely compel their ablest men to attend Congress; and that they would instruct them to go into a thorough investigation of the causes, that have produced so many disagreeable effects in the army and Country; in a word, that public abuses should be corrected & an entire reformation worked. Without these, it does not in my Judgment require the spirit of divination to foretell the consequences of the present administration; nor to how little purpose the States individually are framing constitutions, providing laws, and filling offices with the abilities of their ablest men. These, if the great whole is mismanaged, must sink in the general wreck, and will carry with it the remorse of thinking, that we are lost by our own folly and negligence, or the desire perhaps of living in ease and tranquillity during the expected accomplishment of so great a revolution, in the effecting of which the greatest abilities, and the honestest men our (i.e. the American) world affords, ought to be employed.

It is much to be feared, my dear Sir, that the States, in their separate capacities, have very inadequate ideas of the present danger. Removed (some of them) far distant from the scene of action, and seeing and hearing such publications only, as flatter their wishes, they conceive that the contest is at an end, and that to regulate the government and police of their own State is all that remains to be done; but it is devoutly to be wished, that a sad reverse of this may not fall upon them like a thunder-clap, that is little expected. I do not mean to designate particular States. I wish to cast no reflections upon any one. The Public believe (and, if they do *believe* it, the fact might almost as well be so), that the States at this time are badly represented, and that the great and important concerns of the nation are horribly conducted, for want either of abilities or application in the members, or through the discord & party views of some individuals. That they should be so, is to be lamented more at this time than formerly, as we are far advanced in the dispute, and, in the opinn. of many, drawg. to a happy period; have the eyes of Europe upon us, and I am persuaded many political spies to watch, discover our situation and give information of our weaknesses and wants. The story you have related, of a proposal to redeem ye paper money at its present depreciated value, has also come to my ears; but I cannot vouch for the authenticity of it.

I am very happy to hear, that the Assembly of Virginia have put the completion of their regiments upon a footing so apparently certain; but, as one great defect of your past Laws for this purpose has lain in the mode of getting men to the army, I hope that effectual measures are pointed out in the present to remedy the evil, and bring forward all that shall be raised. The embargo upon provisions is a most salutary measure, as I am afraid a sufficiency of flour will not be obtained, even with money of higher estimation than ours. Adieu, my dear Sir. I am, &c.

P. S. Phila: 30th. This letter was to have gone by Post from Middlebrook but missed that conveyance, since which I have come to this place at the request of Congress whence I shall soon return.

I have seen nothing since I came here (on the 22d Inst.) to change my opinion of Men or Measrs., but abundant reason to be convinced that our affairs are in a more distressed, ruinous, and deplorable condition than they have been in since the commencement of the War.—By a faithful laborer then in the cause—By a

Man who is daily injuring his private Estate without even the smallest earthly advantage not common to all in case of a favorable Issue to the dispute—By one who wishes the prosperity of America most devoutly and sees or thinks he sees it, on the brink of ruin, you are beseeched most earnestly, my dear Colo. Harrison, to exert yourself in endeavoring to rescue your Country by (let me add) sending your ablest and best Men to Congress—these characters must not slumber nor sleep at home in such times of pressing danger—they must not content themselves in the enjoyment of places of honor or profit in their own Country while the common interests of America are mouldering and sinking into irretrievable (if a remedy is not soon applied) ruin in which theirs also must ultimately be involved. If I was to be called upon to draw a picture of the times and of Men, from what I have seen, and heard, and in part know, I should in one word say that idleness, dissipation & extravagance seems to have laid fast hold of most of them.—That speculation—peculation—and an insatiable thirst for riches seems to have got the better of every other consideration and almost of every order of Men.—That party disputes and personal quarrels are the great business of the day whilst the momentous concerns of an empire—a great and accumulated debt —ruined finances—depreciated money—and want of credit (which in their consequences is the want of everything) are but secondary considerations and postponed from day to day—from week to week as if our affairs wear the most promising aspect—after drawing this picture, which from my Soul I believe to be a true one, I need not repeat to you that I am alarmed and wish to see my Countrymen roused.—I have no resentments, nor do I mean to point at any particular characters,—this I can declare upon my honor for I have every attention paid me by Congress that I can possibly expect and have reason to think that I stand well in their estimation, but in the present situation of things I cannot help asking—Where is Mason—Wythe—Jefferson—Nicholas—Pendleton—Nelson—and another I could name—and why, if you are sufficiently impressed with your danger do you not (as New Yk. has done in the case of Mr. Jay) send an extra member or two for at least a certain limited time till the great business of the Nation is put upon a more respectable and happy establishmt.—Your Money is now sinking 5 pr. ct. a day in this city; and I shall not be surprized if in the course of a few months a total stop is put to the currency of it.—And yet an Assembly—a concert—a Dinner—or supper (that will cost three or four hundred pounds) will not only take Men off from acting in but even from thinking of this business while a great part of the Officers of ye Army from absolute necessity are quitting the service and ye more virtuous few rather than do this are sinking by sure degrees into beggary and want.—I again repeat to you that this is not an exaggerated acct.; that it is an alarming one I do not deny, and confess to you that I feel more real distress on acct. of the prest. appearances of things than I have done at any one time since the commencement of the dispute—but it is time to bid you once more adieu. Providence has heretofore taken me up when all other means and hope seemed to be departing from me in this. I will confide.—Yours.

Managing Public Opinion

To John Jay,[4] Middlebrook, March 1, 1779

I have been a little surprised, that the several important pieces of intelligence lately received from Europe (such parts I mean, as are circulated without reserve in conversation), have been given to the public in a manner calculated to attract the attention and impress the minds of the people. As they are now propagated, they run through the country in a variety of forms, are confounded in the common mass of general rumors, and lose a great part of their effect. It would certainly be attended with many valuable consequences if they could be given to the people in some more authentic and pointed manner. It would assist the measures taken to restore our currency, promote the recruiting of the army and our other military arrangements, and give a certain spring to our affairs in general. Congress may have particular reasons for not communicating the intelligence officially (which would certainly be the best mode if it could be done); but, if it cannot, it were to be wished,

[4] President of Congress.

that as much as is intended to be commonly known, could be published in as striking a way, and with as great an appearance of authority as may be consistent with propriety.

I have taken the liberty to trouble you with this hint, as sometimes things the most obvious escape attention.

Arming Slaves

To Henry Laurens, Middlebrook, March 20, 1779

The policy of our arming slaves is in my opinion a moot point, unless the enemy set the example. For, should we begin to form Battalions of them, I have not the smallest doubt, if the war is to be prosecuted, of their following us in it, and justifying the measure upon our own ground. The upshot then must be, who can arm fastest. And where are our arms? Besides, I am not clear that a discrimination will not render slavery more irksome to those who remain in it. Most of the good and evil things in this life are judged of by comparison; and I fear a comparison in this case will be productive of much discontent in those, who are held in servitude. But, as this is a subject that has never employed much of my thoughts, these are no more than the first crude Ideas that have struck me upon ye occasion.

Liberties in Danger

To George Mason, Middlebrook, March 27, 1779

. . . Though it is not in my power to devote much time to a private correspondence owing to the multiplicity of public Letters & other business I have to read, write, & transact; yet, I can with great truth assure you that it would afford me very singular pleasure to be favored at all times with your sentiments in a leizure hour upon public matters of general concernment, as well as those which more immediately respect your own State, if proper conveyances would render prudent a free communication. I am particularly desirous of it at this time because I view things very differently, I fear, from what the people in general do, who seem to think the contest is at an end, & to make money, and get places the only things now remaining to do. I have seen without despondency even for a momt.—the hours which America have stiled her gloomy ones, but I have beheld no day since the commencement of hostilities that I have thought her liberties in such eminent danger as at present.

Friends and Foes seem now to combine to pull down the goodly fabric we have hitherto been raising at the expense of so much time, blood, & treasure—& unless the bodies politic will exert themselves to bring things back to first principles—correct abuses —& punish our internal Foes inevitable ruin must follow,—indeed we seem to be verging so fast to destruction that I am filled with sensations to which I have been a stranger till within these three months.

Our Enemy, behold with exultation & joy, how effectually we labor for their benefit; and from being in a state of absolute despair, and on the point of evacuating America, are now on tiptoe—nothing therefore, in my judgement, can save us but a total reformation in our own conduct or some decisive turn to affairs in Europe. The former alas! to our shame be it spoken! is less likely to happen than the latter; as it is more consistent with the views of the speculators—various tribes of money makers & stock jobbers of all denominations to continue the War for their own private emolument without considering that their avarice & thirst for gain must plunge every thing, including themselves in one common ruin.

Were I to endulge my present feelings, & give a loose to that freedom of expression which my unreserved friendship for you would prompt me to, I should say a great deal on this subject.

But letters are liable to so many accidents, & the sentiments of men in office sought after by the enemy with so much avidity, & besides, conveying useful knowledge (if they get into their hands) for the superstructure of their plans, if often perverted to the wors[t] of purposes that I shall be somewhat reserved notwithstanding this letter goes by a private hand to Mount Vernon.—I cannot refrain lamenting, however, in the most poignant terms, the fatal policy too prevalent in most of the States of employing their ablest men at home in posts of honor or profit, till the great National Interest is fixed upon a solid basis.—To me, it appears no unjust simile to compare the affairs of this great Continent to the mechanism of a clock, each state representing some one or other of the smaller parts of it which they are endeavoring to put in fine order without considering how useless & unavailing their labor is unless the great Wheel, or Spring which is to set the whole in motion is also well attended to—& kept in good order—I allude to no particular state—nor do I mean to cast reflections upon any of them—nor ought I, it may be said to do so upon their representatives; but, as it is a fact too notorious to be concealed that C—— [Congress] is rent by Party—that much business of a trifling nature & personal concernment withdraw their attention from matters of great national moment at this critical period.—When it is also known that idleness & dissipation take place of close attention & application, a man who wishes well to the liberties of his Country and desires to see its rights established cannot avoid crying out where are our men of abilities? Why do they not come forth to save their Country? let this voice my dear Sir call upon you—Jefferson & others—do not from a mistaken opinion that we are about to set down under our own vine, & our own fig tree, let our hitherto noble struggle end in ignom'y—believe me when I tell you there is danger of it—I have pretty good reasons for thinking that Administration a little while ago had resolved to give the matter up, and negotiate a peace with us upon almost any terms; but I shall be much mistaken if they do not now from the present state of our currency dissentions & other circumstances push matters to the utmost extremity—nothing I am sure will prevent it but the interposition of Spain, & their disappointed hope from Russia.

I thank you most cordially for your kind offer of rendering me services. I shall without reserve, as heretofore, call upon you whenever instances occur that may require it, being with the sincerest regard, &c.

Decay of Public Virtue

To James Warren, March 31, 1779

. . . Our conflict is not likely to cease so soon as every good man would wish. The measure of iniquity is not yet filled; and, unless we can return a little more to first principles, and act a little more upon patriotic grounds, I do not know when it will, or what may be the issue of the contest. Speculation, Peculation, Engrossing, forestalling, with all their concomitants, afford too many melancholy proofs of the decay of public virtue, and too glaring instances of its being the interest and desire of too many, who would wish to be thought friends, to continue the war. Nothing, I am convinced, but the depreciation of our currency, proceeding in a great measure from the foregoing causes, aided by stockjobbing and party dissensions, has fed the hopes of the Enemy and kept the B. arms in America to this day. They do not scruple to declare this themselves, and add, that we shall be our own conquerors. Cannot our common country, Ama., possess virtue enough to disappoint them? Is the paltry consideration of a little dirty pelf to individuals to be placed in competition with the essential rights and liberties of the present generation, and of millions yet unborn? Shall a few designing men, for their own aggrandizement, & to gratify their own avarice, overset the goodly fabric we have been rearing at the expense of so much time, blood, & treasure? And shall we at last become the victims of our own abominable lust of gain? Forbid it Heaven! Forbid it all & every State in the Union! by enacting & enforcing efficacious laws for checking the growth of these monstrous evils, & restoring matters in some degree to the pristine state they were in at the commencement of the war!

Our cause is noble. It is the cause of mankind, and the danger to it is to be apprehended from ourselves. Shall we slumber and sleep, then, while we should be punishing those miscreants, who have brot. these troubles upon us, & who are aimg. to continue us in them; while we should be striving to fill our battalions, & devising ways and means to appreciate the currency, on the credit of wch. every thing depends? I hope not. Let vigorous measures be adopted; not to limit the prices of articles, for this I believe is inconsistent with the very nature of things, and impracticable in itself; but to punish speculators, forestallers, & extortioners, and above all to sink the money by heavy taxes, to promote public & private economy. Encourage manufactures &c. Measures of this sort, gone heartily into by the several States, would strike at once at the root of all our evils, & give the *coup de grace* to British hope of subjugating this continent, either by their arms or their arts. The first, as I have before observed, they acknowledge is unequal to the task; the latter I am sure will be so, if we are not lost to every thing that is good & virtuous.

Drinks for Army

To the President of Congress, H. Q., New Windsor, June 27, 1779

I have frequent applications from the officers for allowances of spirits; supported by a plea that it is done elsewhere. I am informed that the officers at Providence are supplied with rum at the rate of nine shilgs @ gallon. I think it highly reasonable and necessary, that they should be supplied at a moderate rate proportioned to their pay; but as there is no authority for doing it, I do not think myself at liberty to adopt the measure; at the same time I should be happy to see so reasonable a request gratified, and the whole put upon an equal footing by some general regulation . . . My situation, as the affair now stands, is delicate and disagreeable. The officers of this Army will not be satisfied with less indulgence than is enjoyed by those of other troops. They may view the refusal on my part as too punctilious and rigid. This concurs with other reasons to make me anxious a speedy determination should take place, either to make the allowance general or prevent it everywhere.

Contempt for British Policy and Corruption

To Major General Robert Howe, West Point, November 20, 1779

Herewith you will receive Mr. Pulteney's lucubrations,[5] and my thanks for the perusal of them. He has made, I perceive, the dependence of America essential to the existence of Great Britain, as a powerful nation. This I shall not deny, because I am in sentiment with him in thinking her fallen state in consequence of the separation, too obvious to be disputed. It was of magnitude sufficient to have made a wise and just people look before they leaped. But I am glad to find that he has placed the supplies necessary to support that dependence upon three things which I am persuaded will never again exist in his nation—namely, public virtue, public economy, and public union in her grand council.

Stock jobbing, speculation, dissipation, luxury and venality, with all their concomitants, are too deeply rooted to yield to virtue and the public good. *We* that are not yet hackneyed in vice—but infants, as it were, in the arts of corruption . . . find it almost, if not quite impossible to preserve virtue enough to keep the body politic and corporate in tolerable tune. It is scarcely to be expected therefore that a people who have reduced these things to a system and have actually interwoven them into their constitution should at once become immaculate.

I do not know which rises highest—my indignation or contempt, for the sentiments which pervade the ministerial writings of this day—these hireling scribblers labor to describe and prove the ingratitude of America in not breaking faith with France—& returning to her allegiance to the Crown of Great Britain after its having offered such advantageous terms of accommodation. Such sentiments as these are insulting to common sense and affrontive to every principle of sound policy and common honesty. Why has she offered these terms?—because after a bloody contest, carried on with unrelenting and savage fury on her part the issue (which was somewhat doubtful while we stood alone) is now become certain

[5] *Thoughts on the Present State of Affairs with America, and the Means of Conciliation,* a British pamphlet that went through many editions.

by the aid we derive from our Alliance. Notwithstanding . . . we are told with an effrontery altogether unparalleled that every cause of complaint is now done away by the generous offers of a tender parent—that it is ungrateful in us not to accept the proffered terms, and impolitic not to abandon a power . . . which held out a saving hand to us in the hour of our distress. What epithet does such sentiments merit? How much should a people possessed of them be despised? From my soul I abhor them! A manly struggle, had it been conducted upon liberal ground, and honest confession that they were unequal to conquest, and wished for our friendship, would have had its proper weight—but their cruelties . . . the wanton depredations committed by themselves and their faithful allies, the Indians—their low and dirty practices of counterfeiting our money—forging letters—and condescending to adopt such arts as the meanest villain in private life would blush at being charged with, has made me their fixed enemy.

Military Order and Discipline

To Lord Stirling, Morristown, March 5, 1780

Orders, unless they are followed by close attention to the performance of them, are of little avail. They are read by some, only heard of by others, and inaccurately attended to by all, whilst by a few they are totally disregarded . . .

Example, whether it be good or bad, has a powerful influence, and the higher in Rank the officer is, who sets it, the more striking it is. Hence, and from all military experience, it has been found necessary for officers of every denomination to inspect narrowly the conduct of such parts of the army and corps, as are committed to their care. . . . Of course neglect of discipline, want of order, irregularity, waste, abuse, and embezzlement of public property, insensibly creep in . . . But, if the Persons issuing them [orders] would devote, as duty indispensably requires, a reasonable portion of their time to a personal and close inspection into the affairs of their respective commands; would frequently parade their Regiments, and compare the actual strength of them, their arms, accoutrements, and clothes, with the returns, and have the deficiencies (if any there be) satisfactorily accounted for and provided . . . would see that the regulations, the general orders, and their own, were carried into execution, where practicable, or report the cause of failure when they cannot; that all returns are made in due form, in proper time, and correctly, comparing one return with another, in order to prevent mistakes, correct abuses, and do justice to the public; and that, in visiting such parts of the line, and such particular corps, as are entrusted to their care, praise is bestowed on the deserving, reprehension, and (where necessary) punishment on the negligent; the good effect would be almost instantaneously felt. Frequent visits and inspection into matters of this kind would produce more real good in one month, than volumes of the best digested orders, that the wit of man can devise, wd. accomplish in seven years.

Army Morale

To the President of Congress, H. Q., Morristown, April 3, 1780

. . . Before I conclude, I think it my duty to touch upon the general situation of the army at this juncture. It is absolutely necessary Congress should be apprized of it, for it is difficult to foresee what may be the result; and, as very serious consequences are to be apprehended, I should not be justified in preserving silence. There never has been a stage of the war, in which the dissatisfaction has been so general or alarming. It has lately, in particular instances, worn features of a very dangerous complexion. A variety of causes has contributed to this; The diversity in the terms of enlistments, the inequality of the rewards given for entering into the service, but still more the disparity in the provision made by the several States for the respective Troops. The system of State supplies, however in the commencement dictated by necessity, has proved in its operation pernicious beyond description. An army must be raised, paid, subsisted, and regulated upon an equal and uniform principle, or the confusions and discontents are endless. Little less than the dissolution of the army would have been long since the consequence of a different plan, had it not been for a spirit of patriotic virtue, both in officers and men, of which there are few examples, seconded by the unremitting pains that have been taken to compose and reconcile them to their situation. But these will not be able to hold out much longer against the influence of causes constantly operating, and every day with some new aggravation.

Some States, from their internal ability and local advantages, furnish their Troops pretty amply, not only with cloathing, but with many little comforts and conveniences; others supply them with some necessaries, but on a more contracted scale; while others have it in their power to do little or nothing at all. The officers and men in the routine of duty mix dayly and compare circumstances. Those, who fare worse than others, of course are dissatisfied, and have their resentment excited, not only against their own State, but against the Confederacy. They become disgusted with a service that makes such injurious distinctions. No arguments can persuade an officer it is justice he should be obliged to pay £— a yard for cloth, and other things in proportion, while another is furnished at part of the price. The officers resign, and we have now scarcely a sufficient number left to take care even of the fragments of corps which remain. The men have not this resource. They murmur, brood over their discontents, and have lately shown a disposition to enter into seditious combinations.

A new scene is now opening, which I fear will be productive of more troublesome effects, than any thing that has hitherto taken place. Some of the States have adopted the measure of making good the depreciation of the money to their Troops, as well for the past as for the future. If this does not become general, it is so striking a point, that the consequences must be unspeakably mischievous. I enter not into the propriety of this measure in the view of finance, but confine myself to its operation upon the army. Neither do I mean to insinuate, that the liberality of particular States has been carried to a blamable length. The evil I mean to point out is the inequality of the different provisions, and this is inherent in the present system. It were devoutly to be wished, a plan could be devised by which every thing relating to the army could be conducted on a general principle, under the direction of Congress. This alone can give harmony and consistence to our military establishment, and I am persuaded it will be infinitely conducive to public economy. I hope I shall not be thought to have exceeded my duty in the unreserved manner in which I have exhibited our situation. Congress, I flatter myself, will have the goodness to believe, that I have no other motives than a zeal for the public service, a desire to give them every necessary information, and an apprehension for the consequences of the evils we now experience. I have the honor to be, &c.

To the President of Congress, H. Q., Morristown, May 27, 1780

It is with infinite pain I inform Congress, that we are reduced again to a situation of extremity for want of meat. On several days of late, the Troops have been entirely destitute of any, and for a considerable time past they have been at best, at half, a quarter, an Eighth allowance of this essential article of provision. The men have borne their distress in general with a firmness and patience never exceeded, and every commendation is due the officers for encouraging them to it, by exhortation and by example. They have suffered equally with the men, and their relative situations considered, rather more. But such reiterated, constant instances of want are too much for the soldiery, and cannot but lead to alarming consequences. Accordingly Two Regiments of the Connecticut line mutinied, and got under arms on Thursday night. And but for the timely exertions of some of their officers, who got notice of it, it might have been the case with the whole, with a determination to return home, or at best to gain subsistence at the point of the bayonet. After a good deal of expostulation by their officers and some of the Pennsylvania line, who had come to their assistance, and after parading their regiments upon the occasion, the men were prevailed on to go to their huts; but a few nevertheless turned out again with their packs, who are now confined. Colonel Meigs, who acted with great propriety in endeavoring to suppress the mutiny, was struck by one of the soldiers. I wish our situation was better with respect to provision in other quarters, but it is not. They are in as great distress at West Point to the full; and, by a Letter of the 19th from Colo. Van Schaick at Albany, he informs me, that the Garrison of Fort Schuyler had then only a month's supply on hand, and that there was no more provision to send them. From this detail Congress will see how distressing our situation is; but there are other matters which still contribute to render it more alarming.

To Fielding Lewis, July 6, 1780

I may lament in the bitterness of my soul, that the fatal policy which has pervaded all our measures from the beginning of the war, and which no experience however dear bought can change, should have reduced our army to so low an ebb, as not to have given a more effectual opposition to those movements than we did; or that we should be obliged to be removing our stores from place to place to keep them out of the way of the enemy instead of driving that enemy from our country—but our weakness invited these insults, and why they did not *attempt at least* to do more than they did, I cannot conceive. Nor will it be easy to make any one at the distance of 400 miles believe that our army, weakened as it is by the expiration of men's enlistments, should at times be five or six days together without meat—then as many without bread—and once or twice, two or three days together without either—and that, in the same army, there should be numbers of men with scarcely as much cloathing as would cover their nakedness, and at least a fourth of the whole with not even the shadow of a blanket, severe as the winter has been. Under these circumstances it is no difficult matter to conceive what a time I must have had to keep up appearances and prevent the most disastrous consequences.

It may be asked how these things have come to pass? the answer is plain—and may be ascribed to the want of system, not to say foresight—originally (if it is not still the case with some) to a fatal jealousy (under our circumstances) of a standing army—by which means we neglected to obtain soldiers for the war when zeal and patriotism run high, and men were eager to engage for a trifle or for nothing; the consequence of which has been that we have protracted the war—expended millions and tens of millions of pounds which might have been saved, and have a new army to raise and discipline once or twice a year, and with which we can undertake nothing because we have nothing to build upon, as the men are slipping from us every day by means of their expiring enlistments. To these fundamental errors, may be added another which I expect will prove our ruin, and that is the relinquishment of Congressional powers to the States individually—all the business is now *attempted,* for it is not done, by a timid kind of recommendation from Congress to the States; the consequence of which is, that instead of pursuing one uniform system, which in the execution shall corrispond in time and manner, each State undertakes to determine—

1st. Whether they will comply or not.

2nd. In what manner they will do it, and

3d. In what time—by which means scarcely any one measure is, or can be executed, while great expences are incurred and the willing and zealous States ruined. In a word our measures are not under the influence and direction of one council, but thirteen, each of which is actuated by local views and politics, without considering the fatal consequences of not complying with plans which the united wisdom of America in its representative capacity have digested, or the unhappy tendency of delay, mutilation or alteration. I do not scruple to add, and I give it decisively as my opinion—that unless the States will content themselves with a full and well-chosen representation in Congress and vest that body with absolute powers in all matters relative to the great purposes of war, and of general concern (by which the States unitedly are affected, reserving to themselves all matters of local and internal polity for the regulation of order and good government) we are attempting an impossibility, and very soon shall become (if it is not already the case) a many-headed monster—a heterogenious mass—that never will or can steer to the same point. The contest among the different States *now* is not which shall do most for the common cause—but which shall do least, hence arise disappointments and delay, one State waiting to see what another will or will not do, through fear of doing too much, and by their deliberations, alterations, and sometimes refusals to comply with the requisitions of Congress, after that Congress spent months in reconciling (as far as it is possible) jarring interests, in order to frame their resolutions, as far as the nature of the case will admit, upon principles of equality.

There is another source from whence much of our present distress, and past difficulties have flowed, and that is the hope and expectation which seizes the States, and Congress toward the close of every year, that Peace must take place in the Winter— This never fails to produce an apathy which lulls them into ease and security, and involves the most distressing consequences at the opening of every campaign. We may rely upon it that we shall never have Peace till the enemy are convinced that we are in a condition to carry on the war. It is no new maxim in politics that for a nation to obtain Peace, or insure it, it must be prepared for war.

But it is time for me to recollect myself and quit a subject which would require a folio volume to illucidate, and expose the folly of our measures. To rectify past blunders is impossible, but we might profit by the experience of them, tho' even here I doubt, as I am furnished with many instances to the contrary. . . .

No Provisions

To Brigadier General John Cadwalader, October 5, 1780

. . . We have been half of our time without provision, and are likely to continue so. We have no magazines, nor money to form them; and in a little time we shall have no men, if we had money to pay them. We have lived upon expedients till we can live no longer. In a word, the history of the war is a history of false hopes and temporary devices, instead of system and of economy. It is in vain, however, to look back, nor is it our business to do so. Our case is not desperate, if virtue exists in the people, and there is wisdom among our rulers. But to suppose that this great revolution can be accomplished by a temporary army, that this army will be subsisted by State supplies, and that taxation alone is adequate to our wants, is in my opinion absurd, and as unreasonable as to expect an Inversion in the order of nature to accommodate itself to our views. If it was necessary, it could easily be proved to any person of a moderate share of understanding, that an annual army or an army raised on the spur of the occasion, besides being unqualified for the end designed, is, in various ways which could be enumerated, ten times more expensive than a permanent body of men, under good organization and military discipline, which never was nor never will be the case of new Troops. A thousand arguments, resulting from experience and the nature of things, might also be adduced to prove, that the army, if it is to depend upon State supplies, must disband or starve; and that taxation alone, (especially at this late hour,) cannot furnish the means to carry on the War. Is it not time then to retract from error, and benefit by experience? Or do we want further proof of the ruinous system we have pertinaciously adhered to?

Present State of Affairs

To Lieutenant Colonel John Laurens, New Windsor, January 15, 1781

In compliance with your request I shall commit to writing the result of our conferences on the present state of American affairs, in which I have given you my ideas with that freedom and explicitness, which the objects of your commission, my entire confidence in you, and the exigency demand. To me it appears evident:

1st. That, considering the diffused population of these States, the consequent difficulty of drawing together its resources, the composition and temper of *a part* of the inhabitants, the want of a sufficient stock of national wealth as a foundation for revenue, and the almost total extinction of commerce, the efforts we have been compelled to make for carrying on the war have exceeded the natural abilities of this country, and by degrees brought it to a crisis, which renders immediate and efficacious succors from abroad indispensable to its safety.

2dly. That, notwithstanding, from the confusion always attendant on a revolution, from our having had governments to frame and every species of civil and military institutions to create, from that inexperience in affairs necessarily incident to a nation in its commencement, some errors may have been committed in the administration of our finances, to which a part of our embarrassments are to be attributed; yet they are principally to be ascribed to an essential defect of means, to the want of a sufficient stock of wealth, as mentioned in the first article, which, continuing to operate, will make it impossible by any merely interior exertions to extricate ourselves from those embarrassments, restore public credit, and furnish the funds requisite for the support of the war.

3dly. That experience has demonstrated the impracticability long to maintain a paper credit without funds for its redemption. The depreciation of our currency was in the main a necessary effect of the want of those funds; and its restoration is impossible for the same reason, to which the general diffidence that has taken place among the people is an additional and, in the present state of things, an insuperable obstacle.

4thly. That the mode, which for want of money has been substituted for supplying the army, by assessing a proportion of the productions of the earth, has hitherto been found ineffectual, has frequently exposed the army to the most calamitous distress, and, from its novelty and incompatibility with ancient habits, is regarded by the people as burthensome and oppressive, has excited serious discontents, and in some places alarming symptoms of opposition. This mode has, besides, many particular inconveniences, which contribute to make it inadequate to our wants, and ineligible but as an auxiliary.

5thly. That, from the best estimates of the annual expense of the war and the annual revenues which these States are capable of affording, there is a large balance to be supplied by public credit. The resource of domestic loans is inconsiderable, because there are properly speaking few moneyed men, and the few there are can employ their money more profitably otherwise; added to which, the instability of the currency and the deficiency of funds have impaired the public credit.

6thly. That the patience of the army, from an almost uninterrupted series of complicated distress, is now nearly exhausted, and their discontents matured to an extremity, which has recently had very disagreeable consequences, and which demonstrates the absolute necessity of speedy relief, a relief not within the compass of our means. You are too well acquainted with all their sufferings for want of clothing, for want of provisions, for want of pay.

7thly. That, the people being dissatisfied with the mode of supporting the war, there is cause to apprehend, that evils actually felt in the prosecution may weaken those sentiments which began it, founded, not on immediate sufferings, but on a speculative apprehension of future sufferings from the loss of their liberties. There is danger, that a commercial and free people, little accustomed to heavy burthens, pressed by impositions of a new and odious kind, may not make a proper allowance for the necessity of the conjuncture, and may imagine they have only exchanged one tyranny for another.

8thly. That, from all the foregoing considerations result, 1st, absolute necessity of an immediate, ample, and efficacious succor in money, large enough to be a foundation for substantial arrangements of finance, to revive public credit, and give vigor to future operations; 2dly, the vast importance of a decided effort of the allied arms on this continent, the ensuing campaign, to effectuate once for all the great objects of the alliance, the liberty and independence of these States. Without the first we may make a feeble and expiring effort the next campaign, in all probability the period to our opposition. With it, we should be in a condition to continue the war, as long as the obstinacy of the enemy might require. The first is essential to the latter; both combined would bring the contest to a glorious issue, crown the obligations, which America already feels to the magnanimity and generosity of her ally, and perpetuate the union by all the ties of gratitude and affection, as well as mutual advantage, which alone can render it solid and indissoluble.

9thly. That, next to a loan of money, a constant naval superiority on these coasts is the object most interesting. This would instantly reduce the enemy to a difficult defensive, and, by removing all prospect of extending their acquisitions, would take away the motives for prosecuting the war. Indeed, it is not to be conceived how they could subsist a large force in this country, if we had the command of the seas, to interrupt the regular transmission of supplies from Europe. This superiority, (with an aid in money,) would enable us to convert the war into a vigorous offensive. I say nothing of the advantages to the trade of both nations, nor how infinitely it would facilitate our supplies. With respect to us, it seems to be one of *two* deciding points; and it appears, too, to be the interest of our allies, abstracted from the immediate benefits to this country, to transfer the naval war to America. The number of ports friendly to them, hostile to the British, the materials for repairing their disabled ships, the extensive supplies towards the subsistence of their fleet, are circumstances which would give them a palpable advantage in the contest of these seas.

10thly. That an additional succor in troops would be extremely desirable. Besides a reinforcement of numbers, the excellence of French troops, that perfect discipline and order in the corps already sent, which have so happily tended to improve the respect and confidence of the people for our allies, the conciliating disposition and the zeal for the service, which distinguish every rank, sure indications of lasting harmony,—all these considerations evince the immense utility of an accession of force to the corps now here. Correspondent with these motives, the enclosed minutes of a conference between their Excellencies the Count de Rochambeau, the Chevalier de Ternay, and myself will inform you, that an augmentation to fifteen thousand men was judged expedient for the next campaign; and it has been signified to me, that an application has been made to the court of France to this effect. But if the sending so large a succor in troops should necessarily diminish the pecuniary aid, which our allies may be disposed to grant, it were preferable to diminish the aid in men; for the same sum of money, which would transport from France and maintain here a body of troops with all the necessary apparatus, being put into our hands to be employed by us, would serve to give activity to a larger force within ourselves, and its influence would pervade the whole administration.

11thly. That no nation will have it more in its power to repay what it borrows than this. Our debts are hitherto small. The vast and valuable tracts of unlocated lands, the variety and fertility of climates and soils, the advantages of every kind which we possess for commerce, insure to this country a rapid advancement in population and prosperity, and a certainty, its independence being established, of redeeming in a short term of years the comparatively inconsiderable debts it may have occasion to contract.

That, notwithstanding the difficulties under which we labor, and the inquietudes prevailing among the people, there is still a fund of inclination and resource in the country, equal to great and continued exertions, provided we have it in our power to stop the progress of disgust, by changing the present system, and adopting another more consonant with the spirit of the nation, and more capable of activity and energy in public measures; of which a powerful succor of money must be the basis. The people are discontented; but it is with the feeble and oppressive mode of conducting the war, not with the war itself. They are not unwilling to contribute to its support, but they are unwilling to do it in a way that renders private property precarious; a necessary consequence of the fluctuation of the national currency, and of the inability of government to perform its engagements oftentimes coercively made. A large majority are still firmly attached to the independence of these States, abhor a reunion with Great Britain, and are affectionate to the alliance with France; but this disposition cannot supply the place of means customary and essential in war, nor can we rely on its duration amidst the perplexities, oppressions, and misfortunes, that attend the want of them.

Military Discipline

To the President of Congress, H. Q., New Windsor, February 3, 1781

I have on different occasions done myself the honor to represent to Congress the inconveniences arising from the want of a proper gradation of punishments in our military code . . . The highest corporal punishment we are allowed to give is a hundred lashes; between that and death there are no degrees. Instances dayly occurring of offences for which the former is entirely inadequate, Courts-Martial, in order to preserve some proportion between the crime and the punishment, are obliged to pronounce sentence of death. Capital sentences on this account become more frequent in our service, than in most cases expedient; and it happens from this, that the greater offences often escape punishment, while lesser are commonly punished . . .

The inconveniences of this defect are obvious. Congress are sensible of the necessity of punishment in an army, of the justice and policy of a due proportion between the crime and the penalty. . . . It appears to me indispensable that there should be an extension of the present corporal punishment, and also that it would be useful to authorize Courts-Martial to sentence delinquents to labor at public works; perhaps even for some crimes, particularly desertions, to transfer them from the land to the sea service, where they have less opportunity to indulge their inconstancy. A variety in punishment is of utility, as well as a proportion. The number of lashes may either be indefinite, left to the discretion of the Court to fix or limited to a larger number. In this case I would recommend five hundred.

Rejects Monarchy

To Colonel Lewis Nicola, May 22, 1782

With a mixture of great surprise and astonishment, I have read with attention the sentiments [that the Army wished Washington to take the title of king] you have submitted to my perusal. Be assured, Sir, no occurrence in the course of the war has given me more painful sensations, than your information of there being such ideas existing in the army, as you have expressed, and I must view with abhorrence and reprehend with severity. For the present the communication of them will rest in my own bosom, unless some further agitation of the matter shall make a disclosure necessary.

I am much at a loss to conceive what part of my conduct could have given encouragement to an address, which to me seems big with the greatest mischiefs, that can befall my Country. If I am not deceived in the knowledge of myself, you could not have found a person to whom your schemes are more disagreeable. . . . Let me conjure you, then, if you have any regard for your country, concern for yourself or posterity, or respect for me, to banish these thoughts from your mind, and never communicate, as from yourself or anyone else, a sentiment of like nature.

Duties of a Good Officer

To Major Thomas Lansdale, Newburgh, January 25, 1783

I was hurt yesterday at the appearance of the Detachment under your Command, as I conceive you must have been, if you viewed and drew a comparison between it and the Regiment on your Left . . .

Dirt and Trash too, of every denomination was so liberally strewed, even upon your parade, and immediately before the doors of your Hutts, that it was difficult to avoid the Filth.

The true distinction, Sir, between what is called a fine Regiment, and an indifferent one will ever . . . be found to originate in, and depend upon the care, or the inattention, of the Officers . . . That Regiment whose Officers are watchful of their men, and attentive to their wants, who will see that proper use is made, and a proper account taken, of whatever is drawn for them; and that Regimental and Company Inspections are frequent in order to examine into the state of their Arms, ammunition, Clothing, and other necessaries, to prevent loss or embezzlement;—who will see that the Soldiers Clothes are well made, kept whole, and clean; that their Hutts are swept and purified; that the Trash, and all kinds of Offal is either burnt or buried; that Vaults or proper necessaries are erected and every person punished who shall on those occasions go elsewhere in the Camp; that their Provision is in good order well cooked and eat at proper hours;—those Officers, I say, who attend to these things—and their duty strictly enjoins it on them—give health, comfort, and a Military pride to their Men, which fires and fits them for every thing great and noble. It is by this means the character of a Regiment is exalted while sloth, inattention, and neglect produce the reverse of these in every particular and must infallibly lessen the reputation of the Corps.

I observed with concern that none of your officers had espontoons; that some of them were even without side arms; and of those that had, some were so remiss in their duty as not to know they were to salute with them. . . . I . . . recommend in pointed terms to your Officers the necessity and advantage of making themselves perfectly masters of the printed "Regulations for the Order and Discipline of the Troops of the United States." Ignorance of them cannot, nor will it be any excuse . . .

As it is the first time I have seen them under Arms, and some allowance is to be made for the rawness of the Corps, I will substitute admonition in place of reprehension—but it is my desire that you should inform the officers I shall expect to see a very great alteration in the police of the Corps and appearance of the Men before the next Inspection.

Peace

To Theodorick Bland, Newburgh, April 4, 1783

. . . Peace has given rest to speculative opinions respecting the time and terms of it. The first has come as soon as we could well have expected it under the disadvantages which we labored; and the latter is abundantly satisfactory.

It is now the bounden duty of every one to make the blessings thereof as diffusive as possible. Nothing would so effectually bring this to pass as the removal of those local prejudices which intrude upon and embarass that great line of policy which alone can make us a free, happy and powerful People. Unless our Union can be fixed upon such a basis as to accomplish these, certain I am we have toiled, bled and spent our treasure to very little purpose.

We have now a National character to establish, and it is of the utmost importance to stamp favorable impressions upon it; let justice be then one of its characteristics, and gratitude another. Public creditors of every denomination will be comprehended in the first; the Army in a particular manner will have a claim to the latter; to say that no distinction can be made between the claims of public creditors is to declare that there is no difference in circumstances; or that the services of all men are equally alike. This Army is of near eight years' standing, six of which they have spent in the Field without any other shelter from the inclemency of the seasons than Tents, or such Houses as they could build for themselves without expence to the public. They have encountered hunger, cold and nakedness. They have fought many Battles and bled freely. They have lived without pay, and in consequence of it, officers as well as men have subsisted upon their Rations.

They have often, very often, been reduced to the necessity of Eating Salt Porke, or Beef not for a day, or a week only but months together without Vegetables or money to buy them; or a cloth to wipe on.

Many of them to do better, and to dress as Officers have contracted heavy debts or spent their patrimonies. The first see the Doors of Gaols open to receive them—whilst those of the latter are shut against them. Is there no discrimination then—no extra exertion to be made in favor of men in these peculiar circumstances, in the event of their military dissolution? Or, if no worse cometh of it, are they to be turned adrift soured and discontented, complaining of the ingratitude of their Country, and under the influence of these passions, to become fit subjects for unfavorable impressions, and unhappy dissentions? For permit me to add, tho every man in the Army feels his distress—it is not every one that will reason to the cause of it.

I would not from the observations here made, be understood to mean that Congress should (because I know they cannot, nor does the army expect it) pay the full arrearages due to them till Continental or State funds are established for the purpose. They would, from what I can learn, go home contented—nay—*thankful* to receive what I have mentioned in a more public letter of this date, and in the manner there expressed. And surely this may be effected with proper exertions. Or what possibility was there of keeping the army together, if the war had continued, when the victualling, clothing, and other expenses of it were to have been added? Another thing Sir, (as I mean to be frank and free in my communications on this subject) I will not conceal from you—it is the dissimilarity in the payments to men in Civil and Military life. The first receive everything—the other get nothing but bare subsistence—they ask what this is owing to? and reasons have been assigned, which, say they, amount to this—that men in Civil life have stronger passions and better pretensions to indulge them, or less virtue and regard for their Country than us,—otherwise, as we are all contending for the same prize and equally interested in the attainment of it, why do we not bear the burthen equally?

These and other comparisons which are unnecessary to enumerate give a keener edge to their feelings and contribute not a little to sour their tempers. As it is the first wish of my Soul to see the War happily & speedily terminated; and those who are now in arms, returned to Citizenship with good dispositions, I think it a duty which I owe to candor and to friendship, to point you to such things as my opportunities have given me reason to believe will have a tendency to harmony and bring them to pass. I shall only add that with much esteem and regard, I am, &c.

Future of the Army

To Theodorick Bland, H. Q., April 4, 1783

The subject of your private letter is so important and involving so many considerations, that I could not hazard my own opinion *only* for a Reply. I have therefore communicated its contents to some of the most intelligent, well-informed, and confidential officers, whose judgment I have compelled, and endeavored to collect from them, what is the general Line and Expectation of the Army at large respectg. the points you mention—and as this is meant to be equally private and confidential as yours, I shall communicate my sentiments to you without reserve, and with the most entire Freedom.

The idea of the officers in keeping the Army together until Settlement of their accounts is effected, and *Funds established* for their Security, is perhaps not so extensive as the words of their Resolution seem to intimate. When that Idea was first expressed, our prospects of Peace were Distant, and it was supposed that Settlement and Funds might both be effected before a Dissolution of the Army would probably take place. They wished therefore to have both done at once. But since the Expectation of Peace is bro't so near, however desirable it would be to the officers, to have their Ballances secured to them upon sufficient Funds, as well as their Settlement ascertained, yet it is not in Idea, that the Army should be held together for the sole Purpose of enforcing either. Nor do they suppose that, by such Means, they could operate on the *Fears* of the civil power, or of the people at large—the impracticability as well as ill policy of such a mode of Conduct is easily discoverable by every sensible Intelligent officer.—The Tho't is reprobated as ridiculous and inadmissible.

Tho' these are their Ideas on the particular Point you have mentioned, yet they have their Expectations and they are of a very serious Nature and will require all the Attention and consideration of Congress to gratify them. These I will endeavor to explain with freedom and candor.

In the first place, I fix it as an *indispensible* Measure, that previous to the Disbanding of the Army, all their accounts, should be compleatly liquidated and settled—and that every person shall be ascertained of the Ballance due to him; and it is *equally essential,* in my opinion, that this Settlement should be effected, with the Army in its collected Body, without any dispersion of the different Lines to their respective States—for in this way the Accounts will be drawn into one view, properly digested upon one general system, and compared with a variety of circumstances, which will require References upon a much easier plan to be dispersed over all the States. The Settlements will be effected with greater ease, in less Time, and with much more oeconomy in this, than in a scattered situation. At the same Time jealousies will be removed, the minds of the Army will be impressed with greater Ease and Quiet, and they better prepared, with good opinions and proper Dispositions to fall back into the great Mass of Citizens—

But after Settlement is formed, there remains another Circumstance of more importance still, and without which, it will be of little consequence to have the sums due them ascertained; that is, the Payment of some part of the Ballance. The Distresses of Officers and Soldiers, are now driven to the extreme, and without this provision will not be lessened by the prospect of Dissolution. It is therefore universally expected that three months' pay at least, must be given them before they are disbanded—this Sum it is confidently imagined may be procured and is absolutely indispensable.

They are the rather confirmed in a Belief of the practicability of obtaining it—as the pay of the Army, has formed great part of the Sum in the Estimates which have been made for the Expences of the War—and altho' this has been obliged to give way to more necessary Claims, yet when those Demands cease, as many will upon the Disbanding the Army—the Pay will then come into view, and have its equal claim to Notice.

They will not however be unreasonable in this Expectation. If the whole cannot be obtained before they are dispersed, the Receipt of one month in Hand, with an absolute assurance of having the other two months in a short Time, will be satisfactory—Should Mr. Morris not be able to assure them the two last Months from the Treasury, it is suggested that it may be obtained in the States, by Drafts from him upon their several Continental Receivers, to be collected by the Individual Officers and Soldiers, out of the last year's Arrears due from the several States apportionments, and for which Taxes have long since been assessed by the Legislatures —This mode, tho' troublesome to the officer, and perhaps inconvenient for the financier, yet from the Necessity of circumstances may be adopted, and might be a means of collecting more Taxes from the people than would in any other way be done. This is only hinted as an Expedient. The Financier will take his own measures.

But I repeat it, as an indispensable point, that this Sum at least, must by some means be procured.—Without this provision, it will be absolutely impossible for many to get from Camp, or to return to their friends—and driven to such necessities it is impossible to foresee what may be the consequences of their not obtaining it. But the worst is to be apprehended.—A Credit, built by their Friends & such others as have been good eno' to supply their wants upon the Expectation of being refunded at the close of the War, out of the large Sums which by their Toils in the course of many Years hard Service, have become due to them from the public, has supported the greatest Number of them to the present Time —and that Debt now remains upon them. But to be disbanded at last, without this little pittance (which is necessary to quit Quarters) like a Sett of Beggars, Needy, distressed and without Prospect will not only blast the Expectations of their Creditors, and expose the officers to the utmost Indignity and the worst of consequences;—but will drive every man of Honor and Sensibility to the extremest Horrors of Despair. On the other Hand to give them this Sum, however small in comparison of their Dues, yet, by fulfiling their Expectations, will sweeten their Tempers, cheer their hopes of the future—enable them to submit themselves 'till they can cast about for some future means of Business—it will gratify their pressing Creditors, and will throw the officer back with Ease and Confidence into the Bosom of this Country, and enable him to mix with cordiality and affection among the mass of useful, happy and contented Citizens—an object of the most desirable importance. I cannot at this point of Distance, know the arrangements of the financier, what have been his anticipations, or what his prospects—but the necessity of fulfilling this Expectation of the Army affects me so exceeding forcibly, that I can not help dwelling upon it, nor is there in my present apprehensions a point of greater consequence or that requires more serious attention. Under this Impression I have thought, if a spirited, pointed, and well adapted Address was framed by Congress, and sent to the States on this Occasion, that Gratitude, Justice, Honor, National Pride, and every Consideration, would operate upon them to strain every Nerve, and exert every endeavor to throw into the Public Treasury, a Sum equal to this Requisition—It cannot be denied, especially when they reflect, how small the Expectation is, compared with the large sum of arrears which is due—and tho' I know that Distinctions are commonly odious, and are looked upon with a jealous and envious Eye—yet it is impossible, that in this case, it can have this operation; for whatever the feelings of Individuals at large may be in contemplating on their own Demands—yet upon a candid Comparison, every man, even the most interested, will be forced to yield to the superior merit and sufferings of the Soldier, who for a course of Years, has contributed his Services in the field, not only at the Expence of his fortune and former Employment, but at the Risque of Ease, domestic happiness, comfort and even Life. After all these Considerations, how must he be struck with the mediocrity of his demand, when, instead of the Pay due him for four, five, perhaps six years hard earned Toil and Distress, he is content for the present with receiving three months, only—and is willing to risque the Remainder upon the same Basis of Security, with the general mass of other public Creditors.—

Another Expectation seems to have possessed the minds of the officers. That, as the objects above mentioned are not the only ones which must occupy the attention of Congress, in Connexion with the Army, it may probably be tho't advisable that Congress should send to the Army, a respectable, well-chosen, and well instructed Committee, of their own Body; with liberal Power, to confer with the Army, to know their Sentiments, their Expectations, their Distresses, their Necessities, and the Impossibility of their falling back from the Soldier to Citizenship without some gratification to their most reasonable Demands. This would be considered as a compliment. And to add still greater satisfaction and advantage, it is tho't very advisable, that the Secretary at War, and the Financier should be of this Delegation. Previous to a Dissolution of the Army, many arrangements will doubtless be necessary in both those Departments, to procure a happy and honorable close to the War, and to introduce Peace, with a prospect of National Glory, Stability, and Benefit. It is not for me to dictate, but I should suppose some Peace Establishment will be necessary; some posts will be kept up and garrisoned; Arsenals for the Deposit of Ordnance and Military Stores, will be determined on, and the Stores collected and deposited; arrangements will be necessary for the Discharge of the Army; at what periods and under what circumstances. The Terms of the Soldiers Service are on different Grounds;—those for the War will suppose and they have a right to do so, their periods of Service to expire at the Close of War, and Proclamation of Peace. What period shall be fixed for these? The Levy men may be retained while the British force remain in our Country if it shall be judged advisable. If I am not consulted in these matters, it will be necessary for me to have an early Knowledge of the Intentions of Congress on these and many other points. But I can think of no mode so effectual as the one suggested of a Committee accompanied by the Financier and Secretary at War. Plans which to us appear feasible and practicable, may be attended with insurmountable difficulties. On the other hand measures may be adopted at Philadelphia which cannot be carried into execution. But here in the manner proposed something might be hit upon which would accommodate itself to the Ideas of both, with greater Ease and Satisfaction, than may now be expected, and which could not be effected by writing Quires of paper, and spending a Length of Time.—

Upon the whole, you will be able to collect from the foregoing Sentiments what are the Expectations of the Army—that they will involve compleat Settlement and partial payment *previous* to any Dispersion. (This they suppose may be done within the Time that they must necessarily remain together.) Upon the fulfillment of these two, they will readily retire, in full assurance that ample Security at the earliest period, and on the best ground it can be had will be obtained for the Remainder of their Ballances.

If the Idea of a Committee to right the Army should not be adopted,—and you find it necessary to pass any further Resolutions, you will easily collect from the foregoing Sentiments what will be satisfactory—without my troubling you any further—I pray you to communicate the Contents of this Letter to Colo. Hamilton, from whom I received a request similar to yours. I have &c.

Circular Letter to the Governors of All the States on Disbanding the Army

June 8, 1783

The great object, for which I had the honor to hold an appointment in the service of my country, being accomplished, I am now preparing to resign it into the hands of Congress, and to return to that domestic retirement, which, it is well known, I left with the greatest reluctance; a retirement for which I have never ceased to sigh, through a long and painful absence, and in which (remote from the noise and trouble of the world) I meditate to pass the remainder of my life, in a state of undisturbed repose. But before I carry this resolution into effect, I think it a duty incumbent on me to make this my last official communication; to congratulate you on the glorious events which Heaven has been pleased to produce in our favor; to offer my sentiments respecting some important subjects, which appear to me to be intimately connected with the tranquillity of the United States; to take my leave of your Excellency as a public character; and to give my final blessing to that country, in whose service I have spent the prime of my life, for whose sake I have consumed so many anxious days and watchful nights, and whose happiness, being extremely dear to me, will always constitute no inconsiderable part of my own.

Impressed with the liveliest sensibility on this pleasing occasion, I will claim the indulgence of dilating the more copiously on the subjects of our mutual felicitation. When we consider the magnitude of the prize we contended for, the doubtful nature of the contest, and the favorable manner in which it has terminated, we shall find the greatest possible reason for gratitude and rejoicing. This is a theme that will afford infinite delight to every benevolent and liberal mind, whether the event in contemplation be considered as the source of present enjoyment, or the parent of future happiness; and we shall have equal occasion to felicitate ourselves on the lot which Providence has assigned us, whether we view it in a natural, a political, or moral point of light.

The citizens of America, placed in the most enviable condition, as the sole lords and proprietors of a vast tract of continent, comprehending all the various soils and climates of the world, and abounding with all the necessaries and conveniences of life, are now, by the late satisfactory pacification, acknowledged to be possessed of absolute freedom and independency. They are, from this period, to be considered as the actors on a most conspicuous theatre, which seems to be peculiarly designated by Providence for the display of human greatness and felicity. Here they are not only surrounded with every thing, which can contribute to the completion of private and domestic enjoyment; but Heaven has crowned all its other blessings, by giving a fairer opportunity for political happiness, than any other nation has ever been favored with. Nothing can illustrate these observations more forcibly, than a recollection of the happy conjuncture of times and circumstances, under which our republic assumed its rank among the nations. The foundation of our empire was not laid in the gloomy age of ignorance and superstition; but at an epoch when the rights of mankind were better understood and more clearly defined, than at any former period. The researches of the human mind after social happiness have been carried to a great extent; the treasures of knowledge, acquired by the labors of philosophers, sages, and legislators, through a long succession of years, are laid open for our use, and their collected wisdom may be happily applied in the establishment of our forms of government. The free cultivation of letters, the unbounded extension of commerce, the progressive refinement of manners, the growing liberality of sentiment, and, above all, the pure and benign light of Revelation, have had a meliorating influence on mankind and increased the blessings of society. At this auspicious period, the United States came into existence as a nation; and, if their citizens should not be completely free and happy, the fault will be entirely their own.

Such is our situation, and such are our prospects; but notwithstanding the cup of blessing is thus reached out to us; notwithstanding happiness is ours, if we have a disposition to seize the occasion and make it our own; yet it appears to me there is an option still left to the United States of America, that it is in their choice, and depends upon their conduct, whether they will be respectable and prosperous, or contemptible and miserable, as a nation. This is the time of their political probation; this is the moment when the eyes of the whole world are turned upon them; this is the moment to establish or ruin their national character for ever; this is the favorable moment to give such a tone to our federal government, as will enable it to answer the ends of its institution, or this may be the ill-fated moment for relaxing the powers of the Union, annihilating the cement of the confederation, and exposing us to become the sport of European politics, which may play one State against another, to prevent their growing importance, and to serve their own interested purposes. For, according to the system of policy the States shall adopt at this moment, they will stand or fall; and by their confirmation or lapse it is yet to be decided, whether the revolution must ultimately be considered as a blessing or a curse; a blessing or a curse, not to the present age alone, for with our fate will the destiny of unborn millions be involved.

With this conviction of the importance of the present crisis, silence in me would be a crime. I will therefore speak to your Excellency the language of freedom and of sincerity without disguise. I am aware, however, that those who differ from me in political sentiment, may perhaps remark, I am stepping out of the proper line of my duty, and may possibly ascribe to arrogance or ostentation, what I know is alone the result of the purest intention. But the rectitude of my own heart, which disdains such unworthy motives; the part I have hitherto acted in life; the determination I have formed, of not taking any share in public business hereafter; the ardent desire I feel, and shall continue to manifest, of quietly enjoying, in private life, after all the toils of war, the benefits of a wise and liberal government, will, I flatter myself, sooner or later convince my countrymen, that I could have no sinister views in delivering, with so little reserve, the opinions contained in this address.

There are four things, which, I humbly conceive, are essential to the well-being, I may even venture to say, to the existence of the United States, as an independent power.

First. An indissoluble union of the States under one federal head.

Secondly. A sacred regard to public justice.

Thirdly. The adoption of a proper peace establishment; and,

Fourthly. The prevalence of that pacific and friendly disposition among the people of the United States, which will induce them to forget their local prejudices and policies; to make those mutual concessions, which are requisite to the general prosperity; and, in some instances, to sacrifice their individual advantages to the interest of the community.

These are the pillars on which the glorious fabric of our independency and national character must be supported. Liberty is the basis; and whoever would dare to sap the foundation, or overturn the structure, under whatever specious pretext he may attempt it, will merit the bitterest execration, and the severest punishment, which can be inflicted by his injured country.

On the three first articles I will make a few observations, leaving the last to the good sense and serious consideration of those immediately concerned.

Under the first head, although it may not be necessary or proper for me, in this place, to enter into a particular disquisition on the principles of the Union, and to take up the great question which has been frequently agitated, whether it be expedient and requisite for the States to delegate a larger proportion of power to Congress, or not; yet it will be a part of my duty, and that of every true patriot, to assert without reserve, and to insist upon, the following positions. That, unless the States will suffer Congress to exercise those prerogatives they are undoubtedly invested with by the constitution, every thing must very rapidly tend to anarchy and confusion. That it is indispensable to the happiness of the individual States, that there should be lodged somewhere a supreme power to regulate and govern the general concerns of the confederated republic, without which the Union cannot be of long duration. That there must be a faithful and pointed compliance, on the part of every State, with the late proposals and demands of Congress, or the most fatal consequences will ensue. That whatever measures have a tendency to dissolve the Union, or contribute to violate or lessen the sovereign authority, ought to be considered as hostile to the liberty and independency of America, and the authors of them treated accordingly. And lastly, that unless we can be enabled, by the concurrence of the States, to participate of the fruits of the revolution, and enjoy the essential benefits of civil society, under a form of government so free and uncorrupted, so happily guarded against the danger of oppression, as has been devised and adopted by the articles of confederation, it will be a subject of regret, that so much blood and treasure have been lavished for no purpose, that so many sufferings have been encountered without a compensation, and that so many sacrifices have been made in vain.

Many other considerations might here be adduced to prove, that, without an entire conformity to the spirit of the Union, we cannot exist as an independent power. It will be sufficient for my purpose to mention but one or two, which seem to me of the greatest importance. It is only in our united character, as an empire, that our independence is acknowledged, that our power can be regarded, or our credit supported, among foreign nations. The treaties of the European powers with the United States of America will have no validity on a dissolution of the Union. We shall be left nearly in a state of nature; or we may find, by our own unhappy experience, that there is a natural and necessary progression from the extreme of anarchy to the extreme of tyranny, and that arbitrary power is most easily established on the ruins of liberty, abused to licentiousness.

As to the second article, which respects the performance of public justice, Congress have, in their late address to the United States, almost exhausted the subject; they have explained their ideas so fully, and have enforced the obligations the States are under, to render complete justice to all the public creditors, with so much dignity and energy, that, in my opinion, no real friend to the honor or independency of America can hesitate a single moment, respecting the propriety of complying with the just and honorable measures proposed. If their arguments do not produce conviction, I know of nothing that will have greater influence: especially when we recollect, that the system referred to, being the result of the collected wisdom of the continent, must be esteemed, if not perfect, certainly the least objectionable of any that could be devised; and that, if it shall not be carried into immediate execution, a national bankruptcy, with all its deplorable consequences, will take place, before any different plan can possibly be proposed and adopted. So pressing are the present circumstances, and such is the alternative now offered to the States.

The ability of the country to discharge the debts, which have been incurred in its defence, is not to be doubted; an inclination, I flatter myself, will not be wanting. The path of our duty is plain before us; honesty will be found, on every experiment, to be the best and only true policy. Let us then, as a nation, be just; let us fulfil the public contracts, which Congress had undoubtedly a right to make for the purpose of carrying on the war, with the same good faith we suppose ourselves bound to perform our private engagements. In the mean time, let an attention to the cheerful performance of their proper business, as individuals and as members of society, be earnestly inculcated on the citizens of America; then will they strengthen the hands of government, and be happy under its protection; every one will reap the fruit of his labors, every one will enjoy his own acquisitions, without molestation and without danger.

In this state of absolute freedom and perfect security, who will grudge to yield a very little of his property to support the common interest of society, and insure the protection of government? Who does not remember the frequent declarations, at the commencement of the war, that we should be completely satisfied, if, at the expense of one half, we could defend the remainder of our possessions? Where is the man to be found, who wishes to remain indebted for the defence of his own person and property to the exertions, the bravery, and the blood of others, without making one generous effort to repay the debt of honor and gratitude? In what part of the continent shall we find any man, or body of men, who would not blush to stand up and propose measures purposely calculated to rob the soldier of his stipend, and the public creditor of his due? And were it possible, that such a flagrant instance of injustice could ever happen, would it not excite the general indignation, and tend to bring down upon the authors of such measures the aggravated vengeance of Heaven? If, after all, a spirit of disunion, or a temper of obstinacy and perverseness should manifest itself in any of the States; if such an ungracious disposition should attempt to frustrate all the happy effects that might be expected to flow from the Union; if there should be a refusal to comply with the requisition for funds to discharge the annual interest of the public debts; and if that refusal should revive again all those jealousies, and produce all those evils, which are now happily removed, Congress, who have, in all their transactions, shown a great degree of magnanimity and justice, will stand justified in the sight of God and man; and the State alone, which puts itself in opposition to the aggregate wisdom of the continent, and follows such mistaken and pernicious counsels, will be responsible for all the consequences.

For my own part, conscious of having acted, while a servant of the public, in the manner I conceived best suited to promote the real interests of my country; having, in consequence of my fixed belief, in some measure pledged myself to the army, that their country would finally do them complete and ample justice; and not wishing to conceal any instance of my official conduct from the eyes of the world, I have thought proper to transmit to your Excellency the enclosed collection of papers, relative to the half-pay and commutation granted by Congress to the officers of the army. From these communications, my decided sentiments will be clearly comprehended, together with the conclusive reasons which induced me, at an early period, to recommend the adoption of this measure, in the most earnest and serious manner. As the proceedings of Congress, the army, and myself, are open to all, and contain, in my opinion, sufficient information to remove the prejudices and errors, which may have been entertained by any, I think it unnecessary to say any thing more than just to observe, that the resolutions of Congress, now alluded to, are undoubtedly as absolutely binding upon the United States, as the most solemn acts of confederation or legislation.

As to the idea, which, I am informed, has in some instances prevailed, that the half-pay and commutation are to be regarded merely in the odious light of a pension, it ought to be exploded for ever. That provision should be viewed, as it really was, a reasonable compensation offered by Congress, at a time when they had nothing else to give to the officers of the army for services then to be performed. It was the only means to prevent a total dereliction of the service. It was a part of their hire. I may be allowed to say, it was the price of their blood, and of your independency; it is therefore more than a common debt, it is a debt of honor; it can never be considered as a pension or gratuity, nor be cancelled until it is fairly discharged.

With regard to a distinction between officers and soldiers, it is sufficient that the uniform experience of every nation of the world, combined with our own, proves the utility and propriety of the discrimination. Rewards, in proportion to the aids the public derives from them, are unquestionably due to all its servants. In some lines, the soldiers have perhaps generally had as ample a compensation for their services, by the large bounties which have been paid to them, as their officers will receive in the proposed commutation; in others, if, besides the donation of lands, the payment of arrearages of clothing and wages (in which articles all the component parts of the army must be put upon the same footing), we take into the estimate the douceurs many of the soldiers have received, and the gratuity of one year's full pay, which is promised to all, possibly their situation (every circumstance being duly considered) will not be deemed less eligible than that of the officers. Should a further reward, however, be judged equitable, I will venture to assert, no one will enjoy greater satisfaction than myself, on seeing an exemption from taxes for a limited time, (which has been petitioned for in some instances,) or any other adequate immunity or compensation granted to the brave defenders of their country's cause; but neither the adoption or rejection of this proposition will in any manner affect, much less militate against, the act of Congress, by which they have offered five years' full pay, in lieu of the half-pay for life, which had been before promised to the officers of the army.

Before I conclude the subject of public justice, I cannot omit to mention the obligations this country is under to that meritorious class of veteran non-commissioned officers and privates, who have been discharged for inability, in consequence of the resolution of Congress of the 23d of April, 1782, on an annual pension for life. Their peculiar sufferings, their singular merits, and claims to that provision, need only be known, to interest all the feelings of humanity in their behalf. Nothing but a punctual payment of their annual allowance can rescue them from the most complicated misery; and nothing could be a more melancholy and distressing sight, than to behold those, who have shed their blood or lost their limbs in the service of their country, without a shelter, without a friend, and without the means of obtaining any of the necessaries or comforts of life, compelled to beg their daily bread from door to door. Suffer me to recommend those of this description, belonging to your State, to the warmest patronage of your Excellency and your legislature.

It is necessary to say but a few words on the third topic which was proposed, and which regards particularly the defence of the republic; as there can be little doubt but Congress will recommend a proper peace establishment for the United States, in which a due attention will be paid to the importance of placing the militia of the Union upon a regular and respectable footing. If this should be the case, I would beg leave to urge the great advantage of it in the strongest terms. The militia of this country must be considered as the palladium of our security, and the first effectual resort in case of hostility. It is essential, therefore, that the same system should pervade the whole; that the formation and discipline of the militia of the continent should be absolutely uniform, and that the same species of arms, accoutrements, and military apparatus, should be introduced in every part of the United States. No one, who has not learned it from experience, can conceive the difficulty, expense, and confusion, which result from a contrary system, or the vague arrangements which have hitherto prevailed.

If, in treating of political points, a greater latitude than usual has been taken in the course of this address, the importance of the crisis, and the magnitude of the objects in discussion, must be my apology. It is, however, neither my wish or expectation, that the preceding observations should claim any regard, except so far as they shall appear to be dictated by a good intention, consonant to the immutable rules of justice, calculated to produce a liberal system of policy, and founded on whatever experience may have been acquired by a long and close attention to public business. Here I might speak with the more confidence, from my actual observations; and, if it would not swell this letter (already too prolix) beyond the bounds I had prescribed to myself, I could demonstrate to every mind open to conviction, that in less time, and with much less expense, than has been incurred, the war might have been brought to the same happy conclusion, if the resources of the continent could have been properly drawn forth; that the distresses and disappointments, which have very often occurred, have, in too many instances, resulted more from a want of energy in the Continental government, than a deficiency of means in the particular States; that the inefficacy of measures arising from the want of an adequate authority in the supreme power, from a partial compliance with the requisitions of Congress in some of the States, and from a failure of punctuality in others, while it tended to damp the zeal of those, which were more willing to exert themselves, served also to accumulate the expenses of the war, and to frustrate the best concerted plans; and that the discouragement occasioned by the complicated difficulties and embarrassments, in which our affairs were by this means involved, would have long ago produced the dissolution of any army, less patient, less virtuous, and less persevering, than that which I have had the honor to command. But, while I mention these things, which are notorious facts, as the defects of our federal constitution, particularly in the prosecution of a war, I beg it may be understood, that, as I have ever taken a pleasure in gratefully acknowledging the assistance and support I have derived from every class of citizens, so shall I always be happy to do justice to the unparalleled exertions of the individual States on many interesting occasions.

I have thus freely disclosed what I wished to make known, before I surrendered up my public trust to those who committed it to me. The task is now accomplished. I now bid adieu to your Excellency as the chief magistrate of your State, at the same time I bid a last farewell to the cares of office, and all the employments of public life.

It remains, then, to be my final and only request, that your Excellency will communicate these sentiments to your legislature at their next meeting, and that they may be considered as the legacy of one, who has ardently wished, on all occasions, to be useful to his country, and who, even in the shade of retirement, will not fail to implore the Divine benediction upon it.

I now make it my earnest prayer, that God would have you, and the State over which you preside, in his holy protection; that he would incline the hearts of the citizens to cultivate a spirit of subordination and obedience to government; to entertain a brotherly affection and love for one another, for their fellow citizens of the United States at large, and particularly for their brethren who have served in the field; and finally, that he would most graciously be pleased to dispose us all to do justice, to love mercy, and to demean ourselves with that charity, humility, and pacific temper of mind, which were the characteristics of the Divine Author of our blessed religion, and without an humble imitation of whose example in these things, we can never hope to be a happy nation.

I have the honor to be, with much esteem and respect, Sir, your Excellency's most obedient and most humble servant.

Chapter 7
UNION AND CONSTITUTION

CONSTITUTION

To John Augustine Washington, May 31, 1776

To form a new government requires infinite care and unbounded attention; for if the foundation is badly laid, the superstructure must be bad. Too much time, therefore, cannot be bestowed in weighing and digesting matters well. We have, no doubt, some good parts in our present constitution; many bad ones we know we have. Wherefore, no time can be misspent that is employed in separating the wheat from the tares. My fear is, that you will all get tired and homesick; the consequence of which will be that you will patch up some kind of a constitution as defective as the present. This should be avoided. Every man should consider, that he is lending his aid to frame a constitution, which is to render millions happy or miserable, and that a matter of such moment cannot be the work of a day.

NEED FOR UNION

To Alexander Hamilton, Newburgh, March 31, 1783

I have duly received your favors of the 17th and 24th ultimo. I rejoice most exceedingly that there is an end to our warfare, and that such a field is opening to our view, as will, with wisdom to direct the cultivation of it, make us a great, a respectable, and happy people; but it must be improved by other means than State politics, and unreasonable jealousies and prejudices, or (it requires not the second sight to see that) we shall be instruments in the hands of our enemies, and those European powers, who may be jealous of our greatness in union, to dissolve the confederation. But, to obtain this, although the way seems extremely plain, is not so easy.

My wish to see the union of these States established upon liberal and permanent principles, and inclination to contribute my mite in pointing out the defects of the present constitution, are equally great. All my private letters have teemed with these sentiments, and, whenever this topic has been the subject of conversation, I have endeavored to diffuse and enforce them; but how far any further essay by me might be productive of the wished-for end, or appear to arrogate more than belongs to me, depends so much upon popular opinions, and the temper and dispositions of the people, that it is not easy to decide. I shall be obliged to you, however, for the thoughts, which you promised me on this subject, and as soon as you can make it convenient.

No man in the United States is or can be more deeply impressed with the necessity of a reform in our present confederation than myself. No man perhaps has felt the bad effects of it more sensibly; for to the defects thereof, and want of powers in Congress, may justly be ascribed the prolongation of the war, and consequently the expenses occasioned by it. More than half the perplexities I have experienced in the course of my command, and almost the whole of the difficulties and distress of the army, have their origin here. But still, the prejudices of some, the designs of others, and the mere machinery of the majority, make address and management necessary to give weight to opinions, which are to combat the doctrines of those different classes of men in the field of politics. . . .

To the Marquis de Lafayette, H. Q., Newburgh, April 5, 1783

. . . We stand, now, an Independent People, and have yet to learn political Tactics. We are placed among the nations of the Earth, and have a character to establish; but how we shall acquit ourselves, time must discover. The probability (at least I fear it), is that local or State politics will interfere too much with the more liberal and extensive plan of government, which wisdom and foresight, freed from the mist of prejudice, would dictate; and that we shall be guilty of many blunders in treading this boundless theatre, before we shall have arrived at any perfection in this art; in a word, that the experience, which is purchased at the price of difficulties and distress, will alone convince us that the honor, power, and true Interest of this Country must be measured by a Continental scale, and that every departure therefrom weakens the Union, and may ultimately break the band that holds us together. To avert these evils, to form a Constitution, that will give consistency, stability, and dignity to the Union, and sufficient powers to the great Council of the nation for general purposes, is a duty which is incumbent upon every man, who wishes well to his Country, and will meet with my aid as far as it can be rendered in the private walks of life: for hence forward my mind shall be unbent and I will endeavor to glide gently down the stream of life till I come to that abyss from whence no traveller is permitted to return. . . .

To Dr. William Gordon, H. Q., Newburgh, July 8, 1783

. . . It now rests with the Confederated Powers, by the line of conduct they mean to adopt, to make this Country great, happy, and respectable; or to sink it into littleness—worse perhaps—into Anarchy and confusion; for certain I am, that unless adequate Powers are given to Congress for the *general* purposes of the Federal Union, that we shall soon moulder into dust and become contemptible in the eyes of Europe, if we are not made the sport of their Politicks. To suppose that the general concerns of this Country can be directed by thirteen heads, or one head without competent powers, is a solecism, the bad effects of which every man who has had the practical knowledge to judge from, that I have, is fully convinced of; tho' none perhaps has felt them in so forcible and distressing a degree. The People at large, and at a distance from the theatre of action, who only know that the machine was kept in motion, and that they are at last arrived at the first object of their wishes, are satisfied with the event, without investigating the causes of the slow progress to it, or of the expences which have accrued, and which they have been unwilling to pay—great part of which has arisen from that want of energy in the Federal Constitution, which I am complaining of, and which I wish to see given to it by a Convention of the People, instead of hearing it remarked that, as we have worked through an arduous contest with the powers Congress already have (but which, by the by, have been gradually diminishing,) why should they be invested with more?

To say say nothing of the invisible workings of Providence, which has conducted us through difficulties where no human foresight could point the way; it will appear evident to a close examiner, that there has been a concatenation of causes to produce this event; which in all probability, at no time, or under any other circumstances, will combine again—We deceive ourselves therefore by the mode of reasoning, and, what would be much worse, we may bring ruin upon ourselves by attempting to carry it into practice.

We are known by no other character among nations than as the United States—Massachusetts or Virginia is no better defined, nor any more thought of by Foreign Powers than the County of Worcester in Massachusetts is by Virginia, or Gloucester County in Virginia is by Massachusetts, (respectable as they are); and yet these counties with as much propriety might oppose themselves to the Laws of the State in which they are, as an Individual State can oppose itself to the Federal Government, by which it is, or ought to be bound. Each of these counties has, no doubt, its local polity and Interests. These should be attended to, and brought before their respective legislatures with all the force their importance merits; but when they come in contact with the general Interest of the State, when superior considerations preponderate in favor of the whole, their voices should be heard no more. So should it be with individual States when compared to the Union, otherwise I think it may properly be asked for what purpose do we farcically pretend to be United? Why do Congress spend months together in deliberating upon, debating, and digesting plans, which are made as palatable, and as wholesome to the Constitution of this country as the nature of things will admit of, when some States will pay no attention to them, and others regard them but partially; by which means all those evils which proceed from delay, are felt by the whole; while the compliant States are not only suffering by these neglects, but in many instances are injured most capitally by their own exertions; which are wasted for want of the united effort. A hundred thousand men, coming one after another, cannot move a Ton weight; but the united strength of 50 would transport it with ease. So has it been with great part of the expence which has been incurred [in] this War. In a word, I think the blood and treasure, which has been spent in it, has been lavished to little purpose, unless we can be better cemented; and that is not to be effected while so little attention is paid to the recommendations of the Sovereign Power.

To me it would seem not more absurd, to hear a traveller, who was setting out on a long journey, declare he would take no money in his pocket to defray the Expences of it, but rather depend upon Chance and Charity, lest he should misapply it—than are the expressions of so much fear of the powers and means of Congress.

For Heaven's sake, who are Congress? are they not the creatures of the People, amenable to them for their conduct, and dependent from day to day on their breath? Where then can be the danger of giving them such Powers as are adequate to the great ends of Government, and to all the general purposes of the Confederation (I repeat the word *general,* because I am no advocate for their having to do with the particular policy of any state, further than it concerns the Union at large)? What may be the consequences if they have not these Powers, I am at no loss to guess; and deprecate the worst; for sure I am, we shall, in a little time become as contemptible in the great scale of Politicks, as we now have it in our power to be respectable. And that, when the band of Union gets once broken, every thing ruinous to our future prospects is to be apprehended. The best that can come of it, in my humble opinion is, that we shall sink into obscurity, unless our Civil broils should keep us in remembrance and fill the page of history with the direful consequences of them.

You say that, Congress loose time by pressing a mode that does not accord with the genius of the People, and will thereby, endanger the Union, and that it is the quantum they want. Permit me to ask if the quantum has not already been demanded? Whether it has been obtained? and whence proceeds the accumulated evils, and poignant distresses of many of the public Creditors—particularly in the Army? For my own part I hesitate not a moment to confess, that I see nothing wherein the Union is endangered by the late requisition of that body, but a prospect of much good, justice, and prosperity from the compliance with it. I know of no tax more convenient, none so agreeable, as that which every man may pay,—or let it alone, as his convenience, abilities, or Inclination shall prompt. I am therefore a warm friend to the impost. . . .

To Benjamin Harrison, Mount Vernon, January 18, 1784

. . . That the prospect before us is, as you justly observe, fair, none can deny; but what use we shall make of it is exceedingly problematical; not but that I believe all things will come right at last, but like a young heir, come a little prematurely to a large inheritance, we shall wanton and run riot until we have brought our reputation to the brink of ruin, and then like him shall have to labor with the current of opinion, when *compelled* perhaps to do what prudence and common policy pointed out, as plain as any problem in Euclid, in the first instance.

The disinclination of the individual States to yield competent powers to Congress for the federal government, their unreasonable jealousy of that body and of one another, and the disposition, which seems to pervade each, of being all-wise and all-powerful within itself, will, if there is not a change in the system, be our downfall as a nation. This is as clear to me as the A, B, C; and I think we have opposed Great Britain, and have arrived at the present state of peace and independency, to very little purpose, if we cannot conquer our own prejudices. The powers of Europe begin to see this, and our newly acquired friends, the British, are already and professedly acting upon this ground; and wisely too, if we are determined to persevere in our folly. They know that individual opposition to their measures is futile, and boast that we are not sufficiently united as a nation to give a general one! Is not the indignity alone of this declaration, while we are in the very act of peacemaking and conciliation, sufficient to stimulate us to vest more extensive and adequate powers in the sovereign of these United States?

For my own part, although I am returned to, and am now mingled with, the class of private citizens, and like them must suffer all the evils of a tyranny, or of too great an extension of federal powers, I have no fears arising from this source, in my mind; but I have many, and powerful ones indeed, which predict the worst consequences, from a half-starved, limping government, that appears to be always moving upon crutches, and tottering at every step. Men chosen as the delegates in Congress are, cannot officially be dangerous. They depend upon the breath, nay, they are so much the creatures of the people, under the present constitution, that they can have no views, (which could possibly be carried into execution,) nor any interests distinct from those of their constituents. My political creed, therefore, is, to be wise in the choice of delegates, support them like gentlemen while they are our representatives, give them competent powers for all federal purposes, support them in the due exercise thereof, and, lastly, to compel them to close attendance in Congress during their delegation. These things, under the present mode for and termination of elections, aided by annual instead of constant sessions, would, or I am exceedingly mistaken, make us one of the most wealthy, happy, respectable, and powerful nations, that ever inhabited the terrestrial globe. Without them, we shall, in my opinion, soon be every thing which is the direct reverse of them. . . .

To James McHenry, Mount Vernon, August 22, 1785

. . . As I have ever been a friend to adequate powers of Congress, without which it is evident to me we never shall establish a national character, or be considered as on a respectable footing by the powers of Europe, I am sorry I cannot agree with you in sentiment not to enlarge them for the regulating of commerce. I have neither time nor abilities to enter into a full discussion of this subject; but it should seem to me, that your arguments against it, principally that some States may be more benefited than others by a commercial regulation, apply to every matter of general utility. Can there be a case enumerated, in which this argument has not its force in greater or less degree? We are either a united people under one head and for federal purposes, or we are thirteen independent sovereignties, eternally counteracting each other. If the former, whatever such a majority of the States, as the constitution points out, conceives to be the benefit of the whole, should, in my humble opinion, be submitted to by the minority. Let the southern States always be represented; let them act more in union; let them declare freely and boldly what is for the interest of, and what is prejudicial to, their constituents; and there will, there must be, an accommodating spirit. In the establishment of a navigation act, this in a particular manner ought, and will doubtless be attended to. If the assent of nine, or as some propose of eleven States, is necessary to give validity to a commercial system, it insures this measure, or it cannot be obtained.

Wherein then lies the danger? But if your fears are in danger of being realized, cannot certain provisos in the ordinance guard against the evil; I see no difficulty in this, if the southern delegates would give their attendance in Congress, and follow the example, if it should be set them, of hanging together to counteract combinations. I confess to you candidly, that I can foresee no evil greater than disunion; than those *unreasonable* jealousies, (I say *unreasonable,* because I would have a *proper* jealousy always awake, and the United States on the watch to prevent individual States from infracting the constitution with impunity,) which are continually poisoning our minds and filling them with imaginary evils to the prevention of real ones.

As you have asked the question, I answer, I do not know that we can enter upon a war of imposts with Great Britain, or any other foreign power; but we are certain, that this war has been waged against us by the former; *professedly* upon a belief that we never could unite in opposition to it; and I *believe* there is no way of putting an end to, or at least of stopping the increase of it, but to convince them of the contrary. Our trade, in all points of view, is as essential to Great Britain, as hers is to us; and she will exchange it upon reciprocal and liberal terms, if better cannot be had. It can hardly be supposed, I think, that the carrying business will devolve wholly on the States you have named, or remain long with them if it should; for either Great Britain will depart from her present contracted system, or the policy of the southern States in framing the act of navigation, or by laws passed by themselves individually, will devise ways and means to encourage seamen for the transportation of the product of their respective countries or for the encouragement of. But, admitting the contrary, if the Union is considered as permanent, and on this I presume all superstructures are built, had we not better encourage seamen among ourselves, with less imports, than divide it with foreigners, and by increasing the amount of them ruin our merchants, and greatly injuring the mass of our citizens.

To sum up the whole, I foresee, or think I do it, the many advantages which will arise from giving powers of this kind to Congress (if a sufficient number of States are required to exercise them), without any evil, save that which may proceed from inattention, or want of wisdom in the formation of the act; whilst, without them, we stand in a ridiculous point of view in the eyes of the nations of the world, with whom we are attempting to enter into commercial treaties, without means of carrying them into effect; who must see and feel, that the Union or the States individually are sovereigns, as best suits their purposes, in a word, that we are one nation today and thirteen tomorrow.

To John Jay, May 18, 1786

We are certainly in a delicate situation; but my fear is, that the people are not yet sufficiently *misled* to retract from error. To be plainer, I think there is more wickedness than ignorance mixed in our councils. Under this impression I scarcely know what opinion to entertain of a general convention. That it is necessary to revise and amend the articles of confederation, I entertain no doubt; but what may be the consequences of such an attempt is doubtful. Yet something must be done, or the fabric must fall, for it certainly is tottering.

Ignorance and design are difficult to combat. Out of these proceed illiberal sentiments, improper jealousies, and a train of evils which oftentimes in republican governments must be sorely felt before they can be removed. The former, that is ignorance, being a fit soil for the latter to work in, tools are employed by them which a generous mind would disdain to use; and which nothing but time, and their own puerile or wicked productions, can show the inefficacy and dangerous tendency of. I think often of our situation, and view it with concern. From the high ground we stood upon, from the plain path which invited our footsteps, to be so fallen! so lost! it is really mortifying. But virtue, I fear, has in a great degree taken its departure from our land, and the want of a disposition to do justice is the source of the national embarrassments; for, whatever guise or colorings are given to them, this I apprehend is the origin of the evils we now feel, and probably shall labor under for some time yet.

To John Jay, Mount Vernon, August 1, 1786

Your sentiments, that our affairs are drawing rapidly to a crisis, accord with my own. What the event will be is beyond the reach of my foresight. We have errors to correct; we have probably had too good an opinion of human nature, in forming our confederation. Experience has taught us that men will not adopt and carry into execution, measures the best calculated for their own good, without the intervention of coercive power. I do not conceive, we can exist long as a nation, without lodging, somewhere, a power which will pervade the whole Union in as energetic a manner, as the authority of the state governments extends over the several states.

To be fearful of investing Congress, constituted as that body is, with ample authorities for national purposes, appears to me the very climax of popular absurdity and madness. Could Congress exert them for the detriment of the people, without injuring themselves in an equal or greater proportion? Are not their interests inseparably connected with those of their constituents? By the rotation of appointments, must they not mingle frequently with the mass of citizens? Is it not rather to be apprehended, if they were not possessed of the powers before described, that the individual members would be induced to use them, on many occasions, very timidly and inefficaciously, for fear of losing their popularity and future election? We must take human nature as we find it; perfection falls not to the share of mortals.

What then is to be done? Things cannot go on in the same strain forever. It is much to be feared, as you observe, that the better kind of people, being disgusted with these circumstances, will have their minds prepared for any revolution whatever. We are apt to run from one extreme to another. To anticipate and prevent disastrous contingencies, would be the part of wisdom and patriotism.

What astonishing changes a few years are capable of producing! I am told that even respectable characters speak of a monarchical form of government without horror. From thinking proceeds speaking: thence to acting is often but a single step. But how irrevocable and tremendous! What a triumph for our enemies, to verify their predictions! What a triumph for the advocates of despotism, to find that we are incapable of governing ourselves, and that systems, founded on the basis of equal liberty, are merely ideal and fallacious. Would to God that wise measures may be taken in time to avert the consequences we have but too much reason to apprehend.

Retired as I am from the world, I frankly acknowledge I cannot feel myself an unconcerned spectator. Yet having happily assisted in bringing the ship into port, and having been fairly discharged, it is not my business to embark again on the sea of troubles. Nor could it be expected that my sentiments and opinions would have much weight on the minds of my countrymen.

Trouble in Massachusetts

To Henry Lee, October 31, 1786

. . . The picture which you have exhibited, and the accounts which are published of the commotions and temper of numerous bodies in the eastern States, are equally to be lamented and deprecated. They exhibit a melancholy proof of what our transatlantic foe has predicted; and of another thing perhaps, which is still more to be regretted, and is yet more unaccountable, that mankind, when left to themselves, are unfit for their own government. I am mortified beyond expression, when I view the clouds, that have spread over the brightest morn that ever dawned upon any country. In a word, I am lost in amazement when I behold what intrigue, the interested views of desperate characters, ignorance and jealousy of the minor part, are capable of effecting, as a scourge on the major part of our fellow citizens of the Union; for it is hardly to be supposed, that the great body of the people, though they will not act, can be so shortsighted or enveloped in darkness, as not to see rays of a distant sun through all this mist of intoxication and folly.

You talk, my good Sir, of employing influence to appease the present tumults in Massachusetts. I know not where that influence is to be found, or, if attainable, that it would be a proper remedy for the disorders. *Influence* is no *government*. Let us have one by which our lives, liberties, and properties will be secured, or let us know the worst at once. Under these impressions, my humble opinion is, that there is a call for decision. Know precisely what the insurgents aim at. If they have *real* grievances, redress them if possible; or acknowledge the justice of them, and your inability to do it in the present moment. If they have not, employ the force of government against them at once. If this is inadequate, *all* will be convinced, that the superstructure is bad, or wants support. To be more exposed in the eyes of the world, and more contemptible than we already are, is hardly possible. To delay one or the other of these, is to exasperate on the one hand, or to give confidence on the other, and will add to their numbers; for, like snow-balls, such bodies increase by every movement, unless there is something in the way to obstruct and crumble them before the weight is too great and irresistible.

These are my sentiments. Precedents are dangerous things. Let the reins of government then be braced and held with a steady hand, and every violation of the constitution be reprehended. If defective, let it be amended, but not suffered to be trampled upon whilst it has an existence. . . .

A Federal Government

To James Madison, Mount Vernon, November 5, 1786

I thank you for the communications in your letter of the 1st instant. The decision of the House on the question respecting a paper emission is portentous, I hope, of an auspicious session. It certainly may be classed with the important questions of the present day, and merited the serious attention of the Assembly. Fain would I hope, that the great and most important of all subjects, the *federal government*, may be considered with that calm and deliberate attention, which the magnitude of it so critically and loudly calls for at this critical moment. Let prejudices, unreasonable jealousies, and local interests, yield to reason and liberality. Let us look to our national character, and to things beyond the present moment. No morn ever dawned more favorably than ours did; and no day was ever more clouded than the present. Wisdom and good examples are necessary at this time to rescue the political machine from the impending storm. Virginia has now an opportunity to set the latter, and has enough of the former, I hope, to take the lead in promoting this great and arduous work. Without an alteration in our political creed, the superstructure we have been seven years in raising, at the expense of so much treasure and blood, must fall. We are fast verging to anarchy and confusion.

By a letter which I have received from General Knox, who had just returned from Massachusetts, whither he had been sent by Congress consequent of the commotions in that State, is replete with melancholy accounts of the temper and designs of a considerable part of that people. Among other things he says:

"Their creed is, that the property of the United States has been protected from the confiscation of Britain by the joint exertions of *all;* and therefore ought to be the *common property of all;* and he that attempts opposition to this creed, is an enemy to equity and justice, and ought to be swept from off the face of the earth." Again: "They are determined to annihilate all debts, public and private, and have agrarian laws, which are easily effected by the means of unfunded paper money, which shall be a tender in all cases whatever." He adds: "The number of these people amount in Massachusetts to about one fifth part of several populous counties, and to them may be collected people of similar sentiments from the States of Rhode Island, Connecticut, and New Hampshire, so as to constitute a body of about twelve or fifteen thousand desperate and unprincipled men. They are chiefly of the young and active part of the community."

How melancholy is the reflection, that in so short a space we should have made such large strides towards fulfilling the predictions of our transatlantic foes! "Leave them to themselves, and their government will soon dissolve." Will not the wise and good strive hard to avert this evil? Or will their supineness suffer ignorance, and the arts of self-interested, designing, disaffected, and desperate characters, to involve this great country in wretchedness and contempt? What stronger evidence can be given of the want of energy in our government, than these disorders? If there is not power in it to check them, what security has a man for life, liberty, or property? To you I am sure I need not add aught on this subject. The consequences of a lax or inefficient government are too obvious to be dwelt upon. Thirteen sovereignties pulling against each other, and all tugging at the federal head, will soon bring ruin on the whole; whereas a liberal and energetic constitution, well guarded and closely watched to prevent encroachments, might restore us to that degree of respectability and consequences, to which we had a fair claim and the brightest prospect of attaining. With sentiments of very great esteem and regard.

I am, dear Sir, &c.

National Representation in Congress

To Bushrod Washington, Mount Vernon, November 15, 1786

That representatives ought to be the mouth of their constituents, I do not deny; nor do I mean to call in question the right of the latter to instruct them. It is to the embarrassment, into which they may be thrown by these instructions in *national matters,* that my objections lie. In speaking of national matters I look to the federal government, which, in my opinion, it is the interest of every State to support; and to do this, as there are a variety of interests in the Union, there must be a yielding of the parts to coalesce the whole. Now a county, a district, or even a State, might decide on a measure, which, though apparently for the benefit of it in its unconnected state, may be repugnant to the interests of the nation, and eventually to the State itself, as part of the confederation. . . . In local matters which concern the district, or things which respect the internal policy of the State, there may be nothing amiss in instructions. In national matters, also, the *sense,* but not the *law* of the district may be given, leaving the delegates to judge from the nature of the case and the evidence before them.

Fears Disorders

To Henry Knox, Mount Vernon, December 26, 1786

. . . I feel, my dear General Knox, infinitely more than I can express to you, for the disorders, which have arisen in these States. Good God! Who, besides a Tory, could have foreseen, or a Briton predicted them? Were these people wiser than others, or did they judge of us from the corruption and depravity of their own hearts? The latter I am persuaded was the case and that notwithstanding the boasted virtue of America we are very little if anything behind them in dispositions to every thing that is bad.

I do assure you, that even at this moment, when I reflect upon the present prospect of our affairs, it seems to me to be like the vision of a dream. My mind can scarcely realize it as a thing in actual existence; so strange, so wonderful does it appear to me. In this, as in most other matters, we are too slow. When this spirit first dawned, probably it might have been easily checked; but it is scarcely within the reach of human ken, at this moment, to say when, where, or how it will terminate. There are combustibles in every State, which a spark might set fire to. In this a perfect calm prevails at present; and a prompt disposition to support and give energy to the federal system is discovered, if the unlucky stirring of the dispute respecting the navigation of the Mississippi does not become a leaven that will ferment and sour the mind of it.

The resolutions of the present session respecting a paper emission, military certificates, &c., have stamped justice and liberality on the proceedings of the Assembly. By a late act, it seems very desirous of a general convention to revise and amend the federal constitution. *Apropos;* what prevented the eastern States from attending the September meeting at Annapolis?[1] Of all the States in the Union it should have seemed to me, that a measure of this sort, (distracted as they were with internal commotions and experiencing the want of energy in the government,) would have been most pleasing to them. What are the prevailing sentiments of the one now proposed to be held in Philadelphia in May next? and how will it be attended? You are at the fountain of intelligence, where the wisdom of the nation, it is to be presumed, is concentred; consequently better able, (as I have had sufficient experience of your intelligence, confidence, and candor,) to solve these questions.

The Maryland Assembly has been violently agitated by the question for a paper emission. It has been carried in the House of Delegates; but what has been or may be the fate of the bill in the Senate, I have not yet heard. The partisans in favor of the measure in the lower House threaten, *it is said,* a secession, if it is rejected by that branch of the legislature. Thus are we advancing. In regretting, which I have often done with the keenest sorrow, the death of our much lamented friend General Greene, I have accompanied it of late with a query, whether he would not have preferred such an exit to the scenes, which, it is more than probable, many of his compatriots may live to bemoan.

In both your letters you intimate, that the men of reflection, principle, and property in New England, feeling the inefficacy of their present government, are contemplating a change; but you are not explicit with respect to its nature. It has been supposed, that the constitution of the State of Massachusetts was amongst the most energetic in the Union. May not these disorders then be ascribed to an indulgent exercise of the powers of administration? If your laws authorized, and your powers are equal to the sup-

[1] At the Annapolis Convention in September, 1786, the only States represented were New York, New Jersey, Pennsylvania, Delaware, and Virginia.

pression of these tumults in the first instance, delay and unnecessary expedients were improper. These are rarely well applied; and the same causes would produce similar effects in any form of government, if the powers of it are not exercised. I ask this question for information. I know nothing of the facts.

That Great Britain will be an unconcerned spectator of the present insurrections, if they continue, is not to be expected. That she is at this moment sowing the seeds of jealousy and discontent among the various tribes of Indians on our frontiers, admits of no doubt in my mind; and that she will improve every opportunity to foment the spirit of turbulence within the bowels of the United States, with a view of distracting our governments and promoting divisions, is with me not less certain. Her first manœuvres in this will no doubt be covert, and may remain so till the period shall arrive when a decided line of conduct may avail her. Charges of violating the treaty, and other pretexts, will then not be wanting to color overt acts, tending to effect the great objects of which she has long been in labor. A man is now at the head of their American affairs, well calculated to conduct measures of this kind, and more than probably was selected for the purpose. We ought not therefore to sleep nor to slumber. Vigilance in watching and vigor in acting is become in my opinion indispensably necessary. If the powers are inadequate, amend or alter them; but do not let us sink into the lowest state of humiliation and contempt, and become a by-word in all the earth. I think with you, that the spring will unfold important and distressing scenes, unless much wisdom and good management is displayed in the interim. Adieu. Be assured no man has a higher esteem and regard for you, than I have; none more sincerely your friend. . . .

Federal Convention

To David Humphreys, December 26, 1786

That the federal government is nearly if not quite at a stand, none will deny. The first question then is, shall it be annihilated or supported? If the latter, the proposed convention is an object of the first magnitude, and should be sustained by all the friends of the present constitution. In the other case, if, on a full and dispassionate revision, the continuance shall be adjudged impracticable or unwise, as only delaying an event which must ere long take place, would it not be better for such a meeting to suggest some other, to avoid if possible civil disorder or other impending evils? I must candidly confess, as we could not remain quiet more than three or four years in time of peace, under the constitutions of our own choosing, which it was believed, in many States at least, were formed with deliberation and wisdom, I see little prospect either of our agreeing upon any other, or that we should remain long satisfied under it if we could. Yet I would wish any thing and every thing essayed to prevent the effusion of blood, and to avert the humiliating and contemptible figure we are about to make in the annals of mankind.

If this second attempt to convene the States, for the purposes proposed by the report of the partial representation at Annapolis in September, should also prove abortive, it may be considered as an unequivocal evidence, that the States are not likely to agree on any general measure, which is to pervade the Union, and of course that there is an end of federal government. The States, therefore, which make the last dying essay to avoid these misfortunes, would be mortified at the issue, and their deputies would return home chagrined at their ill success and disappointment. This would be a disagreeable circumstance for any one of them to be in, but more particularly so for a person in my situation.

To General Henry Knox, February 3, 1787

Thus the matter stands, which is the reason of my saying to you *in confidence,* that at present I retain my first intention not to go. In the mean while, as I have the fullest conviction of your friendship for and attachment to me, know your abilities to judge, and your means of information, I shall receive any communication from you on this subject with thankfulness. My first wish is to do for the best, and to act with propriety. You know me too well to believe, that reserve or concealment of any opinion or circumstance would be at all agreeable to me. The legality of this convention I do not mean to discuss, nor how problematical the issue of it may be. That powers are wanting none can deny. Through what medium they are to be derived will, like other matters, engage the attention of the wise. That, which takes the shortest course to obtain them, in my opinion will, under present circumstances, be found best; otherwise, like a house on fire, whilst the most regular mode of extinguishing the flames is contended for, the building is reduced to ashes. My opinion of the energetic wants of the federal government are well known. My public annunciations and private declarations have uniformly expressed these sentiments; and, however constitutional it may be for Congress to point out the defects of the federal system, I am strongly inclined to believe, that it would not be found the most efficacious channel for the recommendations, more especially the alterations, to flow, for reasons too obvious to enumerate.

To David Humphreys, March 8, 1787

I am still indirectly and delicately pressed by many to attend this meeting; and a thought has run thro' my mind of late attended with more embarrassment than any former one. It is whether my not doing it will not be considered as an implied dereliction to Republicanism—nay more, whether (however injurious the imputation) it may not be ascribed to other motives. My wish is I confess to see this Convention tied [tried?]; after which, if the present form is not made efficient, conviction of the propriety of a change will pervade all ranks, and many [may] be effected by peace. Till then, however necessary it may appear to the more discerning part of the community, my opinion is, that it cannot be accomplished without great contention and much confusion for reasons too obvious to enumerate. It is one of the evils, perhaps not the smallest, of democratical governments that they must feel before they will see or act under this view of matters, and not doubting but you have heard the sentiments of many respectable characters since the date of your letter of the 20th of January on this subject, and perhaps since the business has been moved in Congress of the propriety or impropriety of my attendance, let me pray you, my dear Sir, to give me confidentially the public opinion and expectation as far as it has come to your knowledge of what it is supposed, I will or ought to do on this occasion.

To John Jay, Mount Vernon, March 10, 1787

. . . How far the revision of the federal system, and giving more adequate powers to Congress may be productive of an efficient government, I will not under my present view of the matter, pretend to decide.—That many inconveniences result from the present form, none can deny. Those enumerated in your letter are so obvious and sensibly felt that no logic can controvert, nor is it likely that any change of conduct will remove them, and that attempts to alter or amend it will be like the proppings of a house which is ready to fall, and which no shoars can support (as many seem to think) may also be true. But, is the public mind matured for such an important change as the one you have suggested? What would be the consequences of a premature attempt? My opinion is, that this Country must yet feel and see more, before it can be accomplished.

A thirst for power, and the bantling, I had liked to have said monster for sovereignty, which have taken such fast hold of the States individually, will when joined by the many whose personal consequence in the control of State politics will in a manner be annihilated, form a strong phalanx against it; and when to these the few who can hold posts of honor or profit in the national government, are compared with the many who will see but little prospect of being noticed, and the discontent of others who may look for appointments, the opposition will be altogether irresistible till the mass, as well as the more discerning part of the Community shall see the necessity. Among men of reflection, few will be found I believe, who are not beginning to think that our system is more perfect in theory than in practice; and that notwithstanding the boasted virtue of America it is more than probable we shall exhibit the last melancholy proof, that mankind are not competent to their own government without the means of coercion in the sovereign.

Yet I would fain try what the wisdom of the proposed convention will suggest: and what can be effected by their councils. It may be the last peaceable mode of essaying the practicability of the present form, without a greater lapse of time than the exigency of our affairs will allow. In strict propriety a convention so holden may not be legal. Congress, however, may give it a coloring by recommendation, which would fit it more to the taste without proceeding to a definition of the powers. This, however constitutionally it might be done, would not, in my opinion, be expedient: for delicacy on the one hand, and jealousy on the other, would produce a mere nihil.

My name is in the delegation to this Convention; but it was put there contrary to my desire, and remains contrary to my request. Several reasons at the time of this appointment and which yet exist, conspired to make an attendance inconvenient, perhaps improper, tho' a good deal urged to it. With sentiments of great regard and friendship, &c. . . .

To David Stuart, Philadelphia, July 1, 1787

. . . Rhode Island, from our last accts. still perseveres in that impolitic, unjust, and one might add without much impropriety scandalous conduct, which seems to have marked all her public Councils of late. Consequently, no Representation is yet here from thence. New Hampshire, tho' Delegates have been appointed, is also unrepresented. Various causes have been assigned, whether well, or ill-founded I shall not take upon me to decide. The fact, however, is that they are not here. Political contests, and want of money, are amidst the reasons assigned for the non-attendance of the members.

As the rules of the convention prevent me from relating any of the proceedings of it, and the gazettes contain, more fully than I could detail, other occurrences of a public nature, I have little to communicate to you on the article of news. Happy indeed would it be, if the convention shall be able to recommend such a firm and permanent government for this Union, that all who live under it may be secure in their lives, liberty, and property; and thrice happy would it be, if such a recommendation should obtain. Every body wishes, every body expects something from the convention; but what will be the final result of its deliberation, the book of fate must disclose. Persuaded I am, that the primary cause of all our disorders lies in the different State governments, and in the tenacity of that power, which pervades the whole of their systems. Whilst independent sovereignty is so ardently contended for, whilst the local views of each State, and separate interests, by which they are too much governed, will not yield to a more enlarged scale of politics, incompatibility in the laws of different States, and disrespect to those of the general government, must render the situation of this great country weak, inefficient, and disgraceful. It has already done so, almost to the final dissolution of it. Weak at home and disregarded abroad is our present condition, and contemptible enough it is.

Entirely unnecessary was it to offer any apology for the sentiments you were so obliging as to offer me. I have had no wish more ardent, through the whole progress of this business, than that of knowing what kind of government is best calculated for us to live under. No doubt there will be a diversity of sentiments on this important subject; and, to inform the judgment, it is necessary to hear all arguments that can be advanced. To please all is impossible, and to attempt it would be vain. The only way, therefore, is, under all the views in which it can be placed, and with a due consideration to circumstances, habits, &c., &c., to form such a government as will bear the scrutinizing eye of criticism, and trust it to the good sense and patriotism of the people to carry it into effect. Demagogues, men who are unwilling to lose any of their State consequence, and interested characters in each, will oppose any general government. But let these be regarded rightly, and justice, it is to be hoped, will at length prevail. My best wishes attend Mrs. Stuart, yourself, and the girls. If I can render any service whilst I remain here, I shall be happy in doing it. I am, &c.

To Alexander Hamilton, Philadelphia, July 10, 1787

I thank you for your communication of the 3d. When I refer you to the state of the counsels, which prevailed at the period you left this city, and add that they are now if possible in a worse train than ever, you will find but little ground on which the hope of a good establishment can be formed. In a word, I almost despair of seeing a favorable issue to the proceedings of our convention, and do therefore repent having had any agency in the business.

The men, who oppose a strong and energetic government, are in my opinion narrow-minded politicians, or are under the influence of local views. The apprehension expressed by them, that the *people* will not accede to the form proposed, is the *ostensible,* not the *real* cause of opposition. But, admitting that the present sentiment is as they prognosticate, the proper question ought nevertheless to be, Is it, or is it not, the best form that such a country as this can adopt? If it be the best, recommend it, and it will assuredly obtain, maugre opposition. I am sorry you went away. I wish you were back. The crisis is equally important and alarming, and no opposition, under such circumstances, should discourage exertions till the signature is offered. I will not at this time trouble you with more than my best wishes and sincere regard.

I am, dear Sir, &c.

The Constitution

To Patrick Henry, Mount Vernon, September 24, 1787

In the first moment after my return, I take the liberty of sending you a copy of the constitution, which the federal convention has submitted to the people of these States. I accompany it with no observations. Your own judgment will at once discover the good and the exceptionable parts of it; and your experience of the difficulties, which have ever arisen when attempts have been made to reconcile such variety of interests and local prejudices, as pervade the several States, will render explanation unnecessary. I wish the constitution, which is offered, had been made more perfect; but I sincerely believe it is the best that could be obtained at this time. And, as a constitutional door is opened for amendment hereafter, the adoption of it, under the present circumstances of the Union, is in my opinion desirable.

From a variety of concurring accounts it appears to me, that the political concerns of this country are in a manner suspended by a thread, and that the convention has been looked up to, by the reflecting part of the community, with a solicitude which is hardly to be conceived; and, if nothing had been agreed on by that body, anarchy would soon have ensued, the seeds being deeply sown in every soil. I am, &c.

To Colonel David Humphreys, October 10, 1787

The Constitution that is submitted, is not free from imperfections, but there are as few radical defects in it as could well be expected, considering the heterogeneous mass of which the Convention was composed and the diversity of interests that are to be attended to. As a constitutional door is opened for future amendments and alterations, I think it would be wise in the People to accept what is offered to them and I wish it may be by as great a majority of them as it was by that of the Convention; but this is hardly to be expected because the importance and sinister views of too many characters, will be affected by the change.—Much will depend however upon literary abilities, and the recommendation of it by good pens should be *openly*, I mean, publickly afforded in the Gazettes.—Go matters however as they may, I shall have the consolation to reflect that no objects but the public good—and that peace and harmony which I wished to see prevail in the Convention, obtruded even for a moment in my bosom during the whole Session long as it was.

To Henry Knox, Mount Vernon, October, 1787

. . . The constitution is now before the judgment-seat. It has, as was expected, its adversaries and supporters. Which will preponderate is yet to be decided. The former more than probably will be most active, as the major part of them will, it is to be feared, be governed by sinister and self-important motives, to which every thing in their breasts must yield. The opposition from another class of them may perhaps, (if they should be men of reflection, candor, and information,) subside in the solution of the following simple questions. 1. Is the constitution, which is submitted by the convention, preferable to the government, (if it can be called one,) under which we now live? 2. Is it probable that more confidence would at the time be placed in another convention, provided the experiment should be tried, than was placed in the last one, and is it likely that a better agreement would take place therein? What would be the consequences if these should not happen, or even from the delay, which must inevitably follow such an experiment? Is there not a constitutional door open for alterations or amendments? and is it not likely that real defects will be as readily discovered after as before trial? and will not our successors be as ready to apply the remedy as ourselves, if occasion should require it? To think otherwise will, in my judgment, be ascribing more of the *amor patriae*, more wisdom and more virtue to ourselves, than I think we deserve.

It is highly probable, that the refusal of our Governor [Edmund Randolph] and Colonel Mason to subscribe to the proceedings of the convention will have a bad effect in this State; for, as you well observe, they *must* not only assign reasons for the justification of their own conduct, but it is highly probable that these reasons will be clothed in most terrific array for the purpose of alarming. Some things are already addressed to the fears of the people, and will no doubt have their effect. As far, however, as the sense of this part of the country has been taken, it is strongly in favor of the proposed constitution. Further I cannot speak with precision. If a powerful opposition is given to it, the weight thereof will, I apprehend, come from the south side of the James River, and from the western counties. I am, &c.

To Bushrod Washington, Mount Vernon, November 10, 1787

. . . That the Assembly would afford the people an opportunity of deciding on the proposed constitution, I had scarcely a doubt. The only question with me was, whether it would go forth under favorable auspices, or receive the stamp of disapprobation. The opponents I expected (for it ever has been, that the adversaries to a measure are more active than its friends,) would endeavor to stamp it with unfavorable impressions, in order to bias the judgment, that is ultimately to decide on it. This is evidently the case with the writers in opposition, whose objections are better calculated to alarm the fears, than to convince the judgment, of their readers. They build their objections upon principles, that do not exist, which the constitution does not support them in, and the existence of which has been, by an appeal to the constitution itself, flatly denied; and then, as if they were unanswerable, draw all the dreadful consequences that are necessary to alarm the apprehensions of the ignorant or unthinking. It is not the interest of the major part of those characters to be convinced; nor will their local views yield to arguments, which do not accord with their present or future prospects.

A candid solution of a single question, to which the plainest understanding is competent, does, in my opinion, decide the dispute; namely, Is it best for the States to unite or not to unite? If there are men, who prefer the latter, then unquestionably the constitution which is offered must, in their estimation, be wrong from the words, "*We the people,*" to the signature, inclusively, but those, who think differently, and yet object to parts of it, would do well to consider, that it does not lie with any *one* State, or the *minority* of the States, to superstruct a constitution for the whole. The separate interests, as far as it is practicable, must be consolidated; and local views must be attended to, as far as the nature of the case will admit. Hence it is, that every State has some objection to the present form, and these objections are directed to different points. That which is most pleasing to one is obnoxious to another, and so *vice versâ.* If then the union of the whole is a desirable object, the component parts must yield a little in order to accomplish it. Without the latter, the former is unattainable; for again I repeat it, that not a single State, nor the minority of the States, can force a constitution on the majority. But, admitting the power, it will surely be granted that it cannot be done without involving scenes of civil commotion, of a very serious nature.

Let the opponents of the proposed constitution in this State be asked, and it is a question they certainly ought to have asked themselves, what line of conduct they would advise to adopt, if nine other States, of which I think there is little doubt, should accede to the constitution. Would they recommend, that it should stand single? Will they connect it with Rhode Island? Or even with two others checker-wise, and remain with them, as out casts from the society, to shift for themselves? Or will they return to their dependence on Great Britain? Or, lastly, have the mortification to come in when they will be allowed no credit for doing so?

The warmest friends and the best supporters the constitution has, do not contend that it is free from imperfections; but they found them unavoidable, and are sensible, if evil is likely to arise therefrom, the remedy must come hereafter; for in the present moment it is not to be obtained; and, as there is a constitutional door open for it, I think the people (for it is with them to judge), can, as they will have the advantage of experience on their side, decide with as much propriety on the alterations and amendments which are necessary, as ourselves. I do not think we are more inspired, have more wisdom, or possess more virtue, than those who will come after us.

The power under the constitution will always be in the people. It is intrusted for certain defined purposes, and for a certain limited period, to representatives of their own choosing; and, whenever it is executed contrary to their interest, or not agreeable to their wishes, their servants can and undoubtedly will be recalled. It is agreed on all hands, that no government can be well administered without powers; yet, the instant these are delegated, although those, who are intrusted with the administration, are no more than the creatures of the people, act as it were but for a day, and are amenable for every false step they take, they are, from the moment they receive it, set down as tyrants; their natures, they would conceive from this, immediately changed, and that they can have no other disposition but to oppress. Of these things, in a government constituted and guarded as *ours* is, I have no idea; and do firmly believe, that, whilst many *ostensible* reasons are assigned to prevent the adoption of it, the real ones are concealed behind the curtains, because they are not of a nature to appear in open day. I believe further, supposing them pure, that as great evils result from too great jealousy as from the want of it. We need look, I think, no further for proof of this, than to the constitution of some, if not all, of these States. No man is a warmer advocate for proper restraints and wholesome checks in every department of government, than I am; but I have never yet been able to discover the propriety of placing it absolutely out of the power of men to render essential services, because a possibility remains of their doing ill. . . .

To Edmund Randolph, Governor of Virginia, Mount Vernon, January 8, 1788

. . . The diversity of sentiments upon the important matter, which has been submitted to the people, was as much expected as it is regretted by me. The various passions and *motives,* by which men are influenced, are concomitants of fallibility, engrafted into our nature for the purposes of unerring wisdom; but, had I entertained a latent hope, (at the time you moved to have the constitution submitted to a second convention,) that a more perfect form would be agreed to, in a word, that any constitution would be adopted under the impressions and instructions of the members, the publications, which have taken place since, would have eradicated every form of it. How do the sentiments of the influential characters in this State, who are opposed to the constitution, and have favored the public with their opinions, quadrate with each other? Are they not at variance on some of the most important points? If the opponents in the *same* State cannot agree in their principles, what prospect is there of a coalescence with the advocates of the measure, when the different views and jarring interests of so wide and extended an empire are to be brought forward and combated?

To my judgment it is more clear than ever, that an attempt to amend the constitution, which is submitted, would be productive of more heat and greater confusion than can well be conceived. There are some things in the new form, I will readily acknowledge, which never did, and I am persuaded never will, obtain my cordial approbation; but I then did conceive, and do now most firmly believe, that in the aggregate it is the best constitution, that can be obtained at this epoch, and that this, or a dissolution of the Union, awaits our choice, and are the only alternatives before us. Thus believing, I had not, nor have I now, any hesitation in deciding on which to lean.

I pray your forgiveness for the expression of these sentiments. In acknowledging the receipt of your letter on this subject, it was hardly to be avoided, although I am well-disposed to let the matter rest entirely on its own merits, and men's minds to their own workings. With very great esteem and regard I am, &c.

To the Marquis de Lafayette, Mount Vernon, February 7, 1788

You know it always gives me the sincerest pleasure to hear from you, and therefore I need only say, that your two kind letters of the 9th and 15th of October, so replete with personal affection and confidential intelligence, afforded me inexpressible satisfaction. . . .

You appear to be, as might be expected from a real friend to this country, anxiously concerned about its present political situation. So far as I am able, I shall be happy in gratifying that friendly solicitude. As to my sentiments with respect to the merits of the new constitution, I will disclose them without reserve, (although by passing through the post-office they should become known to all the world,) for in truth I have nothing to conceal on that subject. It appears to me, then, little short of a miracle, that the delegates from so many different States (which States you know are also different from each other), in their manners, circumstances, and prejudices, should unite in forming a system of national government, so little liable to well-founded objections. Nor am I yet such an enthusiastic, partial, or undiscriminating admirer of it, as not to perceive it is tinctured with some real (though not radical) defects. The limits of a letter would not suffer me to go fully into an examination of them; nor would the discussion be entertaining or profitable. I therefore forbear to touch upon it. With regard to the two great points, (the pivots upon which the whole machine must move,) my creed is simply,

1st. That the general government is not invested with more powers, than are indispensably necessary to perform the functions of a good government; and consequently, that no objection ought to be made against the quantity of power delegated to it.

2ly. That these powers, (as the appointment of all rulers will for ever arise from, and at short, stated intervals recur to, the free suffrage of the people,) are so distributed among the legislative, executive, and judicial branches, into which the general government is arranged, that it can never be in danger of degenerating into a monarchy, an oligarchy, an aristocracy, or any other despotic or oppressive form, so long as there shall remain any virtue in the body of the people.

I would not be understood, my dear Marquis, to speak of consequences, which may be produced in the revolution of ages, by corruption of morals, profligacy of manners, and listlessness for the preservation of the natural and unalienable rights of mankind, nor of the successful usurpations, that may be established at such an unpropitious juncture upon the ruins of liberty, however providently guarded and secured; as these are contingencies against which no human prudence can effectually provide. It will at least be a recommendation to the proposed constitution, that it is provided with more checks and barriers against the introduction of tyranny, and those of a nature less liable to be surmounted, than any government hitherto instituted among mortals hath possessed. We are not to expect perfection in this world; but mankind, in modern times, have apparently made some progress in the science of government. Should that, which is now offered to the people of America, be found on experiment less perfect than it can be made, a constitutional door is left open for its amelioration.

Some respectable characters have wished, that the States, after having pointed out whatever alterations and amendments may be judged necessary, would appoint another federal convention to modify it upon those documents. For myself, I have wondered, that sensible men should not see the impracticability of this scheme. The members would go fortified with such instructions, that nothing but discordant ideas could prevail. Had I but slightly suspected, at the time when the late convention was in session, that another convention would not be likely to agree upon a better form of government, I should now be confirmed in the fixed belief that they would not be able to agree upon any system whatever; so many, I may add, such contradictory and in my opinion unfounded objections have been urged against the system in contemplation, many of which would operate equally against every efficient government, that might be proposed. I will only add, as a further opinion founded on the maturest deliberation, that there is no alternative, no hope of alteration, no intermediate resting-place, between the adoption of this, and a recurrence to an unqualified state of anarchy, with all its deplorable consequences. . . .

To the Marquis de Lafayette, Mount Vernon, April 28, 1788

. . . I notice with pleasure the additional immunities and facilities in trade, which France has granted by the late royal *arret* to the United States. I flatter myself it will have the desired effect in some measure of augmenting the commercial intercourse. From the productions and wants of the two countries, their trade with each other is certainly capable of [too?] great amelioration to be actuated by a spirit of unwise policy. For so surely as ever we shall have an efficient government established, so surely will that government impose retaliating restrictions, to a certain degree, upon the trade of Britain. At present, or under our existing form of confederation, it would be idle to think of making commercial regulations on our part. One State passes a prohibitory law respecting some article, another State opens wide the avenue for its admission. One Assembly makes a system, another Assembly unmakes it. Virginia, in the very last session of her legislature, was about to have passed some of the most extravagant and preposterous edicts on the subject of trade, that ever stained the leaves of a legislative code. It is in vain to hope for a remedy of these, and innumerable other evils, until a general government shall be adopted.

The conventions of six States only have as yet accepted the new constitution. No one has rejected it. It is believed that the convention of Maryland, which is now in session, and that of South Carolina, which is to assemble on the 12th of May, will certainly adopt it. It is also since the elections of members of the convention have taken place in this State, more generally believed, that it will be adopted here, than it was before those elections were made. There will, however, be powerful and eloquent speeches on both sides of the question in the Virginia convention; but as Pendleton, Wythe, Blair, Madison, Jones, Nicholas, Innes, and many other of our first characters, will be advocates for its adoption, you may suppose the weight of abilities will rest on that side. Henry and Mason are its great adversaries. The governor, if he approves it at all, will do it feebly.

On the general merits of this proposed constitution, I wrote to you some time ago my sentiments pretty freely. That letter had not been received by you, when you addressed to me the last of yours, which has come to my hands. I had never supposed that perfection could be the result of accommodation and mutual concession. The opinion of Mr. Jefferson and yourself is certainly a wise one, that the constitution ought by all means to be accepted by nine States before any attempt should be made to procure amendments; for, if that acceptance shall not previously take place, men's minds will be so much agitated and soured, that the danger will be greater than ever of our becoming a disunited people. Whereas, on the other hand, with prudence in temper and a spirit of moderation, every essential alteration may in the process of time be expected.

You will doubtless have seen, that it was owing to this conciliatory and patriotic principle, that the convention of Massachusetts adopted the constitution *in toto,* but recommended a number of specific alterations, and quieting explanations as an early, serious, and unremitting subject of attention. Now, although it is not to be expected, that every individual in society will or can be brought to agree upon what is exactly the best form of government, yet there are many things in the constitution, which only need to be explained, in order to prove equally satisfactory to all parties. For example, there was not a member of the convention, I believe, who had the least objection to what is contended for by the advocates for a *Bill of Rights* and *Trial by Jury*. The first, where the people evidently retained every thing, which they did not in the express terms give up, was considered nugatory, as you will find to have been more fully explained by Mr. Wilson and others; and, as to the second, it was only the difficulty of establishing a mode, which should not interfere with the fixed modes of any of the States, that induced the convention to leave it as a matter of future adjustment.

There are other points in which opinions would be more likely to vary. As for instance, on the ineligibility of the same person for president, after he should have served a certain course of years. Guarded so effectually as the proposed constitution is, in respect to the prevention of bribery and undue influence in the choice of president, I confess I differ widely myself from Mr. Jefferson and you, as to the necessity or expediency of rotation in that appointment. The matter was fairly discussed in the convention, and to my full conviction, though I cannot have time or room to sum up the argument in this letter. There cannot in my judgment be the least danger, that the president will by any practicable intrigue ever be able to continue himself one moment in office, much less perpetuate himself in it, but in the last stage of corrupted morals and political depravity; and even then, there is as much danger that any other species of domination would prevail. Though, when a people shall have become incapable of governing themselves, and fit for a master, it is of little consequence from what quarter he comes. Under an extended view of this part of the subject, I can see no propriety in precluding ourselves from the services of any man, who on some great emergency shall be deemed universally most capable of serving the public. . . .

To the Marquis de Lafayette, Mount Vernon, June 18, 1788

. . . I like not much the situation of affairs in France. The bold demands of the parliaments, and the decisive tone of the King, show that but little more irritation would be necessary to blow up the spark of discontent into a flame, that might not easily be quenched. If I were to advise, I should say that great moderation should be used on both sides. Let it not, my dear Marquis, be considered as a derogation from the good opinion, that I entertain of your prudence, when I caution you, as an individual desirous of signalizing yourself in the cause of your country and freedom, against running into extremes and prejudicing your cause. The King, though, I think from every thing I have been able to learn, he is really a good-hearted though a warm-spirited man, if thwarted injudiciously in the execution of prerogatives that belonged to the crown, and in plans which he conceives calculated to promote the national good, may disclose qualities he has been little thought to possess. On the other hand, such a spirit seems to be awakened in the kingdom, as, if managed with extreme prudence, may produce a gradual and tacit revolution much in favor of the subjects, by abolishing *lettres de cachet,* and defining more accurately the powers of government. It is a wonder to me, there should be found a single monarch, who does not realize that his own glory and felicity must depend on the prosperity and happiness of his people. How easy is it for a sovereign to do that, which shall not only immortalize his name, but attract the blessings of millions.

In a letter I wrote you a few days ago by Mr. Barlow, but which might not possibly have reached New York until after his departure, I mentioned the accession of Maryland to the proposed government, and gave you the state of politics to that period. Since which the convention of South Carolina has ratified the constitution by a great majority. That of this State has been sitting almost three weeks; and, so nicely does it appear to be balanced, that each side asserts that it has a preponderancy of votes in its favor. It is probable, therefore, the majority will be small, let it fall on whichever part it may. I am inclined to believe it will be in favor of the adoption. The conventions of New York and New Hampshire both assemble this week. A large proportion of members, with the governor at their head, in the former, are said to be opposed to the government in contemplation. New Hampshire, it is thought, will adopt it without much hesitation or delay. It is a little strange, that the men of large property in the south should be more afraid that the constitution will produce an aristocracy or a monarchy, than the genuine democratical people of the east. Such are our actual prospects. The accession of one State more will complete the number, which, by the constitutional provision, will be sufficient in the first instance to carry the government into effect.

And then, I expect, that many blessings will be attributed to our new government, which are now taking their rise from that industry and frugality, into the practice of which the people have been forced from necessity. I really believe, that there never was so much labor and economy to be found before in the country as at the present moment. If they persist in the habits they are acquiring, the good effects will soon be distinguishable. When the people shall find themselves secure under an energetic government, when foreign nations shall be disposed to give us equal advantages in commerce from dread of retaliation, when the burdens of war shall be in a manner done away by the sale of western lands, when the seeds of happiness which are sown here shall begin to expand themselves, and when every one, (under his own vine and fig-tree,) shall begin to taste the fruits of freedom, then all these blessings (for all these blessings will come) will be referred to the fostering influence of the new government. Whereas many causes will have conspired to produce them. You see I am not less enthusiastic than I ever have been, if a belief that peculiar scenes of felicity are reserved for this country is to be denominated enthusiasm. Indeed, I do not believe, that Providence has done so much for nothing. It has always been my creed, that we should not be left as an awful monument to prove, "that mankind, under the most favorable circumstances for civil liberty and happiness, are unequal to the task of governing themselves, and therefore made for a master."

We have had a backward spring and summer, with more rain and cloudy weather than almost ever has been known; still the appearance of crops in some parts of the country is favorable, as we may generally expect will be the case, from the difference of soil and variety of climate in so extensive a region; insomuch that I hope, some day or another, we shall become a storehouse and granary for the world. In addition to our former channels of trade, salted provisions, butter, and cheese are exported with profit from the eastern States to the East Indies. In consequence of a contract, large quantities of flour are lately sent from Baltimore for supplying the garrison of Gibraltar. I am, &c.

To Thomas Jefferson, August 31, 1788

. . . The merits and defects of the proposed constitution have been largely and ably discussed. For myself, I was ready to have embraced any tolerable compromise, that was competent to save us from impending ruin; and I can say there are scarcely any of the amendments, which have been suggested, to which I have much objection, except that which goes to the prevention of direct taxation. And that, I presume, will be more strenuously advocated and insisted upon hereafter, than any other. I had indulged the expectation, that the new government would enable those entrusted with its administration to do justice to the public creditors, and retrieve the national character. But, if no means are to be employed but requisitions, that expectation was vain, and we may as well recur to the old confederation. If the system can be put in operation, without touching much the pockets of the people, perhaps it may be done; but, in my judgment, infinite circumspection and prudence are yet necessary in the experiment. It is nearly impossible for anybody who has not been on the spot, (from any description) to conceive what the delicacy and danger of our situation have been. Though the peril is not past entirely, thank God the prospect is somewhat brightening.

You will probably have heard, before the receipt of this letter, that the general government has been adopted by eleven States, and that the actual Congress have been prevented from issuing their ordinance for carrying it into execution, in consequence of a dispute about the place at which the future Congress shall meet. It is probable, that Philadelphia or New York will soon be agreed upon.

I will just touch on the bright side of our national state, before I conclude; and we may perhaps rejoice, that the people have been ripened by misfortune for the reception of a good government. They are emerging from the gulf of dissipation and debt, into which they had precipitated themselves at the close of the war. Economy and industry are evidently gaining ground. Not only agriculture, but even manufactures, are much more attended to than formerly. Notwithstanding the shackles under which our trade in general labors, commerce to the East Indies is prosecuted with considerable success. Salted provisions and other produce, (particularly from Massachusetts,) have found an advantageous market there. The voyages are so much shorter, and the vessels are navigated at so much less expense, that we may hope to rival and supply, (at least through the West Indies,) some part of Europe with commodities from thence. This year the exports from Massachusetts have amounted to a great deal more than their imports. I wish this was the case everywhere. . . .

On Accepting the Presidency

To Henry Lee, September 22, 1788

The principal topic of your letter is to me a point of great delicacy indeed, insomuch that I can scarcely without some impropriety touch upon it. In the first place, the event to which you allude may never happen; among other reasons, because, if the partiality of my fellow citizens conceive it to be a means by which the sinews of the new government would be strengthened, it will of consequence be obnoxious to those, who are in opposition to it, many of whom unquestionably will be placed among the electors.

This consideration alone would supersede the expediency of announcing any definite and irrevocable resolution. You are among the small number of those, who know my invincible attachment to domestic life, and that my sincerest wish is to continue in the enjoyment of it solely until my final hour. But the world would be neither so well instructed, nor so candidly disposed, as to believe me uninfluenced by sinister motives, in case any circumstance should render a deviation from the line of conduct I had prescribed to myself indispensable.

Should the contingency you suggest take place, and (for argument's sake alone let me say it) should my unfeigned reluctance to accept the office be overcome by a deference for the reasons and opinions of my friends, might I not, after the declarations I have made (and Heaven knows they were made in the sincerity of my heart), in the judgment of the impartial world and of posterity, be chargeable with levity and inconsistency, if not with rashness and ambition? Nay farther, would there not even be some apparent foundation for the two former charges? Now justice to myself and tranquility of conscience require, that I should act a part, if not above imputation, at least capable of vindication. Nor will you conceive me to be too solicitous for reputation. Though I prize as I ought the good opinion of my fellow citizens, yet, if I know myself, I would not seek or retain popularity at the expense of one social duty or moral virtue.

While doing what my conscience informed me was right, as it respected my God, my country, and myself, I could despise all the party clamor and unjust censure, which must be expected from some, whose personal enmity might be occasioned by their hostility to the government. I am conscious, that I fear alone to give any real occasion for obloquy, and that I do not dread to meet with unmerited reproach. And certain I am, whensoever I shall be convinced the good of my country requires my reputation to be put in risk, regard for my own fame will not come in competition with an object of so much magnitude. If I declined the task, it would lie upon quite another principle. Notwithstanding my advanced season of life, my increasing fondness for agricultural amusements, and my growing love of retirement, augment and confirm my decided predilection for the character of a private citizen, yet it would be no one of these motives, nor the hazard to which my former reputation might be exposed, nor the terror of encountering new fatigues and troubles, that would deter me from an acceptance; but a belief, that some other person, who had less pretence and less inclination to be excused, could execute all the duties full as satisfactorily as myself.

Chapter 8

ADDRESSES AND MESSAGES

ADDRESS TO THE OFFICERS

March, 1783

Gentlemen, By an anonymous summons an attempt has been made to convene you together. How inconsistent with the rules of propriety, how unmilitary, and how subversive of all good order and discipline, let the good sense of the army decide.

In the moment of this summons, another anonymous production was sent into circulation; addressed more to the feelings and passions, than to the reason and judgment of the army. The author of the piece is entitled to much credit for the goodness of his pen, and I could wish he had as much credit for the rectitude of his heart; for, as men see through different optics, and are induced by the reflecting faculties of the mind to use different means to obtain the same end, the author of the address should have had more charity, than to mark for suspicion the man, who should recommend moderation and longer forbearance, or in other words, who should not think as he thinks, and act as he advises. But he had another plan in view, in which candor and liberality of sentiment, regard to justice, and love of country, have no part; and he was right to insinuate the darkest suspicion, to effect the blackest designs.

That the address is drawn with great art, and is designed to answer the most insidious purposes, that it is calculated to impress the mind with an idea of premeditated injustice in the sovereign power of the United States, and rouse all those resentments, which must unavoidably flow from such a belief; that the secret mover of this scheme, whoever he may be, intended to take advantage of the passions, while they were warmed by the recollection of past distresses, without giving time for cool, deliberate thinking, and that composure of mind which is so necessary to give dignity and stability to measures, is rendered too obvious by the mode of conducting the business, to need other proof than a reference to the proceeding.

Thus much, Gentlemen, I have thought it incumbent on me to observe to you, to show upon what principles I opposed the irregular and hasty meeting, which was proposed to be held on Tuesday last, and not because I wanted a disposition to give you every opportunity, consistent with your own honor and the dignity of the army, to make known your grievances. If my conduct heretofore has not evinced to you, that I have been a faithful friend to the army, my declaration of it at this time would be equally unavailing and improper. But, as I was among the first, who embarked in the cause of our common country; as I have never left your side one moment, but when called from you on public duty; as I have been the constant companion and witness of your distresses, and not among the last to feel and acknowledge your merits; as I have ever considered my own military reputation as inseparably connected with that of the army; as my heart has ever expanded with joy, when I have heard its praises, and my indignation has arisen, when the mouth of detraction has been opened against it; it can scarcely be supposed, at this late stage of the war, that I am indifferent to its interests. But how are they to be promoted? The way is plain, says the anonymous addresser; if war continues, remove into the unsettled country; there establish yourselves, and leave an ungrateful country to defend itself. But whom are they to defend? Our wives, our children, our farms and other property, which we leave behind us? Or, in the state of hostile separation, are we to take the two first (the latter cannot be removed) to perish in a wilderness with hunger, cold, and nakedness? If peace takes place, neither sheath your swords, says he, until you have obtained full and ample justice. This dreadful alternative, of either deserting our country in the extremest hour of distress, or turning our arms against it, which is the apparent object, unless Congress can be compelled into instant compliance, has something so shocking in it, that humanity revolts at the idea. My God! What can this writer have in view by recommending such measures. Can he be a friend to the army? Can he be a friend to this country? Rather is he not an insidious foe? Some emissary, perhaps from New York, plotting the ruin of both by sowing the seeds of discord and separation between the civil and military powers of the continent? And what a compliment does he pay to our understandings, when he recommends measures, in either alternative, impracticable in their nature?

But here, Gentlemen, I will drop the curtain, because it would be as imprudent in me to assign my reasons for this opinion, as it would be insulting to your conception to suppose you stood in need of them. A moment's reflection will convince every dispassionate mind of the physical impossibility of carrying either proposal into execution.

There might, Gentlemen, be an impropriety in my taking notice, in this address to you, of an anonymous production; but the manner in which that performance has been introduced to the army, the effect it was intended to have, together with some other circumstances, will amply justify my observations on the tendency of that writing. With respect to the advice given by the author to suspect the man, who shall recommend moderate measures and longer forbearance, I spurn it, as every man who regards that liberty, and reveres that justice, for which we contend, undoubtedly must. For, if men are to be precluded from offering their sentiments on a matter, which may involve the most serious and alarming consequences, that can invite the consideration of mankind, reason is of no use to us; the freedom of speech may be taken away, and, dumb and silent, we may be led away like sheep to the slaughter.

I cannot, in justice to my own belief, and what I have great reason to conceive is the intention of Congress, conclude this address without giving it as my decided opinion, that that honorable body entertain exalted sentiments of the services of the army, and, from a full conviction of its merits and sufferings, will do it complete justice. That their endeavors to discover, and establish funds for this purpose have been unwearied, and will not cease, till they have succeeded, I have no doubt; but, like all other large bodies, where there is a variety of different interests to reconcile, their deliberations are slow. Why then should we distrust them; and, in consequence of that distrust, adopt measures, which may cast a shade over that glory, which has been so justly acquired, and tarnish the reputation of an army, which is celebrated through all Europe for its fortitude and patriotism? And for what is this done? To bring the object we seek nearer? No! Most certainly, in my opinion, it will cast it at a greater distance.

For myself (and I take no merit in giving the assurance, being induced to it from principles of gratitude, veracity, and justice), a grateful sense of the confidence you have ever placed in me, a recollection of the cheerful assistance and prompt obedience I have experienced from you, under every vicissitude of fortune, and the sincere affection I feel for an army I have so long had the honor to command, oblige me to declare in this public and solemn manner, that, in the attainment of complete justice for all your toils and dangers, and in the gratification of every wish, so far as may be done consistently with the great duty I owe to my country, and those powers we are bound to respect, you may freely command my services to the utmost extent of my abilities.

While I give you these assurances and pledge myself in the most unequivocal manner to exert whatever ability I am possessed of in your favor, let me entreat you, Gentlemen, on your part, not to take any measures, which, in the calm light of reason, will lessen the dignity and sully the glory you have hitherto maintained. Let me request you to rely on the plighted faith of your country, and place a full confidence in the purity of the intentions of Congress, that, previous to your dissolution as an army, they will cause all your accounts to be fairly liquidated, as directed in their resolutions, which were published to you two days ago, and that they will adopt the most effectual measures in their power to render ample justice to you for your faithful and meritorious services. And let me conjure you in the name of our common country, as you value your own sacred honor, as you respect the rights of humanity, and as you regard the military and national character of America, to express your utmost horror and detestation of the man, who wishes, under any specious pretences, to overturn the liberties of our country, and who wickedly attempts to open the flood gates of civil discord, and deluge our rising empire in blood.

By thus determining and thus acting, you will pursue the plain and direct road to the attainment of your wishes; you will defeat the insidious designs of our enemies, who are compelled to resort from open force to secret artifice; you will give one more distinguished proof of unexampled patriotism and patient virtue, rising superior to the pressure of the most complicated sufferings; and you will, by the dignity of your conduct, afford occasion for posterity to say, when speaking of the glorious example you have exhibited to mankind, "Had this day been wanting, the world had never seen the last stage of perfection, to which human nature is capable of attaining."

Farewell Orders to the Armies

Rocky Hill, Near Princeton, Sunday, November 2, 1783

The United States in Congress assembled, after giving the most honorable testimony to the merits of the federal armies, and presenting them with the thanks of their country for their long, eminent and faithful services, having thought proper, by their proclamation bearing date the 18th day of October last, to discharge such part of the troops as were engaged for the war, and to permit the officers on furlough to retire from service from and after to-morrow; which proclamation having been communicated in the public papers for the information and government of all concerned, it only remains for the Commander-in-chief to address himself once more, and that for the last time, to the armies of the United States (however widely dispersed the individuals who compose them may be), and to bid them an affectionate, a long farewell.

But before the Commander-in-chief takes his final leave of those he holds most dear, he wishes to indulge himself a few moments in calling to mind a slight review of the past. He will then take the liberty of exploring with his military friends their future prospects, of advising the general line of conduct, which, in his opinion, ought to be pursued; and he will conclude the address by expressing the obligations he feels himself under for the spirited and able assistance he has experienced from them, in the performance of an arduous office.

A contemplation of the complete attainment (at a period earlier than could have been expected) of the object, for which we contended against so formidable a power, cannot but inspire us with astonishment and gratitude. The disadvantageous circumstances on our part, under which the war was undertaken, can never be forgotten. The singular interpositions of Providence in our feeble condition were such, as could scarcely escape the attention of the most unobserving; while the unparalleled perseverance of the armies of the United States, through almost every possible suffering and discouragement for the space of eight long years, was little short of a standing miracle.

It is not the meaning nor within the compass of this address, to detail the hardships peculiarly incident to our service, or to describe the distresses, which in several instances have resulted from the extremes of hunger and nakedness, combined with the rigors of an inclement season; nor is it necessary to dwell on the dark side of our past affairs. Every American officer and soldier must now console himself for any unpleasant circumstances, which may have occurred, by a recollection of the uncommon scenes in which he has been called to act no inglorious part, and the astonishing events of which he has been a witness; events which have seldom, if ever before, taken place on the stage of human action; nor can they probably ever happen again. For who has before seen a disciplined army formed at once from such raw materials? Who, that was not a witness, could imagine, that the most violent local prejudices would cease so soon; and that men, who came from the different parts of the continent, strongly disposed by the habits of education to despise and quarrel with each other, would instantly become but one patriotic band of brothers? Or who, that was not on the spot, can trace the steps by which such a wonderful revolution has been effected, and such a glorious period put to all our warlike toils?

It is universally acknowledged, that the enlarged prospects of happiness, opened by the confirmation of our independence and sovereignty, almost exceeds the power of description. And shall not the brave men, who have contributed so essentially to these inestimable acquisitions, retiring victorious from the field of war to the field of agriculture, participate in all the blessings, which have been obtained? In such a republic, who will exclude them from the rights of citizens, and the fruits of their labors? In such a country, so happily circumstanced, the pursuits of commerce and the cultivation of the soil will unfold to industry the certain road to competence. To those hardy soldiers, who are actuated by the spirit of adventure, the fisheries will afford ample and profitable employment; and the extensive and fertile regions of the West will yield a most happy asylum to those, who, fond of domestic enjoyment, are seeking for personal independence. Nor is it possible to conceive, that any one of the United States will prefer a national bankruptcy, and a dissolution of the Union, to a compliance with the requisitions of Congress, and the payment of its just debts; so that the officers and soldiers may expect considerable assistance, in recommencing their civil occupations, from the sums due to them from the public, which must and will most inevitably be paid.

In order to effect this desirable purpose, and to remove the prejudices, which may have taken possession of the minds of any of the good people of the States, it is earnestly recommended to all the troops, that, with strong attachments to the Union, they should carry with them into civil society the most conciliating dispositions, and that they should prove themselves not less virtuous and useful as citizens, than they have been persevering and victorious as soldiers. What though there should be some envious individuals, who are unwilling to pay the debt the public has contracted, or to yield the tribute due to merit; yet let such unworthy treatment produce no invective, or any instance of intemperate conduct. Let it be remembered, that the unbiassed voice of the free citizens of the United States has promised the just reward and given the merited applause. Let it be known and remembered, that the reputation of the federal armies is established beyond the reach of malevolence; and let a consciousness of their achievements and fame still incite the men, who composed them, to honorable actions; under the persuasion that the private virtues of economy, prudence, and industry, will not be less amiable in civil life, than the more splendid qualities of valor, perseverance, and enterprise were in the field. Every one may rest assured, that much, very much, of the future happiness of the officers and men, will depend upon the wise and manly conduct, which shall be adopted by them when they are mingled with the great body of the community. And, although the General has so frequently given it as his opinion in the most public and explicit manner, that, unless the principles of the Federal Government were properly supported, and the powers of the Union increased, the honor, dignity, and justice of the nation would be lost forever; yet he cannot help repeating, on this occasion, so interesting a sentiment, and leaving it as his last injunction to every officer and every soldier, who may view the subject in the same serious point of light, to add his best endeavors to those of his worthy fellow citizens towards effecting these great and valuable purposes, on which our very existence as a nation so materially depends.

The Commander-in-chief conceives little is now wanting, to enable the soldier, to change the military character into that of the citizen, but that steady and decent tenor of behavior, which has generally distinguished, not only the army under his immediate command, but the different detachments and separate armies, through the course of the war. From their good sense and prudence he anticipates the happiest consequences; and, while he congratulates them on the glorious occasion, which renders their services in the field no longer necessary, he wishes to express the strong obligations he feels himself under for the assistance he has received from every class and in every instance. He presents his thanks in the most serious and affectionate manner to the general officers, as well for their counsel on many interesting occasions, as for their ardor in promoting the success of the plans he had adopted; to the commandants of regiments and corps, and to the other officers, for their great zeal and attention in carrying his orders promptly into execution; to the staff, for their alacrity and exactness in performing the duties of their several departments; and to the non-commissioned officers and private soldiers, for their extraordinary patience and suffering, as well as their invincible fortitude in action. To the various branches of the army, the General takes this last and solemn opportunity of professing his inviolable attachment and friendship. He wishes more than bare professions were in his power; that he were really able to be useful to them all in future life. He flatters himself, however, they will do him the justice to believe, that whatever could with propriety be attempted by him has been done.

And being now to conclude these his last public orders, to take his ultimate leave in a short time of the military character, and to bid a final adieu to the armies he has so long had the honor to command, he can only again offer in their behalf his recommendations to their grateful country, and his prayers to the God of armies. May ample justice be done them here, and may the choicest of Heaven's favors, both here and hereafter, attend those, who, under the Divine auspices, have secured innumerable blessings for others. With these wishes and this benediction, the Commander-in-chief is about to retire from service. The curtain of separation will soon be drawn, and the military scene to him will be closed for ever.

Address to Congress on Resigning His Commission

Annapolis, December 23, 1783

Mr. President,

The great events, on which my resignation depended, having at length taken place, I have now the honor of offering my sincere congratulations to Congress, and of presenting myself before them, to surrender into their hands the trust committed to me, and to claim the indulgence of retiring from the Service of my Country.

Happy in the confirmation of our Independence and Sovereignty, and pleased with the opportunity afforded the United States of becoming a respectable nation, I resign with satisfaction the appointment I accepted with diffidence; a diffidence in my abilities to accomplish so arduous a task, which, however, was superseded by a confidence in the rectitude of our cause, the support of the supreme Power of the Union, and the patronage of Heaven.

The successful termination of the war has verified the most sanguine expectations; and my gratitude for the interposition of

Providence, and the assistance I have received from my Countrymen, encreases with every review of the momentous contest.

While I repeat my obligations to the Army in general, I should do injustice to my own feelings not to acknowledge, in this place, the peculiar services and distinguished merits of the Gentlemen, who have been attached to my person during the war. It was impossible that the choice of confidential officers to compose my family should have been more fortunate. Permit me, Sir, to recommend in particular those, who have continued in Service to the present moment, as worthy of the favorable notice and patronage of Congress.

I consider it an indispensable duty to close this last solemn act of my official life, by commending the Interests of our dearest country to the protection of Almighty God, and those who have the superintendence of them to his holy keeping.

Having now finished the work assigned me, I retire from the great theatre of action; and, bidding an affectionate farewell to this august body, under whose orders I have so long acted, I here offer my commission, and take my leave of all the employments of public life.

First Inaugural Address

New York, April 30, 1789

Fellow-Citizens of the Senate and of the House of Representatives:

Among the vicissitudes incident to life no event could have filled me with greater anxieties than that of which the notification was transmitted by your order, and received on the 14th day of the present month. On the one hand, I was summoned by my country, whose voice I can never hear but with veneration and love, from a retreat which I had chosen with the fondest predilection, and, in my flattering hopes, with an immutable decision, as the asylum of my declining years—a retreat which was rendered every day more necessary as well as more dear to me by the addition of habit to inclination, and of frequent interruptions in my health to the gradual waste committed on it by time. On the other hand, the magnitude and difficulty of the trust to which the voice of my country called me, being sufficient to awaken in the wisest and most experienced of her citizens a distrustful scrutiny into his qualifications, could not but overwhelm with despondence one who (inheriting inferior endowments from nature and unpracticed in the duties of civil administration) ought to be peculiarly conscious of his own deficiencies. In this conflict of emotions all I dare aver is that it has been my faithful study to collect my duty from a just appreciation of every circumstance by which it might be affected. All I dare hope is that if, in executing this task, I have been too much swayed by a grateful remembrance of former instances, or by an affectionate sensibility to this transcendent proof of the confidence of my fellow-citizens, and have thence too little consulted my incapacity as well as disinclination for the weighty and untried cares before me, my error will be palliated by the motives which mislead me, and its consequences be judged by my country with some share of the partiality in which they originated.

Such being the impressions under which I have, in obedience to the public summons, repaired to the present station, it would be peculiarly improper to omit in this first official act my fervent supplications to that Almighty Being who rules over the universe, who presides in the councils of nations, and whose providential aids can supply every human defect, that His benediction may consecrate to the liberties and happiness of the people of the United States a Government instituted by themselves for these essential purposes, and may enable every instrument employed in its administration to execute with success the functions allotted to his charge. In tendering this homage to the Great Author of every public and private good, I assure myself that it expresses your sentiments not less than my own, nor those of my fellow-citizens at large less than either. No people can be bound to acknowledge and adore the Invisible Hand which conducts the affairs of men more than those of the United States. Every step by which they have advanced to the character of an independent nation seems to have been distinguished by some token of providential agency; and in the important revolution just accomplished in the system of their united government the tranquil deliberations and voluntary consent of so many distinct communities from which the event has resulted can not be compared with the means by which most governments have been established without some return of pious gratitude, along with an humble anticipation of the future blessings which the past seem to presage. These reflections, arising out of the present crisis, have forced themselves too strongly on my mind to be suppressed. You will join with me, I trust, in thinking that there are none under the influence of which the proceedings of a new and free government can more auspiciously commence.

By the article establishing the executive department it is made the duty of the President "to recommend to your consideration such measures as he shall judge necessary and expedient." The circumstances under which I now meet you will acquit me from entering into that subject further than to refer to the great constitutional charter under which you are assembled, and which, in defining your powers, designates the objects to which your attention is to be given. It will be more consistent with those circumstances, and far more congenial with the feelings which actuate me, to substitute, in place of a recommendation of particular measures, the tribute that is due to the talents, the rectitude, and the patriotism which adorn the characters selected to devise and adopt them. In these honorable qualifications I behold the surest pledges that as on one side no local prejudices or attachments, no separate views nor party animosities, will misdirect the comprehensive and equal eye which ought to watch over this great assemblage of communities and interests, so, on another, that the foundation of our national policy will be laid in the pure and immutable principles of private morality, and the preeminence of free government be exemplified by all the attributes which can win the affections of its citizens and command the respect of the world. I dwell on this prospect with every satisfaction which an ardent love for my country can inspire, since there is no truth more thoroughly established than that there exists in the economy and course of nature an indissoluble union between virtue and happiness; between duty and advantage; between the genuine maxims of an honest and magnanimous policy and the solid rewards of public prosperity and felicity; since we ought to be no less persuaded that the propitious smiles of Heaven can never be expected on a nation that disregards the eternal rules of order and right which Heaven itself has ordained; and since the preservation of the sacred fire of liberty and the destiny of the republican model of government are justly considered, perhaps, as *deeply,* as *finally,* staked on the experiment intrusted to the hands of the American people.

Besides the ordinary objects submitted to your care, it will remain with your judgment to decide how far an exercise of the occasional power delegated by the fifth article of the Constitution is rendered expedient at the present juncture by the nature of objections which have been urged against the system, or by the degree of inquietude which has given birth to them. Instead of undertaking particular recommendations on this subject, in which I could be guided by no lights derived from official opportunities, I shall again give way to my entire confidence in your discernment and pursuit of the public good; for I assure myself that whilst you carefully avoid every alteration which might endanger the benefits of an united and effective government, or which ought to await the future lessons of experience, a reverence for the characteristic rights of freemen and a regard for the public harmony will sufficiently influence your deliberations on the question how far the former can be impregnably fortified or the latter be safely and advantageously promoted.

To the foregoing observations I have one to add, which will be most properly addressed to the House of Representatives. It concerns myself, and will therefore be as brief as possible. When I was first honored with a call into the service of my country, then on the eve of an arduous struggle for its liberties, the light in which I contemplated my duty required that I should renounce every pecuniary compensation. From this resolution I have in no instance departed; and being still under the impressions which produced it, I must decline as inapplicable to myself any share in the personal emoluments which may be indispensably included in a permanent provision for the executive department, and must accordingly pray that the pecuniary estimates for the station in which I am placed may during my continuance in it be limited to such actual expenditures as the public good may be thought to require.

Having thus imparted to you my sentiments as they have been awakened by the occasion which brings us together, I shall take my present leave; but not without resorting once more to the benign Parent of the Human Race in humble supplication that, since He has been pleased to favor the American people with opportunities for deliberating in perfect tranquillity, and dispositions for deciding with unparalleled unanimity on a form of government for the security of their union and the advancement of their happiness, so His divine blessing may be equally *conspicuous* in the enlarged views, the temperate consultations, and the wise measures on which the success of this Government must depend.

First Annual Address to Congress

United States, January 8, 1790

Fellow-Citizens of the Senate and House of Representatives:

I embrace with great satisfaction the opportunity which now presents itself of congratulating you on the present favorable prospects of our public affairs. The recent accession of the important State of North Carolina to the Constitution of the United States (of which official information has been received), the rising credit and respectability of our country, the general and increasing good will toward the Government of the Union, and the concord, peace, and plenty with which we are blessed are circumstances auspicious in an eminent degree to our national prosperity.

In resuming your consultations for the general good you can not but derive encouragement from the reflection that the measures of the last session have been as satisfactory to your constituents as the novelty and difficulty of the work allowed you to hope. Still further to realize their expectations and to secure the blessings which a gracious Providence has placed within our reach will in the course of the present important session call for the cool and deliberate exertion of your patriotism, firmness, and wisdom.

Among the many interesting objects which will engage your attention that of providing for the common defense will merit particular regard. To be prepared for war is one of the most effectual means of preserving peace.

A free people ought not only to be armed, but disciplined; to which end a uniform and well-digested plan is requisite; and their safety and interest require that they should promote such manufactories as tend to render them independent of others for essential, particularly military, supplies.

The proper establishment of the troops which may be deemed indispensable will be entitled to mature consideration. In the arrangements which may be made respecting it it will be of importance to conciliate the comfortable support of the officers and soldiers with a due regard to economy.

There was reason to hope that the pacific measures adopted with regard to certain hostile tribes of Indians would have relieved the inhabitants of our Southern and Western frontiers from their depredations, but you will perceive from the information contained in the papers which I shall direct to be laid before you (comprehending a communication from the Commonwealth of Virginia) that we ought to be prepared to afford protection to those parts of the Union, and, if necessary, to punish aggressors.

The interests of the United States require that our intercourse with other nations should be facilitated by such provisions as will enable me to fulfill my duty in that respect in the manner which circumstances may render most conducive to the public good, and to this end that the compensations to be made to the persons who may be employed should, according to the nature of their appointments, be defined by law, and a competent fund designated for defraying the expenses incident to the conduct of our foreign affairs.

Various considerations also render it expedient that the terms on which foreigners may be admitted to the rights of citizens should be speedily ascertained by a uniform rule of naturalization.

Uniformity in the currency, weights, and measures of the United States is an object of great importance, and will, I am persuaded, be duly attended to.

The advancement of agriculture, commerce, and manufactures by all proper means will not, I trust, need recommendation; but I can not forbear intimating to you the expediency of giving effectual encouragement as well to the introduction of new and useful inventions from abroad as to the exertions of skill and genius in producing them at home, and of facilitating the intercourse between the distant parts of our country by a due attention to the post-office and post-roads.

Nor am I less persuaded that you will agree with me in opinion that there is nothing which can better deserve your patronage than the promotion of science and literature. Knowledge is in every country the surest basis of public happiness. In one in which the measures of government receive their impressions so immediately from the sense of the community as in ours it is proportionably essential. To the security of a free constitution it contributes in various ways—by convincing those who are intrusted with the public administration that every valuable end of government is best answered by the enlightened confidence of the people, and by teaching the people themselves to know and to value their own rights; to discern and provide against invasions of them; to distinguish between oppression and the necessary exercise of lawful authority; between burthens proceeding from a disregard to their convenience and those resulting from the inevitable exigencies of society; to discriminate the spirit of liberty from that of licentiousness—cherishing the first, avoiding the last—and uniting a speedy but temperate vigilance against encroachments, with an inviolable respect to the laws.

Whether this desirable object will be best promoted by affording aids to seminaries of learning already established, by the institution of a national university, or by any other expedients will be well worthy of a place in the deliberations of the Legislature.

Second Annual Address

United States, December 8, 1790

Fellow-Citizens of the Senate and House of Representatives:

In meeting you again I feel much satisfaction in being able to repeat my congratulations on the favorable prospects which continue to distinguish our public affairs. The abundant fruits of another year have blessed our country with plenty and with the means of a flourishing commerce. The progress of public credit is witnessed by a considerable rise of American stock abroad as well as at home, and the revenues allotted for this and other national purposes have been productive beyond the calculations by which they were regulated. This latter circumstance is the more pleasing, as it is not only a proof of the fertility of our resources, but as it assures us of a further increase of the national respectability and credit, and, let me add, as it bears an honorable testimony to the patriotism and integrity of the mercantile and marine part of our citizens. The punctuality of the former in discharging their engagements has been exemplary.

In conformity to the powers vested in me by acts of the last session, a loan of 3,000,000 florins, toward which some provisional measures had previously taken place, has been completed in Holland. As well the celerity with which it has been filled as the nature of the terms (considering the more than ordinary demand for borrowing created by the situation of Europe) give a reasonable hope that the further execution of those powers may proceed with advantage and success. The Secretary of the Treasury has my directions to communicate such further particulars as may be requisite for more precise information.

Since your last sessions I have received communications by which it appears that the district of Kentucky, at present a part of Viginia, has concurred in certain propositions contained in a law of that State, in consequence of which the district is to become a distinct member of the Union, in case the requisite sanction of Congress be added. For this sanction application is now made. I shall cause the papers on this very important transaction to be laid before you. The liberality and harmony with which it has been conducted will be found to do great honor to both the parties, and the sentiments of warm attachment to the Union and its present Government expressed by our fellow-citizens of Kentucky can not fail to add an affectionate concern for their particular welfare to the great national impressions under which you will decide on the case submitted to you.

It has been heretofore known to Congress that frequent incursions have been made on our frontier settlements by certain banditti of Indians from the northwest side of the Ohio. These, with some of the tribes dwelling on and near the Wabash, have of late been particularly active in their depredations, and being emboldened by the impunity of their crimes and aided by such parts of the neighboring tribes as could be seduced to join in their hostilities or afford them a retreat for their prisoners and plunder, they have, instead of listening to the humane invitations and overtures made on the part of the United States, renewed their violences with fresh alacrity and greater effect. The lives of a number of valuable citizens have thus been sacrificed, and some of them under circumstances peculiarly shocking, whilst others have been carried into a deplorable captivity.

These aggravated provocations rendered it essential to the safety of the Western settlements that the aggressors should be made sensible that the Government of the Union is not less capable of punishing their crimes than it is disposed to respect their rights and reward their attachments. As this object could not be effected by defensive measures, it became necessary to put in force the act which empowers the President to call out the militia for the protection of the frontiers, and I have accordingly authorized an expedition in which the regular troops in that quarter are combined with such drafts of militia as were deemed sufficient. The event of the measure is yet unknown to me. The Secretary of War is directed to lay before you a statement of the information on which it is founded, as well as an estimate of the expense with which it will be attended.

The disturbed situation of Europe, and particularly the critical posture of the great maritime powers, whilst it ought to make us the more thankful for the general peace and security enjoyed by the United States, reminds us at the same time of the circumspection with which it becomes us to preserve these blessings. It requires also that we should not overlook the tendency of a war, and even of preparations for a war, among the nations most concerned in active commerce with this country to abridge the means, and thereby at least enhance the price, of transporting its valuable productions to their proper markets. I recommend it to your serious reflections how far and in what mode it may be expedient to guard against embarrassments from these contingencies by such encouragements to our own navigation as will render our commerce and agriculture less dependent on foreign bottoms, which may fail us in the very moments most interesting to both of these great objects. Our fisheries and the transportation of our own produce offer us abundant means for guarding ourselves against this evil.

Your attention seems to be not less due to that particular branch of our trade which belongs to the Mediterranean. So many circumstances unite in rendering the present state of it distressful to us that you will not think any deliberations misemployed which may lead to its relief and protection.

The laws you have already passed for the establishment of a judiciary system have opened the doors of justice to all descriptions of persons. You will consider in your wisdom whether improvements in that system may yet be made, and particularly whether an uniform process of execution on sentences issuing from the Federal courts be not desirable through all the States.

The patronage of our commerce, of our merchants and seamen, has called for the appointment of consuls in foreign countries. It seems expedient to regulate by law the exercise of that jurisdiction and those functions which are permitted them, either by express convention or by a friendly indulgence, in the places of their residence. The consular convention, too, with His Most Christian Majesty has stipulated in certain cases the aid of the national authority to his consuls established here. Some legislative provision is requisite to carry these stipulations into full effect.

The establishment of the militia, of a mint, of standards of weights and measures, of the post-office and post-roads are subjects which I presume you will resume of course, and which are abundantly urged by their own importance.

Third Annual Address

United States, October 25, 1791

Fellow-Citizens of the Senate and of the House of Representatives:

I meet you upon the present occasion with the feelings which are naturally inspired by a strong impression of the prosperous situation of our common country, and by a persuasion equally strong that the labors of the session which has just commenced will, under the guidance of a spirit no less prudent than patriotic, issue in measures conducive to the stability and increase of national prosperity.

Numerous as are the providential blessings which demand our grateful acknowledgments, the abundance with which another year has again rewarded the industry of the husbandman is too important to escape recollection.

Your own observations in your respective situations will have satisfied you of the progressive state of agriculture, manufactures, commerce, and navigation. In tracing their causes you will have remarked with particular pleasure the happy effects of that revival of confidence, public as well as private, to which the Constitution and laws of the United States have so eminently contributed; and you will have observed with no less interest new and decisive proofs of the increasing reputation and credit of the nation. But you nevertheless can not fail to derive satisfaction from the confirmation of these circumstances which will be disclosed in the several official communications that will be made to you in the course of your deliberations.

The rapid subscriptions to the Bank of the United States, which completed the sum allowed to be subscribed in a single day, is among the striking and pleasing evidences which present themselves, not only of confidence in the Government, but of resource in the community.

In the interval of your recess due attention has been paid to the execution of the different objects which were specially provided for by the laws and resolutions of the last session.

Among the most important of these is the defense and security of the Western frontiers. To accomplish it on the most humane principles was a primary wish.

Accordingly, at the same time that treaties have been provisionally concluded and other proper means used to attach the wavering and to confirm in their friendship the well-disposed tribes of Indians, effectual measures have been adopted to make those of a hostile description sensible that a pacification was desired upon terms of moderation and justice.

Those measures having proved unsuccessful, it became necessary to convince the refractory of the power of the United States to punish their depredations. Offensive operations have therefore been directed, to be conducted, however, as consistently as possible with the dictates of humanity. Some of these have been crowned with full success and others are yet depending. The expeditions which have been completed were carried on under the authority and at the expense of the United States by the militia of Kentucky, whose enterprise, intrepidity, and good conduct are entitled to peculiar commendation.

Overtures of peace are still continued to the deluded tribes, and considerable numbers of individuals belonging to them have lately renounced all further opposition, removed from their former situations, and placed themselves under the immediate protection of the United States.

It is sincerely to be desired that all need of coercion in future may cease and that an intimate intercourse may succeed, calculated to advance the happiness of the Indians and to attach them firmly to the United States.

In order to do this it seems necessary—

That they should experience the benefits of an impartial dispensation of justice.

That the mode of alienating their lands, the main source of discontent and war, should be so defined and regulated as to obviate imposition and as far as may be practicable controversy concerning the reality and extent of the alienations which are made.

That commerce with them should be promoted under regulations tending to secure an equitable deportment toward them, and that such rational experiments should be made for imparting to them the blessings of civilization as may from time to time suit their condition.

That the Executive of the United States should be enabled to employ the means to which the Indians have been long accustomed for uniting their immediate interests with the preservation of peace.

And that efficacious provision should be made for inflicting adequate penalties upon all those who, by violating their rights, shall infringe the treaties and endanger the peace of the Union.

A system corresponding with the mild principles of religion and philanthropy toward an unenlightened race of men, whose happiness materially depends on the conduct of the United States, would be as honorable to the national character as conformable to the dictates of sound policy.

The powers specially vested in me by the act laying certain duties on distilled spirits, which respect the subdivisions of the districts into surveys, the appointment of officers, and the assignment of compensations, have likewise been carried into effect. In a matter in which both materials and experience were wanting to guide the calculation it will be readily conceived that there must have been difficulty in such an adjustment of the rates of compensation as would conciliate a reasonable competency with a proper regard to the limits prescribed by the law. It is hoped that the circumspection which has been used will be found in the result to have secured the last of the two objects; but it is probable that with a view to the first in some instances a revision of the provision will be found advisable.

The impressions with which this law has been received by the community have been upon the whole such as were to be expected among enlightened and well-disposed citizens from the propriety and necessity of the measure. The novelty, however, of the tax in a considerable part of the United States and a misconception of some of its provisions have given occasion in particular places to some degree of discontent; but it is satisfactory to know that this disposition yields to proper explanations and more just apprehensions of the true nature of the law, and I entertain a full confidence that it will in all give way to motives which arise out of a just sense of duty and a virtuous regard to the public welfare.

If there are any circumstances in the law which consistently with its main design may be so varied as to remove any well-intentioned objections that may happen to exist, it will consist with a wise moderation to make the proper variations. It is desirable on all occasions to unite with a steady and firm adherence to constitutional and necessary acts of Government the fullest evidence of a disposition as far as may be practicable to consult the wishes of every part of the community and to lay the foundations of the public administration in the affections of the people.

Pursuant to the authority contained in the several acts on that subject, a district of 10 miles square for the permanent seat of the Government of the United States has been fixed and announced by proclamation, which district will comprehend lands on both sides of the river Potomac and the towns of Alexandria and Georgetown. A city has also been laid out agreeably to a plan which will be placed before Congress, and as there is a prospect, favored by the rate of sales which have already taken place, of ample funds for carrying on the necessary public buildings, there is every expectation of their due progress.

The completion of the census of the inhabitants, for which provision was made by law, has been duly notified (excepting one instance in which the return has been informal, and another in which it has been omitted or miscarried), and the returns of the officers who were charged with this duty, which will be laid before you, will give you the pleasing assurance that the present population of the United States borders on 4,000,000 persons.

It is proper also to inform you that a further loan of 2,500,000 florins has been completed in Holland, the terms of which are similar to those of the one last announced, except as to a small reduction of charges. Another, on like terms, for 6,000,000 florins, had been set on foot under circumstances that assured an immediate completion.

Fourth Annual Address

United States, November 6, 1792

Fellow-Citizens of the Senate and of the House of Representatives:

It is some abatement of the satisfaction with which I meet you on the present occasion that, in felicitating you on a continuance of the national prosperity generally, I am not able to add to it information that the Indian hostilities which have for some time past distressed our Northwestern frontier have terminated.

You will, I am persuaded, learn with no less concern than I communicate it that reiterated endeavors toward effecting a pacification have hitherto issued only in new and outrageous proofs of persevering hostility on the part of the tribes with whom we are in contest. An earnest desire to procure tranquillity to the frontier, to stop the further effusion of blood, to arrest the progress of expense, to forward the prevalent wish of the nation for peace has led to strenuous efforts through various channels to accomplish these desirable purposes; in making which efforts I consulted less my own anticipations of the event, or the scruples which some considerations were calculated to inspire, than the wish to find the object attainable, to ascertain unequivocally that such is the case.

A detail of the measures which have been pursued and of their consequences, which will be laid before you, while it will confirm to you the want of success thus far, will, I trust, evince that means as proper and as efficacious as could have been devised have been employed. The issue of some of them, indeed, is still depending, but a favorable one, though not to be despaired of, is not promised by anything that has yet happened.

In the course of the attempts which have been made some valuable citizens have fallen victims to their zeal for the public service. A sanction commonly respected even among savages has been found in this instance insufficient to protect from massacre the emissaries of peace. It will, I presume, be duly considered whether the occasion does not call for an exercise of liberality toward the families of the deceased.

It must add to your concern to be informed that, besides the continuation of hostile appearances among the tribes north of the Ohio, some threatening symptoms have of late been revived among some of those south of it.

A part of the Cherokees, known by the name of Chickamaugas, inhabiting five villages on the Tennessee River, have long been in the practice of committing depredations on the neighboring settlements.

It was hoped that the treaty of Holston, made with the Cherokee Nation in July, 1791, would have prevented a repetition of such depredations; but the event has not answered this hope. The Chickamaugas, aided by some banditti of another tribe in their vicinity, have recently perpetrated wanton and unprovoked hostilities upon the citizens of the United States in that quarter. The information which has been received on this subject will be laid before you. Hitherto defensive precautions only have been strictly enjoined and observed.

It is not understood that any breach of treaty or aggression whatsoever on the part of the United States or their citizens is even alleged as a pretext for the spirit of hostility in this quarter.

I have reason to believe that every practicable exertion has been made (pursuant to the provision by law for that purpose) to be prepared for the alternative of a prosecution of the war in the event of a failure of pacific overtures. A large proportion of the troops authorized to be raised have been recruited, though the number is still incomplete, and pains have been taken to discipline and put them in condition for the particular kind of service to be performed. A delay of operations (besides being dictated by the measures which were pursuing toward a pacific termination of the war) has been in itself deemed preferable to immature efforts. A statement from the proper department with regard to the number of troops raised, and some other points which have been suggested, will afford more precise information as a guide to the legislative consultations, and among other things will enable Congress to judge whether some additional stimulus to the recruiting service may not be advisable.

In looking forward to the future expense of the operations which may be found inevitable I derive consolation from the information I receive that the product of the revenues for the present year is likely to supersede the necessity of additional burthens on the community for the service of the ensuing year. This, however, will be better ascertained in the course of the session, and it is proper to add that the information alluded to proceeds upon the supposition of no material extension of the spirit of hostility.

I can not dismiss the subject of Indian affairs without again recommending to your consideration the expediency of more adequate provision for giving energy to the laws throughout our interior frontier and for restraining the commission of outrages upon the Indians, without which all pacific plans must prove nugatory. To enable, by competent rewards, the employment of qualified and trusty persons to reside among them as agents would also contribute to the preservation of peace and good neighborhood. If in addition to these expedients an eligible plan could be devised for promoting civilization among the friendly tribes and for carrying on trade with them upon a scale equal to their wants and under regulations calculated to protect them from imposition and extortion, its influence in cementing their interest with ours could not but be considerable.

The prosperous state of our revenue has been intimated. This would be still more the case were it not for the impediments which in some places continue to embarrass the collection of the duties on spirits distilled within the United States. These impediments have lessened and are lessening in local extent, and, as applied to the community at large, the contentment with the law appears to be progressive.

But symptoms of increased opposition having lately manifested themselves in certain quarters, I judged a special interposition on my part proper and advisable, and under this impression have issued a proclamation warning against all unlawful combinations and proceedings having for their object or tending to obstruct the operation of the law in question, and announcing that all lawful ways and means would be strictly put in execution for bringing to justice the infractors thereof and securing obedience thereto.

Measures have also been taken for the prosecution of offenders, and Congress may be assured that nothing within constitutional and legal limits which may depend upon me shall be wanting to assert and maintain the just authority of the laws. In fulfilling this trust I shall count entirely upon the full cooperation of the other departments of the Government and upon the zealous support of all good citizens.

I can not forbear to bring again into the view of the Legislature the subject of a revision of the judiciary system. A representation from the judges of the Supreme Court, which will be laid before you, points out some of the inconveniences that are experienced. In the course of the execution of the laws considerations arise out of the structure of that system which in some cases tend to relax their efficacy. As connected with this subject, provisions to facilitate the taking of bail upon processes out of the courts of the United States and a supplementary definition of offenses against the Constitution and laws of the Union and of the punishment for such offenses will, it is presumed, be found worthy of particular attention.

Observations on the value of peace with other nations are unnecessary. It would be wise, however, by timely provisions to guard against those acts of our own citizens which might tend to disturb it, and to put ourselves in a condition to give that satisfaction to foreign nations which we may sometimes have occasion to require from them. I particularly recommend to your consideration the means of preventing those aggressions by our citizens on the territory of other nations, and other infractions of the law of nations, which, furnishing just subject of complaint, might endanger our peace with them; and, in general, the maintenance of a friendly intercourse with foreign powers will be presented to your attention by the expiration of the law for that purpose, which takes place, if not renewed, at the close of the present session.

In execution of the authority given by the Legislature measures have been taken for engaging some artists from abroad to aid in the establishment of our mint. Others have been employed at home. Provision has been made of the requisite buildings, and these are now putting into proper condition for the purposes of the establishment. There has also been a small beginning in the coinage of half dimes, the want of small coins in circulation calling the first attention to them.

The regulation of foreign coins in correspondency with the principles of our national coinage, as being essential to their due operation and to order in our money concerns, will, I doubt not, be resumed and completed.

It is represented that some provisions in the law which establishes the post-office operate, in experiment, against the transmission of newspapers to distant parts of the country. Should this, upon due inquiry, be found to be the fact, a full conviction of the importance of facilitating the circulation of political intelligence and information will, I doubt not, lead to the application of a remedy.

The adoption of a constitution for the State of Kentucky has been notified to me. The Legislature will share with me in the satisfaction which arises from an event interesting to the happiness of the part of the nation to which it relates and conducive to the general order.

It is proper likewise to inform you that since my last communication on the subject, and in further execution of the acts severally making provision for the public debt and for the reduction thereof, three new loans have been effected, each for 3,000,000 florins—one at Antwerp, at the annual interest of 4½ per cent, with an allowance of 4 per cent in lieu of all charges, and the other two at Amsterdam, at the annual interest of 4 per cent, with an allowance of 5½ per cent in one case and of 5 per cent in the other in lieu of all charges. The rates of these loans and the circumstances under which they have been made are confirmations of the high state of our credit abroad.

Among the objects to which these funds have been directed to be applied, the payment of the debts due to certain foreign officers, according to the provision made during the last session, has been embraced.

Second Inaugural Address

March 4, 1793

Fellow-Citizens:

I am again called upon by the voice of my country to execute the functions of its Chief Magistrate. When the occasion proper for it shall arrive, I shall endeavor to express the high sense I entertain of this distinguished honor, and of the confidence which has been reposed in me by the people of united America.

Previous to the execution of any official act of the President the Constitution requires an oath of office. This oath I am now about to take, and in your presence: That if it shall be found during my administration of the Government I have in any instance violated willingly or knowingly the injunctions thereof, I may (besides incurring constitutional punishment) be subject to the upbraidings of all who are now witnesses of the present solemn ceremony.

Fifth Annual Address

Philadelphia, December 3, 1793

Fellow-Citizens of the Senate and of the House of Representatives:

Since the commencement of the term for which I have been again called into office no fit occasion has arisen for expressing to my fellow-citizens at large the deep and respectful sense which I feel of the renewed testimony of public approbation. While on the one hand it awakened my gratitude for all those instances of affectionate partiality with which I have been honored by my country, on the other it could not prevent an earnest wish for that retirement from which no private consideration should ever have torn me. But influenced by the belief that my conduct would be estimated according to its real motives, and that the people, and the authorities derived from them, would support exertions having nothing personal for their object, I have obeyed the suffrage which commanded me to resume the Executive power; and I humbly implore that Being on whose will the fate of nations depends to crown with success our mutual endeavors for the general happiness.

As soon as the war in Europe had embraced those powers with whom the United States have the most extensive relations there was reason to apprehend that our intercourse with them might be interrupted and our disposition for peace drawn into question by the suspicions too often entertained by belligerent nations. It seemed, therefore, to be my duty to admonish our citizens of the consequences of a contraband trade and of hostile acts to any of the parties, and to obtain by a declaration of the existing legal state of things an easier admission of our right to the immunities belonging to our situation. Under these impressions the proclamation which will be laid before you was issued.

In this posture of affairs, both new and delicate, I resolved to adopt general rules which should conform to the treaties and assert the privileges of the United States. These were reduced into a system, which will be communicated to you. Although I have not thought myself at liberty to forbid the sale of the prizes permitted by our treaty of commerce with France to be brought into our ports, I have not refused to cause them to be restored when they were taken within the protection of our territory, or by vessels commissioned or equipped in a warlike form within the limits of the United States.

It rests with the wisdom of Congress to correct, improve, or enforce this plan of procedure; and it will probably be found expedient to extend the legal code and the jurisdiction of the courts of the United States to many cases which, though dependent on principles already recognized, demand some further provisions.

Where individuals shall, within the United States, array themselves in hostility against any of the powers at war, or enter upon military expeditions or enterprises within the jurisdiction of the United States, or usurp and exercise judicial authority within the United States, or where the penalties on violations of the law of nations may have been indistinctly marked, or are inadequate—these offenses can not receive too early and close an attention, and require prompt and decisive remedies.

Whatsoever these remedies may be, they will be well administered by the judiciary, who possess a long-established course of investigation, effectual process, and officers in the habit of executing it.

In like manner, as several of the courts have doubted, under particular circumstances, their power to liberate the vessels of a nation at peace, and even of a citizen of the United States, although seized under a false color of being hostile property, and have denied their power to liberate certain captures within the protection of our territory, it would seem proper to regulate their jurisdiction in these points. But if the Executive is to be the resort in either of the two last-mentioned cases, it is hoped that he will be authorized by law to have facts ascertained by the courts when for his own information he shall request it.

I can not recommend to your notice measures for the fulfillment of our duties to the rest of the world without again pressing upon you the necessity of placing ourselves in a condition of complete defense and of exacting from them the fulfillment of their duties toward us. The United States ought not to indulge a persuasion that, contrary to the order of human events, they will forever keep at a distance those painful appeals to arms with which the history of every other nation abounds. There is a rank due to the United

States among nations which will be withheld, if not absolutely lost, by the reputation of weakness. If we desire to avoid insult, we must be able to repel it; if we desire to secure peace, one of the most powerful instruments of our rising prosperity, it must be known that we are at all times ready for war. The documents which will be presented to you will shew the amount and kinds of arms and military stores now in our magazines and arsenals; and yet an addition even to these supplies can not with prudence be neglected, as it would leave nothing to the uncertainty of procuring of warlike apparatus in the moment of public danger.

Nor can such arrangements, with such objects, be exposed to the censure or jealousy of the warmest friends of republican government. They are incapable of abuse in the hands of the militia, who ought to possess a pride in being the depository of the force of the Republic, and may be trained to a degree of energy equal to every military exigency of the United States. But it is an inquiry which can not be too solemnly pursued, whether the act "more effectually to provide for the national defense by establishing an uniform militia throughout the United States" has organized them so as to produce their full effect; whether your own experience in the several States has not detected some imperfections in the scheme, and whether a material feature in an improvement of it ought not to be to afford an opportunity for the study of those branches of the military art which can scarcely ever be attained by practice alone.

The connection of the United States with Europe has become extremely interesting. The occurrences which relate to it and have passed under the knowledge of the Executive will be exhibited to Congress in a subsequent communication.

When we contemplate the war on our frontiers, it may be truly affirmed that every reasonable effort has been made to adjust the causes of dissension with the Indians north of the Ohio. The instructions given to the commissioners evince a moderation and equity proceeding from a sincere love of peace, and a liberality having no restriction but the essential interests and dignity of the United States. The attempt, however, of an amicable negotiation having been frustrated, the troops have marched to act offensively. Although the proposed treaty did not arrest the progress of military preparation, it is doubtful how far the advance of the season, before good faith justified active movements, may retard them during the remainder of the year. From the papers and intelligence which relate to this important subject you will determine whether the deficiency in the number of troops granted by law shall be compensated by succors of militia, or additional encouragements shall be proposed to recruits.

An anxiety has been also demonstrated by the Executive for peace with the Creeks and the Cherokees. The former have been relieved with corn and with clothing, and offensive measures against them prohibited during the recess of Congress. To satisfy the complaints of the latter, prosecutions have been instituted for the violences committed upon them. But the papers which will be delivered to you disclose the critical footing on which we stand in regard to both those tribes, and it is with Congress to pronounce what shall be done.

After they shall have provided for the present emergency, it will merit their most serious labors to render tranquillity with the savages permanent by creating ties of interest. Next to a rigorous execution of justice on the violators of peace, the establishment of commerce with the Indian nations in behalf of the United States is most likely to conciliate their attachment. But it ought to be conducted without fraud, without extortion, with constant and plentiful supplies, with a ready market for the commodities of the Indians and a stated price for what they give in payment and receive in exchange. Individuals will not pursue such a traffic unless they be allured by the hope of profit; but it will be enough for the United States to be reimbursed only. Should this recommendation accord with the opinion of Congress, they will recollect that it can not be accomplished by any means yet in the hands of the Executive.

Sixth Annual Address

November 19, 1794

Fellow-Citizens of the Senate and of the House of Representatives:

When we call to mind the gracious indulgence of Heaven by which the American people became a nation; when we survey the general prosperity of our country, and look forward to the riches, power, and happiness to which it seems destined, with the deepest regret do I announce to you that during your recess some of the citizens of the United States have been found capable of an insurrection. It is due, however, to the character of our Government and to its stability, which can not be shaken by the enemies of order, freely to unfold the course of this event.

During the session of the year 1790 it was expedient to exercise the legislative power granted by the Constitution of the United States "to lay and collect excises." In a majority of the States scarcely an objection was heard to this mode of taxation. In some, indeed, alarms were at first conceived, until they were banished by reason and patriotism. In the four western counties of Pennsylvania a prejudice, fostered and imbittered by the artifice of men who labored for an ascendency over the will of others by the guidance of their passions, produced symptoms of riot and violence. It is well known that Congress did not hesitate to examine the complaints which were presented, and to relieve them as far as justice dictated or general convenience would permit. But the impression which this moderation made on the discontented did not correspond with what it deserved. The arts of delusion were no longer confined to the efforts of designing individuals. The very forbearance to press prosecutions was misinterpreted into a fear of urging the execution of the laws, and associations of men began to denounce threats against the officers employed. From a belief that by a more formal concert their operation might be defeated, certain self-created societies assumed the tone of condemnation. Hence, while the greater part of Pennsylvania itself were conforming themselves to the acts of excise, a few counties were resolved to frustrate them. It was now perceived that every expectation from the tenderness which had been hitherto pursued was unavailing, and that further delay could only create an opinion of impotency or irresolution in the Government. Legal process was therefore delivered to the marshal against the rioters and delinquent distillers.

No sooner was he understood to be engaged in this duty than the vengeance of armed men was aimed at *his* person and the person and property of the inspector of the revenue. They fired upon the marshal, arrested him, and detained him for some time as a prisoner. He was obliged, by the jeopardy of his life, to renounce the service of other process on the west side of the Allegheny Mountain, and a deputation was afterwards sent to him to demand a surrender of that which he *had* served. A numerous body repeatedly attacked the house of the inspector, seized his papers of office, and finally destroyed by fire his buildings and whatsoever they contained. Both of these officers, from a just regard to their safety, fled to the seat of Government, it being avowed that the motives to such outrages were to compel the resignation of the inspector, to withstand by force of arms the authority of the United States, and thereby to extort a repeal of the laws of excise and an alteration in the conduct of Government.

Upon the testimony of these facts an associate justice of the Supreme Court of the United States notified to me that "in the counties of Washington and Allegheny, in Pennsylvania, laws of the United States were opposed, and the execution thereof obstructed, by combinations too powerful to be suppressed by the ordinary course of judicial proceedings or by the powers vested in the marshal of that district." On this call, momentous in the extreme, I sought and weighed what might best subdue the crisis. On the one hand the judiciary was pronounced to be stripped of its capacity to enforce the laws; crimes which reached the very existence of social order were perpetrated without control; the friends of Government were insulted, abused, and overawed into silence or an apparent acquiescence; and to yield to the treasonable fury of so small a portion of the United States would be to violate the fundamental principle of our Constitution, which enjoins that the will of the majority shall prevail. On the other, to array citizen against citizen, to publish the dishonor of such excesses, to encounter the expense and other embarrassments of so distant an expedition, were steps too delicate, too closely interwoven with many affecting considerations, to be lightly adopted. I postponed, therefore, the summoning the militia immediately into the field, but I required them to be held in readiness, that if my anxious endeavors to reclaim the deluded and to convince the malignant of their danger should be fruitless, military force might be prepared to act before the season should be too far advanced.

My proclamation of the 7th of August last was accordingly issued, and accompanied by the appointment of commissioners, who were charged to repair to the scene of insurrection. They were authorized to confer with any bodies of men or individuals. They were instructed to be candid and explicit in stating the sensations which had been excited in the Executive, and his earnest wish to avoid a resort to coercion; to represent, however, that, without submission, coercion *must* be the resort; but to invite them, at the same time, to return to the demeanor of faithful citizens, by such accommodations as lay within the sphere of Executive power. Pardon, too, was tendered to them by the Government of the United States and that of Pennsylvania, upon no other condition than a satisfactory assurance of obedience to the laws.

Although the report of the commissioners marks their firmness and abilities, and must unite all virtuous men, by shewing that the means of conciliation have been exhausted, all of those who had committed or abetted the tumults did not subscribe the mild form which was proposed as the atonement, and the indications of a peaceable temper were neither sufficiently general nor conclusive to recommend or warrant the further suspension of the march of the militia.

Thus the painful alternative could not be discarded. I ordered the militia to march, after once more admonishing the insurgents in my proclamation of the 25th of September last.

It was a task too difficult to ascertain with precision the lowest degree of force competent to the quelling of the insurrection. From a respect, indeed, to economy and the ease of my fellow-citizens belonging to the militia, it would have gratified me to accomplish such an estimate. My very reluctance to ascribe too much importance to the opposition, had its extent been accurately seen, would have been a decided inducement to the smallest efficient numbers. In this uncertainty, therefore, I put into motion 15,000 men, as being an army which, according to all human calculation, would be prompt and adequate in every view, and might, perhaps, by rendering resistance desperate, prevent the effusion of blood. Quotas had been assigned to the States of New Jersey, Pennsylvania, Maryland, and Virginia, the governor of Pennsylvania having declared on this occasion an opinion which justified a requisition to the other States.

As commander in chief of the militia when called into the actual service of the United States, I have visited the places of general rendezvous to obtain more exact information and to direct a plan for ulterior movements. Had there been room for a persuasion that the laws were secure from obstruction; that the civil magistrate was able to bring to justice such of the most culpable as have not embraced the proffered terms of amnesty, and may be deemed fit objects of example; that the friends to peace and good government were not in need of that aid and countenance which they ought always to receive, and, I trust, ever will receive, against the vicious and turbulent, I should have caught with avidity the opportunity of restoring the militia to their families and homes. But succeeding intelligence has tended to manifest the necessity of what has been done, it being now confessed by those who were not inclined to exaggerate the ill conduct of the insurgents that their malevolence was not pointed merely to a particular law, but that a spirit inimical to all order has actuated many of the offenders. If the state of things had afforded reason for the continuance of my presence with the army, it would not have been withholden. But every appearance assuring such an issue as will redound to the reputation and strength of the United States, I have judged it most proper to resume my duties at the seat of Government, leaving the chief command with the governor of Virginia.

Still, however, as it is probable that in a commotion like the present, whatsoever may be the pretense, the purposes of mischief and revenge may not be laid aside, the stationing of a small force for a certain period in the four western counties of Pennsylvania will be indispensable, whether we contemplate the situation of those who are connected with the execution of the laws or of others who may have exposed themselves by an honorable attachment to them. Thirty days from the commencement of this session being the legal limitation of the employment of the militia, Congress can not be too early occupied with this subject.

Among the discussions which may arise from this aspect of our affairs, and from the documents which will be submitted to Congress, it will not escape their observation that not only the inspector of the revenue, but other officers of the United States in Pennsylvania have, from their fidelity in the discharge of their functions, sustained material injuries to their property. The obligation and policy of indemnifying them are strong and obvious. It may also merit attention whether policy will not enlarge this provision to the retribution of other citizens who, though not under the ties of office, may have suffered damage by their generous exertions for upholding the Constitution and the laws. The amount, even if all the injured were included, would not be great, and on future emergencies the Government would be amply repaid by the influence of an example that he who incurs a loss in its defense shall find a recompense in its liberality.

While there is cause to lament that occurrences of this nature should have disgraced the name or interrupted the tranquillity of any part of our community, or should have diverted to a new application any portion of the public resources, there are not wanting real and substantial consolations for the misfortune. It has demonstrated that our prosperity rests on solid foundations, by furnishing an additional proof that my fellow-citizens understand the true principles of government and liberty; that they feel their inseparable union; that notwithstanding all the devices which have been used to sway them from their interest and duty, they are now as ready to maintain the authority of the laws against licentious invasions as they were to defend their rights against usurpation. It has been a spectacle displaying to the highest advantage the value of republican government to behold the most and the least wealthy of our citizens standing in the same ranks as private soldiers, preeminently distinguished by being the army of the Constitution—undeterred by a march of 300 miles over rugged mountains, by the approach of an inclement season or by any other discouragement. Nor ought I to omit to acknowledge the efficacious and patriotic cooperation which I have experienced from the chief magistrates of the States to which my requisitions have been addressed.

To every description of citizens, indeed, let praise be given. But let them persevere in their affectionate vigilance over that precious depository of American happiness, the Constitution of the United States. Let them cherish it, too, for the sake of those who, from every clime, are daily seeking a dwelling in our land. And when in the calm moments of reflection they shall have retraced the origin and progress of the insurrection, let them determine whether it has not been fomented by combinations of men who, careless of consequences and disregarding the unerring truth that those who rouse can not always appease a civil convulsion, have disseminated, from an ignorance or perversion of facts, suspicions, jealousies, and accusations of the whole Government.

Having thus fulfilled the engagement which I took when I entered into office, "to the best of my ability to preserve, protect, and defend the Constitution of the United States," on you, gentlemen, and the people by whom you are deputed, I rely for support.

In the arrangements to which the possibility of a similar contingency will naturally draw your attention it ought not to be forgotten that the militia laws have exhibited such striking defects as could not have been supplied but by the zeal of our citizens. Besides the extraordinary expense and waste, which are not the least of the defects, every appeal to those laws is attended with a doubt on its success.

The devising and establishing of a well-regulated militia would be a genuine source of legislative honor and a perfect title to public gratitude. I therefore entertain a hope that the present session will not pass without carrying to its full energy the power of organizing, arming, and disciplining the militia, and thus providing, in the language of the Constitution, for calling them forth to execute the laws of the Union, suppress insurrections, and repel invasions.

As auxiliary to the state of our defense, to which Congress can never too frequently recur, they will not omit to inquire whether the fortifications which have been already licensed by law be commensurate with our exigencies.

The intelligence from the army under the command of General

Wayne is a happy presage to our military operations against the hostile Indians north of the Ohio. From the advices which have been forwarded, the advance which he has made must have damped the ardor of the savages and weakened their obstinacy in waging war against the United States. And yet, even at this late hour, when our power to punish them can not be questioned, we shall not be unwilling to cement a lasting peace upon terms of candor, equity, and good neighborhood.

Toward none of the Indian tribes have overtures of friendship been spared. The Creeks in particular are covered from encroachment by the interposition of the General Government and that of Georgia. From a desire also to remove the discontents of the Six Nations, a settlement is meditated at Presque Isle, on Lake Erie, has been suspended, and an agent is now endeavoring to rectify any misconception into which they may have fallen. But I can not refrain from again pressing upon your deliberations the plan which I recommended at the last session for the improvement of harmony with all the Indians within our limits by the fixing and conducting of trading houses upon the principles then expressed.

Seventh Annual Address

United States, December 8, 1795

Fellow-Citizens of the Senate and of the House of Representatives:

I trust I do not deceive myself when I indulge the persuasion that I have never met you at any period when more than at the present the situation of our public affairs has afforded just cause for mutual congratulation, and for inviting you to join with me in profound gratitude to the Author of all Good for the numerous and extraordinary blessings we enjoy.

The termination of the long, expensive, and distressing war in which we have been engaged with certain Indians northwest of the Ohio is placed in the option of the United States by a treaty which the commander of our army has concluded provisionally with the hostile tribes in that region.

In the adjustment of the terms the satisfaction of the Indians was deemed an object worthy no less of the policy than of the liberality of the United States as the necessary basis of durable tranquillity. The object, it is believed, has been fully attained. The articles agreed upon will immediately be laid before the Senate for their consideration.

The Creek and Cherokee Indians, who alone of the Southern tribes had annoyed our frontiers, have lately confirmed their pre-existing treaties with us, and were giving evidence of a sincere disposition to carry them into effect by the surrender of the prisoners and property they had taken. But we have to lament that the fair prospect in this quarter has been once more clouded by wanton murders, which some citizens of Georgia are represented to have recently perpetrated on hunting parties of the Creeks, which have again subjected that frontier to disquietude and danger, which will be productive of further expense, and may occasion more effusion of blood. Measures are pursuing to prevent or mitigate the usual consequences of such outrages, and with the hope of their succeeding at least to avert general hostility.

A letter from the Emperor of Morocco announces to me his recognition of our treaty made with his father, the late Emperor, and consequently the continuance of peace with that power. With peculiar satisfaction I add that information has been received from an agent deputed on our part to Algiers imparting that the terms of the treaty with the Dey and Regency of that country had been adjusted in such a manner as to authorize the expectation of a speedy peace and the restoration of our unfortunate fellow-citizens from a grievous captivity.

The latest advices from our envoy at the Court of Madrid give, moreover, the pleasing information that he had received assurances of a speedy and satisfactory conclusion of his negotiation. While the event depending upon unadjusted particulars can not be regarded as ascertained, it is agreeable to cherish the expectation of an issue which, securing amicably very essential interests of the United States, will at the same time lay the foundation of lasting harmony with a power whose friendship we have uniformly and sincerely desired to cultivate.

Though not before officially disclosed to the House of Representatives, you, gentlemen, are all apprised that a treaty of amity, commerce, and navigation has been negotiated with Great Britain, and that the Senate have advised and consented to its ratification upon a condition which excepts part of one article. Agreeably thereto, and to the best judgment I was able to form of the public interest after full and mature deliberation, I have added my sanction. The result on the part of His Britannic Majesty is unknown. When received, the subject will without delay be placed before Congress.

This interesting summary of our affairs with regard to the foreign powers between whom and the United States controversies have subsisted, and with regard also to those of our Indian neighbors with whom we have been in a state of enmity or misunderstanding, opens a wide field for consoling and gratifying reflections. If by prudence and moderation on every side the extinguishment of all the causes of external discord which have heretofore menaced our tranquility, on terms compatible with our national rights and honor, shall be the happy result, how firm and how precious a foundation will have been laid for accelerating, maturing, and establishing the prosperity of our country.

Contemplating the internal situation as well as the external relations of the United States, we discover equal cause for contentment and satisfaction. While many of the nations of Europe, with their American dependencies, have been involved in a contest unusually bloody, exhausting, and calamitous, in which the evils of foreign war have been aggravated by domestic convulsion and insurrection; in which many of the arts most useful to society have been exposed to discouragement and decay; in which scarcity of subsistence has imbittered other sufferings; while even the anticipations of a return of the blessings of peace and repose are alloyed by the sense of heavy and accumulating burthens, which press upon all the departments of industry and threaten to clog the future springs of government, our favored country, happy in a striking contrast, has enjoyed general tranquillity—a tranquillity the more satisfactory because maintained at the expense of no duty. Faithful to ourselves, we have violated no obligation to others. Our agriculture, commerce, and manufactures prosper beyond former example, the molestations of our trade (to prevent a continuance of which, however, very pointed remonstrances have been made) being overbalanced by the aggregate benefits which it derives from a neutral position. Our population advances with a celerity which, exceeding the most sanguine calculations, proportionally augments our strength and resources, and guarantees our future security. Every part of the Union displays indications of rapid and various improvement; and with burthens so light as scarcely to be perceived, with resources fully adequate to our present exigencies, with governments founded on the genuine principles of rational liberty, and with mild and wholesome laws, is it too much to say that our country exhibits a spectacle of national happiness never surpassed, if ever before equaled?

Placed in a situation every way so auspicious, motives of commanding force impel us, with sincere acknowledgment to Heaven and pure love to our country, to unite our efforts to preserve, prolong, and improve our immense advantages. To cooperate with you in this desirable work is a fervent and favorite wish of my heart.

It is a valuable ingredient in the general estimate of our welfare that the part of our country which was lately the scene of disorder and insurrection now enjoys the blessings of quiet and order. The misled have abandoned their errors, and pay the respect to our Constitution and laws which is due from good citizens to the public authorities of the society. These circumstances have induced me to pardon generally the offenders here referred to, and to extend forgiveness to those who had been adjudged to capital punishment. For though I shall always think it a sacred duty to exercise with firmness and energy the constitutional powers with which I am vested, yet it appears to me no less consistent with the public end than it is with my personal feelings to mingle in the operations of Government every degree of moderation and tenderness which the national justice, dignity, and safety may permit.

Gentlemen:

Among the objects which will claim your attention in the course of the session, a review of our military establishment is not the least important. It is called for by the events which have changed, and may be expected still further to change, the relative situation of our frontiers. In this review you will doubtless allow due weight to the considerations that the questions between us and certain foreign powers are not yet finally adjusted, that the war in Europe is not yet terminated, and that our Western posts, when recovered, will demand provision for garrisoning and securing them. A statement of our present military force will be laid before you by the Department of War.

With the review of our Army establishment is naturally connected that of the militia. It will merit inquiry what imperfections in the existing plan further experience may have unfolded. The subject is of so much moment in my estimation as to excite a constant solicitude that the consideration of it may be renewed until the greatest attainable perfection shall be accomplished. Time is wearing away some advantages for forwarding the object, while none better deserves the persevering attention of the public councils.

While we indulge the satisfaction which the actual condition of our Western borders so well authorizes, it is necessary that we should not lose sight of an important truth which continually receives new confirmations, namely, that the provisions heretofore made with a view to the protection of the Indians from the violences of the lawless part of our frontier inhabitants are insufficient. It is demonstrated that these violences can now be perpetrated with impunity, and it can need no argument to prove that unless the murdering of Indians can be restrained by bringing the murderers to condign punishment, all the exertions of the Government to prevent destructive retaliations by the Indians will prove fruitless and all our present agreeable prospects illusory. The frequent destruction of innocent women and children, who are chiefly the victims of retaliation, must continue to shock humanity, and an enormous expense to drain the Treasury of the Union.

To enforce upon the Indians the observance of justice it is indispensable that there shall be competent means of rendering justice to them. If these means can be devised by the wisdom of Congress, and especially if there can be added an adequate provision for supplying the necessities of the Indians on reasonable terms (a measure the mention of which I the more readily repeat, as in all the conferences with them they urge it with solicitude), I should not hesitate to entertain a strong hope of rendering our tranquility permanent. I add with pleasure that the probability even of their civilization is not diminished by the experiments which have been thus far made under the auspices of Government. The accomplishment of this work, if practicable, will reflect undecaying luster on our national character and administer the most grateful consolations that virtuous minds can know.

Eighth Annual Address

United States, December 7, 1796

Fellow-Citizens of the Senate and of the House of Representatives:

In recurring to the internal situation of our country since I had last the pleasure to address you, I find ample reason for a renewed expression of that gratitude to the Ruler of the Universe which a continued series of prosperity has so often and so justly called forth.

The acts of the last session which required special arrangements have been as far as circumstances would admit carried into operation.

Measures calculated to insure a continuance of the friendship of the Indians and to preserve peace along the extent of our interior frontier have been digested and adopted. In the framing of these care has been taken to guard on the one hand our advanced settlements from the predatory incursions of those unruly individuals who can not be restrained by their tribes, and on the other hand to protect the rights secured to the Indians by treaty—to draw them nearer to the civilized state and inspire them with correct conceptions of the power as well as justice of the Government.

The meeting of the deputies from the Creek Nation at Colerain, in the State of Georgia, which had for a principal object the purchase of a parcel of their land by that State, broke up without its being accomplished, the nation having previous to their departure instructed them against making any sale. The occasion, however, has been improved to confirm by a new treaty with the Creeks their preexisting engagements with the United States, and to obtain their consent to the establishment of trading houses and military posts within their boundary, by means of which their friendship and the general peace may be more effectually secured.

The period during the late session at which the appropriation was passed for carrying into effect the treaty of amity, commerce, and navigation between the United States and His Britannic Majesty necessarily procrastinated the reception of the posts stipulated to be delivered beyond the date assigned for that event. As soon, however, as the Governor-General of Canada could be addressed with propriety on the subject, arrangements were cordially and promptly concluded for their evacuation, and the United States took possession of the principal of them, comprehending Oswego, Niagara, Detroit, Michilimackinac, and Fort Miami, where such repairs and additions have been ordered to be made as appeared indispensable.

The commissioners appointed on the part of the United States and of Great Britain to determine which is the river St. Croix mentioned in the treaty of peace of 1783, agreed in the choice of Egbert Benson, esq., of New York, for the third commissioner. The whole met at St. Andrews, in Passamaquoddy Bay, in the beginning of October, and directed surveys to be made of the rivers in dispute; but deeming it impracticable to have these surveys completed before the next year, they adjourned to meet at Boston in August, 1797, for the final decision of the question.

Other commissioners appointed on the part of the United States, agreeably to the seventh article of the treaty with Great Britain, relative to captures and condemnation of vessels and other property, met the commissioners of His Britannic Majesty in London in August last, when John Trumbull, esq., was chosen by lot for the fifth commissioner. In October following the board were to proceed to business. As yet there has been no communication of commissioners on the part of Great Britain to unite with those who have been appointed on the part of the United States for carrying into effect the sixth article of the treaty.

The treaty with Spain required that the commissioners for running the boundary line between the territory of the United States and His Catholic Majesty's provinces of East and West Florida should meet at the Natchez before the expiration of six months after the exchange of the ratifications, which was effected at Aranjuez on the 25th day of April; and the troops of His Catholic Majesty occupying any posts within the limits of the United States were within the same period to be withdrawn. The commissioner of the United States therefore commenced his journey for the Natchez in September, and troops were ordered to occupy the posts from which the Spanish garrisons should be withdrawn. Information has been recently received of the appointment of a commissioner on the part of His Catholic Majesty for running the boundary line, but none of any appointment for the adjustment of the claims of our citizens whose vessels were captured by the armed vessels of Spain.

In pursuance of the act of Congress passed in the last session for the protection and relief of American seamen, agents were appointed, one to reside in Great Britain and the other in the West Indies. The effects of the agency in the West Indies are not yet fully ascertained, but those which have been communicated afford grounds to believe the measure will be beneficial. The agent destined to reside in Great Britain declining to accept the appointment, the business has consequently devolved on the minister of the United States in London, and will command his attention until a new agent shall be appointed.

After many delays and disappointments arising out of the European war, the final arrangements for fulfilling the engagements made to the Dey and Regency of Algiers will in all present appearance be crowned with success, but under great, though inevitable, disadvantages in the pecuniary transactions occasioned by that war, which will render further provision necessary. The actual liberation of all our citizens who were prisoners in Algiers, while it gratifies every feeling heart, is itself an earnest of a satisfactory termination of the whole negotiation. Measures are in operation for effecting treaties with the Regencies of Tunis and Tripoli.

To an active external commerce the protection of a naval force is indispensable. This is manifest with regard to wars in which a State is itself a party. But besides this, it is in our own experience that the most sincere neutrality is not a sufficient guard against the depredations of nations at war. To secure respect to a neutral flag requires a naval force organized and ready to vindicate it from insult or aggression. This may even prevent the necessity of going to war by discouraging belligerent powers from committing such violations of the rights of the neutral party as may, first or last, leave no other option. From the best information I have been able to obtain it would seem as if our trade to the Mediterranean without a protecting force will always be insecure and our citizens exposed to the calamities from which numbers of them have but just been relieved.

These considerations invite the United States to look to the means, and to set about the gradual creation of a navy. The increasing progress of their navigation promises them at no distant period the requisite supply of seamen, and their means in other respects favor the undertaking. It is an encouragement, likewise, that their particular situation will give weight and influence to a moderate naval force in their hands. Will it not, then, be advisable to begin without delay to provide and lay up the materials for the building and equipping of ships of war, and to proceed in the work by degrees, in proportion as our resources shall render it practicable without inconvenience, so that a future war of Europe may not find our commerce in the same unprotected state in which it was found by the present?

Congress have repeatedly, and not without success, directed their attention to the encouragement of manufactures. The object is of too much consequence not to insure a continuance of their efforts in every way which shall appear eligible. As a general rule, manufactures on public account are inexpedient; but where the state of things in a country leaves little hope that certain branches of manufacture will for a great length of time obtain, when these are of a nature essential to the furnishing and equipping of the public force in time of war, are not establishments for procuring them on public account to the extent of the ordinary demand for the public service recommended by strong considerations of national policy as an exception to the general rule? Ought our country to remain in such cases dependent on foreign supply, precarious because liable to be interrupted? If the necessary article should in this mode cost more in time of peace, will not the security and independence thence arising form an ample compensation? Establishments of this sort, commensurate only with the calls of the public service in time of peace, will in time of war easily be extended in proportion to the exigencies of the Government, and may even perhaps be made to yield a surplus for the supply of our citizens at large, so as to mitigate the privations from the interruption of their trade. If adopted, the plan ought to exclude all those branches which are already, or likely soon to be, established in the country, in order that there may be no danger of interference with pursuits of individual industry.

It will not be doubted that with reference either to individual or national welfare agriculture is of primary importance. In proportion as nations advance in population and other circumstances of maturity this truth becomes more apparent, and renders the cultivation of the soil more and more an object of public patronage. Institutions for promoting it grow up, supported by the public purse; and to what object can it be dedicated with greater propriety? Among the means which have been employed to this end none have been attended with greater success than the establishment of boards (composed of proper characters) charged with collecting and diffusing information, and enabled by premiums and small pecuniary aids to encourage and assist a spirit of discovery and improvement. This species of establishment contributes doubly to the increase of improvement by stimulating to enterprise and experiment, and by drawing to a common center the results everywhere of individual skill and observation, and spreading them thence over the whole nation. Experience accordingly has shewn that they are very cheap instruments of immense national benefits.

I have heretofore proposed to the consideration of Congress the expediency of establishing a national university and also a military academy. The desirableness of both these institutions has so constantly increased with every new view I have taken of the subject that I can not omit the opportunity of once for all recalling your attention to them.

The assembly to which I address myself is too enlightened not to be fully sensible how much a flourishing state of the arts and sciences contributes to national prosperity and reputation.

True it is that our country, much to its honor, contains many seminaries of learning highly respectable and useful; but the funds upon which they rest are too narrow to command the ablest professors in the different departments of liberal knowledge for the institution contemplated, though they would be excellent auxiliaries.

Amongst the motives to such an institution, the assimilation of the principles, opinions, and manners of our countrymen by the common education of a portion of our youth from every quarter well deserves attention. The more homogeneous our citizens can be made in these particulars the greater will be our prospect of permanent union; and a primary object of such a national institution should be the education of our youth in the science of *government*. In a republic what species of knowledge can be equally important and what duty more pressing on its legislature than to patronize a plan for communicating it to those who are to be the future guardians of the liberties of the country?

The institution of a military academy is also recommended by cogent reasons. However pacific the general policy of a nation may be, it ought never to be without an adequate stock of military knowledge for emergencies. The first would impair the energy of its character, and both would hazard its safety or expose it to greater evils when war could not be avoided; besides that, war might often not depend upon its own choice. In proportion as the observance of pacific maxims might exempt a nation from the necessity of practicing the rules of the military art ought to be its care in preserving and transmitting, by proper establishments, the knowledge of that art. Whatever argument may be drawn from particular examples superficially viewed, a thorough examination of the subject will evince that the art of war is at once comprehensive and complicated, that it demands much previous study, and that the possession of it in its most improved and perfect state is always of great moment to the security of a nation. This, therefore, ought to be a serious care of every government, and for this purpose an academy where a regular course of instruction is given is an obvious expedient which different nations have successfully employed.

The compensations to the officers of the United States in various instances, and in none more than in respect to the most important stations, appear to call for legislative revision. The consequences of a defective provision are of serious import to the Government. If private wealth is to supply the defect of public retribution, it will greatly contract the sphere within which the selection of character for office is to be made, and will proportionally diminish the probability of a choice of men able as well as upright. Besides that, it would be repugnant to the vital principles of our Government virtually to exclude from public trusts talents and virtue unless accompanied by wealth.

While in our external relations some serious inconveniences and embarrassments have been overcome and others lessened, it is with much pain and deep regret I mention that circumstances of a very unwelcome nature have lately occurred. Our trade has suffered and is suffering extensive injuries in the West Indies from the cruisers and agents of the French Republic, and communications have been received from its minister here which indicate the danger of a further disturbance of our commerce by its authority, and which are in other respects far from agreeable.

It has been my constant, sincere, and earnest wish, in conformity with that of our nation, to maintain cordial harmony and a perfectly friendly understanding with that Republic. This wish remains unabated, and I shall persevere in the endeavor to fulfill it to the utmost extent of what shall be consistent with a just and indispensable regard to the rights and honor of our country; nor will I easily cease to cherish the expectation that a spirit of justice, candor, and friendship on the part of the Republic will eventually insure success.

In pursuing this course, however, I can not forget what is due to the character of our Government and nation, or to a full and entire confidence in the good sense, patriotism, self-respect, and fortitude of my countrymen.

I reserve for a special message a more particular communication on this interesting subject.

Thanksgiving Proclamation

Whereas it is the duty of all nations to acknowledge the providence of Almighty God, to obey His will, to be grateful for His benefits, and humbly to implore His protection and favor; and

Whereas both Houses of Congress have, by their joint committee, requested me "to recommend to the people of the United States a day of public thanksgiving and prayer, to be observed by acknowledging with grateful hearts the many and signal favors of Almighty God, especially by affording them an opportunity peaceably to establish a form of government for their safety and happiness:"

Now, therefore, I do recommend and assign Thursday, the 26th day of November next, to be devoted by the people of these States to the service of that great and glorious Being who is the beneficent author of all the good that was, that is, or that will be; that we may then all unite in rendering unto Him our sincere and humble thanks for His kind care and protection of the people of this country previous to their becoming a nation; for the signal and manifold mercies and the favorable interpositions of His providence in the course and conclusion of the late war; for the great degree of tranquillity, union, and plenty which we have since enjoyed; for the peaceable and rational manner in which we have been enabled to establish constitutions of government for our safety and happiness, and particularly the national one now lately instituted; for the civil and religious liberty with which we are blessed, and the means we have of acquiring and diffusing useful knowledge; and, in general, for all the great and various favors which He has been pleased to confer upon us.

And also that we may then unite in most humbly offering our prayers and supplications to the great Lord and Ruler of Nations, and beseech Him to pardon our national and other transgressions; to enable us all, whether in public or private stations, to perform our several and relative duties properly and punctually; to render our National Government a blessing to all the people by constantly being a Government of wise, just, and constitutional laws, discreetly and faithfully executed and obeyed; to protect and guide all sovereigns and nations (especially such as have shown kindness to us), and to bless them with good governments, peace, and concord; to promote the knowledge and practice of true religion and virtue, and the increase of science among them and us; and, generally, to grant unto all mankind such a degree of temporal prosperity as He alone knows to be best.

Given under my hand, at the city of New York, the 3rd day of October, A. D. 1789.

Go. Washington

Message to Senate

September 17, 1789

It doubtless is important that all treaties and compacts formed by the United States with other nations, whether civilized or not, should be made with caution and executed with fidelity.

It is said to be the general understanding and practice of nations, as a check on the mistakes and indiscretions of ministers or commissioners, not to consider any treaty negotiated and signed by such officers as final and conclusive until ratified by the sovereign or government from whom they derive their powers. This practice has been adopted by the United States respecting their treaties with European nations, and I am inclined to think it would be advisable to observe it in the conduct of our treaties with the Indians; for though such treaties, being on their part made by their chiefs or rulers, need not be ratified by them, yet, being formed on our part by the agency of subordinate officers, it seems to be both prudent and reasonable that their acts should not be binding on the nation until approved and ratified by the Government. It strikes me that this point should be well considered and settled, so that our national proceedings in this respect may become uniform and be directed by fixed and stable principles.

The treaties with certain Indian nations, which were laid before you with my message of the 25th May last, suggested two questions to my mind, viz: First, whether those treaties were to be considered as perfected and consequently as obligatory without being ratified. If not, then secondly, whether both or either, and which, of them ought to be ratified. On these questions I request your opinion and advice.

You have, indeed, advised me "*to execute and enjoin an observance of*" the treaty with the Wyandottes, etc. You, gentlemen, doubtless intended to be clear and explicit, and yet, without further explanation, I fear I may misunderstand your meaning, for if by my *executing* that treaty you mean that I should make it (in a more particular and immediate manner than it now is) the act of Government, then it follows that I am to ratify it. If you mean by my *executing it* that I am to see that it be carried into effect and operation, then I am led to conclude either that you consider it as being perfect and obligatory in its present state, and therefore to be executed and observed, or that you consider it as to derive its completion and obligation from the silent approbation and ratification which my proclamation may be construed to imply. Although I am inclined to think that the latter is your intention, yet it certainly is best that all doubts respecting it be removed.

Permit me to observe that it will be proper for me to be informed of your sentiments relative to the treaty with the Six Nations previous to the departure of the governor of the Western territory, and therefore I recommend it to your early consideration.

Message to the House of Representatives

March 30, 1796

Gentlemen of the House of Representatives:

With the utmost attention I have considered your resolution of the 24th instant, requesting me to lay before your House a copy of the instructions to the minister of the United States, who negotiated the treaty with the King of Great Britain, together with the correspondence and other documents relative to that treaty, excepting such of the said papers as any existing negotiation may render improper to be disclosed.

In deliberating upon this subject, it was impossible for me to lose sight of the principle, which some have avowed in its discussion, or to avoid extending my views to the consequences, which must flow from the admission of that principle.

I trust that no part of my conduct has ever indicated a disposition to withhold any information which the constitution has enjoined upon the President as a duty to give, or which could be required of him by either House of Congress as a right; and with truth I affirm, that it has been, as it will continue to be while I have the honor to preside in the government, my constant endeavor to harmonize with the other branches thereof, so far as the trust delegated to me by the people of the United States, and my sense of the obligation it imposes to "preserve, protect, and defend the constitution," will permit.

The nature of foreign negotiations requires caution, and their success must often depend on secrecy; and, even when brought to a conclusion, a full disclosure of all the measures, demands, or eventual concessions which may have been proposed or contemplated, would be extremely impolitic; for this might have a pernicious influence on future negotiations, or produce immediate inconveniences, perhaps danger and mischief, in relation to other powers. The necessity of such caution and secrecy was one cogent reason for vesting the power of making treaties in the President, with the advice and consent of the Senate; the principle on which that body was formed confining it to a small number of members. To admit, then, a right in the House of Representatives to demand, and to have, as a matter of course, all the papers respecting a negotiation with a foreign power, would be to establish a dangerous precedent.

It does not occur, that the inspection of the papers asked for can be relative to any purpose under the cognizance of the House of Representatives, except that of an impeachment, which the resolution has not expressed. I repeat, that I have no disposition to withhold any information which the duty of any station will permit, or the public good shall require, to be disclosed; and, in fact, all the papers affecting the negotiation with Great Britain, were laid before the Senate, when the treaty itself was communicated for their consideration and advice.

The course, which the debate has taken on the resolution of the House, leads to some observations on the mode of making treaties under the constitution of the United States.

Having been a member of the general convention, and knowing the principles on which the constitution was formed, I have ever entertained but one opinion on this subject; and, from the first establishment of the government to this moment, my conduct has exemplified that opinion, that the power of making treaties is exclusively vested in the President, by and with the advice and consent of the Senate, provided two thirds of the Senators present concur; and that every treaty, so made and promulgated, thenceforward became the law of the land. It is thus that the treaty-making power has been understood by foreign nations; and, in all the treaties made with them, we have declared, and they have believed, that, when ratified by the President, with the advice and consent of the Senate, they became obligatory. In this construction of the constitution, every House of Representatives has heretofore acquiesced; and, until the present time, not a doubt or suspicion has appeared, to my knowledge, that this construction was not the true one. Nay, they have more than acquiesced; for till now, without controverting the obligation of such treaties, they have made all the requisite provisions for carrying them into effect.

There is also reason to believe that this construction agrees with the opinions entertained by the State conventions, when they were deliberating on the constitution; especially by those who objected to it, because there was not required, in *commercial treaties*, the consent of two thirds of the whole number of the members of the Senate, instead of two thirds of the Senators present; and because, in treaties respecting territorial and certain other rights and claims, the concurrence of three fourths of the whole number of both Houses respectively was not made necessary.

It is a fact declared by the general convention, and universally understood, that the constitution of the United States was the result of a spirit of amity and mutual concession. And it is well known, that, under this influence, the smaller States were admitted to an equal representation in the Senate with the larger States, and that this branch of the government was invested with great powers; for on the equal participation of those powers the sovereignty and political safety of the smaller States were deemed essentially to depend.

If other proofs than these, and the plain letter of the constitution itself, be necessary to ascertain the point under consideration, they may be found in the journals of the general convention, which I have deposited in the office of the Department of State. In those journals it will appear, that a proposition was made, "that no treaty should be binding on the United States, which was not ratified by a law"; and that the proposition was explicitly rejected.

As, therefore, it is perfectly clear to my understanding, that the assent of the House of Representatives is not necessary to the

Friends, & Fellow-Citizens

The period for a new election of a Citizen, to administer the Executive Government of the United States, being not far distant, and the time actually arrived, when your thoughts must be employed in designating the person, who is to be cloathed with that important trust, it appears to me proper, especially as it may conduce to a more distinct expression of the public voice, that I should now apprise you of the resolution I have formed, to decline being considered among the number of those, out of whom a choice is to be made.—

I beg you, at the same time, to do me the justice to be assured, that this resolution has not been taken, without a strict regard to all the considerations appertaining to the relation, which binds a dutiful citizen to his country—and that, in withdrawing the tender of service which silence in my situation might imply, I am influenced by no diminution of zeal for your future interest, no deficiency of grateful respect for your past kindness; but am supported by a full conviction

A page from George Washington's Farewell Address, September 19, 1776 validity of a treaty; as the treaty with Great Britain exhibits, in itself, all the objects requiring legislative provision, and on these the papers called for can throw no light; and as it is essential to the due administration of the government, that the boundaries, fixed by the constitution between the different departments, should be preserved; a just regard to the constitution and to the duty of my office, under all the circumstances of this case, forbids a compliance with your request.

THE FAREWELL ADDRESS

September 19, 1796

TO THE PEOPLE OF THE UNITED STATES

Friends, and Fellow-Citizens:

The period for a new election of a Citizen, to administer the Executive Government of the United States, being not far distant, and the time actually arrived, when your thoughts must be employed in designating the person, who is to be clothed with that important trust, it appears to me proper, especially as it may conduce to a more distinct expression of the public voice, that I should now apprise you of the resolution I have formed, to decline being considered among the number of those, out of whom a choice is to be made.

I beg you, at the same time, to do me the justice to be assured, that this resolution has not been taken, without a strict regard to all the considerations appertaining to the relation, which binds a dutiful citizen to his country—and that, in withdrawing the tender of service which silence in my situation might imply, I am influenced by no diminution of zeal for your future interest, no deficiency of grateful respect for your past kindness; but am supported by a full conviction that the step is compatible with both.

The acceptance of, and continuance hitherto in, the office to which your suffrages have twice called me, have been a uniform sacrifice of inclination to the opinion of duty, and to a deference for what appeared to be your desire.—I constantly hoped, that it would have been much earlier in my power, consistently with motives, which I was not at liberty to disregard, to return to that retirement, from which I had been reluctantly drawn.—The strength of my inclination to do this, previous to the last election, had even led to the preparation of an address to declare it to you; but mature reflection on the then perplexed and critical posture of our affairs with foreign Nations, and the unanimous advice of persons entitled to my confidence, impelled me to abandon the idea.—

I rejoice that the state of your concerns, external as well as internal, no longer renders the pursuit of inclination incompatible with the sentiment of duty, or propriety; and am persuaded, whatever partiality may be retained for my services, that in the present circumstances of our country, you will not disapprove my determination to retire.

The impressions, with which I first undertook the arduous trust, were explained on the proper occasion.—In the discharge of this trust, I will only say, that I have, with good intentions, contributed towards the organization and administration of the government, the best exertions of which a very fallible judgment was capable.—Not unconscious, in the outset, of the inferiority of my qualifications, experience in my own eyes, perhaps still more in the eyes of others, has strengthened the motives to diffidence of myself; and every day the increasing weight of years admonishes me more and more, that the shade of retirement is as necessary to me as it will be welcome.—Satisfied, that, if any circumstances have given peculiar value to my services, they were temporary, I have the consolation to believe, that, while choice and prudence invite me to quit the political scene, patriotism does not forbid it.

In looking forward to the moment, which is intended to terminate the career of my public life, my feelings do not permit me to suspend the deep acknowledgment of that debt of gratitude, which I owe to my beloved country,—for the many honors it has conferred upon me; still more for the steadfast confidence with which it has supported me; and for the opportunities I have thence enjoyed of manifesting my inviolable attachment, by services faithful and persevering, though in usefulness unequal to my zeal.—If benefits have resulted to our country from these services, let it always be remembered to your praise, and as an instructive example in our annals, that under circumstances in which the Passions agitated in every direction were liable to mislead, amidst appearances sometimes dubious,—vicissitudes of fortune often discouraging,—in situations in which not unfrequently want of success has countenanced the spirit of criticism, the constancy of your support was the essential prop of the efforts and a guarantee of the plans by which they were effected.—Profoundly penetrated with this idea, I shall carry it with me to the grave, as a strong incitement to unceasing vows that Heaven may continue to you the choicest tokens of its beneficence—that your union and brotherly affection may be perpetual—that the free constitution, which is the work of your hands, may be sacredly maintained—that its administration in every department may be stamped with wisdom and virtue—that, in fine, the happiness of the people of these States, under the auspices of liberty, may be made complete, by so careful a preservation and so prudent a use of this blessing as will acquire to them the glory of recommending it to the applause, the affection, and adoption of every nation, which is yet a stranger to it.

Here, perhaps, I ought to stop.—But a solicitude for your welfare, which cannot end but with my life, and the apprehension of danger, natural to that solicitude, urge me on an occasion like the present, to offer to your solemn contemplation, and to recommend to your frequent review, some sentiments; which are the result of much reflection, of no inconsiderable observation, and which appear to me all-important to the permanency of your felicity as a People.—These will be offered to you with the more freedom, as you can only see in them the disinterested warnings of a parting friend, who can possibly have no personal motive to bias his counsels.—Nor can I forget, as an encouragement to it your indulgent reception of my sentiments on a former and not dissimilar occasion.

Interwoven as is the love of liberty with every ligament of your hearts, no recommendation of mine is necessary to fortify or confirm the attachment.—

The Unity of Government which constitutes you one people, is also now dear to you.—It is justly so;—for it is a main Pillar in the Edifice of your real independence; the support of your tranquillity at home; your peace abroad; of your safety; of your prosperity; of that very Liberty, which you so highly prize.—But as it is easy to foresee, that from different causes, and from different quarters, much pains will be taken, many artifices employed, to weaken in your minds the conviction of this truth;—as this is the point in your political fortress against which the batteries of internal and external enemies will be most constantly and actively (though often covertly and insidiously) directed, it is of infinite moment, that you should properly estimate the immense value of your national Union to your collective and individual happiness;—that you should cherish a cordial, habitual, and immoveable attachment to it; accustoming yourselves to think and speak of it as of the Palladium of your political safety and prosperity; watching for its preservation with jealous anxiety; discountenancing whatever may suggest even a suspicion that it can in any event be abandoned, and indignantly frowning upon the first dawning of every attempt to alienate any portion of our Country from the rest, or to enfeeble the sacred ties which now link together the various parts.

For this you have every inducement of sympathy and interest.—Citizens by birth or choice of a common country, that country has a right to concentrate your affections.—The name of AMERICAN, which belongs to you, in your national capacity, must always exalt the just pride of Patriotism, more than any appellation derived from local discriminations.—With slight shades of difference, you have the same Religion, Manners, Habits, and political Principles.—You have in a common cause fought and triumphed together.—The Independence and Liberty you possess are the work of joint councils, and joint efforts—of common dangers, sufferings and successes.—

But these considerations, however powerfully they address themselves to your sensibility, are greatly outweighed by those which apply more immediately to your Interest.—Here every portion of our country finds the most commanding motives for carefully guarding and preserving the Union of the whole.

The *North* in an unrestrained intercourse with the *South*, protected by the equal Laws of a common government, finds in the productions of the latter great additional resources of maritime and commercial enterprise—and precious materials of manufacturing industry.—The *South* in the same intercourse, benefiting by the agency of the *North,* sees its agriculture grow and its commerce expand. Turning partly into its own channels the seamen of the *North,* it finds its particular navigation envigorated;—and, while it contributes, in different ways, to nourish and increase the general mass of the national navigation, it looks forward to the protection of a maritime strength to which itself is unequally adapted.—The *East,* in a like intercourse with the *West,* already finds, and in the progressive improvement of interior communications, by land and water, will more and more find, a valuable vent for the commodities which it brings from abroad, or manufactures at home.—The *West* derives from the *East* supplies requisite to its growth and comfort, —and what is perhaps of still greater consequence, it must of necessity owe the *secure* enjoyment of indispensable *outlets* for its own productions to the weight, influence, and the future maritime strength of the Atlantic side of the Union, directed by an indissoluble community of interest, as *one Nation.*—Any other tenure by which the *West* can hold this essential advantage, whether derived from its own separate strength, or from an apostate and unnatural connexion with any foreign power, must be intrinsically precarious.

While then every part of our Country thus feels an immediate and particular interest in Union, all the parts combined cannot fail to find in the united mass of means and efforts, greater strength, greater resource, proportionably greater security from external danger, a less frequent interruption of their Peace by foreign Nations; and, what is of inestimable value! they must derive from Union an exemption from those broils and wars between themselves, which so frequently afflict neighbouring countries, not tied together by the same government; which their own rivalships alone would be sufficient to produce; but which opposite foreign alliances, attachments, and intrigues would stimulate and embitter.—Hence likewise they will avoid the necessity of those overgrown Military establishments, which under any form of government, are inauspicious to liberty, and which are to be regarded as particularly hostile to Republican Liberty: In this sense it is, that your Union ought to be considered as a main prop of your liberty, and that the love of the one ought to endear to you the preservation of the other.

These considerations speak a persuasive language to every reflecting and virtuous mind,—and exhibit the continuance of the UNION as a primary object of Patriotic desire.—Is there a doubt, whether a common government can embrace so large a sphere? —Let experience solve it.—To listen to mere speculation in such a case were criminal.—We are authorized to hope that a proper organization of the whole, with the auxiliary agency of governments for the respective subdivisions, will afford a happy issue to the experiment. 'T is well worth a fair and full experiment. With such powerful and obvious motives to Union, affecting all parts of our country, while experience shall not have demonstrated its impracticability, there will always be reason to distrust the patriotism of those, who in any quarter may endeavor to weaken its bands.—

In contemplating the causes which may disturb our Union, it occurs as matter of serious concern, that any ground should have been furnished for characterizing parties by *Geographical* discriminations—*Northern* and *Southern*—*Atlantic* and *Western;* whence designing men may endeavor to excite a belief, that there is a real difference of local interests and views. One of the expedients of Party to acquire influence, within particular districts, is to misrepresent the opinions and aims of other districts.—You cannot shield yourselves too much against the jealousies and heart-burnings which spring from these misrepresentations;—They tend to render alien to each other those who ought to be bound together by fraternal affection.—The inhabitants of our Western country have lately had a useful lesson on this head.—They have seen, in the negotiation by the Executive, and in the unanimous ratification by the Senate, of the Treaty with Spain, and in the universal satisfaction at that event, throughout the United States, a decisive proof how unfounded were the suspicions propagated among them of a policy in the General Government and in the Atlantic States unfriendly to their interests in regard to the MISSISSIPPI.—They have been witnesses to the formation of two Treaties, that with G. Britain, and that with Spain, which secure to them every thing they could desire, in respect to our Foreign Relations, towards confirming their prosperity.—Will it not be their wisdom to rely for the preservation of these advantages on the UNION by which they were procured?—Will they not henceforth be deaf to those advisers, if such there are, who would sever them from their Brethren, and connect them with Aliens?—

To the efficacy and permanency of your Union, a Government for the whole is indispensable.—No alliances however strict between the parts can be an adequate substitute.—They must inevitably experience the infractions and interruptions which all alliances in all times have experienced.—Sensible of this momentous truth, you have improved upon your first essay, by the adoption of a Constitution of Government, better calculated than your former for an intimate Union, and for the efficacious management of your common concerns.—This government, the offspring of our own choice uninfluenced and unawed, adopted upon full investigation and mature deliberation, completely free in its principles, in the distribution of its powers, uniting security with energy, and containing within itself a provision for its own amendment, has a just claim to your confidence and your support.—Respect for its authority, compliance with its Laws, acquiescence in its measures, are duties enjoined by the fundamental maxims of true Liberty.—The basis of our political systems is the right of the people to make and to alter their Constitutions of Government.—But the Constitution which at any time exists, 'till changed by an explicit and authentic act of the whole people, is sacredly obligatory upon all.—The very idea of the power and the right of the people to establish Government, presupposes the duty of every individual to obey the established Government.

All obstructions to the execution of the Laws, all combinations and associations, under whatever plausible character, with the real design to direct, controul, counteract, or awe the regular deliberation and action of the constituted authorities, are destructive of this fundamental principle, and of fatal tendency.—They serve to organize faction, to give it an artificial and extraordinary force—to put, in the place of the delegated will of the Nation, the will of a party;—often a small but artful and enterprizing minority of the community;—and, according to the alternate triumphs of different parties, to make the public administration the mirror of the ill-concerted and incongruous projects of faction, rather than the organ of consistent and wholesome plans digested by common councils, and modified by mutual interests.—However combinations or associations of the above description may now and then answer popular ends, they are likely, in the course of time and things, to become potent engines, by which cunning, ambitious, and unprincipled men will be enabled to subvert the Power of the People and to usurp for themselves the reins of Government; destroying afterwards the very engines which have lifted them to unjust dominion.—

Towards the preservation of your Government and the permanency of your present happy state, it is requisite, not only that you steadily discountenance irregular oppositions to its acknowledged authority, but also that you resist with care the spirit of innovation upon its principles, however specious the pretexts.—One method of assault may be to effect, in the forms of the Constitution, alterations which will impair the energy of the system, and thus to undermine what cannot be directly over-thrown.—In all the changes to which you may be invited, remember that time and habit are at least as necessary to fix the true character of Governments, as of other human institutions—that experience is the surest standard, by which to test the real tendency of the existing Constitution of a Country—that facility in changes upon the credit of mere hypothesis and opinion exposes to perpetual change, from the endless variety of hypothesis and opinion:—and remember, especially, that for the efficient management of your common interests, in a country so extensive as ours, a Government of as much vigour as is consistent with the perfect security of Liberty is indispensable.—Liberty itself will find in such a Government, with powers properly distributed and adjusted, its surest Guardian.—It is indeed little else than a name, where the Government is too feeble to withstand the enterprises of faction, to confine each member of the Society within the limits prescribed by the laws, and to maintain all in the secure and tranquil enjoyment of the rights of person and property.

I have already intimated to you the danger of Parties in the State, with particular reference to the founding of them on

Geographical discriminations.—Let me now take a more comprehensive view, and warn you in the most solemn manner against the baneful effects of the Spirit of Party, generally.

This Spirit, unfortunately, is inseparable from our nature, having its root in the strongest passions of the human mind.—It exists under different shapes in all Governments, more or less stifled, controuled, or repressed; but, in those of the popular form, it is seen in its greatest rankness, and is truly their worst enemy.—

The alternate domination of one faction over another, sharpened by the spirit of revenge natural to party dissension, which in different ages and countries has perpetrated the most horrid enormities, is itself a frightful despotism.—But this leads at length to a more formal and permanent despotism.—The disorders and miseries, which result, gradually incline the minds of men to seek security and repose in the absolute power of an Individual: and sooner or later the chief of some prevailing faction, more able or more fortunate than his competitors, turns this disposition to the purposes of his own elevation, on the ruins of Public Liberty.

Without looking forward to an extremity of this kind, (which nevertheless ought not to be entirely out of sight,) the common and continual mischiefs of the spirit of Party are sufficient to make it the interest and duty of a wise People to discourage and restrain it.—

It serves always to distract the Public Councils, and enfeeble the Public administration.—It agitates the community with ill-founded jealousies and false alarms, kindles the animosity of one part against another, foments occasionally riot and insurrection.—It opens the doors to foreign influence and corruption, which find a facilitated access to the Government itself through the channels of party passions. Thus the policy and the will of one country, are subjected to the policy and will of another.

There is an opinion that parties in free countries are useful checks upon the Administration of the Government, and serve to keep alive the Spirit of Liberty.—This within certain limits is probably true—and in Governments of a Monarchical cast, Patriotism may look with indulgence, if not with favour, upon the spirit of party.—But in those of the popular character, in Governments purely elective, it is a spirit not to be encouraged.—From their natural tendency, it is certain there will always be enough of that spirit for every salutary purpose,—and there being constant danger of excess, the effort ought to be, by force of public opinion, to mitigate and assuage it.—A fire not to be quenched; it demands a uniform vigilance to prevent its bursting into a flame, lest, instead of warming, it should consume.—

It is important, likewise, that the habits of thinking in a free country should inspire caution in those entrusted with its administration, to confine themselves within their respective constitutional spheres; avoiding in the exercise of the powers of one department to encroach upon another.—The spirit of encroachment tends to consolidate the powers of all the departments in one, and thus to create, whatever the form of government, a real despotism.—A just estimate of that love of power, and proneness to abuse it, which predominates in the human heart, is sufficient to satisfy us of the truth of this position.—The necessity of reciprocal checks in the exercise of political power, by dividing and distributing it into different depositories, and constituting each the Guardian of the Public Weal against invasions by the others, has been evinced by experiments ancient and modern; some of them in our country and under our own eyes.—To preserve them must be as necessary as to institute them. If in the opinion of the People, the distribution or modification of the Constitutional powers be in any particular wrong, let it be corrected by an amendment in the way which the Constitution designates.—But let there be no change by usurpation; for though this, in one instance, may be the instrument of good, it is the customary weapon by which free governments are destroyed.—The precedent must always greatly overbalance in permanent evil any partial or transient benefit which the use can at any time yield.—

Of all the dispositions and habits, which lead to political prosperity, Religion and morality are indispensable supports.—In vain would that man claim the tribute of Patriotism, who should labour to subvert these great Pillars of human happiness, these firmest props of the duties of Men and Citizens.—The mere Politician, equally with the pious man, ought to respect and to cherish them.—A volume could not trace all their connexions with private and public felicity.—Let it simply be asked where is the security for property, for reputation, for life, if the sense of religious obligation *desert* the oaths, which are the instruments of investigation in Courts of Justice? And let us with caution indulge the supposition, that morality can be maintained without religion.—Whatever may be conceded to the influence of refined education on minds of peculiar structure—reason and experience both forbid us to expect, that national morality can prevail in exclusion of religious principle.—

'T is substantially true, that virtue or morality is a necessary spring of popular government.—The rule indeed extends with more or less force to every species of Free Government.—Who that is a sincere friend to it, can look with indifference upon attempts to shake the foundation of the fabric?—

Promote, then, as an object of primary importance, institutions for the general diffusion of knowledge.—In proportion as the structure of a government gives force to public opinion, it is essential that public opinion should be enlightened.—

As a very important source of strength and security, cherish public credit.—One method of preserving it is to use it as sparingly as possible:—avoiding occasions of expense by cultivating peace, but remembering also that timely disbursements to prepare for danger frequently prevent much greater disbursements to repel it—avoiding likewise the accumulation of debt, not only by shunning occasions of expense, but by vigorous exertions in time of Peace to discharge the debts which unavoidable wars may have occasioned, not ungenerously throwing upon posterity the burthen which we ourselves ought to bear. The execution of these maxims belongs to your Representatives, but it is necessary that public opinion should coöperate.—To facilitate to them the performance of their duty, it is essential that you should practically bear in mind, that towards the payment of debts there must be Revenue—that to have Revenue there must be taxes—that no taxes can be devised which are not more or less inconvenient and unpleasant—that the intrinsic embarrassment inseparable from the selection of the proper objects (which is always a choice of difficulties) ought to be a decisive motive for a candid construction of the conduct of the Government in making it, and for a spirit of acquiescence in the measures for obtaining Revenue which the public exigencies may at any time dictate.—

Observe good faith and justice towards all Nations. Cultivate peace and harmony with all.—Religion and Morality enjoin this conduct; and can it be that good policy does not equally enjoin it?—It will be worthy of a free, enlightened, and, at no distant period, a great nation, to give to mankind the magnanimous and too novel example of a People always guided by an exalted justice and benevolence.—Who can doubt that in the course of time and things, the fruits of such a plan would richly repay any temporary advantages, which might be lost by a steady adherence to it? Can it be, that Providence has not connected the permanent felicity of a Nation with its virtue? The experiment, at least, is recommended by every sentiment which ennobles human nature.—Alas! is it rendered impossible by its vices?

In the execution of such a plan nothing is more essential than that permanent, inveterate antipathies against particular nations and passionate attachments for others should be excluded; and that in place of them just and amicable feelings towards all should be cultivated.—The Nation, which indulges towards another an habitual hatred or an habitual fondness, is in some degree a slave. It is a slave to its animosity or to its affection, either of which is sufficient to lead it astray from its duty and its interest.—Antipathy in one nation against another disposes each more readily to offer insult and injury, to lay hold of slight causes of umbrage, and to be haughty and intractable, when accidental or trifling occasions of dispute occur.—Hence frequent collisions, obstinate, envenomed and bloody contests.—The Nation promoted by ill-will and resentment sometimes impels to War the Government, contrary to the best calculations of policy.—The Government sometimes participates in the national propensity, and adopts through passion what reason would reject;—at other times, it makes the animosity of the Nation subservient to projects of hostility instigated by pride, ambition, and other sinister and pernicious motives.—The peace often, sometimes perhaps the Liberty, of Nations has been the victim.—

So likewise a passionate attachment of one Nation for another produces a variety of evils.—Sympathy for the favourite nation, facilitating the illusion of an imaginary common interest in cases where no real common interest exists, and infusing into one the enmities of the other, betrays the former into a participation in the quarrels and wars of the latter, without adequate inducement or justification: It leads also to concessions to the favourite Nation of privileges denied to others, which is apt doubly to injure the Nation making the concessions; by unnecessarily parting with what ought to have been retained, and by exciting jealousy, ill-will, and a disposition to retaliate, in the parties from whom equal privileges are withheld; and it gives to ambitious, corrupted, or deluded citizens, (who devote themselves to the favourite Nation) facility to betray, or sacrifice the interests of their own country, without odium, sometimes even with popularity:—gilding with the appearances of a virtuous sense of obligation, a commendable deference for public opinion, or a laudable zeal for public good, the base or foolish compliances of ambition, corruption or infatuation.—

As avenues to foreign influence in innumerable ways, such attachments are particularly alarming to the truly enlightened and independent Patriot.—How many opportunities do they afford to tamper with domestic factions, to practise the arts of seduction, to mislead public opinion, to influence or awe the public councils! Such an attachment of a small or weak, towards a great and powerful nation, dooms the former to be the satellite of the latter.

Against the insidious wiles of foreign influence, I conjure you to believe me, fellow-citizens, the jealousy of a free people ought to be *constantly* awake, since history and experience prove that foreign influence is one of the most baneful foes of Republican Government.—But that jealousy to be useful must be impartial; else it becomes the instrument of the very influence to be avoided, instead of a defence against it.—Excessive partiality for one foreign nation and excessive dislike of another, cause those whom they actuate to see danger only on one side, and serve to veil and even second the arts of influence on the other.—Real Patriots, who may resist the intrigues of the favourite, are liable to become suspected and odious; while its tools and dupes usurp the applause and confidence of the people, to surrender their interests.—

The great rule of conduct for us, in regard to foreign Nations, is, in extending our commercial relations, to have with them as little *Political* connection as possible.—So far as we have already formed engagements, let them be fulfilled with perfect good faith.—Here let us stop.—

Europe has a set of primary interests, which to us have none, or a very remote relation.—Hence she must be engaged in frequent controversies, the causes of which are essentially foreign to our concerns.—Hence therefore it must be unwise in us to implicate ourselves, by artificial ties in the ordinary vicissitudes of her politics, or the ordinary combinations and collisions of her friendships, or enmities.

Our detached and distant situation invites and enables us to pursue a different course.—If we remain one People, under an efficient government, the period is not far off, when we may defy material injury from external annoyance; when we may take such an attitude as will cause the neutrality we may at any time resolve upon to be scrupulously respected.—When belligerent nations, under the impossibility of making acquisitions upon us, will not lightly hazard the giving us provocation; when we may choose peace or war, as our interest guided by our justice shall counsel.—

Why forego the advantages of so peculiar a situation?—Why quit our own to stand upon foreign ground?—Why, by interweaving our destiny with that of any part of Europe, entangle our peace and prosperity, in the toils of European ambition, rivalship, interest, humour, or caprice?—

'T is our true policy to steer clear of permanent alliances, with any portion of the foreign world;—so far, I mean, as we are now at liberty to do it—for let me not be understood as capable of patronizing infidelity to existing engagements, (I hold the maxim no less applicable to public than to private affairs, that honesty is always the best policy).—I repeat it therefore let those engagements be observed in their genuine sense.—But in my opinion it is unnecessary and would be unwise to extend them.—

Taking care always to keep ourselves, by suitable establishments, on a respectably defensive posture, we may safely trust to temporary alliances for extraordinary emergencies.—

Harmony, liberal intercourse with all nations, are recommended by policy, humanity, and interest.—But even our commercial policy should hold an equal and impartial hand:—neither seeking nor granting exclusive favours or preferences;—consulting the natural course of things;—diffusing and diversifying by gentle means the streams of commerce, but forcing nothing;—establishing with Powers so disposed—in order to give trade a stable course, to define the rights of our Merchants, and to enable the Government to support them—conventional rules of intercourse, the best that present circumstances and mutual opinion will permit; but temporary, and liable to be from time to time abandoned or varied, as experience and circumstances shall dictate; constantly keeping in view, that 't is folly in one nation to look for disinterested favors from another,—that it must pay with a portion of its independence for whatever it may accept under that character—that by such acceptance, it may place itself in the condition of having given equivalents for nominal favours and yet of being reproached with ingratitude for not giving more.—There can be no greater error than to expect, or calculate upon real favours from Nation to Nation.—'T is an illusion which experience must cure, which a just pride ought to discard.

In offering to you, my Countrymen, these counsels of an old and affectionate friend, I dare not hope they will make the strong and lasting impression, I could wish,—that they will controul the usual current of the passions, or prevent our Nation from running the course which has hitherto marked the destiny of Nations.—But if I may even flatter myself, that they may be productive of some partial benefit; some occasional good; that they may now and then recur to moderate the fury of party spirit, to warn against the mischiefs of foreign intrigue, to guard against the impostures of pretended patriotism, this hope will be a full recompense for the solicitude for your welfare, by which they have been dictated.—

How far in the discharge of my official duties, I have been guided by the principles which have been delineated, the public Records and other evidences of my conduct must witness to You, and to the World.—To myself, the assurance of my own conscience is, that I have at least believed myself to be guided by them.

In relation to the still subsisting War in Europe, my Proclamation of the 22d of April 1793 is the index to my plan.—Sanctioned by your approving voice and by that of Your Representatives in both Houses of Congress, the spirit of that measure has continually governed me:—uninfluenced by any attempts to deter or divert me from it.

After deliberate examination with the aid of the best lights I could obtain, I was well satisfied that our country, under all the circumstances of the case, had a right to take, and was bound in duty and interest, to take a Neutral position.—Having taken it, I determined, as far as should depend upon me, to maintain it, with moderation, perseverance, and firmness.—

The considerations which respect the right to hold this conduct, it is not necessary on this occasion to detail. I will only observe, that according to my understanding of the matter, that right, so far from being denied by any of the Belligerent Powers, has been virtually admitted by all.—

The duty of holding a neutral conduct may be inferred, without any thing more, from the obligation which justice and humanity impose on every Nation, in cases in which it is free to act, to maintain inviolate the relations of Peace and Amity towards other Nations.—

The inducements of interest for observing that conduct will best be referred to your own reflections and experience.—With me, a predominant motive has been to endeavour to gain time to our country to settle and mature its yet recent institutions, and to progress without interruption to that degree of strength and consistency, which is necessary to give it, humanly speaking, the command of its own fortunes.

Though, in reviewing the incidents of my Administration, I am unconscious of intentional error—I am nevertheless too sensible of my defects not to think it probable that I may have committed many errors.—Whatever they may be I fervently beseech the Almighty to avert or mitigate the evils to which they may tend.—I shall also carry with me the hope that my country will never cease to view them with indulgence; and that after forty-five years of my life dedicated to its service, with an upright zeal, the faults of incompetent abilities will be consigned to oblivion, as myself must soon be to the mansions of rest.

Relying on its kindness in this as in other things, and actuated by that fervent love towards it, which is so natural to a man, who views in it the native soil of himself and his progenitors for several generations;—I anticipate with pleasing expectation that retreat, in which I promise myself to realize, without alloy, the sweet enjoyment of partaking, in the midst of my fellow-citizens, the benign influence of good Laws under a free Government,—the ever favourite object of my heart, and the happy reward, as I trust, of our mutual cares, labours, and dangers.

Chapter 9
GENERAL IDEAS

Agriculture
(Extracts from Diaries)

Fertilizers (April, 1760)

Monday, 14. Fine warm day, Wind So'ly and clear till the Even'g when it clouded; No Fish were to be catchd to day neither.

Mixd my Composts in a box with ten Apartments in the following manner, viz: in No. 1 is three pecks of the Earth brought from below the Hill out of the 46 Acre Field without any mixture; in No. 2 is two pecks of the said Earth and one of Marle taken out of the said Field, which Marle seemed a little Inclinable to Sand;

3. Has 2 Pecks of sd. Earth and 1 of Riverside Sand;
4. Has a Peck of Horse Dung;
5. Has mud taken out of the Creek;
6. Has Cow Dung;
7. Marle from the Gullys on the Hill side, wch. seemed to be purer than the other;
8. Sheep Dung;
9. Black Mould taken out of the Pocoson on the Creek side;
10. Clay got just below the Garden.

All mixd with the same quantity and sort of Earth in the most effectual manner by reducing the whole to a tolerable degree of fineness and ju[m]bling them well together in a Cloth.

In each of these divisions were planted three grains of Wheat, 3 of Oats and as many of Barley—all at equal distances in Rows, and of equal depth (done by a machine made for the purpose).

The Wheat Rows are next the Numberd side, the Oats in the

Middle and the Barley on that side next the upper part of the Garden.

Two or three hours after sowing in this manner, and about an hour before Sunset I watered them all equally alike with water that had been standing in a Tub abt. two hours exposed to the Sun. . . .

Finished Harrowing the Clover Field, and began reharrowing of it. Got a new harrow made of smaller, and closer Tinings for Harrowing in Grain—the other being more proper for preparing the Ground for sowing.

Cook Jack's plow was stopd he being employd in setting the Lime Kiln.

Grain crops (May, 1760)

Thursday, 1st. Got over early in the Morning and reachd home before Dinner time, and upon inquiry found that my Clover Field was finished sowing and Rolling the Saturday I left home—as was sowing of my Lucerne: and that on the [ ] they began sowing the last field of Oats and finished it the 25th.

That in box No. 6, two grains of wheat appeared on the 20th, one an Inch high; on the 22d a grain of Wheat in No 7 and 9 appeard; on the 23 after a good deal of Rain the Night before some Stalks appeard in Nos. 2. 3. 4. 5. and 6, but the Ground was so hard bakd by the drying winds when I came home that it was difficult to say which Nos. lookd most thriving. However in

No. 1 there was nothing come up;

2	2 Oats		1 barley;
3	1 Oat		2 barley;
4	1 Oat;		
5	1 Wheat	2 Oats;	
6	1 Do.	3 Do.	1 Do.
7	1 Do.	2 Do.	2 Do.
8	1 Do.	1 Do.	
9	2 Do.	3 Do.	2 Do.
10			1 Do.

The two Grains in No. 8 were I think rather the strongest, but upon the whole No. 9 was the best.

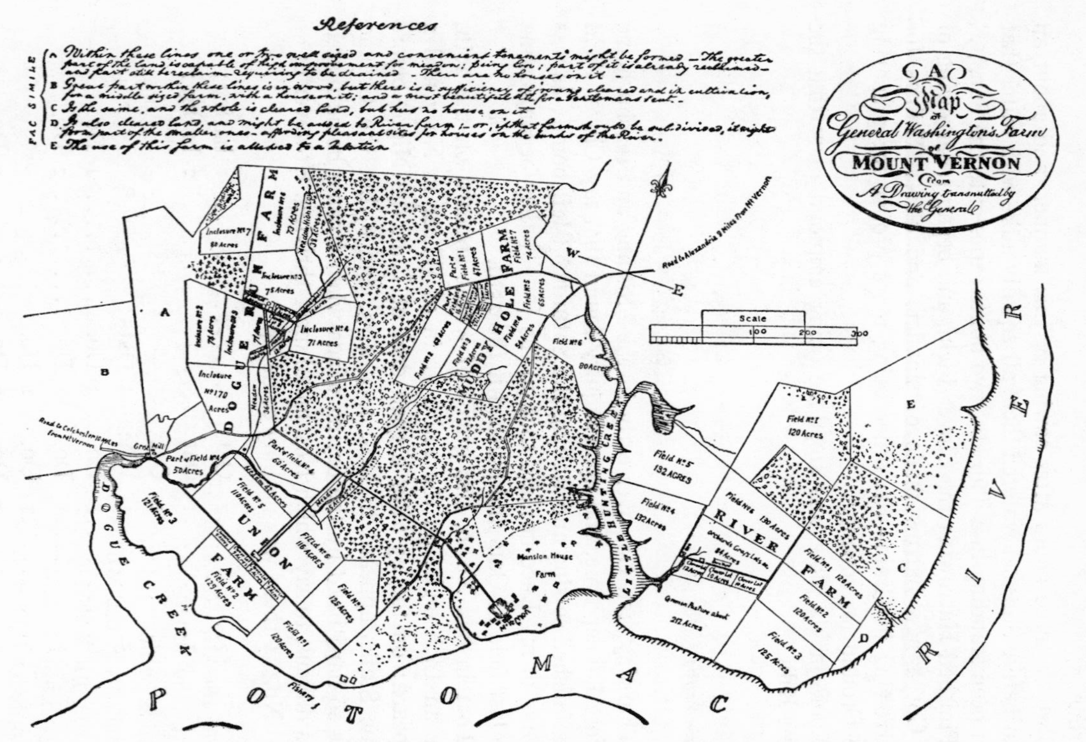

A map of George Washington's Farm at Mount Vernon

Orchard (March, 1765)

5th. Grafted 15 English Mulberrys on wild Mulberry Stocks on the side of the Hill near the Spring Path. Note, the Stocks were very Milkey.

6th. Grafted 10 Carnation Cherrys on growing Stocks in the Garden. . . tree, 1 on a Stock in the middle of the border of the last square, and just above the 2d. fall (Note, this Graft is on the Northernmost fork) of Do.; on the Westernmost one is a Bullock Heart, and on the Easternmost one is a May Cherry out of the Cherry Walk. 1 other on a Stock just above the 2d. Gate. Note this is on the Northernmost prong; the other Graft on the said stock is of the May Cherry in the Cherry Walk.

15. Grafted 6 Early May duke Cherrys on the Nursery, begin'g at that end of the first Row next to the Lane—the Row next the Quarter is meant; at the end of this a Stake drove in.

15. Also Grafted joining to these in the same Row 6 of the latter May dukes—which are all the Cherrys in the Row. Also Grafted 7 Bullock Heart Cherrys in the last Row.

30. Grafted 48 Pears which stand as follows, viz. in the 3d Row beging. at the end next the Cherry Walk are 12 Spanish Pears; next to these are 8 Early June Pears; then 10 latter Bergamy; then 8 Black Pear or Worcester; and lastly 10 Early Bergamy. Note, all these Pears came from Colo. Mason's: and between each sort a Stick is drove down. The Rows are counted from the end of the Quarter.

30. This day also I grafted 39 New Town Pippins, which compleat the 5th Row and which Row are all of this kind of Fruit now.

30. The 6th Row is compleated with Grafts of the Maryland Red Strick, which are all of this sort of Fruit, and contains [ ] trees; so is the 8th Row of this Apple, also 54 in number and 20 in the 9th Row beginning next the Cherry Walk.

30 The 7th. Row has 25 Graffs of the Gloster white Apple which compleats this Row with that sort of Fruit.

Grain drills (April, 1786)

Saturday, 8th. Rid a little after Sun rise to Muddy [hole], to try my drill plow again, which with the alteration of the harrow yesterday, I find will fully answer my expectation, and that it drops the grains thicker, or thinner in proportion to the quantity of seed in the Barrel. The less there is in it the faster it issues from the holes. The weight of a quantity in the barrel, occasions (I presume) a pressure on the holes that do not admit of a free discharge of the Seed through them, whereas a small quantity (sufficient at all times to cover the bottom of the barrel) is, in a manner sifted through them by the revolution of the Barrel.

I sowed with the barrel to day, in drills, about 3 pints of a white well looking Oat, brought from Carolina last year by G. A. Washington in 7 rows running from the path leading from the Overseer's Ho. to the Quarter to the West fence of the field, which the ground was in the best order. Afterwards I sowed in such other parts of the adjoining ground as could at any rate be worked the common Oat of the Eastern shore (after picking out the Wild onion); but in truth nothing but the late Season could warrant sowing in ground so wet.

None of the ground in wch. these Oats were sown had received any improvement from manure, but all of it had been twice plowed, and then listed, after which the harrow had gone over it twice before the seed harrowing. This, had it not been for the frequent rains, etca., which has fallen would have put the ground in fine order.

Transplanted as many of the large Magnolio into the Grove at the No. end of the Ho. as made the number there.

Also transplanted from the same box, 9 of the live Oak, viz. 4 in the bends of the lawn before the House, and five on the East of the grove (within the yard) at the No. end of the House.

Plowed up my last years turnip patch (at home) to sow Orchard grass seeds in.

No fish caught to day. . . .

Monday, 10th. Began my brick work to day, first taking away the foundations of the Garden Houses as they were first placed, and repairing the damages in the Walls occasioned by their removal; and also began to put up my pallisades (on the Wall).

Compleated Sowing with 20 quarts the drilled Oats in the ground intended for experiments at Muddy hole; which amounted to 38 rows, ten feet apart (including the parts of rows sowed on Saturday last). In the afternoon I began to sow Barley, but finding there were too many Seeds discharged from the Barrel, notwithstanding I stopped every other hole, I discontinued the sowing until another Barrel with smaller holes cd. be prepared. The ground, in which these Oats have been sowed and in which the Barley seeding had commenced, has been plowed, cross plowed, listed (as it is called, that is 3 furrow ridges) and twice harrowed before the drill plow was put into it; with this the furrow is made and the seed harrowed in with the manure afterwds.

Began also to sow the Siberian Wheat which I had obtained from Baltimore by means of Colo. Tilghman, at the Ferry Plantation in the ground laid apart there for experiments. This was done upon ground which, sometime ago, had been marked off by furrows 8 feet apart, in which a second furrow had been run to deepen them. 4 furrows were then plowed to these, which made the whole 5 furrow Ridges. These being done sometime ago, and by frequent rains prevented sowing at the time intended had got hard, I therefore before the seed was sowed, split these Ridges again, by running twice in the same furrow. After wch. I harrowed the ridges, and where the ground was lumpy run my spiked Roller with the Harrow at the tale over it, wch. I found very efficacious in breaking the clods and pulverising the earth; and wd. have done it perfectly if there had not been too much moisture remaining of the late rains; after this harrowing and rolling where necessary, I sowed the Wheat with my drill plow on the reduced ridges in rows 8 feet apart. But I should have observed that, after the ridges were split by the furrow in the middle, and before the furrows were closed again by the harrow, I sprinkled a little dung in them. Finding the barrel discharged the Wheat too fast, I did, after sowing 9 of the shortest (for we began at the furthest corner of the field) rows, I stopped every other hole in the barrel, and in this manner sowed 5 rows more, and still thinking the seed too liberally bestowed, I stopped 2, and left one hole open, alternately, by which 4 out of 12 holes only, discharged seeds; and this, as I had taken the strap of leather off, seemed to give seed enough (though not so regular as were to be wished) to the ground.

Report on a Threshing Machine (January, 1790)

Friday, 22d. Exercised on horseback in the forenoon.

Called in my ride on the Baron de Polnitz, to see the operation of his [Winlaw's] threshing machine. The effect was, the heads of the wheat being seperated from the straw, as much of the first was run through the mill in 15 minutes as made half a bushel of clean wheat—allowing 8 working hours in the 24, this would yield 16 bushels pr. day. Two boys are sufficient to turn the wheel, feed the mill, and remove the threshed grain after it has passed through it. Two men were unable, by winnowing, to clean the wheat as it passed through the mill, but a common Dutch fan, with the usual attendance, would be *more* than sufficient to do it. The grain passes through without bruising and is well separated from the chaff. Women, or boys of 12 to 14 years of age, are fully adequate to the management of the mill or threshing machine. Upon the whole, it appears to be an easier, more expeditious, and much cleaner way of getting out grain than by the usual mode of threshing; and vastly to be preferred to treading, which is hurtful to horses, filthy to the wheat, and not more expeditious, considering the numbers that are employed in the process from the time the head is begun to be formed until the grain has passed finally through the fan.

Wheat

July 25, 1768. Took Wheat of three differt. degrees of Ripeness . . . and observd after they had lain 2 or 3 days in the sun . . . by wch. it evidently appears that to cut Wheat Knot green is not only safe but the most desirable state it can be cut in . . . The question is, whether it may not be better to begin while the Wheat is colouring from the upper joint, as the grain will loose but little (if any) than to cut in an overripe state, when it may loose a good deal more by shattering. For my part I am clear it is better to cut it green and shall have no reluctance to practice where the whole cannot be cut at the exact period one would choose it.

July 15, 1769. It appeard evident that 10, and sometimes 9, Cradlers (according as the Wheat was thick or thin) were full suff. to keep the rest of my hands employ'd; and it likewise appeard, that it was evidently to my advantage to employ my own hands to Cradle the Wheat rather than to hire any at all, as these may be got for 2 Shillgs. or half a Crown a day, whereas the Wages of the White Cradlers are exorbitantly high. But if Wheat of different kinds are sowed so as to prevent the Harvest coming on at once, it is my opinion that hirelings of all kinds may be dispensed with. The Rakers in the generality of the Wheat is sufficient to Rake and bind after a Cradle, and the rest of the hands can manage (after the water Carriers and Cooks are taken out) to get the Wheat into convent. places and attend the Stackers. Two, and sometimes three, Stackers will Stack as fast as it is cut and I am of opinion that two brisk hands is sufft. for this purpose. From experience it has been found advantageous to put the Cradlers and their attendants into at least 3 Gangs. The Stops and delays by this means are not so frequent, and the Work much better attended to, as every Mans work is distinguishable, and the whole Cradles not always stopping for every little disorder that happens to each respective one, as is the case when they cut altogether.

Agriculture on Long Island (1790)

April. 24. This Island (as far as I went) from West to East seems to be equally divided between flat and Hilly land, the former on the South next the Seaboard, and the latter on the No. next the Sound. The highland they say is best and most productive, but the other is the pleasantest to work, except in wet seasons when from the levelness of them they are sometimes, (but not frequently having a considerable portion of Sand) incommoded by heavy and continual rains. From a comparative view of their crops they may be averaged as follows:—Indian Corn 25 bushels—Wheat 15—

Rye 12—Oats 15 bushels to the acre. According to their accts. from Lands highly manured they sometimes get 50 of the first, 25 of the 2d and 3d, and more of the latter.

Their general mode of Cropping is,—first Indian Corn upon a lay, manured in the hill, half a shovel full in each hole—(some scatter the dung over the field equally)—2d. Oats and Flax—3d. Wheat with what manure they can spare from the Indian Corn land—with the wheat, or on it, towards close of the Snows, they sow Clover from 4 to 6 lb; and a quart of Timothy Seed. This lays from 3 to 6 years according as the grass remains, or as the condition of the ground is, for so soon as they find it beginning to bind, they plow. Their first plowing (with the Patent tho' they call it the Dutch plow) is well executed at the depth of about 3 or at most 4 inches—the cut being 9 or 10 Inches and the sod neatly and very evenly turned. With Oxen they plough mostly. They do no more than turn the ground in this manner for Indian Corn before it is planted; making the holes in which it is placed with hoes the rows being marked off by a stick—two or three workings afterwards with the Harrows or Plough is all the cultivation it receives *generally*. Their fences, where there is no Stone, are very indifferent; frequently of plashd trees of *any* and *every* kind which have grown by chance; but it exhibits an evidence that very good fences may be made in this manner either of white Oak or Dogwood which from this mode of treatment grows thickest, and most stubborn.—This however, would be no defence against Hogs.

Agriculture
(Letters)

To Marbois, July 9, 1783

To cultivate Exotics for the purpose of making Wine, or for my amusement, was never contemplated by me. The spontaneous growth of the Vine in all parts of this country, the different qualities of them and periods for maturation, led me to conclude, that by a happy choice of the species I might succeed better than those who had attempted the foreign vine. Accordingly, a year or two before hostilities commenced, I selected about two thousand cuttings of a kind which does not ripen with us [in Virginia] till repeated frosts in the Autumn meliorate the Grape and deprive the Vines of their leaves. It is then, and not before, the grape (which is never very pallitable) can be Eaten.

Several little Essays have been made by Gentlemen of my acquaintance to cultivate the foreign grape, for Vine; but none had well succeeded; owing either to an improper kind, or the want of skill in the management. For the most part, their Wine soon contracted an acidity, which rendered it unfit for use; one cause of which I ascribed to the ripening of their grape in our Summer or Autumnal heats, and to the too great fermentation occasioned thereby. This consideration led me to try the wild grape of the Country, and to fix upon the species which I have already described, and which in the Eight years I have been absent from my Estate has been little attended to. Had I remained at home, I should ere this, have perfected the experiment which was all I had in view.

To Arthur Young, August 6, 1786

Agriculture has ever been amongst the most favourite amusements of my life, though I never possessed much skill in the art; and nine years total inattention to it, has added nothing to a knowledge which is best understood from practice; but with the means you have been so obliging as to furnish me, I shall return to it (though rather late in the day) with hope and confidence.

The system of agriculture, if the epithet of system can be applied to it, which is in use in this part of the United States, is as unproductive to the practitioners as it is ruinous to the landholders. Yet it is pertinaciously adhered to. To forsake it, to pursue a course of husbandry which is altogether different and new to the gazing multitude, ever averse to novelty in matters of this sort, and much attached to their old customs, requires resolution; and without a good practical guide, may be dangerous; because, of the many volumes which have been written on this subject, few of them are founded on experimental knowledge—are verbose, contradictory, and bewildering. Your Annals shall be this guide. The plan on which they are published, gives them a reputation which inspires confidence; and for the favour of sending them to me, I pray you to accept my very best acknowledgments. To continue them, will add much to the obligation.

To evince with what avidity, and with how little reserve, I embrace the polite and friendly offer you have made me, of supplying me with "men, cattle, tools, seeds, or any thing else that may add to my rural amusement," I will give you, Sir, the trouble of providing, and sending to the care of Wakelin Welch, Esq. of London, merchant, the following articles:

Two of the simplest and best-constructed ploughs for land which is neither very heavy nor sandy. To be drawn by two horses—to have spare shares and coulters—and a mould on which to form new irons when the old ones are worn out, or will require repairing.

I shall take the liberty in this place to observe, that some years ago, from a description, or recommendation of what was then called the Rotherham, or patent plough, I sent to England for one of them; and till it began to wear, and was ruined by a bungling country smith, that no plough could have done better work, or appeared to have gone easier with two horses; but for want of a mould, which I had neglected to order with the plough, it became useless after the irons which came in with it were much worn.

A little of the best kind of cabbage-seeds, for field culture.

Twenty pounds of the best turnip-seeds, for ditto.

Ten bushels of sainfoin-seeds.

Eight bushels of the winter vetches.

Two bushels of rye-grass seeds.

Fifty pounds of hop clover-seeds.

And, if it is decided, for much has been said for and against it, that burnet, as an early food, is valuable, I should be glad of a bushel of this seed also. Red clover-seeds are to be had on easy terms in this country, but if there are any other kinds of grass-seeds, not included in the above, that you may think valuable, especially for early feeding or cutting, you would oblige me by adding a small quantity of the seeds, to put me in stock. Early grasses, unless a species can be found that will stand a hot sun, and oftentimes severe droughts in the summer months, without much expense of cultivation, would suit our climate best.

You see, Sir, that without ceremony, I avail myself of your kind offer; but if you should find in the course of our correspondence, that I am likely to become troublesome, you can easily check me. Inclosed I give you an order on Wakelin Welch, Esq. for the cost of such things as you may have the goodness to send me. I do not at this time ask for any other implements of husbandry than the ploughs; but when I have read your Annals (for they are but just come to hand) I may request more. In the meanwhile, permit me to ask what a good ploughman might be had for: annual wages, to be found (being a single man) in board, washing, and lodging? The writers upon husbandry estimate the hire of labourers so differently in England, that it is not easy to discover from them, whether one of the class I am speaking of would cost eight or eighteen pounds a year. A good ploughman at low wages, would come very opportunely with the ploughs here requested.

By means of the application I made to my friend Mr. Fairfax, of Bath, and through the medium of Mr. Rack, a bailiff is sent to me, who, if he is acquainted with the best courses of cropping, will answer my purposes as a director or superintendent of my farms. He has the appearance of a plain honest farmer;—is industrious;—and from the character given of him by a Mr. Peacy, with whom he has lived many years, has understanding in the management of stock, and of most matters for which he is employed. How far his abilities may be equal to a pretty extensive concern, is questionable. And what is still worse, he has come over with improper ideas; for instead of preparing his mind to meet a ruinous course of cropping, exhausted lands, and numberless inconveniences into which we had been thrown by an eight years war, he seems to have expected that he was coming to well organized farms, and that he was to have met ploughs, harrows, and all the other implements of husbandry, in as high taste as the best farming counties in England could have exhibited them. How far his fortitude will enable him to encounter these disappointments, or his patience and perseverance will carry him towards the work of reform, remains to be decided.

With great esteem, I have the honour to be, Sir, your most obedient, humble servant, G. WASHINGTON.

To Arthur Young, December 4, 1788

. . . The more I am acquainted with agricultural affairs, the better I am pleased with them; insomuch, that I can no where find so great satisfaction as in those innocent and useful pursuits. In indulging these feelings, I am led to reflect how much more delightful to an undebauched mind is the task of making improvements on the earth, than all the vain glory which can be acquired from ravaging it, by the most uninterrupted career of conquests. The design of this observation, is only to show how much, as a member of human society, I feel myself obliged, by your labours to render respectable and advantageous, an employment which is more congenial to the natural dispositions of mankind than any other. . . .

To Henry Lee, October 16, 1793

[The model of a thresher brought over by English farmers] may also be a good one, but the utility of it among careless negroes and ignorant overseers will depend absolutely upon the simplicity of the construction; for, if there is any thing complex in the machinery, it will be no longer in use than a mushroom is in existence. I have seen so much of the beginning and ending of new inventions, that I have almost resolved to go on in the old way of treading, until I get settled again at home, and can attend myself to the management of one. As a proof in point, of the almost impossibility of putting the overseers of this country out of the track they have been accustomed to walk in, I have one of the most convenient barns in this, or perhaps any other country, where thirty hands may with great ease be employed in threshing. Half of the wheat of the farm was actually stowed in this barn in the straw, by my order, for threshing; notwithstanding, when I came home about the middle of September, I found a treading-yard not thirty feet from the barn-door, the wheat again brought out of the barn, and horses treading it out in an open exposure, liable to the vicissitudes of weather. I am now erecting a building for the express purpose of treading. I have sanguine expectations of its utility.

To Arthur Young, Philadelphia, December 12, 1793

... All my landed property, east of the Appalachian mountains, is under rent, except the estate called Mount Vernon. This, hitherto, I have kept in my own hands: but from my present situation, from my advanced time of life, from a wish to live free from care, and as much at my ease as possible, during the remainder of it, and from other causes, which are not necessary to detail, I have, latterly, entertained serious thoughts of letting this estate also, reserving the mansion-house farm for my own residence, occupation, and amusement in agriculture; provided I can obtain what, in my own judgment, and in the opinion of others whom I have consulted, the low rent which I shall mention hereafter; and provided also I can settle it with good farmers.

The quantity of ploughable land (including meadow), the relative situation of the farms to one another, and the division of these farms into separate inclosures, with the quantity and situation of the woodland appertaining to the tract, will be better delineated by the sketch herewith sent (which is made from actual surveys, subject, nevertheless, to revision and correction), than by a volume of words.

No estate in United America, is more pleasantly situated than this. It lies in a high, dry, and healthy country, three hundred miles by water from the sea, and, as you will see by the plan, on one of the finest rivers in the world. Its margin is washed by more than ten miles of tide-water; from the bed of which, and the innumerable coves, inlets, and small marshes, with which it abounds, an inexhaustible fund of rich mud may be drawn, as a manure, either to be used separately, or in a compost, according to the judgment of the farmer. It is situated in a latitude between the extremes of heat and cold, and is the same distance by land and water, with good roads, and the best navigation (to and) from the Federal City, Alexandria, and Georgetown; distant from the first, fifteen, from the second, nine, and from the last, sixteen miles. The Federal City, in the year 1800, will become the seat of the general government of the United States. It is increasing fast in buildings, and rising into consequence; and will, I have no doubt, from the advantages given to it by nature, and its proximity to a rich interior country, and the western territory, become the emporium of the United States.

The soil of the tract of which I am speaking, is a good loam, more inclined, however, to clay than sand. From use, and I might add, abuse, it is become more and more consolidated, and of course heavier to work. The greater part is a greyish clay; some part is a dark mould; a very little is inclined to sand, and scarcely any to stone. A husbandman's wish would not lay the farms more level than they are; and yet some of the fields (but in no great degree) are washed into gullies, from which all of them have not yet been recovered.

This river, which encompasses the land the distance abovementioned, is well supplied with various kinds of fish, at all seasons of the year; and, in the spring, with the greatest profusion of shad, herrings, bass, carp, perch, sturgeon, &c. Several valuable fisheries appertain to the estate; the whole shore, in short, is one entire fishery.

There are, as you will perceive by the plan, four farms besides that at the mansion-house. These four contain three thousand two hundred and sixty acres of cultivable land, to which some hundreds more, adjoining, as may be seen, might be added, if a greater quantity should be required; but as they were never designed for, so neither can it be said they are calculated to suit, tenants of either the first, or of the lower class; because those who have the strength and resources proportioned to farms of from five hundred to twelve hundred acres (which these contain), would hardly be contented to live in such houses as are thereon: and if they were to be divided and sub-divided, so as to accommodate tenants of small means, say from fifty to one or two hundred acres, there would be none, except on the lots which might happen to include the present dwelling-houses of my overlookers (called bailiffs with you), barns, and negro-cabins: nor would I choose to have the woodland (already too much pillaged of its timber) ransacked, for the purpose of building many more. The soil, however, is excellent for bricks, or for mud-walls; and to the building of such houses there would be no limitation, nor to that of thatch for the cover of them.

The towns already mentioned (to those who might incline to encounter the expense), are able to furnish scantling, plank, and shingles, to any amount, and on reasonable terms; and they afford a ready market also for the produce of the land.

On what is called Union Farm (containing nine hundred and twenty-eight acres of arable and meadow), there is a newly erected brick barn, equal, perhaps, to any in America, and for conveniences of all sorts, particularly for sheltering and feeding horses, cattle, &c. scarcely to be exceeded anywhere. A new house is now building in a central position, not far from the barn, for the overlooker, which will have two rooms, sixteen by eighteen feet below, and one or two above nearly of the same size. Convenient thereto, is sufficient accommodation for fifty odd negroes, old and young; but these buildings might not be thought good enough for the workmen, or day-labourers, of your country.

Besides these, a little without the limits of the farm (as marked in the plan) are one or two other houses, very pleasantly situated, and which, in case this farm should be divided into two (as it formerly was), would answer well for the eastern division. The buildings thus enumerated, are all that stand on the premises.

Dogue Run Farm (six hundred and fifty acres) has a small, but new building for the overlooker; one room only below, and the same above, sixteen by twenty feet each; decent and comfortable for its size. It has also covering for forty odd negroes, similar to what is mentioned on Union Farm. It has a new circular barn, now finishing, on a new construction; well calculated, it is conceived, for getting grain out of the straw more expeditiously than in the usual mode of threshing. There are good sheds also erecting, sufficient to cover thirty work-horses and oxen.

Muddy-hole Farm (four hundred and seventy six acres) has a house for the overlooker, in size and appearance nearly like that at Dogue Run, but older: the same kind of covering for about thirty negroes, and a tolerable good barn, with stables for the work-horses.

River Farm, which is the largest of the four, and separated from the others by Little Hunting Creek, contains twelve hundred and seven acres of ploughable land, has an overlooker's house of one large, and two small rooms below, and one or two above; sufficient covering for fifty or sixty negroes, like those before mentioned; a large barn, and stables, gone much to decay, but will be replaced next year, with new ones.

I have deemed it necessary to give this detail of the buildings, that a precise idea might be had of the conveniences and inconveniences of them; and I believe the recital is just in all its parts. The inclosures are precisely and accurately delineated in the plan; and the fences now are, or soon will be, in respectable order.

I would let these four farms to four substantial farmers, of wealth and strength sufficient to cultivate them, and who would ensure to me the regular payment of the rents; and I would give them leases for seven or ten years, at the rate of a Spanish milled dollar, or other money current at the time, in this country, equivalent thereto, for every acre of ploughable and mowable ground, within the inclosures of the respective farms, as marked in the plan; and would allow the tenants, during that period, to take fuel, and use timber from the woodland, to repair the buildings, and to keep the fences in order until live fences could be substituted in place of dead ones; but in this case no sub-tenants would be allowed.

Or if these farms are adjudged too large, and the rents, of course, too heavy for such farmers as might incline to emigrate, I should have no insuperable objection against dividing each into as many small ones, as a society of them, formed for the purpose, could agree upon, among themselves; even if it should be by the fields, as they are now arranged (which the plan would enable them to do), provided such buildings as they would be content with, should be erected at their own expense, in the manner already mentioned. In which case, as in the former, fuel, and timber for repairs, would be allowed; but, as an inducement to parcel out my grounds into such small tenements, and to compensate me, at the same time, for the greater consumption of fuel and timber, and for the trouble and expense of collecting small rents, I should expect a quarter of a dollar per acre, in addition to what I have already mentioned. But in order to make these small farms more valuable to the occupants, and by way of reimbursing them for the expense of their establishment thereon, I would grant them leases for fifteen or eighteen years; although I have weighty objections to the measure, founded on my own experience, of the disadvantage it is to the lessor, in a country where lands are rising every year in value. As an instance in proof, about twenty years ago, I gave leases for three lives, in land I held above the Blue Mountains, near the Shenandoah river, seventy miles from Alexandria, or any shipping port, at a rent of one shilling per acre (no part being then cleared); and now land of similar quality, in the vicinity, with very trifling improvements thereon, is renting, currently, at five, and more shillings per acre, and even as high as eight.

My motives for letting this estate having been avowed, I will add, that the whole (except the Mansion-House farm), or none, will be parted with, and that upon unequivocal terms; because my object is, to fix my income (be it what it may) upon a solid basis, in the hands of good farmers; because I am not inclined to make a medley of it; and, above all, because I could not relinquish my present course, without a moral certainty of the substitute which is contemplated: for to break up these farms, remove my negroes, and to dispose of the property on them, upon terms short of this, would be ruinous.

Having said thus much, I am disposed to add further, that it would be in my power, and certainly it would be my inclination (upon the principle above), to accommodate the wealthy, or the weak-handed farmer (and upon reasonable terms) with draught-horses, and working mules and oxen; with cattle, sheep, and hogs; and with such implements of husbandry, if they should not incline to bring them themselves, as are in use on the farms. On the four farms there are fifty-four draught-horses, twelve working mules, and a sufficiency of oxen, broke to the yoke; the precise number I am unable this moment to ascertain, as they are comprehended in the aggregate of the black cattle: of the latter, there are three hundred and seventeen; of sheep, six hundred and thirty-four; of hogs, many; but as these run pretty much at large in the woodland (which is all under fence), the number is uncertain. Many of the negroes, male and female, might be hired by the year, as labourers, if this should be preferred to the importation of that class of people; but it deserves consideration, how far the mixing of whites and blacks together is advisable; especially where the former are entirely unacquainted with the latter.

If there be those who are disposed to take these farms in their undivided state, on the terms which have been mentioned, it is an object of sufficient magnitude for them, or one of them in behalf of the rest, to come over and investigate the premises thoroughly, that there may be nothing to reproach themselves, or me, with, if (though unintentionally) there should be defects in any part of the information herein given; or, if a society of farmers are disposed to adventure, it is still more incumbent on them to send over an agent, for the purpose above-mentioned; for with me the measure must be so fixed, as to preclude any cavil or discussion thereafter. And it may not be *mal apropos* to observe in this place, that our overlookers are generally engaged, and all the arrangements for the ensuing crops are made, before the first of September in every year: it will readily be perceived, then, that if this period is suffered to pass away, it is not to be regained until the next year. Possession might be given to the new-comers at the season just mentioned, to enable them to put in their grain for the next crop: but the final relinquishment could not take place until the crops are gathered; which of Indian corn (maize), seldom happens till toward Christmas, as it must endure hard frosts before it can be safely housed.

I have endeavoured, as far as my recollection of facts would enable me, or the documents in my possession allow, to give such information of the actual state of the farms, as to enable persons at a distance to form as distinct ideas as the nature of the thing is susceptible, short of one's own view: and having communicated the motives which have inclined me to a change in my system, I will announce to you the origin of them.

First. Few ships, of late, have arrived from any part of Great Britain, or Ireland, without a number of emigrants; and some of them, by report, very respectable and full-handed farmers. A number of others, they say, are desirous of following, but are unable to obtain passages; but their coming in that manner, even if I was apprized of their arrival in time, would not answer my views, for the reason already assigned; and which, as it is the ultimatum at present, I will take the liberty of repeating, namely, that I must carry my plan into complete execution, or not attempt it; and under such auspices, too, as to leave no doubt of the exact fulfilment: and,

2dly. Because from the number of letters which I have received myself, (and, as it would seem, from respectable people,) inquiring into matters of this sort, with intimations of their wishes, and even intentions, of migrating to this country, I can have no doubt of succeeding. But I have made no reply to these inquiries; or, if any, in very general terms; because I did not want to engage in correspondences of this sort with persons of whom I had no knowledge, nor indeed leisure for them, if I had been so disposed.

I shall now conclude as I began, with a desire, that if you see any impropriety in making these sentiments known to that class of people who might wish to avail themselves of the occasion, that it may not be mentioned. By a law, or by some regulation of your government, artisans, I am well aware, are laid under restraints; and, for this reason, I have studiously avoided any overtures to mechanics, although my occasions called for them. But never having heard that difficulties were thrown in the way of husbandmen by the government, is one reason for my bringing this matter to your view. A second is, that having yourself expressed sentiments which showed that you had cast an eye towards this country, and was not inattentive to the welfare of it, I was led to make by intentions known to you, that if you, or your friends, were disposed to avail yourselves of the knowledge, you might take prompt measures for the execution. And, 3dly, I was sure, if you had lost sight of the object yourself, I could, nevertheless, rely upon such information as you might see fit to give me, and upon such characters, too, as you might be disposed to recommend.

Lengthy as this epistle is, I will crave your patience while I add, that it is written in too much haste, and under too great a pressure of public business, at the commencement of an important session of Congress, to be correct, or properly digested. But the season of the year, and the apprehension of ice, are hurrying away the last vessel bound from this port to London. I am driven, therefore, to the alternative of making the matter known in this hasty manner, and giving a rude sketch of the farms, which is the subject of it; or to encounter delay—the first I preferred. It can hardly be necessary to add, that I have no desire that any formal promulgation of these sentiments should be made. . . .

To Sir John Sinclair, Philadelphia, July 20, 1794

I have read with peculiar pleasure and approbation, the work you patronise, so much to your own honor and the utility of the public.—Such a general view of the agriculture in the several counties of Great Britain is extremely interesting; and cannot fail of being very beneficial to the agricultural concern of your Country and to those of every other wherein they are read, and must entitle you to their warmest thanks for having set such a plan on foot, and for prosecuting it with the zeal & intelligence you do.—

. . . I know of no pursuit in which more real & important service can be rendered to any Country, than by improving its agriculture—its breed of useful animals—and other branches of a husbandman's cares;—nor can I conceive any plan more conducive to this end than the one you have introduced for bringing to view the actual state of them, in all parts of the Kingdom;—by which good & bad habits are exhibited in a manner too plain to be misconceived; for the accounts given to the British board of Agriculture, appear in general, to be drawn up in a masterly manner, so as fully to answer the expectations formed in the excellent plan wch produced them; affording at the same-time a fund of information useful in political oeconomy—serviceable in all countries.

Commons—Tithes—Tenantry (of which we feel nothing in this country) are in the list of impediments I perceive, to perfection in English farming—and taxes are heavy deduction from the profit thereof—Of these we have none, or so light as hardly to be felt.—Your system of Agriculture, it must be confessed, is in a stile superior & of course much more expensive than ours, but when the balance at the end of the year is struck, by deducting the taxes, poor rates, and incidental charges of every kind, from the produce of the land, in the two Countries, no doubt can remain in which Scale it is to be found.

It will be sometime I fear, before an Agricultural Society with Congressional aids will be established in this Country;—we must walk as other countries have done before we can run, Smaller Societies must prepare the way for greater, but with the light before us, I hope we shall not be so slow in maturation as older nations have been.—An attempt, as you will perceive by the enclosed outlines of a plan, is making to establish a State Society in Pennsylvania for agricultural improvements.—If it succeeds, it will be a step in the ladder, at present it is too much in embryo to decide on the result.—

Our domestic animals, as well as our agriculture, are inferior to yours in point of size but this does not proceed from any defect in the stamina of them, but to deficient care in providing for their support; experience having abundantly evinced that where our pasture areas well improved as the soil & climate will admit;—where a competent store of wholesome provender is laid up and proper care used in serving it, that our horses, black cattle, Sheep &c. are not inferior to the best of their respective kinds which have been imported from England.—Nor is the wool of our Sheep inferior to that of the *common* sort with you:—as a proof—after the Peace of Paris in 1783, and my return to the occupations of a farmer, I paid particular attention to my breed of sheep (of which I usually kept about seven or eight hundred).—By this attention, at the shearing of 1789 the fleeces yielded me the average quantity of 5¼£ of wool;—a fleece of which, promiscuously taken, I sent to Mr. Arthur Young, who put it, for examination, into the hands of Manufacturers.—These pronounced it to be equal in quality to the Kentish Wool.—In this same year, i.e. 1789 I was again called from home, and have not had it in my power since to pay any attention to my farm;—The consequence of which is, that my Sheep, at the last shearing, yielded me not more than 2½£.—This is not a single instance of the difference between care and neglect.—Nor is the difference between good & bad management confined to that species of Stock; for we find that good pastures and proper attention, can & does, fill our markets with beef of seven, eight & more hundred weight the four quarters;

whereas from 450 to 500 (especially in the States South of this where less attention hitherto has been paid to grass) may be found about the average weight.—In this market, some Bullocks were killed in the months of March & April last, the weights of wch, as taken from the accounts which were published at the time, you will find in a paper enclosed.—These were pampered steers, but from 800 to a thousand, the four quarters, is no uncommon weight.

Your general history of Sheep, with observations thereon, and the proper mode of managing them, will be an interesting work when compleated; and with the information, & accuracy I am persuaded it will be executed, under your auspices, must be extremely desirable.—The climate of this Country, particularly that of the middle states is congenial to this species of animal; but want of attention to them in most farmers, added to the obstacles which prevent the importation of a better herd, by men who would be at the expence, contributes not a little to the present inferiority we experience. . . .

Both Mr. Adams and Mr. Jefferson had the perusal of the papers which accompanied your note of the 11th of Sep.

With great respect and esteem I have the honor to be Sir, Your Obed Servt. G. WASHINGTON.

To Thomas Jefferson, October 4, 1795

. . . I am much pleased with the account you have given of the succory. This, like all other things of the sort with me, since my absence from home, has come to nothing; for neither my overseers nor manager will attend properly to any thing but the crops they have usually cultivated; and, in spite of all I can say, if there is the smallest discretionary power allowed them, they will fill the land with Indian corn, although even to themselves there are the most obvious traces of its baneful effects. I am resolved, however, as soon as it shall be in my power to attend a little more closely to my own concerns, to make this crop yield in a degree to other grain, to pulses, and to grasses. I am beginning again with chiccory, from a handful of seed given me by Mr. Strickland, which, though flourishing at present, has no appearance of seeding this year. Lucerne has not succeeded better with me than with you; but I will give it another and a fairer trial before it is abandoned altogether. Clover, when I can dress lots well, succeeds with me to my full expectation, but not on the fields in rotation, although I have been at much cost in seeding them. This has greatly disconcerted the system of rotation on which I had decided.

I wish you may succeed in getting good seed of the winter vetch. I have often imported it, but the seed never vegetated, or in so small a proportion, as to be destroyed by weeds. I believe it would be an acquisition, if it was once introduced properly in our farms. The Albany pea, which is the same as the field pea of Europe, I have tried, and found it will grow well; but is subject to the same bug which perforates the garden pea, and eats out the kernel. So it will happen, I fear, with the pea you propose to import. I had great expectation from a green dressing with buckwheat, as a preparatory fallow for a crop of wheat, but it has not answered my expectation yet. I ascribe this, however, more to mismanagement in the times of seeding and ploughing in, than any defect of the system. The first ought to be so ordered, in point of time, as to meet a convenient season for ploughing it in, while the plant is in its most succulent state. But this has never been done on my farms, and consequently has drawn as much from, as it has given to the earth. It has always appeared to me that there were two modes in which buckwheat might be used advantageously as a manure. One, to sow early, and, as soon as a sufficiency of seed is ripened, to stock the ground a second time, to turn the whole in, and when the succeeding growth is getting in full bloom, to turn that in also, before the seed begins to ripen; and, when the fermentation and putrefaction ceases, to sow the ground in that state, and plough in the wheat. The other mode is, to sow the buckwheat so late, as that it shall be generally about a foot high at the usual seeding of wheat; then turn it in, and sow thereon immediately, as on a clover lay, harrowing in the seed lightly to avoid disturbing the buried buckwheat. I have never tried the latter method, but see no reason against its succeeding. The other, as I observed above, I have prosecuted, but the buckwheat has always stood too long, and consequently had got too dry and sticky to answer the end of a succulent plant.

But of all the improving and ameliorating crops, none in my opinion is equal to potatoes, on stiff and hard bound land, as mine is. I am satisfied, from a variety of instances, that on such land a crop of potatoes is equal to an ordinary dressing. In no instance have I failed of good wheat, oats, or clover, that followed potatoes; and I conceive they give the soil a darker hue. I shall thank you for the result of your proposed experiment relative to the winter vetch and pea when they are made.

I am sorry to hear of the depredations committed by the weevil in your parts; it is a great calamity at all times, and this year, when the demand for wheat is so great, and the price so high, must be a mortifying one to the farmers. The rains have been very general, and more abundant since the 1st of August, than ever happened in a summer within the memory of man. Scarcely a mill-dam, or bridge, between this and Philadelphia, was able to resist them, and some were carried off a second and third time.

America and the West

Indians and the West (to James Duane, September 7, 1783)

. . . To suffer a wide-extended Country to be overrun with Land Jobbers, speculators, and monopolizers, or even with scattered settlers, is in my opinion inconsistent with that wisdom and policy, which our true interest dictates, or that an enlightened people ought to adopt; and, besides, is pregnant of disputes both with the Savages and among ourselves, the evils of which are easier to be conceived than described. And for what, but to aggrandize a few avaricious men, to the prejudice of many and the embarrassment of Government? For the People engaged in these pursuits, without contributing in the smallest degree to the support of Government, or considering themselves as amenable to its Laws, will involve it, by their unrestrained conduct, in inextricable perplexities, and more than probably in a great deal of bloodshed.

My ideas, therefore, of the line of conduct proper to be observed, not only towards the Indians, but for the government of the Citizens of America, in their Settlement of the Western Country, (which is intimately connected therewith,) are simply these.

First, and as a preliminary, that all prisoners, of whatever age or sex, among the Indians, shall be delivered up.

That the Indians should be informed, that after a Contest of eight years for the Sovereignty of this Country, Great Britain has ceded all the lands to the United States within the limits described by the—articles of the provisional treaty.

That as they (the Indians), maugre all the advice and admonition which could be given them at the commencement and during the prosecution of the war, could not be restrained from acts of hostility, but were determined to join their arms to those of G. Britain and to share their fortunes, so consequently, with a less generous people than Americans, they would be made to share the same fate, and be compelled to retire along with them beyond the Lakes. But, as we prefer Peace to a state of Warfare; as we consider them as a deluded People; as we persuade ourselves that they are convinced, from experience, of their error in taking up the Hatchet against us, and that their true Interest and safety must now depend upon *our* friendship; as the Country is large enough to contain us all; and as we are disposed to be kind to them and to partake of their Trade, we will, from these considerations and from motives of compassion, draw a veil over what is past, and establish a boundary line between them and us, beyond which we will *endeavor* to restrain our People from Hunting or Settling, and within which they shall not come but for the purposes of Trading, Treating, or other business unexceptionable in its nature.

In establishing this line, in the first instance, care should be taken neither to yield nor to grasp at too much; but to endeavor to impress the Indians with an idea of the generosity of our disposition to accommodate them, and with the necessity we are under, of providing for our warriors, our Young People who are growing up, and strangers who are coming from other Countries to live among us, and if they should make a point of it, or appear dissatisfied with the line we may find it necessary to establish, compensation should be made for their claims within it.

It is needless for me to express more explicitly, because the tendency of my observns. evinces it is my opinion, that, if the legislature of the State of New York should insist upon expelling the Six Nations from all the Country they Inhabited previous to the war, within their Territory, (as General Schuyler seems to be apprehensive of,) it will end in another Indian war. I have every reason to believe from my inquiries, and the information I have received, that they will not suffer their Country (if it were our policy to take it before we could settle it) to be wrested from them without another struggle. That they would compromise for a part of it, I have very little doubt; and that it would be the cheapest way of coming at it, I have no doubt at all. The same observations, I am persuaded, will hold good with respect to Virginia, or any other State, which has powerful tribes of Indians on their Frontiers; and the reason of my mentioning New York is because General Schuyler has expressed his opinion of the temper of its Legislature, and because I have been more in the way of learning the sentimts. of the Six Nations than of any other Tribes of Indians on this Subject.

The limits being sufficiently extensive, in the new ctry., to comply with all the engagements of government, and to admit such emigrations as may be supposed to happen within a given time, not only from the several States of the Union but from Foreign Countries, and, moreover, of such magnitude as to form a distinct and proper government; a Proclamation, in my opinion, should issue, making it Felony (if there is power for the purpose, if not, imposing some very heavy restraint) for any person to Survey or Settle beyond the Line; and the Officers commanding the Frontier Garrisons should have pointed and peremptory orders to see that the Proclamation is carried into effect.

Measures of this sort would not only obtain Peace from the Indians, but would, in my opinion, be the means of preserving it. It would dispose of the Land to the best advantage, People the Country progressively, and check land jobbing and monopolizing, which are now going forward with great avidity, while the door would be open and terms known for every one to obtain what is reasonable and proper for himself, upon legal and constitutional ground.

Every advantage, that could be expected or even wished for, would result from such a mode of procedure. Our settlements would be compact, government well established, and our barrier formidable, not only for ourselves but against our neighs.; and the Indians, as has been observed in Genl. Schuyler's letter, will ever retreat as our settlements advance upon them, and they will be as ready to sell, as we are to buy. That it is the cheapest, as well as the least distressing way of dealing with them, none, who is acquainted with the nature of an Indian warfare, and has ever been at the trouble of estimating the expense of one, and comparing it with the cost of purchasing their Lands, will hesitate to acknowledge.

Unless some such measures, as I have here taken the liberty of suggesting, are speedily adopted, one of two capital evils, in my opinion, will inevitably result, and is near at hand; either that the settling, or rather overspreading, of the western Country will take place by a parcel of Banditti, who will bid defiance to all authority, while they are skimming and disposing of the Cream of the Country at the expense of many suffering officers and soldiers, who have fought and bled to obtain it, and are now waiting the decision of Congress to point them to the promised reward of their past dangers and toils; or a renewal of Hostilities with the Indians, brought about more than probably by this very means.

How far agents for Indian affrs. are indispensably necessary, I shall not take upon me to decide; but, if any should be appointed, their powers should be circumscribed, accurately defined, and themselves rigidly punished for every infraction of them. A recurrence to the conduct of these people, under the British administration of Indian affairs, will manifest the propriety of this caution, as it will be there found that self-Interest was the principle by which their agents was actuated; and to promote this by accumulating Lands and passing large quantities of goods thro' their hands, the Indians were made to speak any language they pleased by their representation, and were pacific or hostile as their purposes were most likely to be promoted by the one or the other. No purchase under any pretence whatever should be made by any other authority than that of the sovereign power, or the Legislature of the State in which such Lands may happen to be; nor should the agents be permitted directly or indirectly to trade, but to have a fixed and ample Salary allowed them, as a full compensation for their trouble.

Whether in practice the measure may answer as well as it appears in theory to me, I will not undertake to say; but I think, if the Indian Trade was carried on, on government acct. and with no greater advance than what would be necessary to defray the expense and risk, and bring in a small profit, that it would supply the Indians upon much easier terms than they usually are, engross their Trade, and fix them strongly in our Interest, and would be a much better mode of treating them, than that of giving presents, where a few only are benefited by them. I confess there is difficulty in getting a man, or set of men, in whose abilities and integrity there can be a perfect reliance, without which the scheme is liable to such abuse as to defeat the salutary ends, which are proposed from it. At any rate, no person should be suffered to Trade with the Indians without first obtaining a license, and giving security to conform to such Rules and Regulations as shall be prescribed, as was the case before the war.

In giving my sentiments in the month of May last (at the request of a Committee of Congress) on a Peace Establishmt., I took the liberty of suggesting the propriety, which in my opinion there appeared, of paying particular attention to the French and other settlers at Detroit and other parts within the limits of the western Country. The perusal of a late pamphlet, entitled "Observations on the Commerce of the American States with Europe and the West Indies," impresses the necessity of it more forcibly than ever on my mind. The author of that Piece strongly recommends a liberal change in the government of Canada; and, tho' he is too sanguine in his expectations of the benefits arising from it, there can be no doubt of the good policy of the measure. It behoves us, therefore, to counteract them by anticipation. These People have a disposition towards us susceptible of favorable impressions; but, as no arts will be left unattempted by the B. to withdraw them from our Interest, the prest, moment should be employed by us to fix them in it, or we may lose them for ever, and with them the advantages or disadvantages consequent of the choice they may make. From the best information and maps of that Country it would appear, that the territory from the mouth of the Great

Miami River, wch. empties into the Ohio, to its confluence with the Mad River, thence by a Line to the Miami fort and Village on the other Miami River, wch. empties into Lake Erie, and Thence by a Line to include the Settlement of Detroit, would, with Lake Erie to the noward, Pensa. to the Eastwd., and the Ohio to the soward, form a governmt. sufficiently extensive to fulfil all the public engagements, and to receive moreover a large population by Emigrants; and to confine the Settlement of the new State within these bounds would, in my opinion, be infinitely better, even supposing no disputes were to happen with the Indians, and that it was not necessary to guard against these other evils which have been enumerated, than to suffer the same number of People to roam over a Country of at least 500,000 Square miles, contributing nothing to the support, but much perhaps to the embarrassment, of the Federal Government.

Was it not for the purpose of comprehending the Settlement of Detroit within the Jurisdn. of the new Governmt., a more compact and better shaped district for a State would be, for the line to proceed from the Miami Fort and Village along the River of that name to Lake Erie; leaving in that case the settlement of Detroit, and all the Territory no. of the Rivers Miami and St. Joseph's between the Lakes Erie, St. Clair, Huron, and Michigan, to form hereafter another State equally large, compact, and water-bounded.[1]

At first view it may seem a little extraneous, when I am called upon to give an opinion upon the terms of a Peace proper to be made with the Indians, that I should go into the formation of New States. But the Settlemt. of the Western Country, and making a Peace with the Indians, are so analogous, that there can be no definition of the one, without involving considerations of the other; for, I repeat it again, and I am clear in my opinion, that policy and oeconomy point very strongly to the expediency of being upon good terms with the Indians, and the propriety of purchasing their Lands in preference to attempting to drive them by force of arms out of their Country; which, as we have already experienced, is like driving the wild Beasts of ye forest, which will return as soon as the pursuit is at an end, and fall perhaps upon those that are left there; when the gradual extension of our settlements will as

[1] These boundaries are roughly those of the present states of Ohio and Michigan.

certainly cause the savage, as the wolf, to retire; both being beasts of prey, tho' they differ in shape. In a word, there is nothing to be obtained by an Indian war, but the soil they live on, and this can be had by purchase at less expense, and without that bloodshed and those distresses, which helpless women and children are made partakers of in all kinds of disputes with them.

If there is any thing in these thoughts, (which I have fully and freely communicated,) worthy of attention, I shall be happy, and am, Sir, your most obedient and most humble servant.

P.S. A formal Address and Memorial from the Oneita Indians when I was on the Mohawk River, setting forth their Grievances and distresses and praying relief, induced me to order a pound of Powder and 3 pounds of Lead to be issued to each man from the Military Magazines in the care of Colo. Willett—This I presume was unknown to Genl. Schuyler at the time he recommended the like measure in his Letter to Congress.

Immigration to America (to Richard Henderson, June 19, 1788)

. . . I must however rather deal in general than particular observations; as I think you will be able, from the length of your residence in the country, and the extensiveness of your acquaintance with its affairs, to make the necessary applications, and add the proper details. Nor would I choose that my interference in the business should be transmitted, lest, in a malicious world, it might be represented that I was officiously using the arts of seduction to depopulate other countries for the sake of peopling our own.

In the first place it is a point conceded, that America, under an efficient government, will be the most favorable country of any in the world for persons of industry and frugality possessed of a moderate capital to inhabit. It is also believed, that it will not be less advantageous to the happiness of the lowest class of people, because of the equal distribution of property, the great plenty of unoccupied lands, and the facility of procuring the means of subsistence. The scheme of purchasing a good tract of freehold estate, and bringing out a number of able-bodied men, indented for a certain time, appears to be indisputably a rational one.

All the interior arrangements of transferring the property and commencing the establishment, you are as well acquainted with as I can possibly be. It might be considered as a point of more difficulty to decide upon the place, which should be most proper for a settlement. Although I believe that emigrants from other countries to this, who shall be well-disposed, and conduct themselves properly, would be treated with equal friendship and kindness in all parts of it; yet, in the old settled States, land is so much occupied, and the value so much enhanced by the contiguous cultivation, that the price would, in general, be an objection. The land in [the] western country, or that on the Ohio, like all others, has its *advantages and disadvantages*. The neighborhood of the savages, and the difficulty of transportation, were the great objections. The danger of the first will soon cease by the strong establishments now taking place; the inconveniences of the second will be, in a great degree, remedied by opening the internal navigation. No colony in America was ever settled under such favorable auspices, as that which has just commenced at the Muskingum. Information, property, and strength, will be its characteristics. I know many of the settlers personally, and that there never were men better calculated to promote the welfare of such a community.

If I was a young man, just preparing to begin the world, or if advanced in life, and had a family to make a provision for, I know of no country where I should rather fix my habitation than in some part of that region, for which the writer of the queries seems to have a predilection. He might be informed that his namesake and distant relation, General St. Clair, is not only in high repute, but that he is governor of all the territory westward of the Ohio, and that there is a gentleman (to wit, Mr. Joel Barlow) gone from New York by the last French packet, who will be in London in the course of this year, and who is authorized to dispose of a very large body of land in that country. The author of the queries may then be referred to the "*Information for those who wish to remove to America,*" and published in Europe in the year 1784, by the great philosopher Dr. Franklin. Short as it is, it contains almost every thing, that needs to be known on the subject of migrating to this country. You may find that excellent little treatise in *"Carey's American Museum,"* for September, 1787. It is worthy of being republished in Scotland, and every other part of Europe.

As to the European publications respecting the United States, they are commonly very defective. The Abbé Raynal is quite erroneous. Guthrie, though somewhat better informed, is not absolutely correct. There is now an *American Geography* preparing for the press by a Mr. Morse of New Haven in Connecticut, which, from the pains the author has taken in travelling through the States, and acquiring information from the principal characters in each, will probably be much more exact and useful. Of books at present existing, Mr. Jefferson's *"Notes on Virginia"* will give the best idea of this part of the continent to a foreigner; and the *"American Farmer's Letters,"* written by Mr. Crevecoeur (commonly called Mr. St. John), the French consul in New York, who actually resided twenty years as a farmer in that State, will afford a great deal of profitable and amusive information, respecting the private life of the Americans, as well as the progress of agriculture, manufactures, and arts, in their country. Perhaps the picture he gives, though founded on fact, is in some instances embellished with rather too flattering circumstances. I am, &c.

Education

A national university (to the Commissioners of the Federal District, Philadelphia, January 28, 1795)

A Plan for the establishment of an university in the Federal City has frequently been the subject of conversation; but, in what manner it is proposed to commence this important institution, on how extensive a scale, the means by which it is to be effected, how it is to be supported, or what progress is made in it, are matters altogether unknown to me.

It has always been a source of serious reflection and sincere regret with me, that the youth of the United States should be sent to foreign countries for the purpose of education. Although there are doubtless many, under these circumstances, who escape the danger of contracting principles unfavorable to republican government, yet we fought to deprecate the hazard attending ardent and susceptible minds, from being too strong and too early prepossessed in favor of other political systems, before they are capable of appreciating their own.

For this reason I have greatly wished to see a plan adopted, by which the arts, sciences, and belles-lettres could be taught in their *fullest* extent, thereby embracing *all* the advantages of European tuition, with the means of acquiring the liberal knowledge, which is necessary to qualify our citizens for the exigencies of public as well as private life; and (which with me is a consideration of great magnitude) by assembling the youth from the different parts of this rising republic, contributing from their intercourse and interchange of information to the removal of prejudices, which might perhaps sometimes arise from local circumstances.

The Federal City, from its centrality and the advantages, which in other respects it must have over any other place in the United States, ought to be preferred, as a proper site for such an university. And if a plan can be adopted upon a scale as *extensive* as I have described, and the execution of it should commence under favorable auspices in a reasonable time, with a fair prospect of success, I will grant in perpetuity fifty shares in the navigation of Potomac River towards the endowment of it.

What annuity will arise from these fifty shares, when the navigation is in full operation, can at this time be only conjectured; and those, who are acquainted with the nature of it, can form as good a judgment as myself.

As the design of this university has assumed no form with which I am acquainted, and as I am equally ignorant who the persons are, that have taken or are disposed to take the maturation of the plan upon themselves, I have been at a loss to whom I should make this communication of my intentions. If the Commissioners of the Federal City have any particular agency in bringing the matter forward, then the information, I now give to them, is in its proper course. If, on the other hand, they have no more to do in it than others, who may be desirous of seeing so important a measure carried into effect, they will be so good as to excuse my using them as the medium for disclosing these intentions.

To Thomas Jefferson, Philadelphia, March 15, 1795

I received your letter of the 23d ultimo; but not at so early a period as might have been expected from the date of it. My mind has always been more disposed to apply the shares in the inland navigation of Potomac and James Rivers, which were left to my disposal by the legislature of Virginia, towards the endowment of an university in the United States, than to any other object it had contemplated. In pursuance of this idea, and understanding that other means are in embryo for establishing so useful a seminary in the Federal City, I did, on the 28th of January last, announce to the commissioners thereof my intention of vesting in perpetuity the fifty shares I hold under that act in the navigation of Potomac, as an additional mean of carrying the plan into effect, provided it should be adopted upon a scale so liberal as to extend to and embrace a *complete* system of education.

I had little hesitation in giving the Federal City a preference of all other places for the institution, for the following reasons. 1st, on account of its being the permanent seat of the government of this Union, and where the laws and policy of it must be better understood than in any local part thereof. 2d, because of its centrality. 3d, because one half (or near it) of the District of Columbia is within the Commonwealth of Virginia, and the whole of the State not inconvenient thereto. 4th, because, as a *part* of the endowment, it would be useful, but *alone* would be inadequate to the end. 5th, because many advantages, I conceive, would result from the jurisdiction, which the general government will have over it, which no other spot would possess. And, lastly, as this seminary is contemplated for the completion of education and study of the sciences, (not for boys in their rudiments,) it will afford the students an opportunity of attending the debates in Congress, and thereby becoming more liberally and better acquainted with the principles of law and government.

My judgment and my wishes point equally strong to the

application of the James River shares to the same object at the same place; but, considering the source from whence they were derived, I have, in a letter I am writing to the executive of Virginia on this subject, left the application of them to a seminary *within the State,* to be located by the legislature.

Hence you will perceive, that I have in a degree anticipated your proposition. I was restrained from going the whole length of the suggestion by the following considerations. 1st, I did not know to what extent or when any plan would be so matured for the establishment of an university, as would enable any assurances to be given to the application of M. D'Ivernois. 2d, the propriety of transplanting the professors *in a body* might be questioned for several reasons; among others, because they might not be all good characters, nor all sufficiently acquainted with our language. And again, having been at variance with the levelling party of their own country, the measure might be considered as an aristocratical movement by more than those, who, without any just cause that I can discover, are continually sounding the bell of aristocracy. And, 3d, because it might preclude some of the first professors in other countries from a participation, among whom some of the most celebrated characters in Scotland, in this line, might be obtained.

Something, but of what nature I am unable to inform you, has been written by Mr. Adams to M. D'Ivernois. Never having viewed my intended donation as more than a part of the means, that were to set this establishment afloat, I did not incline to go too far in the encouragement of professors, before the plan should assume a more formal shape, much less to induce an entire college to migrate. The enclosed is the answer I have received from the commissioners; from which, and the ideas I have here expressed, you will be enabled to decide on the best communication to be made to M. D'Ivernois.

My letter to the commissioners has bound me to the fulfilment of what is therein engaged; and if the legislature of Virginia, in considering the subject, should view it in the same light I do, the James River shares will be added thereto; for I think one good institution of this sort is to be preferred to two imperfect ones, which, without other aid than the shares in *both* navigations, is more likely to fall through, than to succeed upon the plan I contemplate; which, in a few words, is to supersede the necessity of sending the youth of this country abroad for the purpose of education, (where too often principles and habits unfriendly to republican government are imbibed, and not easily discarded,) by instituting such an one of our own, as will answer the end, and associating them in the same seminary, will contribute to wear off those prejudices and unreasonable jealousies, which prevent or weaken friendships and impair the harmony of the Union. With very great esteem, I am, &c.

P. S. Mr. Adams *laid* before me the communications of M. D'Ivernois; but I said nothing to him of my intended donation towards the establishment of an university in the Federal District. My wishes would be to fix this on the Virginia side of the Potomac River; but this would not embrace or accord with those other means, which are proposed for the establishment.

To Robert Brooke, Governor of Virginia, Philadelphia, March 16, 1795

Ever since the General Assembly of Virginia were pleased to submit to my disposal fifty shares in the Potomac, and one hundred in the James River Company, it has been my anxious desire to appropriate them to an object most worthy of public regard.

It is with indescribable regret, that I have seen the youth of the United States migrating to foreign countries, in order to acquire the higher branches of erudition, and to obtain a knowledge of the sciences. Although it would be injustice to many to pronounce the certainty of their imbibing maxims not congenial with republicanism, it must nevertheless be admitted, that a serious danger is encountered by sending abroad among other political systems those, who have not well learned the value of their own.

The time is therefore come, when a plan of universal education ought to be adopted in the United States. Not only do the exigencies of public and private life demand it, but, if it should ever be apprehended, that prejudice would be entertained in one part of the Union against another, an efficacious remedy will be, to assemble the youth of every part under such circumstances as will, by the freedom of intercourse and collision of sentiment, give to their minds the direction of truth, philanthropy, and mutual conciliation.

It has been represented, that a university corresponding with these ideas is contemplated to be built in the Federal City, and that it will receive considerable endowments. This position is so eligible from its centrality, so convenient to Virginia, by whose legislature the shares were granted and in which part of the Federal District stands, and combines so many other conveniences, that I have determined to vest the Potomac shares in that university.

Presuming it to be more agreeable to the General Assembly of Virginia, that the shares in the James River Company should be reserved for a similar object in some part of that State, I intend to allot them for a seminary to be erected at such place as they shall deem most proper. I am disposed to believe, that a seminary of learning upon an enlarged plan, but yet not coming up to the full idea of an university, is an institution to be preferred for the position which is to be chosen. The students who wish to pursue the whole range of science, may pass with advantage from the seminary to the university, and the former by a due relation may be rendered co-operative with the latter.

I cannot however dissemble my opinion, that if all the shares were conferred on an university, it would become far more important, than when they are divided; and I have been constrained from concentring them in the same place, merely by my anxiety to reconcile a particular attention to Virginia with a great good, in which she will abundantly share in common with the rest of the United States.

I must beg the favor of your Excellency to lay this letter before that honorable body, at their next session, in order that I may appropriate the James River shares to the place which they may prefer. They will at the same time again accept my acknowledgements for the opportunity, with which they have favored me, of attempting to supply so important a desideratum in the United States as an university adequate to our necessity, and a preparatory seminary. With great consideration and respect, I am, Sir, &c.[2]

[2] The shares in the James River Company were given to the Liberty Hall Academy, which was afterward called Washington College, and is now Washington and Lee University.

To Alexander Hamilton, Philadelphia, September 1, 1796

[PRIVATE]

About the middle of last week I wrote to you; and that it might escape the eye of the inquisitive (for some of my letters have lately been pried into), I took the liberty of putting it under a cover to Mr. Jay.

Since then, revolving on the paper that was inclosed therein,[3] on the various matters it contained, and of the first expression of the advice or recommendation which was given in it, I have regretted that another subject (which in my estimation is of interesting concern to the well-being of this country) was not touched upon also;—I mean education generally, as one of the surest means of enlightening and giving just ways of thinking to our citizens, but particularly the establishment of a university; where the youth from all parts of the United States might receive the polish of erudition in the arts, sciences, and belles-lettres; and where those who were disposed to run a political course might not only be instructed in the theory and principles, but (this seminary being at the seat of the general government) where the legislature would be in session half the year, and the interests and politics of the nation of course would be discussed, they would lay the surest foundation for the practical part also.

But that which would render it of the highest importance, in my opinion, is, that the juvenal period of life, when friendships are formed, and habits established, that will stick by one; the youth or young men from different parts of the United States would be assembled together, and would by degrees discover that there was not that cause for those jealousies and prejudices which one part of the Union had imbibed against another part:—of course, sentiments of more liberality in the general policy of the country would result from it. What but the mixing of people from different parts of the United States during the war rubbed off these impressions? A century, in the ordinary intercourse, would not have accomplished what the seven years' association in arms did; but that ceasing, prejudices are beginning to revive again, and never will

[3] One of the drafts of the *Farewell Address.*

be eradicated so effectually by any other means as the intimate intercourse of characters in early life,—who, in all probability, will be at the head of the counsels of this country in a more advanced stage of it.

To show that this is no new idea of mine, I may appeal to my early communications to Congress; and to prove how seriously I have reflected on it since, and how well disposed I have been, and still am, to contribute my aid towards carrying the measure into effect, I inclose you the extract of a letter from me to the governor of Virginia on this subject, and a copy of the resolves of the legislature of that State in consequence thereof.

I have not the smallest doubt that this donation (when the navigation is in complete operation, which it certainly will be in less than two years), will amount to £1200 to £1500 sterling a year, and become a rapidly increasing fund. The proprietors of the federal city have talked of doing something handsome towards it likewise; and if Congress would appropriate some of the western lands to the same uses, funds sufficient, and of the most permanent and increasing sort, might be so established as to invite the ablest professors in Europe to conduct it.

Let me pray you, therefore to introduce a section in the address expressive of these sentiments, and recommendatory of the measure, without any mention, however, of my proposed contribution to the plan.

Such a section would come in very properly after the one which relates to our religious obligations, or in a preceding part, as one of the recommendatory measures to counteract the evils arising from geographical discriminations. With affectionate regard, I am always.

Military Academy (to Alexander Hamilton, Mount Vernon, December 12, 1799)

The establishment of an Institution of this kind [Military Academy], upon a respectable and extensive Basis, has ever been considered by me as an object of primary importance to this Country; and while I was in the Chair of Government, I omitted no proper opportunity of recommending it, in my public speeches and other ways, to the attention of the Legislature. But I never undertook to go into a *detail* of the Organization of such an Academy; leaving this task to others whose pursuits in the paths of Science, and attention to the arrangements of such Institutions, had better qualified them for the execution of it.[4]

[4] The Military Academy was established at West Point in 1801.

Chapter 10

COMMENTS ON SOME CONTEMPORARIES

André, John, and Arnold, Benedict

To Lieutenant Colonel John Laurens, October 13, 1780

André has met his fate, and with that fortitude, which was to be expected from an accomplished man and gallant officer; but I am mistaken if, at *this* time, 'Arnold is undergoing the torment of a mental Hell.'[1] He wants feeling. From some traits of his character, which have lately come to my knowledge, he seems to have been so hackneyed in villainy, and so lost to all sense of honor and shame, that, while his faculties will enable him to continue his sordid pursuits, there will be no time for remorse.

Braddock, Edward

To William Fairfax, June 7, 1755

The General, by frequent breaches of contract, has lost all patience; and, for want of that temper and moderation, which should be used by a man of *sense* upon these occasions, will, I fear, represent us in a light we little deserve; for, instead of blaming the individuals, as he ought, he charges all his disappointments to publick supineness, and looks upon the country, I believe, as void

[1] Laurens had written to Washington, October 4: "Arnold must undergo a punishment comparatively more severe in the permanent, increasing torment of a mental hell."

of honour and honesty. We have frequent disputes on this head, which are maintained with warmth on both sides, especially on his, who is incapable of arguing without, or giving up any point he asserts, let it be ever so incompatible with reason or common sense.

Gerry, Elbridge

To Timothy Pickering, February 10, 1799

I am sorry to see Mr. Gerry is pursuing a mischievous path. That he was led astray by his own vanity and self-importance, and was the dupe of *diplomatic skill,* I never had a doubt; but these doubts were accompanied by faint hopes . . . that he possessed candor, fortitude and manliness enough to have come forward with an open declaration that he had been practised upon, and was deceived. But Mr. Gerry's mind is not enlarged enough for such conduct as this.

Hamilton, Alexander

To John Adams, September 25, 1798

I have no hesitation in declaring, that, if the public is to be deprived of the services of Colo. Hamilton in the military line, that the post [of Major General] he was destined to fill will not be easily supplied . . . Although Colo. Hamilton has never acted in the character of a General Officer, yet his opportunities, as the principal and most confidential aid of the commander-in-chief, afforded him the means of viewing every thing on a larger scale than those, whose attentions were confined to Divisions or Brigades . . . These advantages, and his having served with usefulness in the Old Congress, in the General convention, and having filled one of the most important departments of government with acknowledged abilities and integrity, have placed him on high ground, and made him a conspicuous character in the United States, and even in Europe.

. . . By some he is considered as an ambitious man, and therefore a dangerous one. That he is ambitious, I shall readily grant, but it is of that laudable kind, which prompts a man to excel in whatever he takes in hand. He is enterprising, quick in his perceptions, and his judgment intuitively great; qualities essential to a military character.

Huntington, General Jedediah

Opinion of the general officers, March, 1792

Sober, sensible and very discreet.—Has never discover'd much enterprise; yet, no doubt has ever been entertained of his want of spirit, or firmness.

Irvine, General William

Opinion of the general officers, March, 1792

Is sober, tolerably sensible and prudent. It is said he is an oeconomist; and supported his authority whilst he was entrusted with a separate command; but I have no recollection of any circumstance that marks him as a decidedly good, or indifferent officer.

Jefferson, Thomas and Hamilton, Alexander

To Thomas Jefferson, October 18, 1792

I did not require the evidence of the extracts, which you enclosed to me, to convince me of your attachment to the constitution of the United States, or of your disposition to promote the general welfare of this country; but I regret, deeply regret, the difference in opinions, which have arisen and divided you and another principal officer of the government [Alexander Hamilton]; and wish devoutly there could be an accommodation of them by mutual yielding.

A measure of this sort would produce harmony and consequent good in our public councils. The contrary will inevitably introduce confusion and serious mischiefs; and for what? Because mankind cannot think alike, but would adopt different means to attain the same ends. For I will frankly and solemnly declare, that I believe the views of both of you to be pure and well-meant, and that experience only will decide, with respect to the salubrity of the measures, which are the subjects of dispute. Why, then, when some of the best citizens in the United States, men of discernment, uniform and tried patriots, who have no sinister views to promote, but are chaste in their ways of thinking and acting, are to be found, some on one side and some on the other of the questions, which have caused these agitations, should either of you be so tenacious of your opinions, as to make no allowances for those of the other? I could, and indeed was about to add more on this interesting subject, but will forbear, at least for the present, after expressing a wish, that the cup, which has been presented to us may not be snatched from our lips by a discordance of action, when I am persuaded there is no discordance in your views. I have a great, a sincere esteem and regard for you both, and ardently wish that some line could be marked out by which both of you could walk. I am, always, etc.

Knox, General Henry

To John Adams, September 25, 1798

With respect to General Knox, I can say with truth, there is no man in the United States with whom I have been in habits of greater intimacy, no one whom I have loved more sincerely, nor any for whom I have had a greater friendship.

Lincoln, General Benjamin

Opinion of the general officers, March, 1792

Sober, honest, brave and sensible, but infirm, past the vigor of life—

McHenry, James

To Alexander Hamilton, August 9, 1798

Your opinion respecting the unfitness of a certain Gentleman [James McHenry] for the office he holds [Secretary of War], accords with mine, and it is to be regretted, *sorely*, at this time that these opinions are so well founded. I early discovered, after he entered upon the Duties of his office that his talents were unequal to great exertions, or deep resources. In truth they were not expected;—for the fact is, it was a Hobson's choice.

McIntosh, General Lachlan

Opinion of the general officers, March, 1792

Is old and inactive;—supposed to be honest and brave.—Not much known in the Union, and therefore would not obtain much confidence, or command much respect;—either in the community or the army.

MORGAN, GENERAL DANIEL

Opinion of the general officers, March, 1792

Has been fortunate, & has met with eclat.—Yet there are different opinions with respect to his abilities as an officer.—He is accused of using improper means to obtain certificates from the soldiers—. It is said he has been (if the case is not so now) intemperate: that he is troubled with a palpitation which often lays him up; and it is not denied that he is illiterate.

MOULTRIE, GENERAL WILLIAM

Opinion of the general officers, March, 1792

Brave, & it is believed accommodating in his temper—served the whole of the last war; & has been an officer in the preceding one, at least had been engaged in an Expedition against the Cherokees; having defeated them in one or two considerable actions.—What the resources, or powers of his mind are—how active he may be, and whether temperate nor not, are points I cannot speak to with decision, because I have had little or no opportunities to form an opinion of him.

PAINE, THOMAS

To James Madison, Mount Vernon, June 12, 1784

Sir, Can nothing be done in our Assembly for poor Paine? Must the merits and services of *Common Sense* continue to glide down the stream of time unrewarded by this country? His writings certainly have had a powerful effect upon the public mind. Ought they not, then, to meet an adequate return? He is poor, he is chagrined, and almost, if not altogether, in despair of relief. New York, not the least distressed, nor best able State in the Union, has done something for him. This kind of provision he prefers to an allowance from Congress. He has reasons for it, which to him are conclusive; and such, I think, as may be approved by others. His views are moderate; a decent independency is, I believe, all he aims at. Ought he to be disappointed of this?

PINCKNEY, CHARLES COTESWORTH

Opinion of the general officers, March, 1792

A Colonel since Septr. 16th, 1776; but appointed a Brigadr. by brevet at the close of the war, *only*—. In this Gentleman many valuable qualities are to be found.—He is of unquestionable bravery—. Is a man of strict honor, erudition & good sense: and it is said has made Tactics a study—. But what his spirit for enterprise is—whether active or indolent;—or fitted for arrangement, I am unable to say—never having had any opportunity to form a judgment of his talents as a military character.—The capture of Charleston put an end to his military services.

PUTNAM, GENERAL RUFUS

Opinion of the general officers, March, 1792

Possesses a strong mind—and is a discreet man—. No question has ever been made (that has come to my knowledge) of his want of firmness. In short, there is nothing conspicuous in his character—and he is but little known out of his own state, and a narrow circle.

SEVIER, GENERAL JOHN

To James McHenry, July 22, 1798

By what circuitous route did you come at Severe [Sevier] in the wilderness? He may be an estimable character for ought I know; but, from the impression I have of him, he is better qualified to *cut off Indians*,[2] than to discipline an army and lead a Brigade to the mouths of Cannon. But, as I may have mistaken his character, I shall halt here with my strictures on it.

STEUBEN, GENERAL F. W. A. H. F.

Opinion of the general officers, March, 1792

Sensible, sober & brave, well acquainted with Tactics & with the arrangement & discipline of an army.—High in his ideas of subordination—impetuous in his temper—ambitious—and a foreigner.

SULLIVAN, JOHN

To Major General John Sullivan, March 15, 1777

Do not, my dear General Sullivan, torment yourself any longer with imaginary slights, and involve others in the perplexities you feel on that score. No other officer of rank, in the whole army, has so often conceived himself neglected, slighted, and ill treated, as you have done, and none I am sure has had less cause than yourself to entertain such Ideas. Mere accidents, things which have occurred in the common course of service, have been considered by you as designed affronts. . . . Why . . . these unreasonable, these un-

[2] "As to Sevier, the only exploit I ever heard of his performance, was the *murder* of Indians." *Washington to James McHenry, September 14, 1798.*

justifiable suspicions? Suspicions, which can answer no other end, than to poison your own happiness, and add vexation to that of others . . . I have not time to dwell upon subjects of this kind. In quiting [*sic*] it, I shall do it with an earnest exhortation, that you will not suffer yourself to be teased with evils, that only exist in the imagination, and with slights, that have no existence at all; keeping in mind, at the same time, that, if distant armies are to be formed, there are several gentlemen before you, in point of rank, who have a right to claim a preference.

Wayne, General Anthony

Opinion of the general officers, March, 1792

More active & enterprising than Judicious & cautious.—No economist it is feared:—open to flattery—vain—easily imposed upon and liable to be drawn into scrapes. Too indulgent (the effect perhaps of some of the causes just mentioned) to his officers and men.—Whether sober—or a little addicted to the bottle, I know not.

Weedon, General George

Opinion of the general officers, March, 1792

A sensible & judicious man;—his integrity unimpeached;—and was esteemed a pretty good officer.—But if I recollect rightly, not a very active one.—He has never been charged with intemperance to my knowledge;—His name has rarely been mentioned under the present difficulty of chusing an officer to comm'd, but this may, in a great measure be owing to his being at a distance.

White, Anthony Walton

To James McHenry, September 14, 1798

What could have induced the nomination of Walter [Anthony Walton] White to the rank of Brigadier . . . ? Of all the characters in the Revolutionary Army, I believe one more obnoxious to the Officers who composed it could not have been hit upon for a Genl. Officer than White, especially among those to the Southward, where he was best known & celebrated for nothing but frivolity—dress—empty show & something worse—in short for being a notorious L———r. This appointment will . . . exclude many valuable officers, who will not serve as his juniors.

Wilkinson, General James

Opinion of the general officers, March, 1792

Is, by brevet Senr. to those whose names follow—but the appointment to this rank was merely honorary—and as he was but a short time in service, little can be said of his abilities as an Officer.—He is lively, sensible, pompous and ambitious, but whether sober or not, is unknown to me.

Williams, General Otho Holland

Opinion of the general officers, March, 1792

Is a sensible man, but not without vanity. No doubt, I believe, is entertained of his firmness:—and it is thought he does not want activity,—but it is not easy, where there is nothing conspicuous in a character, to pronounce decidedly upon a military man who has always acted under the immediate orders of a superior officer, unless he had been seen frequently in action.—The discipline, interior oeconomy and police of his Corps is the best evidence one can have of his talents in this line, and of this, in the case of Genl. Williams I can say nothing; as he was appointed a Brigadier after he left the Northern to join the Southern army.—But a material objection to him is delicate health (if there has been no change in his constitution),—for he has gone to the Sweet Springs two or three years successively in such bad health as to afford little hope of his ever returning from them.

Part III

MAXIMS, MOTTOS, BRIEF OPINIONS
(including *Rules of Civility*)

Address

In writing or Speaking, give to every Person his due Title According to his Degree & the Custom of the Place.—Rules of Civility, *39th, 1745*

Adjutant-General

The Adjutant-General ought also to be a man of established character, of great activity and experience in the details of an army, and proved integrity, or no alertness can be expected in the execution of the several duties consigned to him on the one hand, and every thing to be feared from treachery or neglect in his office on the other, by which the enemy might be as well informed of our strength as their own.—*To James McHenry, July 4, 1798*

Administration

In every act of my administration, I have sought the happiness of my fellow citizens. My system for the attainment of this object has uniformly been to overlook all personal, local, and partial considerations; to contemplate the United States as one great whole; . . . and to consult only the substantial and permanent interests of our country.—*To Selectmen of Boston, July 28, 1795*

Let me in a friendly way impress the following maxims upon the Executive Officers. In all important matters, to deliberate maturely, but to execute promptly and vigorously; and not to put things off until the morrow, which can be done and require to be done today. Without an adherence to these rules, business never will be *well* done, or done in an easy manner, but will always be in arrear, with one thing treading upon the heels of another. —*To James McHenry, Secretary of War, July 13, 1796*

Agriculture

I know of no pursuit in which more real and important services can be rendered to any country, than by improving its agriculture—its breed of useful animals—and other branches of a husbandman's cares.—*To Sir John Sinclair, July 20, 1794*

America

In short, the foundation of a great empire is laid, and I please myself with a persuasion, that Providence will not leave its work imperfect.—*To Chevalier de la Luzerne, August 1, 1786*

We are *all* the children of the same country—a country great and rich in itself—capable and promising to be, as prosperous and as happy as any the annals of history have ever brought to our view. . . . Our interest, however diversified in local and smaller matters, is the same in all the great and essential concerns of the Nation. . . . The extent of our Country—the diversity of our climate and soil—and the various productions of the States consequent to both, are such as to make one part not only convenient, but perhaps indispensably necessary to the other part;—and may render the whole (at no distant period) one of the most independent in the world. . . . The established government being the work of our own hands, with the seeds of amendment engrafted in the Constitution, may by wisdom, good dispositions, and mutual allowances, aided by experience, bring it as near to perfection as any human institution ever approximated; and therefore, the only strife among us ought to be, who should be foremost in facilitating and finally accomplishing such great and desirable objects . . . However necessary it may be to keep a watchful eye over public servants and public measures, yet there ought to be limits to it; for suspicions unfounded, and jealousies too lively, are irritating to honest feeling; and oftentimes are productive of more evil than good.—*To James Madison, May 20, 1792*

American Character

We have now a National character to establish, and it is of the utmost importance to stamp favorable impressions upon it; let justice be then one of its characteristics, and gratitude another.—*To Theodorick Bland, April 4, 1783*

We [Americans] are apt to run from one extreme into another.—*To John Jay, August 1, 1786*

Notwithstanding the boasted virtue of America we are very little if anything behind them [the British] in dispositions to everything that is bad. —*To Henry Knox, December 26, 1786*

American Future

However unimportant America may be considered at present, and however Britain may affect to despise her trade, there will assuredly come a day, when this country will have some weight in the scales of empires.—*To Lafayette, August 15, 1786*

America, under an efficient government, will be the most favorable country of any in the world for persons of industry and frugality possessed of a moderate capital to inhabit. . . . It will not be less advantageous to the happiness of the lowest class of people, because of the equal distribution of property, the great plenty of unoccupied lands, and the facility of procuring the means of subsistence.—*To Richard Henderson, June 19, 1788*

If this country can steer clear of European politics, stand firm on its bottom, and be wise and temperate in its government, it bids fair to be one of the greatest and happiest nations in the world.—*To Mrs. Sarah Fairfax, May 16, 1798*

Argument

Strive not with your superiors in argument, but always submit your judgment to others with modesty.—Rules of Civility, *40th, 1745*

Arithmetic

Without Arithmetick, the common [affairs of] Life are not to be managed with success.—*To Dr. Boucher, January 2, 1771*

Army

It is a maxim . . . that nothing can be of more importance in an Army than the Clothing and feeding it well.—*To the Committee of Congress, July 19, 1777*

Without [military pride] nothing can be expected from any Army.—*To the Committee of Congress, July 19, 1777*

The consequence of giving rank indiscriminately, is much to be dreaded. . . . The too great liberality practised in this respect, will destroy the pride of rank where it ought to exist, and will not only render it cheap—but contemptible.—*To the Committee of Congress, July 19, 1777*

It is the policy of all Armies to make it [promotion to higher rank] valued and respected as a stimulus to emulation and an incitement to bold and gallant undertaking.—*To the Committee of Congress, July 19, 1777*

My first wish would be, that my military family and the whole army should consider themselves as a band of brothers, willing and ready to die for each other.—*To Henry Knox, October 21, 1798*

From long experience and the fullest conviction, I have been and now am decidedly in favor of a permanent force.—*To John Mathews, October 4, 1780*

Army Engineers

So essential and scientific a part of the army, as the Corps of Artillerists and Engineers, should have an able and respectable officer at their head, without which it would soon sink into ignorance and disrepute.—*To James McHenry, July 4, 1798*

Behavior

However it may be the practice of the World . . . , I have accustomed myself to judge of human Actions very differently and to appreciate them by the manner in which they are conducted, more than by the Event.—*To Major Benjamin Tallmadge, December 10, 1782*

To give opinions unsupported by reasons might appear dogmatical.—*To Alexander Spotswood, November 22, 1798*

Every Action done in Company, ought to be with some Sign of Respect, to those that are Present.—Rules of Civility, *1st, 1745*

In the Presence of Others Sing not to yourself with a humming Noise, nor Drum with your Fingers or Feet.—Rules of Civility, *4th, 1745*

Sleep not when others Speak, Sit not when others stand, Speak not when you should hold your Peace, walk not on when others Stop.—Rules of Civility, *6th, 1745*

At Play and at Fire it's Good manners to Give Place to the last Commer, and affect not to Speak Louder than Ordinary.—Rules of Civility, *8th, 1745*

Reproach none for the Infirmaties [*sic*] of Nature.—Rules of Civility, *21st, 1745*

Behavior in Public Life

Public bodies are not amenable for their Actions. They place and displace at pleasure; and all the satisfaction that an individual can obtain, when he is overlooked [in promotions], is, if innocent, a consciousness that he has not deserved such treatment for his honest exertions.—*To Benedict Arnold, April 3, 1777*

To be disgusted at the decision of questions, because they are not consonant to our own ideas, and to withdraw ourselves from public assemblies, or to neglect our attendance at them . . . , is wrong, because these things may originate in a difference of opinion; but, supposing the fact is otherwise . . . , it is the indispensable duty of every patriot to counteract them by the most steady and uniform opposition.—*To John Parke Custis, February 28, 1781*

We ought not to look back, unless it is to derive useful lessons from past errors, and for the purpose of profiting by dear bought experience. To inveigh against things that are past and irremediable, is unpleasing; but to steer clear of the shelves and rocks we have struck upon, is the part of wisdom. —*To Major-General John Armstrong, March 26, 1781*

Blame

When a man does all he can though it Succeeds not well blame not him that did it. . . .—Rules of Civility, *44th, 1745*

Books

I conceive a knowledge of books is the basis upon which other knowledge is to be built.—*To Dr. Boucher, July 9, 1771*

Borrowing

Great speculations and sometimes trade may be benefited of obtaining money on Interest, but no landed Estate will bear it.—*To Samuel Washington, July 12, 1797*

You may be assured that there is no practice more dangerous than that of borrowing money. . . . For when money can be had in this way, repayment is seldom thought of in time; the Interest becomes a moth; exertions to raise it by dint of Industry ceases—it comes easy and is spent freely. . . . In the meantime the debt is accumulating like a snowball in rolling.—*To Samuel Washington, July 12, 1797*

Buying and Selling

It is your interest, I know to sell high:—it is mine to buy low:—but there is nothing incompatible . . . in both these cases; for when the former is the case, I mean not to become a purchaser—when the latter happens . . ., I mean . . . to avail myself for supplies.—*To P. Marsteller, December 15, 1786*

Capital Punishment

I always hear of capital executions with concern, and regret that there should occur so many instances [desertions] in which they are necessary. —*To General Clinton, December 31, 1778*

Chaplains

The last Assembly . . . provided for a chaplain to our regiment. . . . I now flatter myself, that your Honor will be pleased to appoint a sober, serious man for this duty. Common decency, Sir, in a camp calls for the services of a divine, and which ought not to be dispensed with, altho' the world should be so uncharitable as to think us void of religion, and incapable of good instructions.—*To President of the Council, April 17, 1758*

Character Assassination

To aim a stroke at the reputation of a virtuous character, hazarding his health, . . . is a crime of so deep a dye as no Epithet can convey an adequate idea of to my mind.—*To James McHenry, July 7, 1797*

Charity

Let your heart feel for the afflictions and distresses of every one, and let your hand give in proportion to your purse; remembering . . . that it is not every one who asketh that deserveth charity.—*To Bushrod Washington, January 15, 1783*

Never let an indigent person ask, without receiving *something*, if you have the means.—*To George Washington Parke Custis, November 13, 1796*

Citizens

It is not the part of a good citizen to despair of the republic.—*To Chevalier de la Luzerne, August 1, 1786*

Civil Authority

There is nothing that could add more to my happiness, than to go hand in hand with the civil authority of this, or any other government, to which it may be my lot to be ordered.—*To Committee of Safety of New York, April 17, 1776*

Coercion

Experience has taught us, that men will not adopt and carry into execution measures the best calculated for their own good, without the intervention of a coercive power.—*To John Jay, August 1, 1786*

Company

Associate yourself with Men of good Quality if you Esteem your own Reputation; for 'tis better to be alone than in bad Company. . . .—Rules of Civility, *56th, 1745*

Concealment

Concealment is a species of misinformation.—*To Timothy Pickering, February 10, 1799*

Conduct

We ought not to convert trifling difficulties into insuperable obstacles.—*To Malmedy, May 16, 1777*

It is easy to make acquaintances, but very difficult to shake them off, however irksome and unprofitable they are found, after we have once committed ourselves to them.—*To Bushrod Washington, January 15, 1783*

Ingratitude has been experienced in all ages, and republics in particular have ever been famed for the exercise of that unnatural and sordid vice.—*To Major-General Israel Putnam, June 2, 1783*

Let your promotion result from your own application and from intrinsic merit, not from the labors of others. The last would prove fallacious, and expose you to the reproach of the daw in borrowed feathers.—*To George Washington Parke Custis, November 13, 1796*

Conduct for Women

Nothing short of good sense and an easy unaffected conduct can draw the line between prudery and coquetry.—*To Eleanor Parke Custis, January 16, 1795*

A thorough-faced coquette dies in celibacy, as a punishment for her attempts to mislead others.—*To Eleanor Parke Custis, January 16, 1795*

Congressmen

Representatives ought to be the mouth of their constituents.—*To Bushrod Washington, November 15, 1786*

Conscience

Labour to keep alive in your Breast that Little Spark of Ce[les]tial fire called Conscience.—Rules of Civility, *110th, (last), 1745*

While I feel the most lively gratitude for the many instances of approbation from my country, I can not otherwise deserve it, than by obeying the dictates of my conscience.—*To Selectmen of Boston, July 28, 1795*

Constitution

A constitution, which is to render millions happy or miserable, . . . [is] a matter of such moment [that it] cannot be the work of a day.—*To John Augustine Washington, May 31, 1776*

Should the States reject this excellent Constitution, the probability is that an opportunity will never again offer to cancel another in peace—the next will be drawn in blood.—*Spoken as he signed it, September 17, 1776*

I wish the constitution, which is offered, had been made more perfect; but I sincerely believe it is the best that could be obtained at this time. And, as a constitutional door is opened for amendment hereafter, the adoption of it, under the present circumstances of the Union, is in my opinion desirable.—*To Patrick Henry, September 24, 1787*

The constitution is the guide, which I can never abandon.—*To Selectmen of Boston, July 28, 1795*

Conversation

Let your Conversation be without Malice or Envy, for 'tis a sign of a Tractable and Commendable Nature.—Rules of Civility, *58th, 1745*

Speak not in an unknown Tongue in Company but in your Language and that as those of Quality do and not as ye Vulgar; Sublime matters treat seriously. . . .—Rules of Civility, *72d, 1745*

When you Speak of God or his Attributes, let it be Seriously & [with] Reverence.—Rules of Civility, *108th, 1745*

Courtesy

When you meet with one of Greater Quality than yourself, Stop, and retire especially if it be at a Door or any Straight place to give way for him to Pass.—Rules of Civility, *29th, 1745*

Undertake not to teach your equal in the art himself professes; it savors arrogancy.—Rules of Civility, *41st, 1745*

Criticism

Against the malignancy of the discontented, the turbulent, and the vicious, no abilities, no exertions, nor the most unshaken integrity are any safeguard.—*To John Jay, November 1, 1794*

Danger

It is unfortunate when men cannot or will not see danger at a distance; or, seeing it, are undetermined in the means, which are necessary to avert . . . it.—*To John Trumbull, June 25, 1799*

Debt

To contract new Debts is not the way to pay old ones.—*To James Welch, April 7, 1799*

Democracy

It is to be regretted I confess, that democratical states must always *feel* before they can *see;* it is this that makes their governments slow, but the people will be right at last.—*To Lafayette, July 25, 1785*

Democrats

My opinion is . . . that you could as soon scrub the blackamore white as to change the principle of a profest Democrat, and that he will leave nothing unattempted to overturn the Government of this Country.—*To James McHenry, September 30, 1798*

Despotism

To condemn them [proscribed men] without a hearing, and consign them to punishment more rigorous perhaps than death, is the summit of despotism. —*To John Marshall, December 4, 1797*

Discipline

Be strict in your discipline; that is . . . , require nothing unreasonable of your officers and men, but see that whatever is required be punctually complied with. Reward and punish every man according to his merit, without partiality or prejudice; hear his complaints; if well founded, redress them; if otherwise, discourage them, in order to prevent frivolous ones. Discourage vice in every shape.—*To Col. William Woodford, November 10, 1775*

Discourse

Let your Discourse with Men of Business be Short and Comprehensive. . . .—Rules of Civility, *35th, 1745*

Speak not of doleful Things in a Time of Mirth or at the Table; Speak not of Melancholy Things as Death and Wounds, and if others Mention them Change if you can the Discourse. . . .—Rules of Civility, *62d, 1745*

Be not tedious in discourse or in reading unless you find the company pleased therewith.—Rules of Civility, *80th, 1745*

Dispute

To constitute a dispute there must be two parties. To understand it well, both parties, and all the circumstances, must be fully heard; and, to accommodate differences, temper and mutual forbearance are requisite.—*To David Stuart, March 28, 1790*

Dreams

Tell not your Dreams, but to your intimate Friend . . .—Rules of Civility, *62d, 1745*

Dress

Do not conceive that fine clothes make fine men any more than fine feathers make fine birds. A plain genteel dress is more admired, and obtains more credit than lace and embroidery, in the Eyes of the judicious and sensible.—*To Bushrod Washington, January 15, 1783*

Wear not your cloths foul, unript or dusty, but see they be brushed once every day at least. . . .—Rules of Civility, *51st, 1745*

In Your Apparel be Modest and endeavour to accomodate Nature, rather than to procure Admiration [.] keep to the Fashio[n] of your equals Such as are Civil and orderly with respect to Times and Places. . . .—Rules of Civility, *52d, 1745*

Education

There is nothing, in my opinion more desirable to form the manners and encrease the knowledge of observant youth than [travelling, for the completion of his education].—*To Dr. Boucher, May 13, 1770*

In my opinion, every effort of genius, and all attempts towards improving useful knowledge ought to meet with encouragement in this country.—*To Nicholas Pike, June 20, 1786*

Education generally [is] one of the surest means of enlightening and giving just ways of thinking to our citizens.—*To Alexander Hamilton, September 1, 1796*

Not that I think his [Custis] becoming a mere scholar is a desirable education for a gentleman, but I conceive a knowledge of books is the basis upon which other knowledge is to be built, and that it is men and things more than books he is to be acquainted with by travelling.—*To Dr. Boucher, July 9, 1771*

It has always been a source of serious reflection and sincere regret with me, that the youth of the United States should be sent to foreign countries for the purpose of education. . . . [There is] the danger of contracting principles unfavorable to republican government.—*To Commissioners of Federal District, January 28, 1795*

It is with indescribable regret, that I have seen the youth of the United States migrating to foreign countries, in order to acquire the higher branches of erudition, and to obtain a knowledge of the sciences. . . . A serious danger is encountered by sending abroad among other political systems those, who have not well learned the value of their own.—*To Robert Brooke, March 16, 1795*

Elections

In all free governments, contentions in elections will take place, and, whilst it is confined to our own citizens, it is not to be regretted; but severely indeed ought it to be reprobated, when occasioned by foreign machinations.—*To Jonathan Trumbull, March 3, 1797*

Enemy

Shew not yourself glad at the Misfortune of another though he were your enemy.—Rules of Civility, *22d, 1745*

Among individuals the most certain way to make a man your enemy is to tell him you esteem him such.—*To John Banister, April 21, 1778*

Evil

The lesser evil, where there is a choice of them, should always yield to the greater.—*To Henry Lee, October 31, 1786*

Example

Example, whether it be good or bad, has a powerful influence, and the higher in Rank the officer is, who sets it, the more striking it is.—*To Lord Stirling, March 5, 1780*

Excuses

It is better to offer no excuse than a bad one.—*To Harriot Washington, his niece, October 30, 1791*

Face

Let your countenance be pleasant but in serious matters somewhat grave. —Rules of Civility, *19th, 1745*

Be not Angry at Table whatever happens & if you have reason to be so, shew it not but on a Chearful Countenance especially if there be Strangers, for Good Humour makes one Dish of Meat a Feas[t]. . . .—Rules of Civility, *105th, 1745*

Farming

More good is derived from looking into the Minutiae on a Farm than strikes people at first view; and by examining the Farm yards, fences, and looking into fields—to see that *nothing* is within, but what are *allowed* to be there, produces more good,—or at least avoids more evil, oftentimes, than riding from one working party, or from one Overseer to another, generally accomplishes.—*To James Anderson, December 10, 1799*

Federalists

If principles, instead of men, are not the steady pursuit of the Federalists, their cause will soon be at an end.—*To Gov. Jonathan Trumbull, August 30, 1799*

Flattery

Be no Flaterer [*sic*], neither Play with any that delights not to be Play'd withal.—Rules of Civility, *17th, 1745*

Foreign Policy

I believe it is among nations as with individuals, that the party taking advantage of the distresses of another will lose infinitely more in the opinion of mankind, and in subsequent events, than he will gain by the stroke of the moment.—*To Gouverneur Morris, July 28, 1791*

I have always given it as my decided opinion, that no nation had a right to intermeddle in the internal concerns of another; that every one had a right to form and adopt whatever government they liked best to live under themselves.—*To James Monroe, August 25, 1796*

My ardent desire is, and my aim has been . . . to comply strictly with *all* our engagements, foreign and domestic; but to keep the United States free from political connexions with *every* other country, to see them independent of *all* and under the influence of *none*. In a word, I want an *American* character, that the powers of Europe may be convinced we act for *ourselves*, and not for *others*. This, in my judgment, is the only way to be respected abroad and happy at home; and not, by becoming the partisans of Great Britain or France, create dissensions, disturb the public tranquility, and destroy, perhaps for ever, the cement which binds the union.—*To Patrick Henry, October 9, 1795*

No policy, in my opinion, can be more clearly demonstrated, than that we should do justice to all, and have no political connexion with any of the European powers beyond those, which result from and serve to regulate our commerce with them. Our own experience . . . will soon convince us, that the idea of disinterested favors or friendship from any nation whatever is too novel to be calculated on, and there will always be found a wide difference between the words and actions of any of them.—*To William Heath, May 20, 1797*

I believe it is the sincere wish of United America to have nothing to do with the political intrigues, or the squabbles, of European nations; but, on the contrary, to exchange commodities and live in peace and amity with all the inhabitants of the earth.—*To Earl of Buchan, April 22, 1793*

Foreign Relations

Nations are not influenced, as individuals may be, by disinterested friendship; but, when it is their interest to live in amity, we have little reason to apprehend any rupture.—*To Lafayette, August 15, 1786*

Freedom

[Freedom is] a blessing, on which all the good and evil of life depends. —*To George Mason, April 5, 1769*

French Language

To be acquainted with the French Tongue is become a part of polite Education.—*To Dr. Boucher, January 2, 1771*

Remember, my good friend, that I am unacquainted with your language [French], that I am too far advanced in years to acquire a knowledge of it, and that, to converse through the medium of an interpreter upon common occasions, especially with the Ladies, must appear so extremely awkward, insipid, and uncouth, that I can scarce bear it in idea.—*To Lafayette, September 30, 1779*

Friendship

Shew nothing to your Friend that may affright him.—Rules of Civility, *3d, 1745*

A slender acquaintance with the world must convince every man, that actions, not words, are the true criterion of the attachment of his friends, and that the most liberal professions of good will are very far from being the surest marks of it.—*To Major-General John Sullivan, December 15, 1779*

Be courteous to all, but intimate with few; and let those few be well tried before you give them your confidence. True friendship is a plant of slow growth, and must undergo and withstand the shocks of adversity before it is entitled to the appellation.—*To Bushrod Washington, January 15, 1783*

[During] the juvenal period of life . . . friendships are formed, and habits established, that will stick by one.—*To Alexander Hamilton, September 1, 1796*

Gambling

Avoid Gaming. This is a vice which is productive of every possible evil; equally injurious to the morals and health of its votaries. It is the child of avarice, the brother of iniquity, and father of mischief.—*To Bushrod Washington, January 15, 1783*

General Staff

The General Staff . . . may be considered as so many parts of the Commander-in-Chief.—*To James McHenry, July 4, 1798*

A good choice [of General Staff] is of . . . immense consequence. . . . The Inspector-General, Quartermaster-General, Adjutant-General, and officer commanding the corps of Artillerists and Engineers, ought to be men of the most respectable character, and of first-rate abilities; because, from the nature of their respective offices, and from their being always about the Commander-in-Chief, who is obliged to entrust many things to them *confidentially,* scarcely any movement can take place without their knowledge. . . . Besides possessing the qualifications just mentioned, they ought to have those of Integrity and prudence in an eminent degree, that *entire* confidence might be reposed in them. Without these, and their being on good terms with the Commanding General, his measures, if not designedly thwarted, may be so embarrassed as to make them move heavily on.—*To James McHenry, July 4, 1798*

Generals

Able, well-informed, active, and spirited General Officers are . . . of high importance to the honor, reputation, and success of any army.—*To James McHenry, July 4, 1798*

Germans

They [Germans] are known to be a steady, laborious people.—*To Commissioners of Federal District, December 18, 1792*

Gestures

The gestures of the body must be suited to the discourse you are upon.—Rules of Civility, *20th, 1745*

Gifts

Presents . . . , to me, are of all things the most painful; but I am so well satisfied of the motives which dictated yours my scruples are removed; and I receive the buckles (which are indeed very elegant) as a token of your regard and attachment.—*To David Humphreys, June 26, 1797*

God

The will of Heaven is not to be controverted or scrutinized by the children of this world. It therefore becometh the creatures of it to submit to the will of the Creator, whether it be to prolong or to shorten the number of our days, to bless them with health, or afflict them with pain.—*To George Augustine Washington, January 27, 1792*

Good and Evil

Most of the good and evil things in this life are judged of by comparison. —*to Henry Laurens, March 20, 1779*

Good Men

It is infinitely better to have a *few* good men than *many* indifferent ones. —*To James McHenry, August 10, 1798*

Gossip

Speak not Evil of the Absent for it is unjust. . . .—Rules of Civility, *89th, 1745*

Government

To form a new government requires infinite care and unbounded attention; for if the foundation is badly laid, the superstructure must be bad. Too much time, therefore, cannot be bestowed in weighing and digesting matters well.—*To John Augustine Washington, May 31, 1776*

Candor is not a more conspicuous trait in the character of Governments than it is of individuals.—*To Timothy Pickering, August 29, 1797*

The consequences of a lax or inefficient government are too obvious to be dwelt upon. Thirteen sovereignties pulling against each other, and all tugging at the federal head, will soon bring ruin on the whole.—*To James Madison, November 5, 1786*

Green

Green being a color little apt . . . to fade, and grateful to the eye, I would give it the preference.—*To Robert Cary & Co., June 6, 1768*

Greeting

In Pulling off your Hat to Persons of Distinction, as Noblemen, Justices, Churchmen & make a Reverence, bowing more or less according to the Custom of the Better Bred, and Quality of the Person. Amongst your equals expect not always that they should be with you first, but to Pull of the Hat when there is no need is Affectation. . . .—Rules of Civility, *26th, 1745*

Happiness

Happiness depends more upon the internal frame of a person's own mind, than on the externals in the world.—*To Mrs. Mary Washington, February 15, 1787*

A sensible woman can never be happy with a fool.—*To Eleanor Parke Custis, January 16, 1795*

Happiness of Mankind

In this age of free inquiry and enlightened reason, it is to be hoped, that the condition of the people in every country will be bettered, and the happiness of mankind promoted.—*To David Humphreys, July 20, 1791*

As no one can feel a greater interest in the happiness of mankind than I do, . . . it is the first wish of my heart, that the enlightened policy of the present age may diffuse to all men those blessings, to which they are entitled, and lay the foundation of happiness for future generations.—*To Thomas Paine, May 6, 1792*

Harvard

My opinion always has been, that the university in Massachusetts [Harvard] would have been the most eligible seminary to have sent him

[George Washington Parke Custis]; first, because it is on a larger scale than any other; and secondly, because I believe that the habits of youth there, whether from the discipline of the school, or the greater attention of the people generally to morals, and a more regular course of life, are less prone to dissipation and excess than they are at the colleges south of it.—*To David Stuart, January 22, 1799*

Honesty

It is an old adage, that *honesty is the best policy*. This applies to public as well as private life, to States as well as individuals.—*To James Madison, November 30, 1785*

Hospitality

Virginia hospitality . . . is the most agreeable entertainment we can give, or a stranger expect to find, in an infant, woody country, like ours.—*To Richard Washington, August 10, 1760*

Let the hospitality of the house [Mount Vernon], with respect to the poor, be kept up. Let no one go hungry away. If any of this kind of people should be in want of corn, supply their necessities, provided it does not encourage them in idleness; and I have no objection to your giving my money in charity, to the amount of forty or fifty pounds a year, when you think it well bestowed. What I mean by having no objection is, that it is my desire that it should be done. You are to consider, that neither myself nor wife is now in the way to do these good offices. In all other respect, I recommend it to you, and have no doubt of your observing the greatest economy and frugality; as I suppose you know, that I do not get a farthing for my services here, more than my expenses. It becomes necessary, therefore, for me to be saving at home.—*To Lund Washington, November 26, 1775*

Human Affairs

Human affairs are always chequered and vicissitudes in this life are rather to be expected than wondered at.—*To Robert Stewart, April, 1763*

Human Nature

We may lament that things are not consonant with our wishes, but cannot change the nature of Men, and yet those who are distressed by the folly and perverseness of it, cannot help complaining.—*To Gouverneur Morris, May 29, 1778*

It is the nature of man to be displeased with everything that disappoints a favorite hope or flattering project; and it is the folly of too many of them to condemn without investigating circumstances.—*To Lafayette, September 1, 1778*

A small knowledge of human nature will convince us, that, with far the greatest part of mankind, interest is the governing principle; and that, almost, every man, is more or less under its influence.—*To a Committee of Congress, January 28, 1778*

We must take the passions of men as nature has given them, and those principles as a guide, which are generally the rule of action.—*To John Banister, April 21, 1778*

It is not the public, but private interest, which influences the generality of mankind, nor can the Americans any longer boast an exception.—*To John Laurens, July 10, 1782*

We must take human nature as we find it. Perfection falls not to the share of mortals.—*To John Jay, August 1, 1786*

Unfortunately the nature of man is such, that the experience of others is not attended to as it ought to be. We must *feel*, ourselves, before we can think or perceive the danger that threatens.—*To John Marshall, December 4, 1797*

The views of men can only be known, or guessed at, by their words or actions.—*To Patrick Henry, January 15, 1799*

Ignorance

Ignorance and design are difficult to combat. Out of these proceed illiberal sentiments, improper jealousies, and a train of evils which oftentimes in republican governments must be sorely felt before they can be renewed. —*To John Jay, May 18, 1786*

Immigration

Rather than quarrel about territory, let the poor, the needy, and oppressed of the earth, and those who want land, resort to the fertile plains of our western country, the *second land of promise*, and there dwell in peace, fulfilling the first and great commandment.—*To David Humphreys, July 25, 1785*

If I was a young man, just preparing to begin the world, or if advanced in life, and had a family to make a provision for, I know of no country where I should rather fix my habitation than in some part of that region [the West].—*To Richard Henderson, June 19, 1788*

I have established it as a maxim neither to invite nor to discourage immigrants. My opinion is, that they will come hither as fast as the true interest and policy of the United States will be benefited by foreign population. I believe many of these . . . have been, and I fear will continue to be, imposed on by speculators in land and other things; but I know of no prevention but caution, nor any remedy except the laws.—*To John Jay, November 1, 1794*

Indians

Humanity and good policy must make it the wish of every good citizen of the United States, that husbandry, and consequently civilization, should be introduced among the Indians. So strongly am I impressed with the beneficial effects, which our country would receive from such a thing, that I shall always take a singular pleasure in promoting, as far as may be in my power, every measure which may tend to ensure it.—*To Timothy Pickering, January 20, 1791*

I must confess I cannot see much prospect of living in tranquillity with them [Indians], so long as a spirit of land-jobbing prevails, and our frontier settlers entertain the opinion, that there is not the same crime (or indeed no crime at all) in killing an Indian as in killing a white man.—*To David Humphreys, July 20, 1791*

Influence

Influence is no government.—*To Henry Lee, October 31, 1786*

Inspector-General

If the Inspector-General is not an officer of great respectability of character, firm and strict in discharging the duties of the trust reposed in him, or if he is too pliant in his disposition, he will most assuredly be imposed upon, and the efficient strength and condition of the army will not be known to the Commander-in-Chief. . . . He may form his Plans upon erroneous calculations, and commit fatal mistakes.—*To James McHenry, July 4, 1798*

Invasion

If there be good cause . . . to expect such an event [invasion], delay in preparing for it might be dangerous, improper, and not to be justified by prudence.—*To John Adams, July 4, 1798*

Jesting

Break not a Jest where none take pleasure in mirth. Laugh not loud, nor at all without Occasion, deride no man's Misfortune. . . .—Rules of Civility, *64th, 1745*

Labor

Workmen in most Countries I believe are necessary plagues—in this [country] where entreaties as well as money must be used to obtain their work and keep them to their duty they baffle all calculation in the accomplishment of any plan or repairs they are engaged in;—and require more attention to and looking after than can be well conceived.—*To William Gordon, October 15, 1797*

Land

Lands far removed from the proprietors of them—however valuable in themselves—are very unprofitable.—*To John Lewis, April 17, 1782*

Law

Laws or ordinances unobserved, or partially attended to, had better never have been made; because the first is a mere nihil, and the second is productive of much jealousy and discontent.—*To James Madison, March 31, 1787*

There never was a law yet made . . . that hit the taste *exactly* of every man, or every part of the community.—*To Major-General Daniel Morgan, October 8, 1794*

If the laws are to be so trampled upon with impunity, and a minority (a small one too) is to dictate to the majority, there is an end put . . . to republican government; and nothing but anarchy and confusion is to be expected hereafter. Some other man or society may dislike another law, and oppose it with equal propriety, until all laws are prostrate, and every one (the strongest I presume) will carve for himself.—*To Charles M. Thruston, August 10, 1794*

A proscribing system, or Laws having the same effect, when carried to a great extent, ever appeared to me to be impolitic; and their operation should always cease with the cause, which produced them. Examples, in terrorem are necessary, but to exile many of its Inhabitants cannot be the interest of any State.—*To President of Congress, June 2, 1778*

Liberty

That no man should scruple, or hesitate a moment to use arms in defence of so valuable a blessing [as liberty], on which all the good and evil of life depends, is clearly my opinion. Yet arms . . . should be the last resort.—*To George Mason, April 5, 1769*

Love and Sex

Men and women feel the same inclinations towards each other *now* that they always have done, and which they will continue to do until there is a new order of things, and *you,* as others have done, may find, perhaps, that the passions of your sex are easier raised than allayed. Do not therefore boast too soon or too strongly of your insensibility to, or resistance of, its powers. In the composition of the human frame there is a good deal of inflammable matter, however dormant it may lie for a time, and like an intimate acquaintance of yours, when the torch is put to it, *that* which is *within you* may burst into a blaze; for which reason and especially too, as I have entered upon the chapter of advices, I will read you a lecture drawn from this text.

Love is said to be an involuntary passion, and it is, therefore, contended that it cannot be resisted. This is true in part only, for like all things else, when nourished and supplied plentifully with aliment, it is rapid in its progress; but let these be withdrawn and it may be stifled in its birth or much stinted in its growth. For example, a woman (the same may be said of the other sex) all beautiful and accomplished, will, while her hand and heart are undisposed of, turn the heads and set the circle in which she moves on fire. Let her marry, and what is the consequence? The madness *ceases* and all is quiet again. Why? not because there is any diminution in the charms of the lady, but because there is an end of hope. Hence it follows, that love may and therefore ought to be under the guidance of reason, for although we cannot avoid first impressions, we may assuredly place them under guard; and my motives for treating on this subject are to show you, while you remain Eleanor Parke Custis, spinster, and retain the resolution to love with moderation, the propriety of adhering to the latter resolution, at least until you have secured your game, and the way by which it may be accomplished.

When the fire is beginning to kindle, and your heart growing warm, propound these questions to it. Who is this invader? Have I a competent knowledge of him? Is he a man of good character; a man of sense? For, be assured, a sensible woman can never be happy with a fool. What has been his walk in life? Is he a gambler, a spendthrift, or drunkard? Is his fortune sufficient to maintain me in the manner I have been accustomed to live, and my sisters live, and is he one to whom my friends can have no reasonable objection? If these interrogatories can be satisfactorily answered, there will remain but one more to be asked, that, however, is an important one. Have I sufficient ground to conclude that his affections are engaged by me? Without this the heart of sensibility will struggle against a passion that is not reciprocated—delicacy, custom, or call it by what epithet you will, having precluded all advances on your part. The declaration, without the *most indirect* invitation of yours, must proceed from the man, to render it permanent and valuable, and nothing short of good sense and an easy unaffected conduct can draw the line between prudery and coquetry. It would be no great departure from truth to say, that it rarely happens otherwise than that a thorough-faced coquette dies in celibacy, as a punishment for her attempts to mislead others, by encouraging looks, words, or actions, given for no other purpose than to draw men on to make overtures that they may be rejected.—*To Eleanor Parke Custis, January 16, 1775*

Marriage

I never did, nor do I believe I ever shall, give advice to a woman, who is setting out on a matrimonial voyage; first, because I never could advise one to marry without her own consent; and, secondly, because I know it is to no purpose to advise her to refrain, when she has obtained it. A woman very rarely asks an opinion or requires advice on such an occasion, till her resolution is formed; and then it is with the hope and expectation of obtaining a sanction . . . that she applies.—*To Lund Washington, September 20, 1783*

It has ever been a maxim with me through life, neither to promote nor to prevent a matrimonial connection, unless there should be something indispensably requiring interference in the latter. I have always considered marriage as the most interesting event of one's life, the foundation of happiness or misery.—*To Burwell Bassett, May 23, 1785*

Mathematics

. . . mathematics, than which, so much at least as relates to surveying, nothing can be more essentially necessary to any person possessed of a large landed estate.—*To Dr. Boucher, July 9, 1771*

Merit

Merit rarely goes unrewarded.—*To Bushrod Washington, January 15, 1783*

Military Discipline

A refusal to obey the commands of a superior officer, especially where the duty required was evidently calculated for the good of the service, cannot be justified, without involving consequences subversive of all military discipline.—*To Col. Josias C. Hall, April 3, 1778*

Military Hospitals

I hope your new appointment . . . will make the necessary reform in the [military] hospital and that I shall not, the next campaign, have my ears, and eyes too, shocked with the complaints and looks of poor creatures perishing for want of proper care.—*To the President of Congress, January 26, 1777*

Humanity and feeling for the sick and wounded of an army call loudly for skill, attention, and economy in the director of the hospitals.—*To James McHenry, July 4, 1798*

Military Men

A commanding officer, not having this liberty [of approving the officers under his command], appears to me to be a strange thing.—*To Warner Lewis, August 14, 1755*

It is idle . . . to expect more from military men, than from those discharging the civil departments of government.—*To Joseph Jones, December 14, 1782*

Military Operations

You know that landing men, and procuring horses, are not the work of an hour, a day, or even a week.—*To Major General William Heath, February 3, 1777*

Military Promotions

The consequence of giving rank indiscriminately, is much to be dreaded —great dissatisfaction has already arisen on account of bestowing this on officers in the Civil departments of the Army, on the inferior staffs, Waggon Masters, &, who by custom, propriety, and every other motive are excluded from it in all well regulated Armies. The too great liberality practised in this respect, will destroy the pride of rank where it ought to exist, and will not only render it cheap—but contemptible. It is the policy of all Armies to make it valued and respected as a stimulus to emulation and an incitement to bold and gallant undertaking.—*To Committee of Congress, July 10, 1777*

Military vs Civilian Control

If a commanding officer is amenable to private calls for the discharge of public duty, he has a dagger always at his breast, and can turn neither to the right nor to the left without meeting its point; in a word he is no longer a free agent in office, as there are few military decisions which are not offensive to one party or the other.—*To General Greene, May 20, 1785*

Militia

Militia, . . . here today and gone tomorrow—whose way, like the ways of Providence are almost inscrutable.—*To John Augustine Washington, February 24, 1777*

Morale

Impress upon the mind of every man, from the first to the lowest, the importance of the cause, and what it is they are contending for.—*To Col. William Woodford, November 10, 1775*

National Happiness

The United States are making great progress towards national happiness; and, if it is not attained here in as high a degree as human nature will admit . . . , I think we may then conclude, that political happiness is unattainable.—*To de la Luzerne, September 10, 1791*

Negotiations

It is hardly possible in the early stages of a negotiation to foresee all the results, so much depending upon fortuitous circumstances and incidents, which are not within our control.—*To John Jay, November 1, 1794*

News

Be not apt to relate News if you know not the truth thereof. In Discoursing of things you Have heard Name not your Author always a [se]cret. . . .—Rules of Civility, *79th, 1745*

Newspapers

We get so many details in the Gazettes, and of such different complexions, that it is impossible to know what credence to give to any of them.—*To James McHenry, April 3, 1797*

There is so little dependence on newspaper publications, which take whatever complexion the editors please to give them, that persons at a distance, who have no other means of information, are oftentimes at a loss to form an opinion on the most important occurrences.—*To Oliver Wolcott, May 15, 1797*

If the government and the officers of it are to be the constant theme for newspaper abuse, and this too without condescending to investigate the motives or the facts, it will be impossible, I conceive, for any man living to manage the helm or to keep the machine together.—*To Edmund Randolph, August 26, 1792*

Offense

Offensive operations oftentimes are the *surest,* if not . . . the *only* means of defense.—*To John Trumbull, June 25, 1799*

Office Seekers

[America is] a country where offices bear no proportion to the seekers of them.—*To John Jay, November 1, 1794*

Parents

Honor & Obey your Natural Parents altho they be Poor.—Rules of Civility, *108th, 1745*

Passion

In all causes of Passion [ad]mit Reason to Govern. . . .—Rules of Civility, *58th, 1745*

Patriotism

Every post is honorable, in which a man can serve his country.—*To Benedict Arnold, September 14, 1775*

I will venture to assert, that a great and lasting war can never be supported on this principle [patriotism] alone. It must be aided by a prospect of interest or some reward.—*To John Banister, April 21, 1778*

The approbation of my country is what I wish; and, as far as my abilities and opportunities will permit, I hope I shall endeavor to deserve it. It is the highest reward to a feeling mind; and happy are they, who so conduct themselves as to merit it.—*To Patrick Henry, March 28, 1778*

From the crisis at which our affairs have arrived, . . . I think every man, who does not merely make profession of patriotism is bound by indissoluble ties to remain in the army.—*To Col. Josias C. Hall, April 3, 1778*

Justice requires and a grateful government certainly will bestow those places of honor and profit, which necessity must create, upon those who have risked life, fortune and Home to support its cause.—*To Robert Stewart, August 10, 1783*

. . . my country, whose voice I can never hear but with veneration and love.—First Inaugural, *April 30, 1789*

I have no wish superior to that of promoting the happiness and welfare of this country.—*To Henry Lee, July 21, 1793*

I am clearly in sentiment with you that every man who is in the vigor of life, ought to serve his country, in whatever line it requires and he is fit for.—*To David Humphreys, June 26, 1797*

[It is] incumbent upon every person of every description to contribute at all times to his country's welfare.—*To John Adams, July 13, 1798*

If real danger threatened the country, no young man ought to be an idle spectator of its defence.—*To David Stuart, December 30, 1798*

Peace

Nothing short of a general peace in Europe, will produce tranquility in this country.—*To David Humphreys, June 26, 1797*

Peace with all the world is my sincere wish.—*To Jonathan Boucher, August 15, 1798*

Peace and War

My primary objects, to which I have steadily adhered, have been to preserve the country in peace if I can, and to be prepared for war if I cannot; to effect the first, upon terms consistent with the respect which is due to ourselves, and with honor, justice, and good faith to all the world. —*To Gouverneur Morris, June 25, 1794*

Philosophy

The principles of Philosophy Moral, Natural etc., I should think a very desirable knowledge for a Gentleman.—*To Dr. Boucher, January 2, 1771*

Political Appointments

Wishing to promote the public weal, and to make justice and impartiality the lines by which to walk to accomplish this, every information that can enable me to tread on such firm ground, or which would enable me to investigate with more accuracy the characters of public men . . . , cannot fail of being acceptable to me.—*To Henry Lee, June 30, 1792*

I shall not, whilst I have the honor to administer the government, bring a man into any office of consequence knowingly, whose political tenets are adverse to the measures, which the general government are pursuing; for this, in my opinion, would be a sort of political suicide.—*To Timothy Pickering, September 27, 1793*

In the appointments to the great offices of the government, my aim has been to combine geographical situation, and sometimes other considerations, with abilities and fitness of ***known*** characters.—*To Edward Carrington, October 9, 1795*

[In making appointments] esteem, love, and friendship can have no influence on my mind.—*To John Adams, August 25, 1798*

Political Parties

I was not a party man myself, and the first wish of my heart was, if parties did exist, to reconcile them.—*To Thomas Jefferson, July 6, 1796*

Political Power

Extensive powers not exercised as far as was necessary have, I believe, scarcely ever failed to ruin the possessor.—*To Joseph Reed, July 4, 1780*

Potatoes

Of all the improving and ameliorating crops, none in my opinion are equal to potatoes on stiff and hard bound land.—*To Thomas Jefferson, October 4, 1795*

Precedency

They that are in Dignity or in office have in all places Precedency but whilst they are Young they out [*sic*] to respect those that are their equals in Birth or other Qualitys, though they have no Publick charge.—Rules of Civility, *33d, 1745*

Precedents

Precedents are dangerous things.—*To Henry Lee, October 31, 1786*

Presidency

It was among my first determinations when I entered upon the duties of my present station to visit every part of the United States in the course of my administration of the government. . . . And this determination was accompanied by another: —viz—not, by making my headquarters in private families, to become troublesome to them in any of these tours.—*To Edward Rutledge, January 16, 1791*

The powers of the executive of this country are more definite, and better understood, perhaps, than those of any other country; and my aim has been, and will continue to be, neither to stretch nor relax from them in any instance whatever, unless compelled to it by imperious circumstances.—*To Alexander Hamilton, July 2, 1794*

I suffered every attack that was made upon my Executive Conduct . . . to pass unnoticed while I remained in public office, well knowing that if the general tenor of it wou'd not stand the test of investigation, a newspaper vindication would be of little avail.—*To William Gordon, October 15, 1797*

Presidential Policy

In every act of my administration, I have sought the happiness of my fellow citizens. My system for the attainment of this object has uniformly been to overlook all personal, local, and partial considerations; to contemplate the United States as one great whole; to confide that sudden impressions, when erroneous, would yield to candid reflection; and to consult only the substantial and permanent interests of our country.—*To Selectmen of Boston, July 28, 1795*

Prevention

It is easier to prevent than to remedy an evil.—*To Richard Henry Lee, December 14, 1784*

It is much easier at all times to prevent an evil than to rectify mistakes. —*To James McHenry, August 10, 1798*

Prisoners of War

Prisoners . . . you will treat with as much humanity and kindness, as may be consistent with your own safety and the public interest. Be very particular in restraining . . . your . . . troops . . . from all acts of cruelty and insult, which will disgrace the American arms.—*To Benedict Arnold, September 14, 1775*

You ask my advice as to the propriety of enlisting prisoners of war. I would just observe, that, in my opinion, it is neither consistent with the rules of war, nor politic; nor can I think, that, because our enemies have commited an unjustifiable action, by enticing, and in some instances intimidating, our men into their service, we ought to follow their example. —*To Board of War, November 30, 1776*

Promises

Undertake not what you cannot Perform but be Carefull to keep your Promise. . . .—Rules of Civility, *82d, 1745*

Propaganda

It is well known, that, when one side only of a story is heard and often repeated, the human mind becomes impressed with it insensibly.—*To Edmund Pendleton, January 22, 1795*

Property

It is . . . natural for man to wish to be the absolute Lord and Master of what he holds in occupancy.—*To William Strickland, July 15, 1797*

Providence

It is not for man to scan the wisdom of Providence. The best we can do, is to submit to its decrees. Reason, religion, and philosophy teach us to do this; but 'tis time alone, that can ameliorate the pangs of humanity and soften its woes.—*To Henry Knox, March 2, 1797*

The ways of Providence are inscrutable, and not to be scanned by short-sighted man, whose duty is submission without repining at its decrees.—*To Archibald Blair, June 24, 1799*

Public Life

Men in responsible positions cannot, like those in private life, be governed *solely* by the dictates of their own inclinations, or by such motives as can only affect themselves. . . . A man in public office . . . is accountable for the consequences of his measures to others, and one in private life . . . has no other check than the rectitude of his own action.—*To Duke de Liancourt, August 8, 1796*

Public Opinion

In a free and republican government, you cannot restrain the voice of the multitude. Every man will speak as he thinks.—*To Lafayette, September 1, 1778*

In this country a personal difference in political sentiments is often made to take the garb of general dissensions.—*To Gouverneur Morris, October 20, 1792*

Whatever my own opinion may be on this or any other subject interesting to the community at large, it always has been and will continue to be my earnest desire to learn, and, as far as is consistent, to comply with, the public sentiment; but it is on *great* occasions *only*, and after time has been given for cool and deliberate reflection, that the *real* voice of the people can be known.—*To Edward Carrington, May 1, 1796*

When the situation of this country calls loudly for vigor and unanimity, it is to be lamented that gentlemen of talents and character should disagree in their sentiments for promoting the public weal; but unfortunately this ever has been, and most probably ever will be, the case in the affairs of mankind.—*To Alexander Hamilton, October 18, 1787*

Public Service

In general I esteem it a good maxim, that the best way to preserve the confidence of the people durably is to promote their true interest.—*To Joseph Reed, July 4, 1780*

I have no object in view incompatible with the constitution, and the obvious interests of this country. . . . I only wish, whilst I am a servant of the public, to know the will of my masters, that I may govern myself accordingly.—*To Edmund Pendleton, September 23, 1793*

Quality

It is not the lowest priced goods that are always the cheapest—the quality is, or ought to be as much an object with the purchaser, as the price.—*To P. Marsteller, December 15, 1786*

Reading

Light reading (by this, I mean books of little importance) may amuse for the moment, but leaves nothing solid behind.—*To George Washington Parke Custis, November 13, 1796*

Read no Letters, Books, or Papers in Company but when there is a Necessity for the doing of it you must ask leave: come not near the Books or Writings of Another so as to read them unless desired or give your opinion of them unask'd also look not high when another is writing a letter.—Rules of Civility, *16th, 1745*

Recreation

Let your Recreations be Manfull not Sinfull.—Rules of Civility, *109th, 1745*

Religious Freeedom

As the contempt of the religion of a country by ridiculing any of its ceremonies, or affronting its ministers or votaries, has ever been deeply resented, you are to be particularly careful to restrain every officer and soldier from such imprudence and folly, and to punish every instance of it.

On the other hand, as far as lies in your power, you are to protect and support the free exercise of the religion of the country, and the undisturbed enjoyment of the rights of conscience in religious matters, with your utmost influence and authority.—*To Benedict Arnold, September 14, 1775*

Every man conducting himself as a good citizen, and being accountable to God alone for his religious opinions, ought to be protected in worshipping the Deity according to the dictates of his own conscience. . . . If I could have entertained the slightest apprehension that the Constitution framed in the Convention, where I had the honor to preside, might possibly endanger the religious rights of any ecclesiastical Society, certainly I would never have placed my signature to it; if I could now conceive that the general Government might ever be so administered as to render liberty of conscience insecure, I beg you will be persuaded that no one would be more zealous than myself to establish effectual barriers against the horrors of spiritual tyranny, and every species of religious persecution. . . . Be assured, Gentlemen, that I entertain a proper sense of your fervent supplications to God for my temporal and eternal happiness.—*To United Baptist Churches of Virginia, May, 1789*

Being no bigot myself, I am disposed to indulge the professors of Christianity in the church with that road to Heaven, which to them shall seem most direct, plainest, easiest and least liable to exception.—*To Lafayette, August 15, 1787*

It is now no more that toleration is spoken of, as if it was by the indulgence of one class of people that another enjoyed the exercise of their inherent natural rights. For happily the Government of the United States, which gives to bigotry no sanction, to persecution no assistance, requires only that those who live under its protection should demean themselves as good citizens, in giving it, on all occasions, their effectual support. . . . May the Father of Mercies scatter light and not darkness on our paths, and make us all, in our several vocations useful here, and in his own due time and way everlastingly happy.—*To the Hebrew Congregation of Newport, August, 1790*

Remedies

Desperate diseases require desperate remedies.—*To President of Congress, December 20, 1776*

Republicanism

Republicanism is not the phantom of a deluded imagination. On the contrary, . . . under no form of government, will laws be better supported, liberty and property better secured, or happiness be more effectually dispensed to mankind.—*To Edmund Pendleton, January 22, 1795*

Reputation

A character is valuable to all men, and not less so to a Speculator.—*To James Welch, April 7, 1799*

Saving

No person wishes more to save money to the public, than I do; and no person has aimed more at it. But there are some cases in which parsimony may be ill-placed.—*To President of Congress, April 23, 1776*

Secretary of War

He [Secretary of War] ought to be a man, not only of competent skill in the science of war, but possessing a general knowledge of political subjects, of known attachment to the government we have chosen, and of proved integrity.—*To Charles Cotesworth Pinckney, January 22, 1794*

Slavery

There is not a man living, who wishes more sincerely than I do, to see a plan adopted, for the abolition of slavery. But there is only one proper way and effectual mode by which it can be accomplished, and that is by legislative authority.—*To Robert Morris, April 12, 1786*

To set the slaves afloat, at once would I believe be productive of much inconvenience and mischief; but, by degrees, it certainly might and assuredly ought to be effected, and that, too, by legislative authority.—*To Lafayette, May 10, 1786*

I never mean, unless some particular circumstance should compel me to it, to possess another slave by purchase, it being among my first wishes, to see some plan adopted by which Slavery, in this country may be abolished by law.—*To John Francis Mercer, September 9, 1786*

With respect to the other species of property, concerning which you ask my opinion, I shall frankly declare to you that I do not like even to think, much less talk of it. However, as you have put the question, I shall, in a few words, give you *my ideas* of it. Were it not then, that I am principled against selling negroes, as you would do cattle at a market, I would not in twelve months from this date, be possessed of one, as a slave. I shall be happily mistaken, if they are not found to be very troublesome species of property ere many years pass over our heads.—*To Alexander Spotswood, November 23, 1794*

I had resolved never to become the Master of another slave by purchase. —*To George Lewis, November 13, 1797*

Spain

Spain appears to be so much behind the other nations of Europe in liberal policy, that a long time will undoubtedly elapse, before the people of that kingdom can taste the sweets of liberty, and enjoy the natural advantages of their country.—*To David Humphreys, July 20, 1791*

Suspicions

However necessary it may be to keep a watchful eye over public servants, and public measures, yet there ought to be limits to it; for suspicions unfounded, and jealousies too lively, are irritating to honest feeling; and oftentimes are productive of more evil than good.—*To James Madison, May 20, 1792*

System

Nothing can so effectually obviate the evil [of planlessness], as an established, and regular course of proceeding; made known to *all* who are actors in it; that *all may*, thereby, be enabled to play their parts.—*To James Anderson, December 10, 1799*

Testament

You will act very prudently in having your will revised by some person skilled in the law, as a testator's intentions are often defeated by different interpretations of statutes.—*To John West, January 13, 1775*

Life is always uncertain, and common prudence dictates to every man the necessity of settling his temporal concerns, while it is in his power, and while the mind is calm and undisturbed.—*To Martha Washington, June 18, 1775*

Time

What to me is more valuable, my time, that I most regard.—*To James McHenry, September 14, 1799*

Time is of more importance than is generally imagined.—*To James Anderson, December 10, 1799*

Title

You are pleased to dub me with a title I have no pretensions to—that is, ye Hon[ora]ble.—*To his London agent, April 5, 1758*

Tolerance of Opinion

Without more charity for the opinions and acts of one another in governmental matters, or some more infallible criterion by which the truth of speculative opinions, before they have undergone the test of experience, are to be fore-judged, . . . I believe it will be difficult, if not impracticable, to manage the reins of government.—*To Thomas Jefferson, August 23, 1792*

Differences in political opinions are as unavoidable, as, to a certain point, they may perhaps be necessary. But it is exceedingly to be regretted, that subjects cannot be discussed without temper on the one hand, or decisions submitted to without having the motives . . . improperly implicaed on the other; and this regret borders on chagrin, when we find that men of abilities, zealous patriots, . . . will not exercise more charity in deciding on the opinions and actions of one another.—*To Alexander Hamilton, August 26, 1792*

Travel

Every man, who travels with a view to observing the laws and customs of other countries, should be able to give some description of the situation and government of his own.—*To Dr. Boucher, July 9, 1771*

Treaties

Unless treaties are mutually beneficial to the parties, it is in vain to hope for a continuance of them beyond the moment when the one, which conceives itself overreached, is in a situation to break off the connexion.—*To Gouverneur Morris, July 28, 1791*

Truth

What can be so proper as the truth?—*To Richard Washington, April 15, 1757*

Truth will ultimately prevail where there is pains taken to bring it to light.—*To Charles M. Thruston, August 10, 1794*

Values

Men set different values upon the same thing according to the lights in which it strikes them.—*To Benjamin Dulany, November 17, 1781*

Wants

Imaginary wants are indefinite; and oftentimes insatiable; because they sometimes are boundless, and always changing.—*To John Augustine Washington, January 16, 1783*

War

My first wish is to see this plague to mankind banished from off the earth, and the sons and daughters of this world employed in more pleasing and innocent amusements, than in preparing implements and exercising them for the destruction of mankind.—*To David Humphreys, July 25, 1785*

A century, in the ordinary intercourse, would not have accomplished what the seven years' association in arms did.—*To Alexander Hamilton, September 1, 1796*

Washington, D. C.

On account of its being the permanent seat of the government of this Union, . . . the laws and policy of it must be better understood than in any local part thereof.—*To Thomas Jefferson, March 15, 1795*

A century hence, if this country keeps united, . . . will produce a city, though not as large as London, yet of a magnitude inferior to few others in Europe, on the banks of the Potomac, where one is now establishing for the permanent seat of the government of the United States, . . . a situation not excelled, for commanding prospect, good water, salubrious air, and safe harbour, by any in the world; and where elegant buildings are erecting and in forwardness for the reception of Congress in the year 1800.—*To Mrs. Sarah Fairfax, May 16, 1798*

Women

When once the woman has tempted us, and we have tasted the forbidden fruit, there is no such thing as checking our appetites, whatever the consequences may be.—*To Mrs. Richard Stockton, September 2, 1783*

Work

My observation on every employment in life is, that, wherever and whenever one person is found adequate to the discharge of a duty by close application thereto, it is worse executed by two persons, and scarcely done at all if three or more are employed therein.—*To Henry Knox, September 24, 1792*

Workers

If they are good workmen, they may be from Asia, Africa or Europe; they may be Mahometans, Jews or Christians of any sect, or they may be Atheists. I would, however, prefer middle aged to young men, and those who have good countenances, and good characters . . . to others who have neither.—*To Tench Tilghman, March 24, 1784*

Selected Bibliography

I. *Bibliographies:*

BAKER, W. S., *Bibliotheca Washingtoniana; a Descriptive List of the Biographies and Biographical Sketches of George Washington* (Philadelphia, 1889).

CHANNING, E., HART, A. B., TURNER, F. J., *Guide to the Study and Reading of American History* (Boston, 1912).

GRIFFIN, A. P. C., *Catalogue of the Washington Collection in the Boston Athenaeum* (Cambridge, 1897).

II. *Washington's Writings:*

BROOKE, W. E., ed., *Agricultural Papers of George Washington* (Boston, 1912).

BUTTERFIELD, C. W., ed., *Washington-Crawford Letters . . . , 1767 to 1781* (Cincinnati, 1877).

———, ed., *Washington-Irvine Correspondence . . . , 1781 to 1783* (Madison, 1882).

CONWAY, M. D., ed., *George Washington and Mount Vernon: A Collection of Washington's Unpublished Agricultural and Personal Letters* (Brooklyn, 1889).

———, ed., *George Washington's Rules of Civility, Traced to their Sources and Restored* (New York, 1890).

EVANS, L. B., ed., *Writings of George Washington* (New York, 1908).

FITZPATRICK, J. C., ed., *Calendar of the Correspondence of George Washington, Commander in Chief of the Continental Army* (5 vols., Washington, D. C., 1906-15).

———, ed., *Diaries of George Washington, 1748-99* (4 vols., Boston, 1925).

———, ed., *The Writings of George Washington, 1745-1799* (39 vols., Washington, D. C., 1931-44).

FORD, C. F., ed., *The Writings of George Washington* (14 vols., New York, 1889-93).

———, ed., *Washington-Duché Letters* (Brooklyn, 1890).

MOORE, C., ed., *Rules of Civility and Decent Behaviour in Company and Conversation* (Boston, 1926).

OSBORNE, L. P., ed., *Washington Speaks for Himself* (New York, 1927).

SPARKS, J., ed., *The Writings of George Washington* (12 vols., Boston, 1834-37).

III. *Some Biographies:*

CORBIN, J., *Unknown Washington* (New York, 1930).
CUSTIS, G. W. P., *Recollections and Private Memoirs of Washington* (Philadelphia, 1859).
FORD, P. L., *The True George Washington* (Philadelphia, 1896).
FORD, C. W., *George Washington* (2 vols., New York, 1900).
FREEMAN, D. S., *George Washington, A Biography* (5 vols., New York, 1948-52).
HAPGOOD, N., *George Washington* (New York, 1901).
HUGHES, R., *George Washington* (3 vols., New York, 1926-30).
IRVING, W., *Life of George Washingon* (5 vols., Philadelphia, 1855-59).
LODGE, H. C., *George Washington* (2 vols., Boston, 1930).
MARSHALL, J., *Life of George Washington* (5 vols., Philadelphia, 1804-07).
SEARS, L. M., *George Washington* (New York, 1932).
SPARKS, J., *Life of George Washington* (Boston, 1839).
WILSON, W., *George Washington* (New York, 1903).
WISTER, O., *Seven Ages of Washington: A Biography* (New York, 1907).
WOODWARD, W. E., *George Washington, The Image and the Man* (New York, 1926).

Index

Set in Linotype Old Style No. 7
Format by Edwin H. Kaplin
Manufactured by The Haddon Craftsmen, Inc.
Published by HARPER & BROTHERS, *New York*